LAWRENCE, HARDY, AND AMERICAN LITERATURE

RICHARD SWIGG

London
OXFORD UNIVERSITY PRESS
New York   Toronto
1972

Oxford University Press, Ely House, London W.1

GLASGOW NEW YORK TORONTO MELBOURNE WELLINGTON
CAPE TOWN IBADAN NAIROBI DAR ES SALAAM LUSAKA ADDIS ABABA
DELHI BOMBAY CALCUTTA MADRAS KARACHI LAHORE DACCA
KUALA LUMPUR SINGAPORE HONG KONG TOKYO

ISBN 0 19 212552 4

Thanks are due to the following for permission to quote from copyright material: the Estate of the late Mrs. Frieda Lawrence, Laurence Pollinger Ltd., and William Heinemann Ltd., for works of D. H. Lawrence listed at page 363; the Centaur Press Ltd. for the uncollected versions of *Studies in Classic American Literature*, Copyright 1961 by the Estate of the late Mrs. Frieda Lawrence, published in *The Symbolic Meaning*, edited by Armin Arnold (Centaur Press, 1962); the Trustees of the Hardy Estate, The Macmillan Company of Canada, and Macmillan London and Basingstoke, for works of Thomas Hardy listed at pages 363-4.

Printed in Great Britain
by Hazell Watson & Viney Ltd
Aylesbury, Bucks

To
A. D. FRANKLAND

Contents

Preface

WRITING in 1920, in the preface to his play *Touch and Go*, Lawrence said of tragedy:

If men are no more than implements, it is non-tragic and merely disastrous. In tragedy the man is more than his part. Hamlet is more than Prince of Denmark, Macbeth is more than murderer of Duncan. The man is caught in the wheels of his part, his fate, he may be torn asunder. He may be killed, but the resistant, integral soul in him is not destroyed. He comes through, though he dies. He goes through with his fate, though death swallows him. And it is in the facing of fate, this going right through with it, that tragedy lies. Tragedy is not disaster. It is a disaster when a cart-wheel goes over a frog, but it is not a tragedy. Tragedy is the working out of some passional problem within the soul of man . . . There has to be a supreme *struggle*.

In this view, tragedy is a forward movement undertaken by the soul at a high level of self-responsibility. There has to be struggle with the 'passional problem' in order to yield some conscious realization to the soul so that it can pass forward in moral continuity and integrity, grasping the logic of its fate. Unless there is the struggle into consciousness, unless the soul 'goes through' with things in active awareness, there is mere contingency, the meaninglessness of accident, instrumentality—the process of passive fatalism, not of tragedy.

The distinction between the two processes was very important to Lawrence the novelist: that is, as author of *The Rainbow* and *Women in Love*. But at the time of his early novels, *The White Peacock* and *The Trespasser*, he had hardly begun to tackle the 'passional problem'. Instead, there is an overwhelming sense of passive fatalism, but no way of working free of it, no consciousness by which the individual can be wrested from the drift of blind necessity. The connection between an irresolute tragic sense and a failure in consciousness was something, therefore, which Lawrence knew only too well from his own experience as a young writer. And out of that experience he realized also how the artist can disguise and ennoble his failure of consciousness by patterning his art in such a way that he excludes from view the very terms by which his surrender to fatalism can be questioned or contested. The effort to discover the missing terms and put them back in the argument was for Lawrence, as novelist and as critic, the impetus behind his growth to consciousness. His attack on absolutes in art and the creation of a new kind of moral art in *The Rainbow* and *Women in Love*: all originated from his profound quarrel with inherited forms of fatalism.

Because I believe that Lawrence's development as a novelist cannot be considered without an understanding of his relationship to tragedy, I have tried to make clear in the course of this study the connections between various areas of his creative interest—areas which in the past have usually been discussed separately or only in relation to his criticism. If tragedy was a crucial issue for Lawrence the novelist, then equally so were the expressions of tragic dilemma which he found in other writers whose work he needed in order to focus his perceptions, to crystallize his sense of the 'passional problem'. It was this need, above all, which brought Lawrence to an imaginative engagement with the work of Hardy, Poe, Hawthorne, Melville, and Cooper. Through them Lawrence defined his own evolving purposes as a novelist. Without the other writers as a sharpening force in Lawrence's imagination, *The Rainbow* and *Women in Love* would probably not have emerged in the form in which we have them today.

There seem to have been two stages in Lawrence's reading of Hardy or the Americans. A period of early, general familiarity with their work was followed by a more stringent phase of re-reading and re-assessment. Thus Hardy's novels were known to Lawrence in his youth, and their presence can be felt in his work even as late as *Sons and Lovers*. But then, during the writing of *The Rainbow*, Lawrence turned aside from his work to re-read Hardy and to produce a long critical study of the Wessex novels. And with American literature, there was a similar experience. According to Jessie Chambers's memoir, Lawrence read in his youth Emerson, Thoreau, Longfellow, Whitman, and Cooper (in particular, *The Last of the Mohicans* and *The Pathfinder*). He knew the poems of Poe, and seems[1] to have been acquainted with the *Tales*. I also think it likely that by the time he came to write *The Rainbow*, Lawrence had read Hawthorne's *The Scarlet Letter*. Only in 1916, however, during the writing of *Women in Love*, did American literature take on the kind of imaginative importance for Lawrence's own art which Hardy's novels possessed several years previously. For now Lawrence discovered *Moby Dick* and read (or re-read) *The Deer-slayer*, with, I believe, a profound effect on his understanding of Hawthorne and Poe. In 1917, after completing *Women in Love*, Lawrence moved on to a critical study of American literature, and for this purpose he enlarged his previous knowledge by reading Benjamin Franklin's *Autobiography*, Hector St. John Crèvecœur's *Letters from an*

---

[1] See *Collected Letters*, ed. Harry T. Moore (1962), vol. I, p. 154.

American Farmer, Richard Dana's *Two Years before the Mast*, two novels by Hawthorne (*The House of the Seven Gables* and *The Blithedale Romance*), and Cooper's 'Anglo-American novels' (*Homeward Bound, Home as Found, The Spy, The Pilot*).

The different phases of Lawrence's engagement with Hardy and the Americans have to be understood as a sequence, because then it becomes apparent how far Lawrence's creative needs preceded his formation of critical attitudes. He could not have become a penetrating critic of Hardy and the Americans without having first grappled as a novelist with their meaning. Therefore my discussion of Lawrence's development is mainly concerned with the sequence of writing from *The White Peacock* to *Women in Love* and the essays on American literature, because it is here that his struggle with his own and others' writing is at its most illuminating, not only in what it reveals of Lawrence's purposes but also in what it points to in the work of Hardy and the Americans.

There is a tendency to think of Lawrence's criticism as a kind of brilliant, impressionistic commentary which distances us from his subject, either because of his personal preoccupations or because of a summarizing loftiness of argument whose grand conclusions we cannot usefully relate to the specific local texture of the work he is discussing. But if we look closely at Hardy and the Americans—at first apart from Lawrence's view of them, and then in relation to his work—it will be seen that Lawrence's critical analysis is grounded upon a genuine sense of the specific which is always invisibly there for him even as he moves quickly and unpretentiously to a discussion of the larger implications. The extent to which Lawrence's critical discoveries issue from the substance and grain of a work has never been sufficiently recognized, and therefore I have discussed Hardy and the Americans (initially, at least) in separation from Lawrence. In this way, Lawrence's view of the other writers can, when necessary, be affirmed or challenged, and, at the same time, aspects of their art can be dealt with which have more importance for Lawrence's own art than his explicit critical statements would lead us to believe. By isolating and distinguishing the particular concerns of Hardy and the Americans, I am often resisting Lawrence's critical incursions, because resistance can help to display more usefully than acquiescence the opportunities which lay in the other art for Lawrence's further realization in his own.

But even if one tries to avoid one-sidedness, it is necessary to be ordered and selective as regards the material to be discussed. My aim here has been to concentrate on those works which had particular relevance to Lawrence as novelist rather than as critic, even though at times a work was important to him in both of his capacities. In his

Study of Thomas Hardy he dealt with most of the Wessex novels, but gave his main attention to three—*The Return of the Native, Tess of the d'Urbervilles,* and *Jude the Obscure.* His choice was significant, and therefore my chapter on Hardy in Part One is almost solely devoted to a discussion of these novels. More than any others, they represent the relationship between Hardy's work and Lawrence's which reached its conclusion during the writing of *The Rainbow.* After that came another focus for Lawrence in American literature, but although *Women in Love* reveals the effect of the new vision I have treated the novel within the continuum of Lawrence's work, only then proceeding in Part Two to a discussion of Poe, Hawthorne, Melville, and Cooper. These are the writers who really mattered to Lawrence's creative development, and not the other subjects of his essays on American literature: Franklin, Crèvecœur, and Dana. Whitman, of course, has a prominent place in the essays, but while recognizing his importance throughout Lawrence's entire writing life, I have not been able to discuss him in any depth because that would require a treatment of his and Lawrence's verse, an area which lies outside the range and aims of this book. Cooper's 'Anglo-American novels' have also been omitted from discussion, despite Lawrence's essay on them, because the Leatherstocking novels have the greater claim for detailed attention. Similarly, Melville's novels *Typee* and *Omoo* are not discussed in Part Two because I believe that the place which they occupied for the author of the American *Studies* was filled, for the author of *Women in Love,* by *Moby Dick.* On the other hand I have discussed in Part Two certain tales by Poe which Lawrence never mentions in his essays, but which are relevant to aspects of *Women in Love* and also to the work of the other Americans. In fact, the continuity of themes among the Americans is given particular emphasis in Part Two, and to this end I have gone against chronology in placing the chapter on Cooper where it is.

RICHARD SWIGG

University of Keele
March 1971

Acknowledgements

My principal debt is to Charles Tomlinson for his constant encouragement, generosity, and understanding throughout the various stages of this book. I would also like to thank Catharine Carver for her thorough scrutiny of my typescript, and for the helpful suggestions which she made for its improvement. My thanks as well to Ann and Alfred Hardacre, my typists, and to Derek Lee and Percy Lloyd for the loan of books. My debt to those who granted me permission to quote from the works of Lawrence and Hardy is acknowledged at page iv.

I am also aware of an indebtedness to authors whose books have suggested several valuable starting-points for my own thinking—notably, John Holloway in *The Victorian Sage*, Donald Davie in *The Heyday of Sir Walter Scott*, and D. E. S. Maxwell in *American Fiction*.

Finally, my thanks to my wife for her patience.

R. S.

D. H. Lawrence: Some Relevant Dates

1885   Born in Eastwood, Notts., 11 September
1906–9 Studies for a Teacher's Certificate at Nottingham University College and takes up a teaching post in Croydon. Writes *The White Peacock*.
1910   Begins *The Trespasser*. His mother becomes ill in the summer and dies in December.
1911   '. . . in that year, for me everything collapsed, save the mystery of death, and the haunting of death in life.' January: *The White Peacock* published. Begins *Sons and Lovers*. November: becomes ill and leaves his teaching post.
1912   During convalescence completes *The Trespasser* which is published in May. Meets Frieda Weekley and goes abroad with her, to live for the next two years mainly in Italy. Rewrites *Sons and Lovers*.
1913   By March is working on the first draft of *The Rainbow* (known at this time as *The Sisters*). May: *Sons and Lovers* published. September: begins another draft of *The Rainbow*.
1914   May: sends a completed draft of *The Rainbow* to Edward Garnett. June: returns to England and marries Frieda in July. September–December: writes the *Study of Thomas Hardy*. December: begins the final version of *The Rainbow*.
1915   March: completes *The Rainbow*. Writes 'England, My England'. August or September: writes 'The Crown'. September: revises Italian sketches of 1913 as *Twilight in Italy*. *The Rainbow* published, and banned in November. December: goes to live in Cornwall.
1916   Writes *Women in Love*.
1917   Writes 'The Reality of Peace'.

1917   By August is writing the first versions of essays on American
         literature.
         October: expelled from Cornwall by the police, and lives at
         various times in the next two years in Berkshire and Derby-
         shire.
1918   June: finishes the essays on American literature.
1919   November: goes abroad, and lives mainly in Sicily till
         February 1922.
1920   June: finishes a revision of the essays on American literature.
         November: *The Lost Girl* published (completed in April).
         Women in Love published in a limited edition in New York.
1921   June: completes *Aaron's Rod* (published April 1922).
         December: revises 'England, My England'.
1922   February: sails to Ceylon.
         May–August: lives in Australia and writes *Kangaroo.*
         September: arrives in California, and lives during the next
         three years in New Mexico and Mexico.
         October: *Fantasia of the Unconscious* published.
         Begins the final revision of the essays on American literature
         which are published as *Studies in Classic American Literature* in
         August 1923.
1923   Begins *The Plumed Serpent.*
1924   Completes *St. Mawr,* published in the following year.
1925   Completes *The Plumed Serpent* (published January 1926), and
         in September returns to Europe. For the next five years
         lives at various places in Germany, Austria, Switzerland,
         Italy, and France.
1928   *Lady Chatterley's Lover* published.
1930   Dies in France, 2 March.

PART ONE

Tragedy and the Unconscious

I

Thomas Hardy and the Problem of
the 'Middle Distance'

I T is not difficult to see a confusion of purpose in the art of Hardy's novels, but less easy to describe the source of the unease. We may put aside the philosophic defences by which Hardy seems to be explaining (and misrepresenting) his art, but then we must contend with the nature of the impulses, the strange energies, the tendernesses—all that sensitive knowledge, in fact, which the 'philosophy' is trying to defend. Through this inner knowledge there seems to run a basic misgiving on Hardy's part, a sense of bemusement, something vulnerable in him which winces and falters. It is a hesitancy in the art which denies adequate voice to the latent urgings of the novels and which gives them the shape of an imprecise metaphysic or an approximate 'impression'.

Hardy, however, in letting the approximations remain, seems quite knowingly to tolerate this restricting of his art.[1] But, as a passage from *Jude the Obscure* reveals, there is consistency in his self-limiting. Somewhat like his own Jude he stands at bay behind an intervening filter or 'philosophy', partly sheltered from the harsh sun of contingency:

He pulled his straw hat over his face, and peered through the interstices of the plaiting at the white brightness, vaguely reflecting. Growing

---

[1] See Hardy's note on an article about him in *The Fortnightly Magazine*, April 1917: 'Like so many critics, Mr. Courtney treats my works of art as if they were a scientific system of philosophy, although I have repeatedly stated in prefaces and elsewhere that the views in them are *seemings*, provisional impressions only, used for artistic purposes because they represent approximately the impressions of the age, and are plausible, till somebody produces better theories of the universe' (*The Life of Thomas Hardy, 1840–1928*, by Florence Emily Hardy (1962), p. 375). See also a letter, December 1920: '. . . I have no philosophy—merely what I have often explained to be only a confused heap of impressions, like those of a bewildered child at a conjuring show . . .' (Ibid., p. 410).

up brought responsibilities, he found. Events did not rhyme quite as he had thought. Nature's logic was too horrid for him to care for. That mercy towards one set of creatures was cruelty towards another sickened his sense of harmony. As you got older, and felt yourself to be at the centre of your time, and not at a point in its circumference, as you had felt when you were little, you were seized with a sort of shuddering, he perceived. All around you there seemed to be something glaring, garish, rattling, and the noises and glares hit upon the little cell called your life, and shook it, and warped it.   (P. 23.)[1]

As the 'little cell' shrinks back from the glare of full consciousness, one touches with it the erratic stamina at the heart of the novels—the unreliable energies, the fitful determination, which are ultimately disappointing when they fail to carry Hardy's intuitiveness all the way into firm, mature realization. One touches with Jude the diffident imagination of the earlier novelist, the man who noted in his diary the month that he published *The Return of the Native*: 'Woke before it was light. Felt that I had not enough staying power to hold my own in the world' (28 November 1878; *Life*, p. 124).

I

In contrast, *The Return of the Native* itself does possess a 'staying power' of a circumscribed but decisive kind. By the creation of Egdon Heath, Hardy propounds a mental defensiveness of a quality to be found nowhere else in the novels, for here a stern, undaunted face is turned against the mysterious illogicalities of life. The Heath is as much an outer mental barrier as it is a place, a strange 'philosophic' safeguard for that life and knowledge which is content to stay within the boundary of its attitudes. This 'great inviolate place', 'slighted and enduring'—and doggedly insensitive to the pains of human history—is like the haggard rind grown round the inner, sensitive organism. It is the stubborn, long-distance vision which protects the small satisfactions to be found within the casing, the microscopic joys or contentment of the insects' consciousness—as with the ants toiling and bustling in their Heath thoroughfare, the stupefied wasps creeping or rolling

---

[1] Unless otherwise indicated, page references are to the editions and sources listed in the Bibliography, p. 363

inside the fallen apples, the maggots wallowing in the dried ponds, and the butterfly-acrobats sporting round Clym Yeobright's furze-hook. At this minute level the imagination is stable, free, uninhibited.

But if this sensuous vision is touched by Hardy's defensive consciousness, a blight seems to occur. It is as if all the inner succulence, all the vivid strangeness, become one, in tragic withering, with the outer mental shell, Egdon. When the Heath speaks through the 'mummied heath-bells of the past summer, originally tender and purple, now washed colourless by Michaelmas rains, and dried to dead skins by October suns,' its November winds create a note akin to 'the ruins of human song . . . a worn whisper, dry and papery.' Human aspirations in the novel press for some realization beyond the small satisfactions, beyond the Egdon limits, but this would take Hardy out and into the blinding light of original, perplexing consciousness. The creative energy in him hesitates, and so, like the heath-bells, the aspirations lose their succulence and integrity, passing into dead forms, into dull, inferior motives.

This is the fate of Eustacia and Mrs. Yeobright, who are ultimately assigned a withered expression for their unspecified yearnings. Both women are intuitive in generalized vision as they look beyond the encompassing Heath, and both lack the finer featuring, the more conscious rendering, to champion and give exact shape to their vague desires. Hardy says of Eustacia (p. 78), 'There was no middle distance in her perspective.' What we might say is that he cannot let her progress from her unconscious desire close at hand to the uncertainly-perceived finer form in the far distance, because there is a connecting step missing in his consciousness. At the point in Hardy's thinking where he falters over the problem of conscious shape (and so has to betray the imagination in him), there the bright, fluid vision of Eustacia's dreams must dry and dull. Thus, after hearing Clym's voice on the night of his arrival on the Heath, Eustacia dreams of herself (p. 138) dancing as in Paradise with a man in silver armour, both moving in brilliance and harmony against the background of the Heath. After the dancers have dived into one of the Heath pools and come out 'into an iridescent hollow, arched with rainbows', the silver knight begins to remove his casque to kiss her. But the features are not to be seen, the shape cannot be stabilized: 'At that moment there was a cracking noise, and his figure fell into fragments like a pack of cards.' Daylight has arrived while Eustacia is dreaming, and a maidservant has opened the window-shutter. But the imaginative brilliance again appears (pp. 233–5) in Eustacia's fascination with Clym's talk of the Louvre and of the room filled with glittering treasure: ' "... a perfect blaze of splendour. The rays bristle and dart from the encrustations of gilding to the magnificent inlaid coffers ... till there is a perfect network of light which quite dazzles the eye." ' And Clym, as the native returned from Paris and the diamond trade, is in Eustacia's eyes the human featuring of these alien riches: ' "Clym, the eclipsed moonlight shines upon your face with a strange foreign colour, and shows its shape as if it were cut out in gold." '

Eustacia's paradisal yearnings are akin to Mrs. Yeobright's less romantic but equally far-gazing intuitive sight. Meditatively flying beyond the limits of her own body, the older woman also lacks a middle distance: 'Communities were seen by her as from a distance ... vast masses of beings, jostling, zigzagging, and processioning in definite directions, but whose features are indistinguishable by the very comprehensiveness of the view.' Her undetailed grasp of mankind in its general, overall shiftings is comparable to Eustacia's dream of free movement and brilliant imaginative treasure, and makes Mrs. Yeobright one of those blind, female seers who 'can watch a world which they never saw, and estimate forces of which they have only heard.' Like Eustacia, she seeks some unembodied larger liberty beyond the hemmings-in of the unthinking Heath routine, and so she must instinctively turn from the sight of the busy ants working across their age-old little track on the Heath, to see (p. 341) a heron flying 'with his face towards the sun'. It is her equivalent of Eustacia's anonymous knight: 'He had come dripping wet from some pool in the valleys, and as he flew the edges and lining of his wings, his thighs, and his breast were so caught by the bright sunbeams that he appeared as if formed of burnished silver.'

Amongst these fluid cravings as they pursue conscious identity or form, one finds the real inner plan of the novel lying dormant or imperfectly construed. At moments Hardy can suggest, almost with the general comprehensiveness of his Mrs. Yeobright, the clear path of aspiration—most notably when he pictures Eustacia (p. 13) standing anonymous and alone on Rainbarrow:

Above the plain rose the hill, above the hill rose the barrow, and above the barrow rose the figure. Above the figure was nothing that could be mapped elsewhere than on a celestial globe.

Significantly it is here, where the imagination needs it—above the 'homogeneous' organism of earth merging with the human figure, above the featureless and unparticularized—that Hardy places the man from heaven in Eustacia's dream, the 'high thinking' Clym Yeobright, heard only as a voice when he first comes back and seen for a moment as the worn, mentally-ridden 'countenance of the future'. His is the face or the human identity in which the anonymous desires of the women locate themselves, but when those desires are directly particularized in relation to Clym, when Hardy interprets them through Clym's mind, the precious metal becomes selfish currency. The aspiring for an enrichment to the spirit, as suggested by the glistening values of the silver knight, the Louvre treasure, and the burnished heron, is translated through the strain upon Clym as the desire for social gain—Eustacia seen as hopelessly romantic in pursuit of a Paris of fashion and pleasure; Mrs. Yeobright seen as more staid in her desire for Clym's enhancement in status and affluence in business. On this level Hardy makes the conflict one of social versus nonsocial purposes, with Clym shared out and broken between the claims of his two loves; but on the level of imagination, the problem is more radical.

What one sees in Clym's breakdown is Hardy's failure to sustain him as the enactor of *any* desires. Hardy can carry the striving dreams no further in Clym, and they must end as shrivelled ideas, taking on the brown gaunt look which both the Heath and Clym come to have. So although Clym is blinded and burnt out by the women's overpowering wishes, the burden he really carries is the strain of the novel's consciousness. His 'culture scheme' displays the impasse in which he and the women are fixed. He comes back to teach the ordinary Egdon people 'that they might rise to a serene comprehensiveness without going through the process of enriching themselves.' But there is no intermediate stage, no middle distance, no method of translating desires into accurate reality, which Clym can give to the women, let alone to his pupils. In terms of the plot-conflict, Mrs. Yeobright and Eustacia are disappointed in Clym as a teacher because their social ambitions have been betrayed; but in terms of imagination his 'culture scheme' betrays them because it has no means of giving stability to their deeper, spiritual ambitions. Therefore Clym must be an implausible figure of consciousness. If the two women are the question of the novel, Clym is the wavering answer.

There is no adequate reply to the aspirings but Hardy fashions a semblance of one when he characterizes the desires inside a simple moral picture. At the same time he leaves himself free not to have to confirm the accuracy of the picture. When the unfulfilled ambitions are seen through the eyes of the ordinary Heath people, when they are interpreted through the obviously approximate 'impression' of custom, humour, ignorance, and superstition, then the vital desires of the aspirers can be evaluated and given the appearance of being more manageable than they really are—all without Hardy's having to take explicit responsibility for the crude moral shaping and identification which he uses.

Thus the actors, Egdon people and aspirers, are assigned their parts in a primitive drama in which, as with the defiant bonfires at the beginning of the novel and the mummers' play later, the small community defeats evil menaces from the outer darkness: so on Rainbarrow the Devil is tempted into the small area of firelight, and at Christmas St. George is victorious over the Saracen. Yet though this primitive, superstitious morality allows Hardy to simplify the issues, he does not give complete, creative assent to the work of the morality's agents, Venn and Susan Nonsuch. These covert protectors of the innocent in the little commonwealth remain suspiciously like the devils and witches they actively war upon—Venn, the faithful defender of Thomasin's honour, the constant knight, appears on Rainbarrow like a red demon summoned up by the wild dance of the community; Susan Nonsuch, the proclaimer of Eustacia as a witch, remains the superstitious victimizer, not the victim.

But although Hardy will not support these agents when they carry the moral verdict beyond the narrow system of values and strike out in real violence, with Susan's knife attack on Eustacia in the church and Venn's gun assault on Wildeve, he will happily establish the simple moral arena from which they are only extending its judgements. There, with sanction, it seems, Eustacia and Wildeve in their passion can be more clearly seen as threats to the peace of Thomasin and Clym. Once brought within the bounds of the moral ordering, their identity becomes that of intruders, controlled by their traditionally doomed roles in a predictable folk play. The desires which create the silver knight of Eustacia's dream cannot be met by the ultimately disappointing higher consciousness of Clym but they can be replied to by the crude moral consciousness. Therefore, Eustacia in pursuit of Clym as the knight of her romantic dream, intrudes into the Christmas mumming as the Turkish knight, slays the Valiant Soldier, and is finally killed after a 'gradual sinking to earth' by St. George. In the same way, Wildeve intrudes on Christian Cantle's mission with Mrs. Yeobright's guineas, and the small circle of heath where they gamble by lantern-light becomes another morality arena, inside which Christian cries out against the dice as 'the devil's play-things' and fears damnation: ' "The devil will toss me into the flames." ' This Valiant Soldier is easily cleared of his money, but as he falls, Venn appears as another St. George to win back the guineas from the Devil in a burst of intense play.

Hardy almost admits that the moral ordering is a travesty of passion, a device which whittles energy down to the size of caricature. His imagination cannot help suggesting this of the gambling fury—'their eyes being concentrated upon the little flat stone, which to them was an arena vast and important as a battle-field.' Nevertheless, Hardy retreats to this small-scale simplicity in order to make acceptable those events which are really caused by the failure of consciousness in his aspirers, as one sees with the death of Mrs. Yeobright. After being excluded from her son's house because Eustacia feared Wildeve's discovery there, Mrs. Yeobright dies from an adder's bite and from fatigued despair on the Heath. But one feels that the character is over-whelmed by a lack of 'staying power', by Hardy's withdrawal of energy from a cause that cannot hold its own in the merciless glare of the sun—the blinding light which parches the imagination dry. Brought to the ground from her spiritual and social aloofness, she reaches the level of the creeping things previously unconsidered in her vision and the level of the morality at which her decline can be more easily interpreted.

At the gathering in the turf-hut (pp. 347–50) where they attempt to revive her, the morality arena again appears—at first in Christian Cantle's remark on the snake, like the ' "old serpent in God's garden, that gied the apple to the young woman with no clothes" ', and later when the indictment of unseen evil reaches out beyond the small group round Mrs. Yeobright in the flickering light of the hut and implicates Eustacia and Wildeve, standing in the shadows. It is from these simple terms of moral reference, by which the fierce glare which *really* kills Mrs. Yeobright is lit more manageably, that Clym ultimately takes his consciousness. He is worn by remorse and his discovery of Eustacia's part in the affair, yielding up his high thinking to accept in exhaustion the superstitious, conforming judgements of the ignorant: ' "How bewitched I was! How could there be any good in a woman that everybody spoke ill of?" ' He hesitates in regret after he has driven Eustacia away, but the primitive judgement remains in force, to be finally executed by her drowning.

Nevertheless, the double-sided method of presenting her death —Eustacia pulled under, exhausted and protesting against fate, while at the same moment Susan Nonsuch works vindictive magic against her—suggests more openly than in the death of Mrs. Yeobright that Hardy is leaving in doubt the justice of his moral explanation. On one side Eustacia complains (p. 420) of her unfair treatment by life, her lack of fulfilment and Wildeve's inadequacy as a passionate equal: ' "He's not *great* enough for me to give myself to—he does not suffice for my desire! . . . I was capable of much; but I have been injured and blighted and crushed by things beyond my control!" ' With her one looks up towards that blank in development which Hardy cannot bridge with his unstable, unenriched Clym. But against her, in the sinking vision, where Eustacia can be viewed as too self-willed, proud, and socially ambitious, she is scaled down to the terms of the reductive morality, made the size of the little wax image that Susan moulds, stabs, and finally melts in the fire. In spacing out the complaints Hardy is free to endorse neither Eustacia's protest against the incomprehensible nor the vengeful retort of the primitive morality. When he creates (p. 419) the impression that Eustacia is inevitably engulfed by the Heath, so that she 'ceased to stand erect, gradually crouching down under the umbrella as if she were drawn into the Barrow by a hand from beneath', the moral, fatalistic effect is kept deliberately approximate—a 'seeming' which speaks only vaguely for what Hardy cannot define: the real inevitability of her fall. Eustacia must die because he cannot develop her beyond his own gaunt mental consciousness, and so she must be absorbed by Egdon, the grim expression of that consciousness.

There is a similar wavering effect in the account of Clym's fall. He comes (p. 230) at the moment of the moon's eclipse as the lover and as the 'high thinking' and mentally straining progressive. His spiritual eye travels at long distance over the lunar shape as if it were an image of an unreachable world where personal development can freely take place, unhindered by society's crass demand for status and ambition. What the silver knight and the heron are to the women, so the moon is to Clym. Yet the bright, ghastly geography of 'the silvery globe'—'the Bay of Rainbows, the sombre Sea of Crises, the Ocean of Storms, the Lake of Dreams, the vast Walled Plains, and the wondrous Ring Mountains'—is the very picture of his own ravaged consciousness, stretched to its uttermost limit. One reaches with Clym the bounds of the novel's own consciousness, for the 'far-removed landscape' of the moon, with its wild, barren deserts, is really the 'gaunt waste in Thule' which is Egdon, the outermost mental crust in which the unresolved strivings take on their final, rigid moulding. At the exact moment that Clym's limits as a developing individual are fixed, a 'tawny stain' begins to grow on the moon's edge, and the cloaked figure of Eustacia arrives to eclipse her lover's mind by a sensual darkening. So stamina falters, Clym the silver knight begins to collapse, while in the moral framework the Valiant Soldier is overwhelmed by the Turkish knight in her powerful egotism. In the same way Hardy allows a possible shift of interpretation when he recounts Eustacia's meeting (p. 99) with Wildeve on the Heath, watched from his hiding-place by Venn: 'They were as two horns which the sluggish heath had put forth from its crown, like a mollusc, and had now again drawn in.' They can be seen as abortive creations, hesitantly venturing beyond the protective shell of Egdon, but unable to survive as stable, larger figures in an atmosphere where there is no further consciousness to support them, no 'intervening . . . ether'[1] through which to pass to fulfilment. Or Eustacia and Wildeve can be viewed through the judging eyes of Venn who is disguised as part of the Heath and

[1] Yeobright's preaching 'was not unlike arguing to ancient Chaldeans that in ascending from earth to the pure empyrean it was not necessary to pass first into the intervening heaven of ether' (p. 204).

who submerges them within it by his moral vision, as he recalls the adventured aberrations.

The aspirers who seek paradisal harmony cannot escape from Hardy's 'tragical' stoicism and his perplexed stubbornness, his view of life's illogicalities and discords. It is only underneath that attitude, underneath the hard Egdon shell, that life begins to make strange sense and harmony, amongst the beautiful, blind movements of the purely instinctive life. But harmony can only be found at this level if the upper layer of stoicism is forgotten, if the crude moral picturing is abandoned, and if the human spirit submits to an intense restriction. So, in the gambling scene, the human intensity of the play tightens the moral consciousness of the scene to the point where it disappears, snuffed out by the moth in its blind flight into the lantern flame, and is replaced, almost immediately and unthinkingly, by the light from the glow-worms, the insect consciousness.

But Hardy's suggestion of a *quid pro quo* interchange between man and the small life of the Heath is not presented in all its astonishing variety until the description of Clym's new life as the temporarily blinded furze-cutter, 'not more distinguishable from the scene around him than the green caterpillar from the leaf it feeds on.' Here, through Clym's mindless absorption, is the sensitive inner landscape of Egdon with its strange lustres and movements, like a minute paradise, a non-human community, the only *real* place on earth where concern for social aggrandizement does not exist. Perhaps its strangest aspect arises from the inclusion of the human figure and hence the normalizing of the alien vision round him, so that the scene is more extraordinary in proportion to the unself-remarking manner:

His daily life was of a curious microscopic sort, his whole world being limited to a circuit of a few feet from his person. His familiars were creeping and winged things, and they seemed to enroll him in their band. Bees hummed around his ears with an intimate air, and tugged at the heath and the furze-flowers at his side in such numbers as to weigh them down to the sod. The strange amber-coloured butterflies which Egdon produced, and which were never seen elsewhere, quivered in the breath of his lips, alighted upon his bowed back, and sported with the glittering point of his hook as he flourished it up and down. Tribes of emerald-green grasshoppers leaped over his feet, falling awkwardly on their backs, heads, or hips, like unskilful acrobats, as chance might rule; or engaged themselves in noisy flirtations under the fern-fronds with silent ones of homely hue. Huge flies, ignorant of larders and wire-netting, and quite in a savage state, buzzed about him without knowing that he was a man. In and out of the fern-dells snakes glided in their most brilliant blue and yellow guise, it being the season immediately following the shedding of their old skins, when their colours are brightest. Litters of young rabbits came out from their forms to sun themselves upon hillocks, the hot beams blazing through the delicate tissue of each thin-fleshed ear, and firing it to a blood-red transparency in which the veins could be seen. None of them feared him.   (P. 296.)

But the unendangered, unknowing freedom of this vision, in all its curious features and relaxed knowledge, retains a tinge of the fantastic because while the human mind is being assimilated and consoled Hardy is still aware in Mrs. Yeobright of a responsibility to higher consciousness. One senses that the 'intimate air' of Clym's 'familiars' is due to Hardy's normalizing and presenting as acceptable Clym's new mindless identity in defence against the larger view in Mrs. Yeobright which (p. 327), in disappointment, makes her 'scarcely able to familiarize herself with this strange reality.' Even though the playfulness of the microscopic world is expanded in acuteness and precise delicacy against Mrs. Yeobright's long-range generalizing vision (and social scheming), something of Hardy's own dissatisfaction with Clym as a failed human being remains in the women's disappointment and the tragic sympathy allowed them. Their disillusion, although partly accounted for by their social hopes, persists as an implicit charge of failure from which Hardy will not defend Clym. To live on, Clym must be less than a human being in his restriction; so latterly his life 'creeps like a snail'. Burnt out as a lover but dutifully he offers himself as a husband to Thomasin, and lastly becomes a preacher on 'morally unimpeachable subjects'. But 'Some believed him, and some believed not', and Hardy, as throughout the novel, refuses to confirm the truth of his moral ordering and its spokesmen.

2

This hesitancy continues in the later novel, *Tess of the d'Urbervilles; A Pure Woman Faithfully Presented* (1891). But *Tess* displays a different attitude towards imaginative yearnings and their un-fulfilment. The change is revealed if one compares Clym's furze-cutting scene and its harmonies with the moment when Angel Clare's harp-playing entrances Tess across the garden at Tal-bothays. In an atmosphere of 'delicate equilibrium', where there is 'no distinction between the near and the far, and an auditor felt close to everything within the horizon,' Tess is captured, a hypnotized creature:

The outskirt of the garden in which Tess found herself had been left uncultivated for some years, and was now damp and rank with juicy grass which sent up mists of pollen at a touch; and with tall blooming weeds emitting offensive smells—weeds whose red and yellow and purple hues formed a polychrome as dazzling as that of cultivated flowers. She went stealthily as a cat through this profusion of growth, gathering cuckoo-spittle on her skirts, cracking snails that were under-foot, staining her hands with thistle-milk and slug-lime, and rubbing off upon her naked arms sticky blights which, though snow-white on the apple-tree trunks, made madder stains on her skin; thus she drew quite near to Clare, still unobserved of him.

Tess was conscious of neither time nor space. The exaltation which she had described as being producible at will by gazing at a star, came now without any determination of hers; she undulated upon the thin notes of the second-hand harp, and their harmonies passed like breezes through her, bringing tears into her eyes. The floating pollen seemed to be his notes made visible, and the dampness of the garden the weeping of the garden's sensibility. Though near nightfall, the rank-smelling weed-flowers glowed as if they would not close for intentness, and the waves of colour mixed with the waves of sound.   (Pp. 159–60.)

The furze-cutting momentum can enroll Clym into its small peace and innocence provided that he yields up his mind and provided that these minute satisfactions are hidden from the scrutiny of Mrs. Yeobright's aspiring vision. But in *Tess* a moment of paradisal balance is gained by merging the small and larger visions; by interpenetrating the spiritual hope and the physical limits to create a wavering whole. The sense of the earth-bound, of ugly physicality, is not destroyed, but it has enough of its gross force enervated by spiritual infusions for Hardy to make new, bizarre harmonies.

He has, in fact, moved towards an aesthetic, compensatory

method, something foreshadowed by the deliberately hesitant
moralizing in *The Return of the Native*, but more clearly seen in a
note of June 1877, twelve years before *Tess* was begun. In it
Hardy says he is interested in a new idea of beauty, in making a
'sweet pattern' from Nature's 'defects': 'I think the art lies in
making these defects the basis of a hitherto unperceived beauty,
by irradiating them with "the light that never was" on their
surface, but is seen to be latent in them by the spiritual eye'
(*Life*, p. 114). The sense of 'defects' in life—or the inability to
reconcile the pressures of spirit and flesh, social and non-social
aims—makes Clym's mind and Hardy's long-range view of Egdon
into one 'slighted and enduring' shell. But the reference to Wordsworth's 'Elegiac Stanzas' suggests something of Hardy's growing
inclination to make the predicament spiritually acceptable. In
this poem Wordsworth imagines that if he had painted Peele
Castle he would not have created Beaumont's storm picture—
'That Hulk which labours in the deadly swell . . . Cased in the
unfeeling armour of old time'—but once, in a calmer mood than
now, out of 'the fond illusion of my heart', would have made a
picture of 'Elysian quiet, without toil or strife',

> . . . if mine had been the Painter's hand,
> To express what then I saw; and add the gleam,
> The light that never was, on sea or land,
> The consecration, and the Poet's dream.

But Hardy wants to add the tranquil gleam to the sense of strife
and treat the repulsive and the agonizing as if it were beautiful.
Therefore Wordsworth's contribution to the spiritualizing aesthetic is only partial. Probably it was in Turner's paintings that
Hardy saw how 'the light that never was' could dissolve the impact
of the mentally-perceived tragic limitations. A note of January
1887 reveals:

The much decried, mad, late-Turner rendering is now necessary to
create my interest. The exact truth as to material fact ceases to be of
importance in art—it is a student's style—the style of a period when
the mind is serene and unawakened to the tragical mysteries of life;
when it does not bring anything to the object that coalesces with and
translates the qualities that are already there,—half hidden, it may
be—and the two united are depicted as the All. (*Life*, p. 185.)

However, if the spiritual light in *Tess* brings out the 'tragical mysteries' in order to neutralize them, the aesthetic union must be made at the cost of lowering intellectual intensity or resistant energies—hence the fluid light of the garden scene and of others in the novel, where the 'exact truth as to material fact' or the 'defects' can be sufficiently blurred to allow the pitying irony to embrace the poignant inevitability of it all. The entranced surrender of Tess in her advance through the weird tones of the garden belongs with other hazily lit, somnambulistic scenes, where tragic yieldings are passively conceded in fog or in the intervals between sleep and waking, in the twilights before complete night or day. At the fog in the Chase, Tess, a 'pale nebulousness' in white muslin, becomes a spirit betrayed by the flesh in Alec's seduction. But in Angel's vision of Tess in the 'spectral, half-compounded, aqueous light' of the dairy fields before daybreak, it is the animal in Tess which is betrayed by Angel's spiritual seduction; to him she appears 'ghostly, as if she were merely a soul at large.' This is to lead, after the revelations of Tess's past, to the half-conscious events of the sleep-walking episode, when Tess acquiesces in Angel's carrying her off to burial in the abbot's coffin. With kisses, one dream sweetly puts away the results of another dream—each a sanctified surrender to the 'tragical mysteries'.

The confused sexuality of such 'mysteries' is viewed through a haze of consciousness because in thus translating sensuality into a spiritually acceptable diffuseness Hardy creates a vigourless 'seeming' which is not only aesthetic but moral. The taint with which Tess is smeared as she listens to Angel's harp is no more than an enfeebled indictment of her guilt. The fecund 'dampness' becomes 'the weeping of the garden's sensibility' in which consciousness of the flesh is decomposed, thinned out into the sexual implicitness of the pollen mists and stains. Through all this moves the spiritual dreamer, unharmed and just lightly impeded, towards the illusion where the sexual cloud and the 'thin notes' of the harp sanctify each other in bodiless harmony. It is Hardy's way of not being morally bound to the 'exact truth' of 'material fact'.

As he casts his luminous ambivalence over the question of innocence and guilt, he is deliberately weakening what in *The Return of the Native* was an unconfident compulsion to assign moral evaluation to his characters. In the other novel the rudimentary morality was confined but intensely lit within the greater darkness surrounding the Christmas mumming, the Heath gambling, the furze-hut at Mrs. Yeobright's death, and Susan's house when Eustacia dies. It was the sun in miniature, the failure of energy writ small, but *Tess* writes it diffusely. Here the light is unconfined, less intense, so scattered that there is no energy to make moral distinctions: all are victims and murderers by turns in a helpless somnambulism. Tess is one moment the 'fascinated bird' who is hypnotized by Angel's music, the next she is a stealthy cat drawing near her unaware prey; one moment she is seen as the victim of Angel's and Alec's mistreatment, the next she is seen as their unwitting, beguiling huntress. It is that twilight blurring of the distinction between culpable will and blameless passivity which leads to the wavering of value in the verbs —'gathering cuckoo-spittle on her skirts, cracking snails that were underfoot'—and which is responsible for the uncertain evaluation of Tess, stained yet the 'Pure Woman Faithfully Presented'.

How 'faithfully' Hardy presents her depends on the degree to which he can control, by his moral-aesthetic method, his sense of impure physicality working its gross compulsions on human life. As one sees, when he sanctifies the country people after the drunken, sensual dance at Trantridge (pp. 78–86), the 'defects' are most easily beautified when they are of sufficiently low emotional charge not to resist their glamorizing. In the dance, as in the garden scene later, the fecund meaning is decomposed to a hot, suggestive steam or mist, so that the 'floating, fusty *débris* of peat and hay, mixed with the perspirations and warmth of the dancers' forms 'a sort of vegeto-human pollen'. Distinctions between the flesh's clumsy blundering and the spirit's unimpeded liberty are now so weakened that when the dancers stagger home Hardy can say that though to the 'mean unglamoured eye' they seem 'terrestrial and lumpy', yet in their own eyes they have risen into the sublimity of the moon and stars, 'themselves and surrounding nature forming an organism of which all the parts harmoniously and joyously interpenetrated each other.' These 'children of the open air' are purified still further when Hardy adds a spiritual gleam so that the moonlight in the dew of the fields forms a 'circle of opalized light' round the shadow of each person's head, a halo which adheres whatever the 'vulgar unsteadiness' of the shadow and which 'persistently beautified it.' The sinners are dressed in saintly vapours, and the fumes from drunken breaths mingle as one with the night mist.

In other episodes, however, the force of impurity is much stronger, so intractable that Hardy, in attempting to create a sentimental beautifying, is subtly overwhelmed and hypnotized by the horror. It is this which seems to occur (p. 37) after the death of the family horse on the road to market before dawn. As Tess dreams of a 'grimacing personage' laughing at her family pretensions to aristocracy, Prince is killed by collision with the mailcart. The girl is splashed from face to skirt with the blood of the dying horse, and as the sun rises on the coagulating pool of blood on the road, it becomes iridescent: 'a hundred prismatic hues were reflected from it.' Here the sense of foulness is not lessened by the spiritual irradiation; instead, the spirituality administers to the triumph of ubiquitous foulness as it disperses it throughout the novel as a persistent contamination, a 'grimacing' elusiveness. The stain, by being prismatically disintegrated, is spiritually multiplied into many more lurking, insidious taints.

From confusion such as this, where physicality and blood are distorted by an unfocused vision, Hardy derives his tragic sense. As can be seen in the biography which he helped his second wife to write, and in her quotations from his notes, Hardy in 1876 had arrived at the perception which was only later to be fully, artistically realized in the blurred consciousness of *Tess*. Mrs. Hardy writes (*Life*, p. 110) that on his travels in Germany Hardy remarked 'on a singular optical effect that was almost tragic. Owing to mist the wide landscape itself was not visible, but "the Rhine glared like a riband of blood, as if it serpentined through the atmosphere above the earth's surface." ' It is that same effect, the flesh as a red blur, or as a snaking, stealthy vileness, which is superstitiously half-discerned through the smoke and fogs of the garden scenes in *Tess*—gardens like defiled Paradises, where man, woman, and sex are the Adam, Eve, and Serpent. But, because the light is diffuse, the sensual horror can mockingly overpower the vague spiritual ordering, and since Hardy has effectively nullified any tendency towards clear, moral scrutiny, it is inevitable that Alec d'Urberville should assume an hypnotic dominance in the novel.

Alec is more a blotch of emotional meaning than a character, an impure impulse who is confusedly seen through the 'blue narcotic haze' of his cigar smoke as the future 'blood-red ray in the spectrum of her young life', when Tess gathers strawberries in the d'Urberville garden. Hardy may attempt to regulate the intractable impulse inside a pictorial stereotype, but it is only with secondary creative interest that he gives Alec features and attributes: hence the cigars, moustache, cane, and town suits of the seducing cad, the plunderer of the countryside. None of this can bind Alec's meaning or fix the lurking satire or diminish the force which he exerts on Hardy's imagination as a repulsive, aristocratic power. The emotional unrest to which Alec's name is attached flits behind the clothes and roles, never anchored for long to one or the other, as he changes from the fashionable urban seducer to the black-clothed evangelist and then back again, only to appear in the disguise of a country labourer or pretend to be one of Tess's ancestors sleeping in a tomb. He is the constant surprise which follows Tess, catching her out everywhere like 'a ghastly *bizarrerie*, a grim incongruity'. He is the diffused stain, like the impure 'polychrome' of colours in the Talbothays garden, which is present even when he does not appear as a character. Such appearances are only momentary identifications, for the possibilities for impurity seem boundless. In the dairyman's tale at Talbothays a seducer hides in the milk churn. It takes merely one garlic weed in the pasture to give all the butter a tang. The discovery at Flintcomb-Ash of chalk flints 'in bulbous, cusped, and phallic shapes' brings on Marian's uncontrollable shrieks of laughter.

In such hysterical responses the moral-aesthetic method seems to yield to the 'defect' and to satirize its own spirituality. Alec, for instance, in the Marlott allotments, is allowed to laugh (p. 450) at the role assigned him as the sensual snake in the paradisal garden. Just as Eustacia and Wildeve are brought into the simple scheme of the 'timeworn drama' in order to merit traditional defeat as traditional intruders, so Alec in pursuit of Tess is dressed in the old-fashioned smock of the country man, but with 'a ghastly comicality' which is revealed when the smoky fire lights up his face or glints on the steel prongs of his fork. Alec mocks the simple moral scheme in which he is dressed up for condemnation: ' "If I were inclined to joke I should say, How much this seems like Paradise! . . . You are Eve, and I am the old

Other One come to tempt you in the disguise of an inferior animal." '

Hardy is impelled to the same kind of insidious satire in a more important scene (pp. 283–90), whose outcome provokes Angel's hideous laughter. Here the sensual in Tess (especially in relation to Alec's seduction) is dressed in condemning clothes, ready for the effect of her confession to Angel after their marriage. Angel's spiritualizing imagination makes him adorn her with the ornamental heirlooms which befit her descent as a d'Urberville aristocrat. Yet this beautifying of Tess with spiritual riches is soon betrayed into sinister glamour as the fire burns low and confessions begin. In the half-light the gems on her skin assume an unfocused sensual value—'a constellation of white, red, and green flashes'—and as she bends forward 'each diamond on her neck gave a sinister wink like a toad's.'

It is in this change in valuation that one sees the novel's essential difference from *The Return of the Native*. There the sap is dried out of the fluid imaginativeness by the mental translation of the spiritual desires: the blaze of silver knight, far-off jewels, or the glittering heron, is mentally converted into cheaper currency, so that the dancers emerging from the Heath pool in Eustacia's dream become those victims of the moral interpretation, the drowned figures of Eustacia and Wildeve—sodden like the roll of wet banknotes which are dried out to crispness in front of the fire. In *Tess*, there is no scorching of the values to a disintegrating pack of cards, crisp money, or dried heath-bells, but instead, in a different kind of failure of consciousness, there is a loss of faith, a betrayal of spiritual worth, which is due to an uncertainty in valuing individual natures.

It is an uncertainty, a sickly wavering light of consciousness which, diffused over the question of right and wrong, produces both Alec's immoral dominance and Angel's uneven affirmation of imaginative, spiritual values. Both characters are expressions of the faithlessness to which Hardy's method lends itself. The diluted poignancy, the widespread and 'beautified' sense of incrimination can so easily slip into the grotesque ironies of universal contamination. Then in this surrender all values are poisoned: the economic aristocrat, possessor of concrete power, mockingly invades the peasant dress and all the simple virtues associated with it; the peasant girl, whose mere spiritual aristocracy is weighed unfavourably against its actual modern shape, is decorated as noble and almost immediately betrayed in the faithless laughter.

As in Hardy's sanctifying of the drunken dancers, these 'defects' —the sense of strife between subjective belief and concrete actualities—can best be harmonized when they have a low emotional power and when Hardy can defend faith in spiritual imaginativeness without risk, at an unambitious, indulgent level. His defence is therefore most readily exercised on behalf of the country people and of Tess when seen as a simple village girl. When Tess baptizes her dead child (p. 121), without the Church's proper sanction, objections are waived in deference to this personal illusion of rightness. Thus the spiritual light upon her face sentimentally condones and respects the belief, showing her face 'as a thing of immaculate beauty, with a touch of dignity which was almost regal.' It is a similar recompense, an affirming of the inner value of the country workers, which Angel pays when he learns in the dairy (pp. 200–1) 'that the magnitude of lives is not as to their external displacements, but as to their subjective experiences.' So his spiritual feeling for Tess seems to make her personality expand throughout the dairy and the world, and it can be seen that 'the impressionable peasant leads a larger, fuller, more dramatic life than the pachydermatous king', while in this subjective estimate of size Tess's life 'to herself who endured or enjoyed it, possessed as great a dimension as the life of the mightiest to himself.' As with his treatment of Clym on summery Egdon, Hardy needs to inflate the value of the seemingly insignificant specks who, like Tess, move and labour on vast landscapes, 'like a fly on a billiard-table . . . and of no more consequence to the surroundings than that fly.'

It is as though in asserting the subjective importance of individual lives, Hardy is impelled to make the most of moments of happiness against the dwarfing perspectives in which his art deals. His redressing of the imbalance is comparable to that of Henchard's daughter in *The Mayor of Casterbridge* who learns at the end (p. 405) the secret lesson in life of 'making limited opportunities endurable . . . in the cunning enlargement, by a species of microscopic treatment, of those minute forms of satisfaction that offer themselves to everybody not in positive pain.' By the 'cunning enlargement' in *Tess* the ordinary, humble workers are given a limited consolation, as in Hardy's account (pp. 239–41) of Tess and Angel driving with their milk cans one night for transport to London, reaching the 'feeble light' of the lamp at the little railway station: 'a poor enough terrestrial star, yet in one sense of more importance to Talbothays Dairy and mankind than the celestial ones to which it stood in such humiliating contrast.' In Angel's torment after Tess has confessed, Hardy goes further (p. 297) in an adjustment of the lost balance, raising subjective feeling through pity to bizarre proportions, as if the spiritualizing imagination has to expand thus far in order to contain the huge, sensual discovery: Angel weeps 'a tear so large that it magnified the pores of the skin over which it rolled, like the object lens of a microscope' through which one sees his 'reillumination as to the terrible and total change that her confession had wrought in his life, in his universe.'

But when Hardy wishes to carry further the belief in subjective experience—to make it more than licensed illusion or lugubrious magnifying of the humble—then his faith in his purpose becomes confused and erratic. The central difficulty is in upholding Tess's individuality as a spiritual aristocrat, without falling prey to the disillusionment which Alec's presence invites as the social, moneyed power of scorn. Hardy seems at one moment to insist on Tess's integrity because a peasant's inner life is as high as a king's; the next moment, more boldly, Tess's worth is seen as noble, without needing any special privileges granted her by sentimental recompense. Then she is seen as proud because that is her aristo-cratic nature by right, not because she is a peasant girl whom Hardy honours out of illusion, in defiance of those who occupy the modern position of aristocrats. Indeed, the uncertainty in Hardy's valuing of Tess's nature seems to stem from his inability to get past the fact that Alec's kind of aristocracy, though financial and base, is at least rational, plausible, socially true. Hardy cannot bring himself to an unambiguous assertion of Tess's spiritual aristocracy, because Alec usurps the reality of such a wish and denies it. This is so even when Tess's integrity provokes Alec's surprised remarks, that she is 'mighty sensitive for a cottage girl' or ' "One would think you were a princess from your manner, in addition to a true and original d'Urberville." '

There is, of course, a sardonic hesitation in Alec's comments which refuses to confirm the imaginative idea even as he poses it as a possibility. A similar hesitation is displayed by Angel in his wandering between rational and imaginative attitudes towards Tess's aristocracy: 'Perhaps Tess's lineage had more value for himself than for anybody in the world besides.' The 'perhaps' is the mark of the privately allowed fancy, the subjective feeling which hesitates to proceed into full consciousness. Rationally Angel sees aristocracy as a foolish illusion which mischievously lures poor people on to a social aggrandizement they cannot attain. The old aristocracy he sees as an exhausted, degenerate stock, spent in blood and as a political force. Yet, for all that, ' "lyrically, dramatically, and even historically, I am tenderly attached to them." ' This indulgent antiquarianism which adorns Tess as an aristocrat cannot survive as a powerful faith after the confession, when the suggestion of sinister degeneracy in her lineage is one of the factors which drives Angel to the refuge of prudish disgust. Only after the wider experience abroad, when his disgust is worn away with his own physical erosion as a man, can Tess's aristocracy be viewed again as an unspecified quality, independent of rational qualms about modern social status. Now he sees the difference between 'the political value and the imaginative value' of Tess's descent: imaginatively it 'was a fact of great dimensions; worthless to economics, it was a most useful ingredient to the dreamer.'

Although this insight and Angel's realization of Tess's ancestral 'flash of dignity' still makes Tess's rich individuality no more than a thing of subjective fancy, the murder of Alec takes the imaginative value further. Tess's killing of the modern, sham version of the aristocrat is the most defiant act committed by the spiritual imagination against mocking, denying actuality, even though Hardy curbs its meaning inside a pattern of helpless guilt and fatalism, so that Angel is still allowed to wonder after he has been re-united with Tess 'what obscure strain in the d'Urberville blood had led to this aberration—if it were an aberration.' Yet the doomed outcome is postponed until Hardy has acquiesced in the fanciful idyll of the couple's flight. It is presented as an escape into an interlude of childlike peace, 'temporary and unforefending', watched over by a weakened, permissive irony, an indulgent pity. When they sleep in the great four-poster bed in the New Forest mansion, the 'imaginative' aristocracy of Tess is fulfilled, but only under cover of the momentarily protected dream. This 'fact of

great dimensions' is granted recognition at last by poignant subterfuge, attended by a respectful (if ultimately treacherous)
rationalism.

3

The episode in the sanctuary of the mansion closely approaches
the viewpoint of *Jude the Obscure* (1895). In Tess's unwillingness to
move on and in the lovers' peering out at the world through the
chinks in the shutters—'within was affection, union, error forgiven: outside was the inexorable'—Jude's plight is sketched, as
the child behind the plaiting of the straw hat who is afraid to
grow up. But for him the human predicament is more naked: in
Jude's uprooted, jolting world, there can be no cleaving to a
steadfast rural ethic of modest endurance, no defensive, armoured
Egdon to be the mental refuge for failed desires: nor does Hardy's
mood permit a spiritualizing compensation to sanctify human
dreams amidst the 'defects' of existence. Aspirations must now
struggle courageously against all illogicalities, as if Hardy is
determined to clash beliefs and realities against each other with a
rough, jarring extravagance which becomes throughout the novel
an ironic pattern of fracturing. A kind of reckless vehemence is
constantly grating actual conduct against professed theory, so that
degradation seems to wrench at aspiration and the physical hurls
itself at the spiritual. From such a mood come the vulgarities and
clumsiness of certain episodes. The farmer beats Jude. Arabella
forces him to kill the pig, flings the pig's pizzle at him, and throws
down his books with her greasy fingers. Miss Fontover smashes
Sue's pagan images. Arabella's child hangs the children of Sue
and Jude.

In this world of unmuzzled inconsistencies and restlessness, the
factors which mock at spiritual desires are blunter, less insidious,
than the defiling things in *Tess*, just as Arabella's coarse robust-
ness grabs where Alec only lurks. Sexual needs, blood, beer, and
cruelty make up the lurid mixture which 'stains' and implicates
Jude, but the very roughness by which the world drags down its
aspirers has a vigour that saves it from being a subtler, deeper
menace. In fact, the reckless energy in Hardy which enforces
harsh oppositions[1] is the same energy which spurs on the spiritual

[1] 'Of course the book is all contrasts—or was meant to be in its original
conception . . . e.g. Sue and her heathen gods set against Jude's reading the

imagination to seek persistently for a harmony, often without care for the ironic assaults. Because there can be no adhesion, as with Clym and Tess, to meaningful rural work as a consoling centre of stability, the spiritual dreamer is set free to attempt an actualization of vague desires, and, conversely, the dislocated, urbanizing world with its 'glaring, garish, rattling' forces is set free to wreak its disillusions.

In this loosening of traditional restraints, Jude's yearning 'to find something to anchor on, to cling to . . . without fear of farmers, or hindrance, or ridicule' has sufficient blind stamina to persist through and beyond the disasters. It is, therefore, a measure of the novel's mood that Christminster's vague glow should be seen by Jude only when he has passed again (p. 27) through the field where the farmer beat him: 'Through the solid barrier of cold cretaceous upland to the northward he was always beholding a gorgeous city—the fancied place he had likened to the new Jerusalem'. There is strength enough to support the subjective belief of Jude throughout the changes of maturity, so that right to the end he must still take his bearings on this 'centre of the universe', this ideal of unity and meaning, which the spirit obsessively demands. It is as though in Jude's vision of the Celestial City, 'a castle, manned by scholarship and religion', a place of harmonies and strange tongues, with its roofs and spires gleaming like topaz through the mist, Hardy combines and upholds Eustacia's yearning for spiritual riches and Clym's for 'serene comprehensiveness'. The aspirer can now move across the connecting step which is absent from the consciousness of *The Return of the Native*. Because Paris remains unapproachable for Eustacia, her yearning is condemned as a lust for lone self-enhancement. But Christminster, reached and entered by the dreamer, now reveals, if confusedly, what Paris symbolizes: the full range of conditions by which human fulfilment has to be struggled for. Stability and unity in the self can only be achieved in dependent and hurtful relation with others.

These are the conditions which Christminster symbolically suggests, because living, endeavouring human beings populate

---

Greek testament; Christminster academical, Christminster in the slums; Jude the saint, Jude the sinner; Sue the Pagan, Sue the saint; marriage, no marriage; &c., &c.' (Letter from Hardy, 20 November 1895; *Life*, p. 272).

the framework of its meaning, and because spiritually and physically it holds together the conflicting aspects of Jude's desires. Early in the novel, Christminster is Phillotson in his attempt to be a university graduate: for Jude (p. 27) 'the city acquired a tangibility, a permanence, a hold on his life, mainly from the one nucleus of fact that the man for whose knowledge and purposes he had so much reverence was actually living there.' When Jude first works in the city, it is Sue Bridehead who is the spiritual centre of Christminster, 'the one thing uniting him to the emotions of the living city'. On a later visit, he thinks of her as the 'City phantom'. But she is not the only centre which holds him, for, when his spiritual ambitions are fatigued, he must turn for relief to the low, beery life of the poor quarter, 'one of the great palpitating centres of Christminster life.' This other source of strength, the vitality of the 'struggling men and women', is shared by Arabella, herself a sensual centre in Jude's life. So he reacts against his unspiritual needs, and regards them as a moral weakness and a smirching.

Christminster remains for Jude a vision of wholeness and consistency at the same time as he is thrust into inconsistencies, constantly forced to adjust his goals and principles in order to fit his actual behaviour or to keep conscious pace with his real, living wants. So powerful are the demands of the spirit and the senses that neither will accept forms offered to it by the other. The spirit sees Christminster society (and therefore society in general) as ethically crude and superficial: its tyrannous enforcement of Mosaic Law, its insistence on the flesh as the central basis of marriage, is as outdated as the crumbling fabric of its religious buildings. The sensual viewpoint also disdains the joyless morality of the marriage rituals, but raucously affirms the physical idea of marriage as a vital, natural value. It is Jude's fate to share both viewpoints, through Sue and Arabella, so that he is continually refused rest on a form, principle, or expression which satisfies either view.

In his early immaturity his childish instinct leads him naturally to worship pagan Greek gods, while his logic leads him to study the Greek New Testament and reverence the outworn Anglicanism of modern Christminster. In the same way, he at first believes that his relationship with Sue is solely one of intellectual companionship, even though in following her as an unrecognized lover he must refuse 'to meditate on the life of inconsistency he was leading.' It is Sue who points out to him (p. 174) another inconsistency, that the very Christian doctrines he reveres are those which condemn him for abandoning his marriage with Arabella: ' "Your theories are not so advanced as your practice!" ' At Shaston his ideal of apostleship is finished with the burning of his religious books when he sees (p. 226) the anomaly of his theoretical attachment to precepts that debar his love for Sue: 'it was glaringly inconsistent for him to pursue the idea of becoming the soldier and servant of a religion in which sexual love was regarded as at its best a frailty, and at its worst damnation.' One sees in the great inconsistency between his actual work and his high ambitions, that Jude is forced to deal with old forms as he remakes the structures of the past, whether in renewing the crumbling masonry of Christminster and Melchester Cathedral, or in making the model of Cardinal College and selling Christminster cakes. Even though he is moved on intellectually by Sue's influence, away from the Gothic Revival to modern Classical forms, from Anglican gloom to Sue's ideal of 'Greek joyousness', he must instinctively return to Christminster as a repairer, 'as if he had known no wish to do otherwise.' Now worn out by his drudgery, he is left devoid of his previous principles and possessed of Sue's intellectual courage. But his instinct remains strong for the ideal of harmony glimpsed as a child, as though in the Christminster vision, whatever the realities of dead religious and social form, something remained unexpressed. At the end for Jude there can be no moral or conscious position to cover his behaviour: he is (pp. 337–8) ' "in a chaos of principles—groping in the dark—acting by instinct and not after example . . . I perceive there is something wrong somewhere in our social formulas: what it is can only be discovered by men and women with greater insight than mine,—if, indeed, they ever discover it —at least in our time." '

Indeed, the danger in *Jude* is not that Hardy will accept an inferior moral interpretation of desires but that the spiritual imagination will disdain any binding form offered. With Sue Bridehead Jude's strong instinct becomes a hypersensitive vitality, too fast and nervous to allow the settling of a moral identification upon her: 'An exciting thought would make her walk ahead so fast that he could hardly keep up with her.' It is this spiritual restlessness that resists any fixing matrix, much as Alec's sensual meaning does, whether it is a dry interpretation of the Song of Solomon or (p. 214) the ties of marriage: ' "the social moulds civilization fits us into have no more relation to our actual shapes than the conventional shapes of the constellations have to the real star-patterns." ' She is not to be identified as Mrs. Richard Phillotson but as ' "a woman tossed about, all alone, with aberrant passions, and unaccountable antipathies." ' It is this unwillingness to be held by social form, body, even gender, which makes her recoil and flee at the slightest hint that her dream of freedom is assuming a fabric, that spiritual love is giving way to physical. In flight she runs from one trap to blunder into another, only to break out again, ruining in turn the student in London, Phillotson, and Jude. In Sue, the 'light that never was' of *Tess* becomes a character, with its mixture of treachery and pity, its poignancy when the physical danger is lessened and its hysteria when it overbalances into the sensual. When Jude tells her of his marriage to Arabella, Sue is impelled by reaction into marriage with Phillotson, cruelly making Jude give her away at the ceremony. She is safe from one danger on the condition of risking another, as she is when, after her flight from marriage with Phillotson into an uncertain safety with Jude, she returns to her sick husband and inflicts more hurt by awakening already wounded feelings.

As a 'maddening compound of sympathy and averseness', Sue in her alternations seems, like the spiritual light in *Tess*, to be forever seeking an impossible balance, trying to assuage the results of her aversions with a pity which inevitably (p. 183) brings on further aversions: 'Possibly she would go on inflicting such pains again and again, and grieving for the sufferer again and again, in all her colossal inconsistency.' But Sue's 'inconsistency' is only Jude's nervously intensified, and she, more speedily than he can, exhausts all the 'conventional shapes' as the advanced thinker of the novel; but like Clym and Angel, her unstable consciousness cannot discover 'the real star-patterns'. In creating her, Hardy discards for Jude so many principles and wrong shapes that no pattern of being can be assembled. Jude drives on without a mental or social form for inner desires, while Sue finally spends her mental strength. Only in exhaustion does she rest at last, betraying herself to the fabric of flesh and the despised marriage-contract.

Sue's nervous shifts of feeling characterize at its keenest the energetic unease of the novel as a whole, the erratic movement between contradictory attitudes. Hardy seems to range between 'sympathy and averseness' for the physical or spiritual issues, depending on how he groups the figures in the relationships and weights the different alliances. Now Jude joins Arabella against Sue's spirituality; now Jude and Sue in their spirituality oppose the inferior sensuality of the Arabellas; then finally, against Jude's protests, Sue accepts Arabella as the rightful wife. The shifts of attention and uneasiness stem from the fact that the claims of physical desire in Jude and Arabella have a justice which is not to be completely denied by the spirit, when it counts such wants as basely conventional and gross or when (in the motto from Antoninus for Part Five) it sees itself 'overpowered here in the compound mass the body'. Jude's quotation (p. 290) from 'the Jewish law-giver'—'For what man is he that hath betrothed a wife and hath not taken her?'—is allowed to support his case for marriage with Sue as a natural rather than vulgar idea.

It is in the Aldbrickham episode, when Arabella intervenes between Sue and Jude, and sends them the child of her marriage to Jude, that a distinction becomes apparent between the physical Law seen as an imprisoning social ritual (from which Sue flinches as compelling the individual to feel in a certain way) and the Law seen as right and natural, regardless of the social question. When Arabella disturbs Jude's patient celibacy and prompts his new demands for a physical marriage, Sue can be clearly seen disguising her revulsion from the sexual under the abstract dislike of the social tie. But the distinction between the Law's two aspects is quickly lost, and marriage becomes again a legal trick worked on men by the cunning Arabellas of the world. With the spiritual view reasserted, attention shifts away from the inner problems of Jude's and Sue's relationship, on to the bigots and prudes who uphold such wretched unions as that between Arabella and her second husband. At the Agricultural Show, therefore, when Jude and Sue linger in the flower pavilion and Sue pushes her face in amongst the roses, this 'more exceptional couple' is placed above the scorn and pettiness of Arabella. Their solidarity against growing public criticism conceals for Hardy the need to explore more fully the effect of Sue's giving in to Jude and bearing him children. It is not until after the hanging of the children in the misery of the Christminster slums that the solidarity breaks and the problem comes to the surface. Here Arabella represents the social-physical Law at its most crudely vengeful: for to Sue, in her anguish, the action of young Jude is justified because he seems to her the child of the rightful marriage killing the children of the wrongful marriage; while Arabella has already primed Phillotson (p. 329) to adopt a stern hand when Sue comes flying back— ' "you've got the laws on your side. Moses knew." '

But young Jude can be seen as more than an agent of the implacable Law executing its judgements, for he also expresses for Hardy something beyond Jude's and Sue's realizing. Jude as a child himself sees the discords and illogic but has sufficient heroic stamina to flounder on through the inconsistencies, in a disastrous attempt to make the dream of harmony tangible. Sue, more advanced intellectually, knows that the forms Jude takes to be his goals are already superseded by a new spirit—something that partakes of extreme age and extreme youth, and paradoxically makes Sue a believer in 'Greek joyousness', an untouched pagan innocence. To Jude she is 'one of the women of some grand old civilization.' It is that fastidiousness in Sue, the incongruous mixture of the happy, unknowing child and the adult who has intellectually discarded all the life-forms of her era, which reaches more perfect expression in young Jude, the old child, 'Age masquerading as Juvenility'. Arabella brings him back with her from Australia—' "It is strange, Jude," ' Sue remarks (p. 289), ' "that these preternaturally old boys almost always come from new countries" '—but the child is as much Sue's as Arabella's. He is a further refinement of spiritual flinching before life, so sophisticated that even Sue's 'Greek joyousness' is superseded as an ideal because he has seen through life before he has begun to live it. He is a kind of abbreviation in his grasp of the tragic generalities without the less abstract particulars: in a sense, his hanging of Sue's children and himself is a logical shortening. His coming to Jude and Sue at Aldbrickham, when Jude is urging Sue into physical marriage, is the first emergence of the mood which is to dominate the final chapters of the novel—suicide or self-renunciation.

All conscious life becomes anomalous, and the child born dead from Sue is a further abbreviation: one is finished before one has begun. This hopeless compression of human life makes Jude's career a vain adventure into consciousness and a return to blindness. His last cries (p. 418) come from the Book of Job: ' "Let the day perish wherein I was born. . . . Let that day be darkness. . . . Why died I not from the womb? . . . For now should I have lain still and been quiet. I should have slept: then had I been at rest!" ' Coming from one who, of all the aspirers in the novels, has painfully gone the furthest towards the realizing of his desires, such renunciation has particular force, for what Hardy relinquishes here is the struggle to shape unwieldy conflicts of consciousness, to make meaningful narrative art out of them. It is not in the outraged reception of *Jude* when first published but in Jude's retreat from outer pain that one sees why the novel form, for the purposes of Hardy the artist, became finally unnecessary.

II

The White Peacock and *The Trespasser*

I

HARDY's tragic sense comes out of an irresolute energy, from a confusion in the unconscious, like a growth that is blasted when it touches the mind: so the heath-bells on Egdon and Christminster's worn fabric are the 'dead skins' of a stricken vigour. In *The White Peacock* (1911), Lawrence inherits the link between tragedy and the unconscious, sharing with Hardy the same deference to irresistible collapse, when all problems slip from scrutiny and go into undifferentiated chaos. But even in his first novel Lawrence cannot help suggesting more: a sense of how the irresistible comes about. Not that he can consciously define the failure in human desires and relationships; he can only hint at how the inevitable sorrow is nearly avoided, before he again affirms its sway, dissatisfied but helpless. He wants to resist tragic conclusions, but the terms on which this might be possible are denied him by the flagging powers of the men in the novel. So often he must contradict the tragic mood from the position of a tame, precarious idealism— as when at his sister Lettie's coming-of-age party, Cyril the narrator makes a 'nest' in the window-curtains for one of his female friends, and she sits gazing out at the snow:

'It is lovely,' she said reflectively. 'People must be ill when they write like Maxim Gorky.'

'They live in town,' said I.

'Yes—but then look at Hardy—life seems so terrible—it isn't, is it?'

'If you don't feel it, it isn't—if you don't see it. I don't see it for myself.'   (P. 108.)

This is facile, but another more vital part of Lawrence in the book wants it not to be merely that. It is a part of him which lies beyond the mood of frail cheerfulness in which Cyril speaks at the party: ' "we just live, nothing abnormal, nothing cruel and extragavant—just natural—like doves in a dovecot." ' But the view from the 'dovecot' or the 'nest' seems the only plausible one from which to utter non-tragic thoughts: hence Lawrence's sympathy through Cyril for the scenes of young friends, gathered together in happy tableaux, safe in 'the delightful bond of the lamp-lit tea-table', with the outer darkness shut away and the little civilization in firm female control.

But, as in *The Return of the Native*, the novel also has allegiance to powers outside the moral lamplight, to a world of blind fatalism, blood, haphazard killings, and inarticulate cries of suffering. Such are the cries which come from the dark into the warm 'dovecot' rooms of the novel, where Cyril sits with Leslie or George, 'the peevish, wailing, yarling cry of some beast in the wood.' One recalls the Hardy ethos of helpless incrimination, with Jude forced to kill the pig and Tess stained as she obliviously crushes snails, when Lettie expresses (p. 12) her sense of inexorable suffering: ' "If we move the blood rises in our heel-prints.' " All seems inevitable: the casual slaughter of the bees and shrimps by George; the chick toppling effortlessly into the fire after it has been put to warm; the bloodthirsty hunt which ends in the killing of the rabbits and mice in the cornfield and the wild dog in the woods. But the outer world of confused guilt and suffering brings a closer, more relevant challenge to the ordered 'nest'—the figure of Cyril's and Lettie's father, the parent exiled from the playful scene to make the idealizing possible for Lawrence. As the group of young friends wander through the twilit woods, they find a man asleep in a nightmare, painfully working over an episode from his past, moving his mouth 'in indistinct speech'. This is the inarticulate language of tragedy which Lawrence's art shares here with Hardy's. The unresolved crisis between the men and women of the novel rises up like a persistent question, half-recognized in the twilight as the 'dim uneasiness' which irks Cyril.

Yet there is a groping towards some clearer idea of human suffering, some isolation of the problem, which makes Lawrence separate such issues from the universal sense of pain. When it comes to the wasting of human beings, there is a hesitation about the blind pattern of fate, a standing back from the unrecking flow of death and suffering in woods and farms, as if Lawrence would check the inevitable acceptance of human outcasts as wild beasts. Even though Cyril succumbs to the inexorable drive of events, and in his father's last moments feels himself borne along as 'a

mere fleck drifting unconsciously through the dark', this yielding
is suspended for a while after Mr. Beardsall's death:

The death of the man who was our father changed our lives. It was not
that we suffered a great grief; the chief trouble was the unanswered
crying of failure. But we were changed in our feelings and in our relations; there was a new consciousness, a new carefulness.   (P. 43.)

On the terms of the novel, Lawrence cannot make an adequate
reply to the 'unanswered crying of failure' because the 'consciousness' and 'carefulness' never become an effective moral caution,
and are easily overwhelmed by reckless oblivion or a wasting
sense of frustration. The key to the frustration is found in the
immature novelist and his spokesman Cyril, both of whom shift
between male and female sympathies but who are emotionally
bound (and with helpless reluctance) to regard the women's
position as the ultimate centre. It is as though in attempting to
break the deadlock in the relations between men and women,
Lawrence, in his portrayal of Lettie, must inevitably allow her to
try to do the man's work for him, without at the same time wishing her to dictate the conditions by which freedom is to be
achieved or to dominate the relationship. The position is precarious as regards George and Lettie, because in prompting
George to develop out of his unconscious state, to assume the lead
so that both may begin to move towards some more fulfilled life,
Lettie is seeking a resolution which Lawrence in his portrayal of
George cannot give. She challenges George (p. 27) to come to
consciousness—' "You are blind; you are only half-born; you are
gross with good living and heavy sleeping" '—but he cannot wake
from his bluff, masculine sleep of life, with its careless, almost
callous indifference to the issues. For his part, he can only challenge Lettie (as in the embarrassing scene at the piano) with the
heavy, sensual power of his presence, just as Annable challenges
the 'doves' round the snow-drops with a menacing shape which is
seen 'in the rim of light, darkly.' Different attitudes from male and
female are offered against each other, but neither can move
beyond their respective borderlines. The only stable morality is
the woman's; even against her own will, in Lettie's case, her
standards monopolize the light.

This crippling is evident in the portrayal of Cyril, the figure
who most epitomizes the divided allegiances of the novel. On the

one hand, there is the Cyril who soulfully sympathizes with the neglected wives, who, narrator-novelist, threads the passing moods and prose poems, uncritically accepts his mother's view of his father's rottenness and mourns the evanescence of happiness. September, his month of birth, is seen through a dreamy wash of nostalgia, with the earth 'like a woman married and fading' and the blue mist 'like memory in the eyes of a neglected wife.' But there is also the Cyril who sympathizes with the neglecters and the despised husbands, who wishes to be accorded his place as friend and consoler to the powerful men in their outcast state. This is the Cyril who works with George in the fields and talks to Annable in the darkness. And here again, as with the death of Beardsall, Lawrence seems to move cautiously towards an expressiveness that might unlock the tragedy. There is a sensitive hesitation within the mindless flow of physical labour and the movements of earth and sky which surround Cyril and George in the wide field. As Cyril goes down the wet hillside, carelessness is halted:

I kicked through the drenched grass, crushing the withered cowslips under my clogs, avoiding the purple orchids that were stunted with harsh upbringing . . . crushing the pallid lady smocks, the washed-out wild gillivers. I became conscious of something near my feet, something little and dark, moving indefinitely. I had found again the larkie's nest.   (P. 219.)

The poignant, nostalgic Cyril has already changed to a vigorous, masculine figure, trampling down the feeble, dying soulfulness, yet, as with the orchids, using no wanton force. By a kind of logic, he opens the way for himself to a new 'consciousness': 'In my heart of hearts, I longed for someone to nestle against, someone who would come between me and the coldness and wetness of the surroundings.' But in this spurning of the tragic poignancy (which makes this scene in the grass so different from that in the Talbothays garden) there is an emotional restriction in the new sensitiveness. A high friendship with another man must still be conceived on the terms of motherhood and the nest. Nothing can come of these friendships with George or Annable, as with George and Lettie, because the consciousness to hold them is, like the larks, too 'little and dark, moving indefinitely'.

Even so, this does not make the resistance to misery, although lacking strong definition, a mere falling back all the way to 'dovecot' idealism. There is an urge to deny the total sway of tragedy which comes from something more than tame wishfulness, as one sees immediately after Beardsall's death, when Cyril protests at the withered hopelessness:

It was not true, that sad, colourless face with grey beard, wavering in the yellow candle-light. It was a lie—that wooden bedstead, that deaf woman, they were fading phrases of the untruth. That yellow blaze of sunflowers was true, and the shadow from the sun-dial on the warm old almshouses—that was real.   (P. 40.)

Lawrence is here also 'crushing the pallid lady smocks, the washed-out wild gillivers', with flat contradiction.

He strikes out again in the 'Motif of Suffering' chapter, towards the end of the novel, when George and Cyril see the London outcasts asleep under Waterloo Bridge and hear a socialist speaker on the miseries of the poor. George, already ruined as a man, is soon after attracted to socialism, but Cyril winces from the speaker's vision:

For him the world was all East End, and all the East End was as a pool from which the waters are drained off, leaving the water-things to wrestle in the wet mud under the sun, till the whole of the city seems a heaving, shuddering struggle of black-mudded objects deprived of the elements of life. I felt a great terror of the little man, lest he should make me see all mud, as I had seen before.   (P. 278.)

One recalls the microscopic swarmings which Mrs. Yeobright sees (*Return of the Native*, p. 325) on Egdon: 'All the shallower ponds had decreased to a vaporous mud amid which the maggoty shapes of innumerable obscure creatures could be indistinctly seen, heaving and wallowing with enjoyment.' One also remembers Mrs. Yeobright's soaring comprehensiveness of view, her intuitive understanding of human communities in their distant movements—all of which Hardy distrusts in its ignoring of the little life and yet supports in its visionary grandeur. It is that larger, untrapped movement of life which Lawrence also supports as desirable and which he affirms as an unidentifiable purpose above the insect squirmings. For George (and presumably the socialist), the 'stupendous poetry' of the city and its 'enormous unintelligible lettering' is too large for his reading, but Cyril is entranced by the movement of the Londoners. The rhythmic rise and fall of the larks' bodies in the nest seems pictured at large (p. 282) in 'the come and go of people weaving and intermingling in the complex mesh of their intentions, with all the subtle grace and mystery of their moving, shapely bodies.' But like Mrs. Yeobright's vision of communities, 'whose features are indistinguishable by the very comprehensiveness of the view', Lawrence cannot read the poem more clearly. As with the lark's nest, Cyril remains the affirmer of a movement that his author cannot plausibly enact.

In other parts of the novel, the tragic moods are openly defied by a vitality which makes its short revolt, misses its grasp on a surer consciousness, and fights on destructively, unredeemed and directionless. And so the old sad assumptions of tragedy passively regain control. The assertive gestures of certain episodes merely herald the return of the sorrowing ethic—as in the scene after the killing of the rabbits in the cornfield when Cyril frightens the rats away from the pool. The young people see an autumn moon over the rim of the wood, and Emily says (p. 54): ' "I always think it wants to know something, and I always think I have something to answer, only I don't know what it is." ' The moon seems to challenge to some further consciousness, but the challenge can be answered only imperfectly by the frenzied dance of George and Lettie, stamping over the dead leaves under the moon's gaze. ' "What business have they with their sadness!" ' demands Lettie, flinging into the air petals from the chrysanthemums, the flowers of sorrow and acquiescence; ' "I like things to wink and look wild." ' Lawrence here touches the same kind of mocking extravagance as Hardy pictures in Eustacia Vye (*Return of the Native*, p. 303), when in bold defiance of her depression over her marriage to Clym, she goes out to dance at the moonlit gypsying with Wildeve: ' "No one shall know my suffering. I'll be bitterly merry, and ironically gay, and I'll laugh in derision!" ' But in Lawrence's novel as in Hardy's the extravagance has no higher command by which to steady itself positively. It turns into self-wasting, so that Lettie accepts engagement to Leslie crying, ' "Ah, Fate—Fate! It separates you whether you want it or not" ', and there is an unrestrained slip into careless, purposeless indifference. 'George and Lettie crushed the veined belles of wood-sorrel and broke the silken mosses. What did it matter to them what they broke or crushed . . .when all the great red apples were being shaken from the Tree to be left to rot?' (P. 210.)

Now George and Lettie diverge into their separate marriages, using up their lives in an extravagant sensationalizing of themselves. In her married frustration, Lettie becomes an icily brilliant figure, her early tendency towards the Sarah Bernhardt style of 'raillery and mockery' left unchecked now: at her engagement party she was 'moving as if in a drama', and now 'she seemed to be moving in some alluring figure of a dance.' George, caught within his sensual limits, burns himself out with the 'raw gin' of existence. He is attracted to the suggestion he receives from the opera which he visits (pp. 245–6) with his newly-married wife: 'The gaudy, careless Southern life amazed them. The bold free way in which Carmen played with life startled them with hints of freedom. . . . On the stage the strange storm of life clashed in music towards tragedy and futile death.'

After this nothing can stop George's degeneration. Inevitably, he comes to be set apart, an outcast, like the other ruined 'animals', Beardsall and Annable. In a world where men are infants, unable to rise above their helpless incomprehension, or trapped wild creatures, the women are provoked into a fierce assertion of motherhood, with self-righteous Christianity as its moral weapon; where the men cannot seize their chance, the opportunity is withdrawn and the women must make order by their conditions. When Emily finishes off the wild dog and faces Cyril with blood on her skirts like Tess in a similar atmosphere of guilt and sadness, the twofold allegiance of the novel is again displayed (p. 69) in Cyril's response: 'Emily had the gift of sorrow. It fascinated me, but it drove me to rebellion.' In the outcome, however, the rebellion is a gesture without confidence. The wild dogs are brought to heel or destroyed, and over the helpless irresolution and 'unanswered crying' of the child-men sweeps the pitying, motherly love of the women. With Emily's husband, Tom, in a robust sleep of pure physical contentment; with Lettie's husband bemused and vaguely unaware; with George in an alcoholic stupor, the 'nest' is supreme, dominated by its 'young, arrogant, impervious mothers' and their 'storms of babies'. Like the striking miners who gave in and compromised, the men-folk remain 'imprisoned underground'.

2

The Trespasser (1912) is a fevered extreme after *The White Peacock* —more luridly spectacular in its defiance of tragedy, more degraded in its surrender. One cannot help associating it with the distress in which it was written—Lawrence's illness and half-fascination with death after his mother died—but this would be to miss its significance as a reckless, convulsive work which naturally follows on from the *Carmen* scene (pp. 245–6) in the previous novel. George, in taking the suggestion of forbidden freedoms offered in the abandoned movements of the opera, was 'like a trespassing child' who played dangerously and fatally outside the Nethermere morality of his upbringing. But *The Trespasser*, with its sensual and spiritual wildness, launches more desperately into the heightened danger which Hardy saw of theatrical performers. Quoting from Hardy's notes of June 1890, his wife writes:

At Bizet's opera of *Carmen* he was struck . . . with the manner in which people conducted themselves on the operatic stage; that of being 'possessed, maudlin, distraught, as if they lived on a planet whose atmosphere was intoxicating. . . . The morality of actresses, dancers, etc., cannot be judged by the same standard as that of people who lead slower lives. Living in a throbbing atmosphere they are perforce throbbed by it in spite of themselves.'   (*Life*, pp. 226–7.)

The exalted fret which governs the story of Siegmund's and Helena's love affair and leads to the psychic and physical breakdown of their lives is given an 'operatic' resonance, as personalities merge and overpower each other, as the inflamed imagination flows out from fact to symbol with a grand rashness. Ecstatic, consummate moments give way to exhausted despair, or the feelings rise to sudden, blind cruelty only to fall back with pitying sorrowful tenderness.

At one point in the novel, as Siegmund and Helena lie together by the sea (pp. 35–62), this changing movement of the feelings is particularly marked. At first Siegmund's attack centres on Helena as the spiritual witch, the damned Sue Bridehead of the novel: 'She belonged to that class of "dreaming women" with whom passion exhausts itself at the mouth. . . . For centuries a certain type of woman has been rejecting the "animal" in humanity, till now her dreams are abstract and full of fantasy, and her blood runs in bondage, and her kindness is full of cruelty.' The attack on her grows as she listens to Siegmund's heart beating: 'The throb was strong and deep. It seemed to go through the whole island and the whole afternoon, and it fascinated her: so deep, unheard, with its great expulsions of life. Had the world a heart? Was there also deep in the world a great God thudding out waves of life, like a great heart, unconscious?' The 'waves of life' become the real waves of the sea, beating against a 'tremendous white mass of boulders' on the shore—a frustrated pounding against Helena's white, spiritual desert of rock which gives Siegmund a malicious thrill. It is an exultant game of death—'She clung closer to him, as her hair was blown out damp, and her white dress flapped in the wet wind. Always, against the rock, came the slow thud of the waves, like a great heart beating under the breast.' But then the passionate cruelty against the unsubmissive whiteness, the strength to crush the 'pallid lady smocks', is spent, and the feelings drain away into a tenderness of exhaustion, a fatherly pity for Helena.

As if in revenge, Helena's later act of spiritual assertion duplicates Siegmund's rise and fall of sensual insistence. In the moonlight she also plays near death, making a witch-like incantation over the body of Siegmund, casting a spiritual spell as she leans on him and gradually stops the flow of blood to his thigh. But then (pp. 93–4) her fancy is spent: 'Suddenly she became aware that she must be slowly weighing down the life of Siegmund,' so she withdraws. He is left stunned, enthralled, while she is victorious in motherly pity over him, 'drooping with the strength of her compassion . . . immortal, not a fragile human being, but a personification of the great motherhood of woman.' It is a moment of significant collapse for Siegmund and his author: all the previously established female figures—the daring Lettie, the soulful Emily, the self-righteous matrons—merge into one huge, victorious aggregate in Helena, the ' "Hawwa—Eve—Mother" ' to which Siegmund submits. Together in the moonlit Catholic graveyard Siegmund and Helena bow to the carven Christ, Siegmund surrendering responsibility for his 'small, futile tragedy' beneath the greater tragic authority.

But for all the wild play of sensations and careless expenditure of life, there is a sense of caution in Siegmund which makes him draw away from the hurtful games and combats. On their first day together on the Isle of Wight, he playfully suggests walking over the edge of the cliff, and Helena, though at first horrified, becomes attracted to the idea. She is portrayed as capable in her spiritual fancy of reducing everything to a child's game, the world for her being 'a great wonder-box which hid innumerable sweet toys for surprises'. But Siegmund (p. 54) has qualms: 'What was death to her but one of her symbols, the death of which the sagas talk—something grand, and sweeping, and dark.' He draws back from the cliff edge, refusing to toy with experience and knowing the toll exacted on his own flesh and blood: 'He would not dare to tempt Fate now, having too strong a sense of death to risk it.'

This hesitation becomes later in the novel a groping away from the triumphant spiritual consciousness which in Helena holds all the daylight and devalues Siegmund's individuality, making him just a pitied thing, a little 'personality'. Up above there is no way out, but below there might be another con-sciousness and escape. Therefore, while Helena plays alone in the waves and accepts the warm sun as the ultimate reality behind the material world, Siegmund pushes his fingers into the sand of a beach, passing the surface warmth to touch the 'cold mystery' underneath, the 'almost hurt of the dark, heavy coldness.' The sand becomes for him (p. 81) an image which contains all possible life—a consoling discovery for Siegmund: 'He himself might play with the delicious warm surface of life, but always he recked of the relentless mass of cold beneath—the mass of life which has no sympathy with the individual, no cognizance of him.'

Siegmund, in his wish to submit to an authority deeper than Helena's, in his need to find a stoic comfort behind life and 'a wonderful kindness in death', does not realize that in the small emotional circuit of the novel the urge for relief leads back in image and feeling to Helena again: where the fever blows hot and cold, with Siegmund's sun-burnt intensity and his dream of soothing ice-crystals, Helena is identified not only with the warm, light surface above but also with the 'dark, heavy coldness' be-neath. Without Lawrence's conscious ordering, it seems, Helena's dominant spirituality flows out to overpower and colour all the emotional values of the novel. She is as much the playful waters on which Siegmund rides as the white rocks which graze his flesh and shock him; as much the tender, soulful sun as the harsh sun which breaks down the cells of his blood and chars him. The attempted escape from Helena's one-sided vision must be a doomed, truant gesture when the cool relief sought can only be had from the same source which puts 'a cool hand of absolution' on Helena's moonlit brow. There is no escaping the female power, consciously or unconsciously.

Siegmund confesses as much when he returns (p. 211) to the 'nest' of his wife and children: ' "It seems to me a man needs a mother all his life. I don't feel much like a lord of creation." ' But, looking at the moving stream of London life, rather as Cyril does in the other novel, Siegmund finds a consolation for personal failure by considering its unimportance in the larger whole. As he has felt previously, one man's death isn't the death of life: ' "If the spark goes out, the essence of the fire is there in the darkness." ' The positive is weak, however, when compared even with the town 'poetry' of *The White Peacock*. The pallid affirmation of Siegmund before his suicide—' "Whatever happens, the world is wonderful" '—is a token of that tamed submissiveness in the novel which marks a greater defeat for the male cause than all the yieldings of *The White Peacock*.

The human ideal which Cyril glimpsed, 'the subtle grace and mystery', is lost from definition in *The Trespasser* by the 'heaving, shuddering struggle'. But that struggle in the novels brings out a metaphor of tragic failure, an image of danger which was to stay with Lawrence even after he had written the *Study* of Hardy and had there looked directly at the concept at the back of his imagination—Hardy's Egdon Heath. As an immature or mature novelist, there persists in Lawrence a basic idea of strength and possible failure: life itself incorruptible, but human life possibly thwarted and deformed, becoming just part of a great 'mass'. For his characters or his own style, the 'mass' in Lawrence's writing often signifies a failure to progress or grow. When life cannot develop as it should, when consciousness is obstructed and unclarified, when an idea or a person cannot be defined beyond a certain stage, then there is a coarsening of texture, so that life sinks into generalization, an undifferentiated, inferior thing. In these early novels there is a blind beating against the mood of tragic generalization, but one sees in *The Trespasser*'s wild foray how the man is so wounded by the battle, so 'stunted by harsh upbringing', that he surrenders his chance to be more than he is—a realization that is passed on to *The Rainbow*, and which *Women in Love* deepens. For Lawrence struggle has to be more than defiance, because that can maim just as much as acceptance can paralyse the will. It is *Sons and Lovers* which clarifies the conditions of struggle in a new way.

III

Sons and Lovers

I

THE sense of a new purposefulness in *Sons and Lovers* (1913), the feeling of recovery after *The Trespasser*, is only partly expressed by Lawrence in a letter written just before the completion of his third novel. 'Tragedy', he says, 'ought really to be a great kick at misery.'[1] As is shown by the strokes of defiance in the previous novels, the 'kick' and the following loss of balance can merely become desperate assents to the misery. Lawrence's remark on tragedy does not express the more anchored determination in *Sons and Lovers*, the firmer mood which seems to refute the inevitability of male failure in the other novels by establishing an ideal of responsible manhood. This, one might say, is the working hypothesis of the will which steels the book—an assumption of eventual success which is dangerous for those who cannot live up to or grow beyond the structure. But at the same time it is an indispensable criterion, a steadying power. And, as the inspirer of the purposefulness, it is Mrs. Morel who embodies its strength and ultimate danger.

When she turns away from her husband's unthinking nature, from the playful, soft sensuality which cannot rise to responsibilities, Mrs. Morel places hope in her sons, those who seem to inherit her Puritan doggedness and who are to fulfil her as 'lovers' or 'knights' battling in her cause upon a larger scene than she can reach herself. So she proudly considers (p. 101) the achievement of having Paul in Nottingham and William in London: 'Now she had two sons in the world. She could think of two places, great centres of industry, and feel that she had put a man into each of them, that these men would work out what *she* wanted.' This is where the holding pattern is too strong, where the

[1] Letter to A. W. McLeod, 6 October 1912 (*The Collected Letters*, ed. Harry T. Moore, 1962, vol. 1, p. 150).

individual wants of the sons must fret against the central will which carries them forward. It is as much a problem as the conflict of Clym Yeobright, in his lack of social ambitions, with his mother's aspirations. Mrs. Yeobright is another of these large-visioned, intuitive women who 'can watch a world which they never saw, and estimate forces of which they have only heard.'

But the pattern itself in *Sons and Lovers* is not immutable; experiment can be made within and beyond it. The world of city and industry, the field of decisive movement, is taken on trust in the novel as the larger, shadowy goal which Lawrence at this point does not care to question or analyse. Therefore, when Paul Morel is forced to look for his first job and is regarded as 'a prisoner of industrialism' this is a false note belying the dominant mood of sturdy optimism and the belief (at times, held with difficulty) that all problems, however puzzling and confused, are open to manly tackling. The town is all right, says Paul (p. 271): ' "it's only temporary. This is the crude, clumsy make-shift we've practised on, till we find out what the idea is." ' The model carries while one reshapes the design.

It sustains the promise, expectation, and sense of possibility in Mrs. Morel's pride and the excited awe of her children when they await the return of William on the 'great train' from London one Christmas, or when they look up the lines one Easter—'one way, to London, and the other way, to Scotland, and they felt the touch of these two magical places.' The railway tracks lead away, flat, practical, concrete, to reachable values; they have that element of stable, progressive endeavour which is seen as the male quality in life when Paul talks (p. 177) to Miriam 'endlessly about his love of horizontals: how they, the great levels of sky and land in Lincolnshire, meant to him the eternality of the will, just as the bowed Norman arches of the church, repeating themselves, meant the dogged leaping forward of the persistent human soul, on and on, nobody knows where.' The soul works its heroic way by stages, marking off significant turning-points, distinguishing between separate experiences and wants, judiciously attempting to allocate roles and purposes. But all the time its travel forward and its flights upward are made on the condition that it is secured to the ground, clinched to the responsibility of its individual form in the world.

Lawrence would break from this anchorage at moments, but it

stabilizes the movement of the novel, as he works through the experience which he cannot face directly in the previous novels; indeed, the 'eternality of the will' resists the tragic leanings almost over-emphatically, when the picture begins to collapse, lose its separate qualities, and sink into a great, confused mass. As Paul gazes out over Nottingham with Clara (p. 273), his brooding lets the focus slip: 'The little, interesting diversity of shapes had vanished from the scene; all that remained was a vast, dark matrix of sorrow and tragedy . . . a dark mass of struggle and pain. The factory, the girls, his mother, the large, uplifted church, the thicket of the town, merged into one atmosphere—dark, brooding, and sorrowful, every bit.' Then the clock strikes two, the signal for work to resume in the factory: 'Paul started, and everything sprang into form, regained its individuality, its forget-fulness, and its cheerfulness.' The soul moves on, recalled. This is the rough, dogged value of the male activity. It is this recall which is asserted by the 'fuming and burning train' as it violates the darkness for a moment and then rushes on to great places, or by the pit-head movement when Paul comes (p. 136) to tell his father bad news. The boy could not 'realise William was dead; it was impossible with such a bustle going on.' Even as Mrs. Morel dies, the hooters call the men to work again, and Paul in his misery, almost crushed from life, turns determinedly once more, not to the 'poetic' city-vision of Cyril or Siegmund, but to the place of busy effort, 'the faintly humming, glowing town'. Here, in the wilful hypothesis, man rises above the mass, above all the unconscious, formless, unresolved things which imprison his developing 'on and on, nobody knows where'.

It is as if Lawrence's imagination had transformed Hardy's Egdon into the industrial Midlands, and Hardy's rural workers, moving unambitiously in their traditional ruts, become the purposeful workmen of pits and factories. As Paul and Mrs. Morel watch by a colliery (p. 123) they see a movement akin to that of Hardy's 'sky-backed pantomime of silhouettes', the laden figures who bring the furze-faggots to make the bonfire on Rainbarrow: 'Along the ridge of the great pit-hill crawled a little group in silhouette against the sky, a horse, a small truck, and a man. They climbed the incline against the heavens.' One remembers the momentary placing of Eustacia's figure over the 'high hill cutting against the still light sky'—'Above the plain rose the hill, above the hill rose the barrow, and above the barrow rose the figure.' But in Hardy's novel that upward movement for the aspirer cannot be held steady, and significantly it is replaced by the more traditional forms of man's self-assertion, the 'Promethean rebelliousness' of the Heath-dwellers, which, in the yearly bonfires, kicks against 'foul times, cold darkness, misery and death.' It is this which is picked up and steadied in Lawrence's anti-tragic version of industrial man's energy—furnaces flaring into the night sky, coal-banks burning, steam rising from pits. Hardy's 'Titanic' Egdon has a strange identity in its changing moods, faces, and voices—the organism which grasps Eustacia into its mass as she stumbles in her exhaustion (*Return of the Native*, p. 418) over 'twisted furze-roots, tufts of rushes, or oozing lumps of fleshy fungi . . . scattered about the heath like the rotten liver and lungs of some colossal animal.' In *Sons and Lovers* it assumes the colliery world's enormity, as seen by Paul in his wonder: ' "Look how it heaps together, like something alive almost—a big creature that you don't know" ' (p. 123).

Like the 'burdened figures' of Egdon, the men of Lawrence's novel are also weighed down, but with the struggle to comprehend the obscure cause of failure, to break a way through their enthrallment. They seem to battle against a riddle in the unconscious. On the day of Paul's birth, Morel is hewing away in the mine at a piece of stubborn rock which obstructs the path to the next day's work, but at last, with a deep, savage dissatisfaction, he must leave the job unfinished. In a sense, the work at this puzzle in the soul is passed on to William; he goes further, but is brought to a strenuous impasse—a baffling expressed in the fevered talk as he dies (p. 135), which significantly brings an image from his working world: ' "Owing to a leakage in the hold of this vessel, the sugar had set, and become converted into rock. It needed hacking—" '. Like Beardsall's fevered dream in the wood, this is the 'indistinct speech', the semi-articulate struggle, which is also suggested by the flickering shadows which are cast on the ceiling of Paul's room as he lies sick in childhood: 'the room seemed full of men who battled silently.' The shadow-men take on a blundering reality when William's coffin is brought home. As they stagger up the stairs (p. 139) with the 'great dark weight' upon them, they seem like unconscious wrestlers with some hidden enemy: 'Paul saw drops of sweat fall from his father's brow. Six men were in the room—six coatless men, with yielding, struggling limbs, filling the room and knocking against the furniture.' After this, the responsibility for the weary struggle into consciousness is peculiarly Paul's. As a child he has already undertaken it, when Mrs. Morel notes (p. 36) 'the peculiar knitting of the baby's brows . . . as if it were trying to understand something that was pain.'

2

The novel as a whole also seeks out the flaws and confusions of the emotional argument that men and women are inevitably doomed to some essential failure in their relationships. There is concern to make a fair appraisal of experience, to discriminate between differing purposes, influences, allegiances. It is as though (in revision, perhaps) Lawrence were applying by hindsight what he had discovered through Paul's experiences as an artist and lover. In Paul's (and Lawrence's) desire to take the relationship with Clara further than the terms of the novel allow—'He had wanted her to be something she could not be'—one may have the origin of the assessment of the Morels' failure: 'The pity was, she was too much his opposite. She could not be content with the little he might be; she would have him the much that he ought to be. So, in seeking to make him nobler than he could be, she destroyed him.' (P. 16.)

This suggests more fairness, a greater narrative adroitness in moving amongst opposing sympathies, than Lawrence's form does, in fact, allow him when he is portraying the first years of the Morels' marriage. His commitment to self-responsible human endeavour through Mrs. Morel is too necessary and too deep for him to swerve aside from priorities and explore fully in Morel all that fails to satisfy such purposefulness. Morel, with his 'dusky, golden softness', his 'sensuous flame of life', can, therefore, be no mitigating critic of his wife's Puritan unyieldingness. So he is cast off, turns roguish, and William is taken into the forward-moving impetus of his mother, only to sink 'puzzled and rather fretted'. By this time, however, Lawrence, through his description of young Paul's friendship with the Leivers family, has begun to introduce a new appraising consciousness into the wilful pattern. Now, by means of comparison, it can be seen that whereas Mrs. Morel's

Puritan ethic of will and responsibility is the dangerous force for Morel and William, the Catholic mystical religion of Mrs. Leivers, with its overtones of humility, selflessness, and submission, also paralyses her sons: they feel themselves 'cut away underneath', unable to establish normal relations with others, and like Morel they retort with brutality and clumsiness.

Such are the cripplings brought about by these determined 'mothers of men'. But Lawrence, in attempting to make a fair evaluation of opposing purposes, also shows the rewards which are gained in the same place where the losses are made. The rarefied atmosphere of the Leivers's household, which is so disastrous for its sons, has the very refining, subtilizing quality which is so beneficial to Paul Morel. His friendship with Mrs. Leivers and her daughter Miriam is marked out as another crucial step in his education; debts and gains are made clear. Paul's growth as a painter is vitally enhanced by Mrs. Leivers's mental discrimination —'Together they seemed to sift the vital fact from an experience' —while his spiritual relationship with Miriam urges him on to a further clarifying of himself, to find out, one might say, 'what the idea is', as he discards the 'clumsy make-shift' model. Paul with Miriam is incited beyond the blinder aims of his mother, and he gains an articulateness: the work is not merely for the sake of dogged accomplishment on its own, but has a larger, if as yet undisclosed, meaning. 'Then he was stimulated into knowledge of the work he had produced unconsciously. In contact with Miriam he gained insight; his vision went deeper. From his mother he drew the life-warmth, the strength to produce; Miriam urged this warmth into intensity like a white light.' (P. 158.)

So runs the onwardness, taking from here, casting off there, and becoming more unsatisfactory as Paul becomes its heroic expression and as Lawrence organizes the novel for his benefit. By clearing the way for Paul's developing spirit and making others serve his needs, Lawrence keeps open the sense of purpose at the cost of disregarding the claims of Miriam upon Paul. The onwardness which demonstrates Miriam's physical inadequacy for Paul and which makes the chapters 'The Test on Miriam' and 'The Defeat of Miriam' into victories of living purpose over its enemies, serves to confirm one's suspicion that Lawrence's previous attempts to be fair and appraising are not rooted confidently in his form—at least, not yet, because in the course of

Sons and Lovers Lawrence is working his way towards an art of more flexible moral sympathies. Meanwhile, in transition, he is caught by the claims of those who suffer from his commitment to Paul's triumph or who are sceptical of Paul's need to drive on towards a new kind of consciousness.

This hampering of endeavour Lawrence attacks as 'personality', but it is a vital discipline. Significantly, for the form of *The Rainbow* and *Women in Love*, it is the 'personality' of the woman that balks the man's adventure—urging on in one way, holding him back in another. Mrs. Morel and Miriam sustain Paul in his growth, yet are uncertain of his ultimate goal, and so Paul must convincingly argue himself away to individuality within their sustaining but confining framework: hence his need to distinguish (using the strength they have given him) the point at which the purposes of the growing man split off from those of the embracing, nurturing female. The arguments with Miriam are attempts to make a conscious assertion of this difference, to establish male sovereignty —as when Paul compares his purpose to Norman arches and Miriam's to Gothic, or where in a letter he describes hers as those of an eternal nun. In a way Paul is arguing with his mother by means of Miriam's spirituality, her clarifying power.

But this is not enough for Paul. He must in the end adventure beyond the upholding frame itself in an attempt to escape the claims of 'personality'—that quality which Miriam shares with Mrs. Morel and makes Paul's sex-relation with Miriam so un-satisfactory: 'Never any relaxing, never any leaving himself to the great hunger and impersonality of passion . . . she called him back to the littleness, the personal relationship' (p. 284). So Paul (with Lawrence) passes on to the 'great' impersonality of the re-lationship with Clara, while his mother and Miriam are left behind to wait, each in her different way confident that he will return to her, each doubting the seriousness of his questing. Miriam's position is nearly identical with Mrs. Morel's: 'She could let him go to Clara, so long as it was something that would satisfy a need in him, and leave him free for herself to possess' (p. 318).

Lawrence is still hindered, however, for Miriam's spiritual disbelief in Paul's further wants, like Clara's later dissatisfaction with him, has a questioning force in the novel which cannot be easily denied. Lawrence splits off the male from the female purposes with Paul's striving for clarity, and yet, because the woman withholds her final blessing from this advance beyond her understanding vision, the adventure lacks the novelist's confident belief. Miriam may be an over-spiritual danger for Paul, drawing herself and Paul back in fear from a further advance, but there is a suspicion of justice in the hesitancy. As with Mr. Morel, there is an unconvincingness about the passionate man which cannot be erased for the woman, even as she delights in his working. A critical spirit seems to partner her encouragement of man in his preoccupied world of labour. When Paul first goes (p. 112) to the factory in Nottingham, 'The man was the work and the work was the man, one thing, for the time being. It was different with the girls. The real woman never seemed to be there at the task, but as if left out, waiting.' The woman is suspended, while the man finds out the 'idea' to bring her. Paul expresses the division when he says (p. 225) ' "a man gets across his bicycle—and goes to work—and does all sorts of things. But a woman broods." '

And so Miriam shyly draws back to watch Paul as he moves forward, rapt in his own activity; she knows her own power to urge him on, and yet there is a fearfulness which Lawrence sees as a grasping 'personality' in the girl, something that claims back the worker for herself. She listens to Paul reading the Bible, while she sits back on the sofa away from him (p. 228): 'As he sat in the arm-chair reading, intent, his voice only thinking, she felt as if he were using her unconsciously as a man uses his tools at some work he is bent on. She loved it. And the wistfulness of his voice was like a reaching to something, and it was as if she were what he reached with.' The situation recurs—the boy reaching out decisively for an undefined beyond, while the girl waits—as when Paul swoops up like a bird on the barn's swing and Miriam hangs back 'in a kind of brooding', or when Paul, precariously rocking in the topmost branches of the cherry tree, reaches for the rich, sensual fruit to throw her.

But one should not interpret the movement of such scenes merely as Paul's sexuality straining against Miriam's spiritual hesitancy. The 'passionate' strains against the 'personal' in a larger sense, with the 'passionate' as the sensual and creative glow which wants to alter the terms of the novel by which it is still confined. When Paul rocks against the stable, rooted frame, he is symbolically venturing just beyond the dimensions of the novel; climbing dangerously high in the cherry tree or swinging almost completely out of the barn into the dull drizzle beyond, he seems to touch and fall back from the new vision of human individuality which Lawrence cannot at the moment establish in firm consciousness. Paul's art gives us further suggestions of this vision which is fully revealed in its incompleteness only when Lawrence portrays Paul's relationship with Clara. Like Paul's painting of pine-trees caught in the sunset glare as 'standing-up pieces of fire', or the corn-shocks which 'stood up as if alive', there is a declaration of new stature, a sense of uprightness, which wants to raise the glowing human figure sheer above the circumscribed environment, above the merging atmosphere of confusion and blindness, above the 'dark mass of struggle and pain'. This is the artistic manifesto which leads into the 'Passion' chapter, dealing with Paul and Clara, and which suggests a crucial altering of the scene: 'He loved to paint large figures, full of light, but not merely made up of lights and cast shadows, like the impressionists; rather definite figures that had a certain luminous quality like some of Michael Angelo's people. And these he fitted into a landscape, in what he thought true proportion.' (P. 301.)

The 'luminous quality' or the 'shimmering protoplasm' of the inner passion must be taken further than the imaginative gusto of Hardy's Prometheans and the high blazings of *The Return of the Native* if it is to survive as more than defiance. Unless Lawrence can infuse his sense of vital, 'impersonal' being with moral realization, the fire may sink, and the man may become a Clym, the tired figure of failed consciousness whom Eustacia critically regards: ' "He's an enthusiast about ideas, and careless about outward things. He often reminds me of the Apostle Paul . . . but the worst of it is that though Paul was excellent as a man in the Bible he would hardly have done in real life." ' (*Return of the Native*, p. 332.) It is inevitable that Hardy's apostle-worker, blindly preoccupied with his smaller vision, absorbed into the Heath mass, should be an intense disappointment to the distantly considering woman, when he appears (p. 326) 'not more distinguishable from the scene around him than the green caterpillar from the leaf it feeds on . . . a mere parasite of the heath, fretting its surface in his daily labour as a moth frets a garment, entirely engrossed with its products, having no knowledge of anything in the world but fern, furze, heath, lichens, and moss.'

Lawrence's working apostle, seen from a distance by Miriam as she rounds the corner in the lane, is involved in a different task —one that now points the crucial divorce between the art of Lawrence and Hardy; for in Miriam's spiritual 'annunciation' of this bowed figure in the road, working 'steadily, patiently, a little hopelessly' at some hidden problem, Paul's visionary purpose is clearly defined (p. 166) by the setting sun—'one rift of rich gold in that colourless grey evening seemed to make him stand out in dark relief.' Coming closer, she sees the very humble but specific task on which Paul is so intently engaged. He is only trying to repair a broken umbrella, which once belonged to his dead brother William. But in a larger sense Lawrence in Paul is working towards a way of mending tragedy, gathering the broken parts together and healing the breach between men and women. It is like a second chance to go over the conflict—an experimental attempt to balance both sides.

3

Therefore, Paul's association with Clara and Baxter Dawes is Lawrence's experiment with form, in which he tries to test out, at greater length, the vision that previously he has only been able to offer in glimpses. Past problems that remained tragically insoluble while they were locked within their original format, are now removed to a new setting, re-expressed and, by being made reachable, now have a chance of being curable. So the deadlock between the Morels, the inability of either man or woman to reconcile himself to the other's being, comes up once more with Clara and Baxter, each aggressive, unhappy, stultified. Each, like Morel in his slackening, has 'denied the God in him'.

Paul senses Clara's misery with immediate intuition. Her militant aloofness and apparent self-sufficiency only conceal the fact that she is a figure 'dethroned' from life as a woman. But coming from extremes of opposed experience—Paul from Miriam's spiritual love, Clara from Baxter's 'animalism'—Paul and Clara meet in a kind of powerful, healing love which reinstates the male or female in each. They are initiated through 'the immensity of passion', helped to stand up in a strange, larger knowledge:

To know their own nothingness, to know the tremendous living flood which carried them always, gave them rest within themselves. If so great a magnificent power could overwhelm them, identify them altogether with itself, so that they knew they were only grains in the tremendous heave that lifted every grass-blade its little height, and every tree, and living thing, then why fret about themselves? They could let themselves be carried by life, and they felt a sort of peace each in the other. There was a verification which they had had together. Nothing could nullify it, nothing could take it away; it was almost their belief in life.

But Clara was not satisfied. Something great was there, she knew; something great enveloped her. But it did not keep her.   (P. 354.)

Nor does this reaction from 'personality' keep Lawrence's complete confidence. As 'blind agents of a great force', Paul and Clara are the figures fitted into the landscape and restoringly carried by a power which is far beyond the old, 'personal' sustaining frame of Mrs. Morel and Miriam. But the question remains of the carelessness in the exulting sweep of 'why fret about themselves?' This adventure into impersonality must be made at the cost of 'true proportion' for the human figures; a consciousness, a responsibility for oneself, is left out in the relaxing, and the woman's dissatisfaction is the essential criticism of this. The relationship of Paul and Clara cannot flourish further, when there still remains the unhealed split between the daytime working personality and the impersonal night forces. Lawrence cannot hold his figures in the great background of space and night when they have so few laws to work by, no moral stature to match their scene. Like Mrs. Morel with her husband, he seeks to make them nobler than they can be, and this results in the uncertain proportioning of the impersonal quality in the figures. In the scene on the Lincolnshire coast, when the lovers go bathing (pp. 357–8), Paul sees Clara against her great background: 'As he watched, he lost her. She was dazzled out of sight by the sunshine. Again he saw her, the merest white speck moving against the white, muttering sea-edge.' She is 'almost nothing among the morning', 'a grain of sand . . . a concentrated speck blown along', and Clara is whittled almost to the nullity which Eustacia is in Clym's eyes on Egdon: 'Clym watched her as she retired towards the sun. The luminous rays wrapped her up with her increasing distance. . . . As he watched, the dead flat of the scenery overpowered him. . . .' (*Return of the Native*, p. 275). But the sense of life's 'oppressive horizontality' which exhausts Hardy's Clym, is resisted by Lawrence's Paul when he rubs Clara down after her swim. Lawrence wants a subjective magnitude for her, but not from pity: ' "she is magnificent, and even bigger than the morning and the sea. Is she—? Is she—?" ' Clara is magnified, ennobled, but Paul's question 'What is she?' is like Lawrence's query to himself as to what real terms support Clara's new importance as a human being.

One is aware that in attempting to offer laws of individuality Lawrence is still arguing with Miriam, and, through her, with his mother and father. Grappling with Clara and Baxter in the dark is like Paul being given an opportunity to go back and reshape the story of his mother and father, to enact in Clara's and Baxter's revival the discoveries he has made through Miriam's influence. ' "It's not religious to be religious" ', Paul had said to Miriam (pp. 250–1); ' "I reckon a crow is religious when it sails across the sky. But it only does it because it feels itself carried to where it's going, not because it thinks it is being eternal . . . God doesn't *know* things, He *is* things. And I'm sure He's not soulful." ' Paul argues himself and his individual being away from Miriam's spiritual Christianity, yet the language of her rapt states, like 'communion' or 'annunciation', is translated to sketch Paul's and Clara's new being, 'carried by life': 'It was almost as if she had gained *herself*, and stood now distinct and complete. She had received her confirmation. . . . Together they had received the baptism of life, each through the other; but now their missions were separate.' (P. 361.)

Again, when he describes Baxter's revival as a man, Lawrence seems to be 'reaching through' for the semi-conscious idea of individuality which will stabilize being on a firm basis. Paul's fight in the darkness with the self-ashamed Baxter, the crippled, idle figure, is another kind of baptism of fire. It leads naturally from Paul's challenge in the Nottingham public-house (p. 342) about the frustrations of the aristocrats in the German army: ' "Till there's a war they are idle good-for-nothings. When there's a war, they are leaders and commanders. There you are then—they *want* war!" ' The fight and the friendly-hostile relationship which follows between the two men is the means by which Baxter gradually regains a dignity, and ability to face himself. For Lawrence in Paul the fight is a final coming to grips with his furtive, ruined father, a completion of the preliminary sparring that William had as a young man with Morel. But Baxter can reach no high aristocracy of spirit as a restored man; he is healed just enough as an ordinary personality to own himself beaten back from the wasting of himself. Humbled, with enough at stake to make him fear death, he comes back to Clara. In his giving in she sees in him 'a certain nobility', the unheroic heroism of the ordinary personality, which she is now ready and tutored to serve.

It is not hard to see that in this new, quiet acceptance of each other, the 'personal' relationship seems to triumph over the impersonal, and Paul, when measured against Baxter's 'manly' humility by Clara, is an unconvincing figure now: 'there seemed something false about him and out of tune . . . something evanescent. . . . He would never make sure ground for any woman to stand on' (pp. 406–7). Lawrence seems to hover between agreeing and suggesting that Clara and Baxter have settled for a lesser destiny than Paul in his stubborn, onward persistence, straining against the terms of the very novel. The illness of his mother is the real factor which sinks Paul into unconvincingness and the novel into contradiction of itself: for Mrs. Morel, behind everything, is the source of the will and responsibility. But Lawrence, for all his reshaping of her in Clara, cannot completely differentiate inside that will, cannot confidently distinguish between its life-strengthening and tyrannic aspects, because the idea of responsibility for oneself has not been given sufficient new value to free itself from its old form. The life that has carried Paul can too easily become the death which sweeps him away.

As he walks home during his mother's last illness (p. 390) one sees again the silent, baffled struggle which his sick-room fire cast as shadows in his childhood—'The furnaces flared in a red blotch over Bulwell; the black clouds were like a low ceiling.' It is as if 'he were walking out of life, between the black levels of the sky and the earth'. He is being squeezed out of life as an individual body and identity: like his father, he is 'shrinking together, getting smaller', 'He was as if trying to get himself into the smallest possible compass' (pp. 406–7). The dark mass of tragic, confused, unconscious forces is gradually working the body down, and carelessly Paul's body is letting itself slip, decomposing, out of focus—as when he came down from the cherry-tree and made love to Miriam, and lay on the ground afterwards (p. 287), oblivious of the rain in his hopeless dissatisfaction with her sacrificial kind of giving: 'he felt as if nothing mattered, as if his living were smeared away into the beyond, near and quite lovable.' One remembers his parents in their moments of surrender to a tragic oblivion—Morel in a field one Wakes week, sleeping for an hour on the ground, and suffering ever afterwards from head-pains; Mrs. Morel, thrust out into the dark garden by her husband with her unborn child within her, drifting out of painful consciousness in the perfume of the white lilies, melting 'in the mixing-pot of moonlight, and she rested with the hills and lilies and houses, all swum together in a kind of swoon'. When she at last comes to bed, she looks (p. 26) at her reflection: 'she smiled faintly to see her face all smeared with the yellow dust of lilies.'

There is the same smearing out of the body and consciousness in Paul's agony of cross-purposes, sustained to live, yet called to die with his mother. It is almost a Hardy conclusion of 'oppressive horizontality', with the individual 'overpowered here in the compound mass the body'. The human figure is crowded tight and crawling pathetically between a big earth and sky, nearly crushed from view in the great background. But the Clym Yeobright fate is again spurned, the carelessness just controlled: 'Where was he?—one tiny upright speck of flesh, less than an ear of wheat lost in the field . . . On every side the immense dark silence seemed pressing him, so tiny a spark, into extinction, and yet, almost nothing, he could not be extinct' (p. 420). Like Paul's half-realization of Clara's importance—'Who is she?'—the uncertainty of 'Where was he?' looks towards a dimension, a time and space, which Lawrence cannot completely establish on the terms of Sons and Lovers. But as Paul, the artist of the novel, strides towards the city's 'gold phosphorescence' it is as if Lawrence were at last nearly within reach of an art which can span and understand the movement once seen so tantalizingly distant in The White Peacock, 'the come and go of people weaving and intermingling in the complex mesh of their intentions'. As one now sees, the effort to identify the terms of his new art is for Lawrence a strenuous but essential undertaking.

IV

The *Study of Thomas Hardy*

I

IN *Sons and Lovers* Lawrence cannot confirm the value that Paul and Clara have, impersonally, as 'grains in the tremendous heave'. But up to the last moments of the novel, in Paul's renewal of coherence as a 'tiny upright speck', Lawrence is still refusing to abandon his intuitive grasp on the impersonal dimension, although as yet he has no conscious metaphysic to justify such persistence. Even after he has completed one of the versions[1] of his new novel, *The Rainbow*, he can only describe the standpoint from which he is now writing ('that which is physic—non-human, in humanity') by using an analogy which is not entirely satisfactory. Writing to Edward Garnett in June 1914, Lawrence says that his new interest as a novelist is not in 'the old stable *ego*—of the character' but in 'another *ego*, according to whose action the individual is unrecognisable, and passes through, as it were, allotropic states' which are 'states of the same single radically unchanged element. (Like as diamond and coal are the same pure single element of carbon. The ordinary novel would trace the history of the diamond —but I say, "Diamond, what! This is carbon." And my diamond might be coal or soot, and my theme is carbon.)' (*Collected Letters*, vol. 1, pp. 279–80.)

The analogy is useful because Lawrence is able to place what

[1] Completed May 1914 and sent to Garnett. In July of the same year Lawrence asked Edward Marsh to lend him some Hardy novels for a book he was about to write on Hardy, and in September he wrote to J. B. Pinker that 'out of sheer rage' about the 'idiocy' of the war he had begun the book on Hardy. By December (see *Collected Letters*, vol. 1, pp. 296–8) the *Study of Thomas Hardy* was finished and Lawrence had begun to write the final version of *The Rainbow* which was completed in March 1915 and published the following September. The *Study* was never published in full until after Lawrence's death, when Edward D. McDonald included it in his *Phoenix* collection (1936) of unpublished Lawrence material.

is enduringly impersonal in humanity, its molecular 'grains', within a general 'physiology of matter'. But the language which he is using (suggested by the essays of the Italian futurist Marinetti) gives him too restricted a set of terms for his descriptive purposes. His sense of the eternal, unchanged 'carbon' has greater potential expression elsewhere: in the Egdon Heath of his imagination. It is not surprising, therefore, that shortly after defending his novel to Garnett, Lawrence should bring himself to a conscious critical encounter with Hardy's novels, with the creative material which has been so intrinsic to his imagination and which gives him, as no other material could do at this time, the stimulus, the framework, the range of possibilities, for him to be able to argue out and define his own artistic principles. Because of the lengths to which Lawrence takes criticism in the *Study of Thomas Hardy*, the final version of *The Rainbow* becomes, in technique and strategy, an emotional generation away from his previous novels. This is not to say that the unique art of *The Rainbow* totally depends on the body of ideas worked out by means of Hardy's novels in the *Study*. Instead, *The Rainbow* benefits from the refining of moral sympathies which gradually takes place in the *Study*. The movements of feeling in the novel are shrewdly clarified not dictated by the criticism of Hardy.

It might seem, however, with so much speculative material in the *Study*, so great a proportion of philosophical exploration out-weighing specific discussion of Hardy, that Lawrence is only using the ostensible subject of his inquiry as an excuse for working out other, unrelated problems. But, as one sees, Lawrence finds that he cannot intelligently discuss Hardy's problems as a novelist without relating them to mankind's artistic and religious prob-lems. Much in the *Study* leads one away from Hardy in order to be able to return to him with enlarged understanding. But even when Lawrence is not discussing Hardy explicitly, Hardy is there as a consistent, implicit presence, providing points of suggestivity which Lawrence thinks through as through a natural, symbolic language. In Chapter II[1], for instance, before Lawrence comes to

---

[1] Page and chapter references throughout are to *Phoenix*, ed. Edward D. McDonald (1961), where the *Study* appears on pp. 398–516. Out of the ten chapters of the *Study*, three deal specifically with Hardy's novels. These are: Chapter III (dealing with the early work, *Desperate Remedies*, *Under the Greenwood Tree*, *A Pair of Blue Eyes*, *Far from the Madding Crowd*, and *The Hand of*

give his first discussion of Hardy's novels in Chapter III, it is an image from *The Return of the Native* which suggests itself, like a talisman to his mind, as he speaks of man's need to struggle towards his own special being: 'I wish we were all like kindled bonfires on the edge of space, marking out the advance-posts.' In Chapter IV, as Lawrence moves away from Hardy's novels and continues to consider his theme—the 'brimming-over' of beings in flower, of riches unrelated to social usefulness and self-preservation—it is an image from Hardy (in particular, the gambling scene between Venn and Wildeve) which comes naturally into his mind: 'When is a glow-worm a glow-worm? When she's got a light on her tail.' Similarly, a man is a man to Lawrence when he is 'alight with life', but if that light is missing (as it is for Hardy's blinded Clym in the furze, 'not more distinguishable from the scene around him than the green caterpillar from the leaf it feeds on'), then 'there is no man, only a creature, a clod, undistinguished'.

If scenes and impressions from Hardy's fiction appear in the *Study* like part of a symbolic vocabulary, Egdon Heath for Lawrence makes up the first large word. It is fundamental, as the groundbase of thinking about tragedy, which spreads out beyond the local confines of the discussion of *The Return of the Native* in Chapter III. In emphasizing the great background in Hardy's novels, the 'vital and vivid' power 'which matters more than the people who move upon it', Lawrence asserts a priority of feeling, an unsentimental corrective, which for the moment can move unimpeded by considerations of Hardy's pity and irony for the failed characters. Hardy's Egdon is stoic, enduring, unchanging; Lawrence's Egdon is also eternal but dynamic. It is inviolate not because it has a hard casing but because it has an indomitable, thrusting creativity. Nothing can diminish its potency, and it gives Lawrence imaginative relief, 'savage satisfaction', to see all the exhausted human figures of the novel contained within the bigger rhythms of an inexhaustible sequence, free of pity's scruple:

Out of the body of this crude earth are born Eustacia, Wildeve, Mistress Yeobright, Clym, and all the others. They are one year's

---

Ethelberta, but giving the main discussion to *The Return of the Native*, 'the first tragic and important novel'); Chapter V (the individualists of all the novels); and Chapter IX (*Tess of the d'Urbervilles* and *Jude the Obscure*).

accidental crop. What matters if some are drowned or dead, and others preaching or married: what matter, any more than the withering heath, the reddening berries, the seedy furze, and the dead fern of one autumn of Egdon. The Heath persists. Its body is strong and fecund, it will bear many more crops beside this.   (P. 415.)

In putting aside the 'worn whisper', the 'ruins of human song', which the wind on Hardy's Heath utters through 'the mummied heath-bells of the past summer'—the plaint to which Eustacia adds her tragic sighing—Lawrence takes a more extravagant consolation from the Heath's persistence than Hardy in his dirge for the slighted and enduring human spirit of the ages. But by correcting the emphasis, with the picture of a rough, surging magnanimity, tossing its human products from its body or reclaiming the undeveloped failures, Lawrence inevitably veers to the large, careless mood which in *The Trespasser* and *Sons and Lovers* nearly wipes out responsibility for the suffering, struggling individual. Yet the swing is essential for him. He cannot accept Hardy's impressionistic moral picturing if he is to think his way through the tragic problem—hence the emphasis on the great background and its 'vast, uncomprehended . . . morality' set above Hardy's 'little human morality play, with its queer frame of morality and its mechanized movement'; hence also the insistence on the superiority of Hardy's sensuous understanding to his smaller social consciousness. These are the priorities Lawrence must roughly claim before he can consider, with later carefulness, why the individualities of these 'spilled and wasted' lives failed to emerge, or only half-grow.

With such re-proportioning, Hardy's universal tragedy is reduced to what Lawrence sees as its proper mental size: the exceptional aspirers of Hardy's novels merely offend against the self-preserving community ethic, and they struggle as 'more or less pioneers' half in, half out of the smaller scheme, 'free and yet unfree, preaching the walled city and looking to the waste.' They die either through their own lack of strength to bear the isolation or by the community's revenge, or both. But to Lawrence theirs are pathetic struggles against a lesser code, not the positive offences of real tragedy, the great crimes against the greater morality of life, which the Greeks and Shakespeare dramatized: Oedipus, Hamlet, and Macbeth actively transgress 'the unfathomed moral forces of nature, and out of this unfathomed force comes their death.'

What the 'unfathomed' morality consists of, what composes the 'unchanged element' at the back of life, is only suggested incompletely at this point in the *Study*, for the emphasis on the fecund background, 'organic as the body of a beast', limits the uncomprehended morality, for the moment, to a physical, sensual significance. And because of this necessary insistence on the fount of life as a great body, Eustacia is treated more sympathetically than Clym; the spiritual has to wait for Lawrence's estimate of Sue Bridehead later in the *Study*, to receive its complete due. Although Lawrence regards Eustacia and Clym as people who are thwarted through their wrong mental conception of their inner desires, Eustacia seems nearer the truth of her wants, her mental disguise frailer, than Lawrence pictures Clym. Both for Lawrence seek aspects of the community—Eustacia the social vanities of Paris, Clym, in a cowardly form of re-entry into the community at a higher level, seeking to live in moral abstraction—but Eustacia's idealizing of Paris through Clym is more acceptable to Lawrence than Clym's idealizing of his teaching scheme through Eustacia.

Lawrence is here not only attacking what he sees as Hardy's falsity of consciousness in the interpretation of Eustacia's dreams in *The Return of the Native*. A vital, imaginative understanding has been gained which is to clarify Lawrence's own depiction of yearning in *The Rainbow*. When Eustacia vows to Clym in the eclipse chapter that if he takes her to Paris as a wife she will 'be something', and when later she disappointedly admits to Wildeve about her young dream, that she thought she 'saw the way to it in my Clym', the invitation is there in Hardy's novel for Lawrence to dismiss the frivolous love of the *beau monde* as a trick of Eustacia's mind and her author's, and see (p. 416) that Eustacia wants some form of self-realization: 'Where was her imagined Paris, the place where her powerful nature could come to blossom? Beside some strong-passioned, unconfined man, her mate.' By the same kind of reading, Lawrence sees later in the *Study* (pp. 499–500) that when Jude studies for Christminster his basic passion is not represented by the conscious, social ambition from the disappointment of which Hardy works the tragedy; like Eustacia's, Jude's deep yearning is not for some petty trophy, Lawrence says, not for 'the vanity of education, a sort of superiority of educational wealth', but 'through familiarity with the true thinkers and poets . . . to find conscious expression for that which he held in his blood.' Sue is the freeing agent in Jude's life, as Lawrence infers Clym might have been in Eustacia's.

But Eustacia has the advantage of Lawrence's sympathy because she is less out of harmony with the 'passionate purpose' than Clym. In Hardy's novel, Clym suffered from the stress of the flesh upon thought, but Lawrence sees the situation in reverse: Clym suffers because he suppresses and mechanizes his emotions by his mental consciousness, and is therefore trapped by false purposes in a way that the more passionate Eustacia isn't. Whereas Eustacia's idealizing of Paris and Clym seems for Lawrence to be an instinctive enlarging movement, Clym's idealizing (his culture-scheme, Hardy says, 'had somehow become glorified. A beautiful woman had been intertwined with it') is seen as a narrowing, in Lawrence's interpretation: 'she had to fit in his system of ideas.' So thoroughly does Lawrence pursue his attack on Hardy's presentation of Clym that out of the eclipse scene in *The Return of the Native* he crystallizes a realization which not only represents for him all that is wrong with the moral consciousness of Hardy's novel but which also has enough symbolic force to be carried over into *The Rainbow*, there to become an essential part of its conception, strategy, and wisdom.

Just before the eclipse (*Return of the Native*, p. 230) Clym gazes at the moon's surface: 'His eye travelled over the length and breadth of that distant country . . . till he almost felt himself to be voyaging bodily through its wild scenes, standing on its hollow hills, traversing its deserts, descending its vales and old sea bottoms, or mounting to the edges of its craters.' Then, as the shadow of the earth moves across the moon, Eustacia's cloaked figure arrives in its wake to darken Clym's mind. But Lawrence will not accept Hardy's 'seeming', with its suggestion that Eustacia's passion saps and blinds the 'high thinking' Clym out of a selfish fervour. For Lawrence, Clym's blindness is self-inflicted:

So he skated over heaven and hell, and having made a map of the surface, thought he knew all. But underneath and among his mapped world, the eternal powerful fecundity worked on heedless of him and his arrogance. . . . What did it matter if he had calculated a moral chart from the surface of life? Could that affect life, any more than a

chart of the heavens affects the stars, affects the whole stellar universe
which exists beyond our knowledge?   (P. 418.)

Because Clym did not know that Eustacia 'existed untouched by
his system and his mind' and 'that she was Egdon, the powerful,
eternal origin seething with production', Lawrence, without
alluding directly to the scene, changes the meaning of the eclipse
of the moon and Clym. It is as if he sees Clym's view of the moon
as the white, abstract picture of the great background of life, the
mental chart of the small moral system projected as if it were the
real geography, over which, in powerful denial, moves the true
background, the physically alive Egdon in Eustacia, obliterating
the map: 'Shortsighted almost to blindness, we pore over the
chart, map out journeys, and confirm them: and we cannot see
life itself giving us the lie the whole time.' Lawrence in his interpretation is assisted not only by Hardy's wavering viewpoint, as
it shifts between passions and morality, neither of which it can
fully endorse ('a hesitating betwixt life and public opinion',
Lawrence sees it), but also by the cry of Sue Bridehead from her
marriage with Phillotson: 'The social moulds civilization fits us
into have no more relation to our actual shapes than the conventional shapes of the constellations have to the real star-
patterns' (*Jude the Obscure*, p. 214).
    So the vanity of the map-maker is exposed, as he works at his
futile purpose surrounded by the greater, incomprehensible
purpose of life, yet the question remains for Lawrence of why a
Clym Yeobright must halt his evolving individuality and shirk
his real purpose for the security of obsolete patterns, 'safe within
the proven, deposited experience, thrilling as he traverses the
fixed channels and courses of life.' But the problem of man's
self-stunting, the deeper motives for his relapse into jaded work,
are questions that Lawrence can only bring himself to tackle by
setting out more explicitly the passionate purpose and the conditions of growth. In trying to suggest these, he moves towards a
more sympathetic understanding of the terms of failure than he
can allow himself to display in his rebuke of Clym.
    Egdon is still the mainstay of his thinking, but changing its
value as his thought develops. A new abstract calm enters the
passionate argument, as if Lawrence were now meditating the
significance of the static scene, which Hardy calls 'strangely

homogeneous', where Eustacia's motionless figure stands on Rain-barrow, above the brooding expectancy of the Heath ('it had waited thus, unmoved, during so many centuries'). Lawrence, in fact, is touching the imaginative plan in the novel which Hardy cannot carry into meaningful action; and he touches it by seeing the Egdon idea anew as a picture of life's origins: at first 'life must have been uniform, a great, unmoved, utterly homogeneous infinity. . . .' In going back, it seems, to the beginning of Hardy's novel, Lawrence is going back to the beginning of life and the embryo form of moral purpose. The crude, dynamic Heath of the earlier discussion is now infiltrated with a subtler movement: Egdon becomes abstract, leavened with discrimination, its 'incomprehensible' morality becoming clearer as Lawrence speaks of clarification:

It seems as though one of the conditions of life is, that life shall con-tinually and progressively differentiate itself, almost as though this differentiation were a Purpose. Life starts crude and unspecified, a great Mass. And it proceeds to evolve out of that mass ever more distinct and definite particular forms, an ever-multiplying number of separate species and orders, as if it were working always to the produc-tion of the infinite number of perfect individuals, the individual so thorough that he should have nothing in common with any other individual. It is as if all coagulation must be loosened, as if the elements must work themselves free and pure from the compound.
(P. 431.)

Here in Chapter V, as Lawrence evolves the more distinct terms of his morality out of the 'crude earth' of his initial premise, as the spirit and consciousness break up the thickened idea, one sees a metaphysic being refined. Full individuality, Lawrence goes on to argue, is the state of singleness where man has come into knowledge of himself and his bounds, of the point where he ends and others begin, so that he knows everything that intrinsically relates to him and that belongs to his special purposes, just as he is also aware of the special singleness in others' lives and all that is *not* related to his purposes. From here Lawrence develops the morality, and, by inference, what he conceives more distinctly as the real tragic possibilities. The sin against the morality stems from the person who is not yet sufficiently distinct and purified out of the mass and who, in confusion or perversity, takes that which does not belong to his nature or intrinsic purposes—violating the integrity of another's being or seizing the wrong knowledge or system for himself. Such, for Lawrence, are the real sinners, the great violators like Oedipus, Agamemnon, Clytemnestra, Orestes, Macbeth, Lear, and Hamlet, who wreak disaster on themselves, either externally by destroying the singleness in others or, internally, by killing the spiritual consciousness or the blood-consciousness in themselves, so that they pervert their special form.

Although in Chapter V Lawrence returns to discuss Hardy's heroic individualists, using these new terms, he will still not allow that Hardy's heroes ever reach as far as the great sinners of Greek and Shakespearian drama. They never transcend the conventional morality frame; they only passively transgress against the larger code. For Lawrence they remain 'unbegotten' heroes, destroyed by the conventions of the small morality, because of the division (he detects) in Hardy. The passionate artist in Hardy is secretly sympathetic to the exceptional figure, the aristocrat, but the conscious moralist, working by timid bourgeois ethics, must show a perversity in Sergeant Troy, Clym, Tess, or Jude, and bring them down.

The division exists, but Lawrence seems to be aware that he has not explained to himself why it should be there in Hardy, why the sensuous understanding should be greater than the conscious metaphysic. He is approaching again the original problem behind Clym's failure of development and the unsure stamina of his author, when he says (p. 439) that for Hardy's flawed aristocrats 'the question of their unfortunate end is begged in the beginning', because they are given a radical frailty from the start, 'a weak life-flow, so that they cannot break away from the old adhesion, they cannot separate themselves from the mass which bore them. . . .' It is almost as if it occurs to Lawrence that in some way their conception by Hardy as innately weak is true, given the democratic age in which they are portrayed: 'In an heroic age they might have lived and more or less triumphed.' If this is so, then the aristocrat's 'certain coldness of temper, inelastic' in Hardy's novels is a larger, cultural problem, brought about by the changes in man's religious and artistic history. In tracing out these changes, Lawrence reaches an explanation of the two difficulties that create the problem of the failing individual—the antagonism of the moral community and Hardy's divided attitude towards it.

2

In Chapter V of the *Study*, Egdon is abstracted from its context in *The Return of the Native* to become a great mass. In Chapters VI and VII, as Lawrence works historically, it assumes the value of a principle, with various attributes—inertia, the unconscious, the utterly sensual, Being. But it is only defined in Lawrence's thinking because he sets against it, in necessary conflict, a movement that opposes this primary fundamental oneness—that is, the principle of activity, consciousness, spirituality, Not-Being, individuality, multiplicity. Egdon, therefore, becomes the 'female' Law of homogeneity, while the stirrings against it are called by the name of 'male' Love.

But for all the widening terminology, Lawrence is only moving away from a direct dealing with Hardy in order to find a level at which he can more satisfactorily set the problems which come out of the novels. There is now a time scale which radically affects Lawrence's way of discussing Hardy's art when he comes to *Tess* and *Jude* in Chapter IX of the *Study*. Across the ages, Lawrence visualizes a struggle between Law and Love, now one in domination, now the other, with historic moments of reconciliation before the balance is again lost. It is really the essential struggle between man and woman—the man with the preponderance of individualistic Love in his make-up, the woman having more of the principle of Law in hers. But, one should make clear, Lawrence conceives of situations where the 'female' Law of physical knowledge is greater in the man than the woman, because the epoch's mood governs the over-development of one principle at the expense of the other. In the same way, a woman may have more 'male' Love in her than the man. And these are the factors which are important for Lawrence when envisaging the religious desires, achievements, and failures of mankind. By 'religious' he suggests a deep desire in man and woman to meet in physical and spiritual fulfilment. They move towards each other throughout the ages, touching in a divine clasp of body and soul, then move apart again, either consummated for that time or tragically disappointed because one principle, Law or Love, has been too strong for the other and overborne it in the weaker man or the weaker woman.

Imbalance or balance has its repercussions in art. Lawrence sees that when art can truthfully express the achieved equilibrium between man and woman, between the 'male' and 'female' principles, then it is the hour of joyful or 'religious art'. But where there is imbalance and failure, then, Lawrence sees, artists may be tempted into various kinds of dishonesty. An artist may truthfully record the victory of one principle over the other, and yet be stuck in a repetitive 'tragic art', forever remembering that past failure and, by his remembrance of what has been, be unable to move forward; or an artist may react against imbalance, against the experience of himself and his age, and falsely picture a reconciliation of the principles. In the latter situation the artist strives to show what should be, but in opposing the *fait accompli* of his times, in making his unfulfilled yearning true only in art, he must inevitably exaggerate or distort to make up the deficiency in himself and his age—adding on a 'male' quality in his art where the epoch is weak in individual consciousness, adding on 'femaleness' where the spiritual mind is in excess.

Lawrence seems to see in Hardy both kinds of artist—the tragic rememberer and the reactionary—each responding to imbalance, each trying to reconcile desire with experience and collapsing into fiasco. It is as if Lawrence is brought to this view by now seeing the downfall of Clym and Eustacia in *The Return of the Native* in the historical terms that Hardy himself suggests in *Jude the Obscure*. In *The Return*, Egdon overwhelms the aspirers 'like some colossal animal', but in *Jude* 'the compound mass the body' which brings down the airy spirits is called the Mosaic Law and attains the precarious status of a religious principle. This is Lawrence's cue in Chapter VII of the *Study* (before he specifically discusses *Jude* in Chapter IX) to take Hardy's 'Law' back to its historical origin. In doing so, Lawrence is breaking up the tragic dilemmas of Hardy's fiction into their separate aspects and distributing them across human history according to their proper epochs.

So the Mosaic Law in *Jude* brings Lawrence to an interpretation of its source in early Judaism. For him it is the epoch of physical Law, the static, unconscious mass, when the 'male' consciousness is undeveloped in man and woman. In Lawrence's reading of Genesis, Eve is born from Adam's flesh but cannot be recognized as separate, because the great 'female' God of the body, the

Law, holds sway. In Biblical art, David's Psalms yearn for a
woman who is conceived still very much in the image of the
homogeneous Law, without separate consciousness. Therefore,
for Lawrence, while the Song of Solomon (Sue Bridehead's
'great and passionate song') is 'religious art', because it
expresses the jubilant contact of man and woman for which
David has yearned, the physical Law must inevitably overwhelm
the weaker Love and its spirituality. Thus stability breaks—a
breach that the Book of Job goes on fixedly remembering in 'tragic
art', dominated by a static, physical vision, held in the Law of the
God of the Ten Commandments who recognizes no other condition of being: 'Thou shalt have no other gods before me.' One
thinks of Hardy's last tragic effect, in Jude's death-scene (*Jude
the Obscure*, p. 418), when he and Sue have been caught back by
their old marriage partners, and the world shouts its victory in
the university celebrations: ' "Ah—yes! The Remembrance
games," he murmured. "And I here. And Sue defiled!" '

Jude's despair in the novel and his cry from the words of Job
are significant to Lawrence later when, in Chapter IX, he portrays Hardy as an artist of self-division, strongly rooted in the
Law and tortured like Job or his Jude: 'It is the same cry all
through Hardy, this curse upon the birth in the flesh, and this
unconscious adherence to the flesh.' But by the time he comes to
that remark (p. 481), Lawrence has grasped the nature of the
conflict historically. In moving on from Judaism to the appearance
of Christ, Lawrence is moving towards that side of Hardy which
makes the Law in him not completely satisfying and which provokes eventually the curse on it. To Lawrence the 'male' spirit
which was suppressed under Judaism arose in Christ to contradict
the absolutist pretensions of the Law and to bring a needed,
balancing interpretation to it. The inexorable commandment of
the jealous God of Law is refined by a new command: 'Thou shalt
love thy neighbour as thyself'—that is, recognize by spiritual
awareness the separate Law in others and in oneself. With this
movement towards articulate individuality, Lawrence now sees
the old 'female' exclusiveness threatened by the still weak but
gradually strengthening 'male' spirit of Christian Love.

It is a new development in the Law and Love dilemma which
reaches, according to Lawrence, a particularly critical stage in
the Middle Ages. And by maintaining his sense of continuity in

time, he is able to realize that what were thought to be two totally opposed desires in Jude—the sensual desire in contrast with the obsession for Gothic Christminster—can now be seen, historically, as different stages of the same process. Therefore, in Lawrence's interpretation, the established art forms of the Middle Ages (whether the cathedrals or the work of Fra Angelico) are a continuation of the old Law but now contain within them a necessary challenge to the Law's authority. This is the historical placing by means of which Lawrence, in his later discussion of *Jude the Obscure*, is able to see the quality of Jude's self-division—'monkish, passionate, medieval, belonging to woman yet striving away from her'—and also to see the value of Sue's intellectual challenge to him. Jude's 'fixed vision' of Christminster can, therefore, be viewed as akin to the medieval, artistic worship of a physical God: he is imprisoned within Job's knowledge of the triumphant flesh and yet, because of Sue, has opportunities of freedom offered to him.

For Hardy, Sue Bridehead is a 'modernist', striving for freedom amongst those worn-out forms of the nineteenth century to which Jude is still attached because of his inability to see that 'mediaevalism was as dead as a fern-leaf in a lump of coal; that other developments were shaping in the world around him, in which Gothic architecture and its associations had no place' (*Jude the Obscure*, p. 91). For Lawrence, however, the historical process which creates a Sue Bridehead begins much earlier in time, and, as with Jude over Mosaic Law and the Gothic Revival of the nineteenth century, he transfers the problem of Sue's 'modernity' to its proper epoch—out of imitation medievalism into the real Middle Ages. To do so he must make a significant alteration in Hardy's conception of Sue, but, as in his treatment of Jude's perplexities, it enables him to deal with different aspects of her problem in separate stages and to adjust his attitude as history shows its changing emphases. Therefore, the depiction of a split between the overall form of medieval art and its rebellious details, enables Lawrence to give the right degree of evaluation to Sue's influence on Jude's labouring, religious instinct. Lawrence can see, in its time and place, the benefit to Jude of Sue's forward-moving critical mind because she makes him aware of the inconsistencies and divisions in himself. Outside that time and place, in a changed situation, Lawrence can be equally sure of his doubts about Sue, but, because of his portrayal of the 'medieval' stage of the problem in Chapter VII, he is able to say later, in Chapter IX, that spiritual marriage with Sue helps Jude 'to overcome the female sensuousness in himself, to transmute his sensuous being into another state, a state of clarity, of consciousness'.

These are the implications which Lawrence draws from certain scenes in *Jude the Obscure*, although he does not mention them specifically. When Jude and Sue visit the art gallery in Wardour Castle (pp. 143-4), Jude is absorbed by the medieval Italian pictures on devotional subjects: 'Sue paused patiently beside him, and stole critical looks into his face as, regarding the Virgins, Holy Families, and Saints, it grew reverent and abstracted. . . . It was evident that her cousin deeply interested her, as one might be interested in a man puzzling out his way along a labyrinth from which one had one's self escaped.' In Melchester previously, Jude had suggested to Sue (p. 141) that they might go and sit in the Cathedral:

'Cathedral? Yes. Though I think I'd rather sit in the railway station,' she answered, a remnant of vexation still in her voice. 'That's the centre of the town life now. The Cathedral has had its day!'

'How modern you are!'

'So would you be if you had lived so much in the Middle Ages as I have done these last few years! The Cathedral was a very good place four or five centuries ago; but it is played out now. . . . I am not modern, either. I am more ancient than mediaevalism, if you only knew.'

What 'ancient' means for Sue is suggested later at Aldbrickham (p. 318), when she upholds classical standards of art in preference to Jude's Gothic.

'Remember the interior of Christminster Cathedral—almost the first place in which we looked in each other's faces. Under the picturesqueness of those Norman details one can see the grotesque childishness of uncouth people trying to imitate the vanished Roman forms, remembered by dim tradition only.'

But the 'grotesque childishness' within the formal structure has a different meaning for Lawrence when he considers (p. 454) the innate criticism made by the 'male' spirit from within the medieval cathedrals of physical Law:

All the little figures, the gargoyles, the imps, the human faces, whilst subordinated within the Great Conclusion of the Whole, still, from their obscurity, jeered their mockery of the Absolute, and declared for multiplicity, polygeny.

The suppressed spirit of Hardy's Sue is for Lawrence not pagan in its rebellion. On the contrary, she expresses the striving of 'male' Love, the Christian urge to individualization and mind. In accordance with this alteration in the meaning of Sue's criticism, Lawrence, when he comes to discuss her later in the *Study*, dismisses Hardy's suggestion of her pagan affinity, when she buys plaster statuettes from the foreign 'image-man', and, with them wrapped in leaves, carries her 'heathen load into the most Christian city in the country'. Lawrence sees it otherwise: 'She turned to look at Venus and Apollo. As if she could know either Venus or Apollo, save as ideas. Nor Venus nor Aphrodite had anything to do with her, but only Pallas and Christ.' (P. 501.)

Lawrence returns implicitly to Sue when he is discussing a later historical period. Meanwhile he is working out a logic in his attempt to understand the course of religion and art. For him the medieval conflict between the old absolute and its rising critic leads momentarily to a point of equilibrium between Law and Love, to the joyful reconciliation which Botticelli's art expresses. But even in Botticelli's pallid, spiritual virgins, the Christian 'maleness' is beginning to assert its domination over the Law of the body, and at the Renaissance the balance finally tips in favour of the mental consciousness and individuality, with the extra weight of the Greek 'male' spirit as the deciding factor which overbears the Law. And here in working out the developments which follow in post-Renaissance art—whether with the artists of the now-subordinated Law like Michelangelo, Raphael, Tolstoy, and Hardy; or with the artists of dominating Love like Correggio, Rembrandt, Turner, Shelley, Flaubert, and the French *symbolistes*—Lawrence seems to be discovering not only the terms on which he can evaluate the strange phenomenon of Sue Bridehead and understand her predicament, but also the mistakes and confusion to which he and Hardy have been led in an epoch of spiritual consciousness.

Now the *Study* traces the artistic effect that results from the worship of mind and spirit in the new religious emphasis of northern Europe. The artists who go with the mainstream of their time, the followers of Christian Love in all its new excess, are tempted towards a new absolutism in their work and a distortion of a different kind from that of the 'reactionaries' like Michelangelo and Raphael. Rembrandt's art, according to Lawrence, tries to marry the impossible, mixing the flesh with the spirit; Turner does without the flesh, denying its presence, and tries to marry spirit with spirit. Turner always sought

to make the light transfuse the body, till the body was carried away, a mere bloodstain, became a ruddy stain of red sunlight within white sunlight. . . . If Turner had ever painted his last picture, it would have been a white, incandescent surface, the same whiteness when he finished as when he began, proceeding from nullity to nullity, through all the range of colour.   (P. 474.)

One has already noticed the attractiveness of Turner to Hardy, the novelist who sees in Turner's last paintings an escape from 'the exact truth as to material fact'; who attempts to leaven the body of the world with his added 'gleam, The light that never was'; who creates the Shelleyan figure of Sue Bridehead—'"you spirit, you disembodied creature . . . hardly flesh at all,"' as Jude calls her. But Hardy cannot suppress his sense of the body in the way that Lawrence suggests Turner is nearly able to do. He cannot reach that stage of illusion: for through the mist, one remembers, there comes the 'almost tragic' insistence of the glaring redness, the Rhine seen on his travels 'like a riband of blood'. The physical knowledge in Hardy becomes insidious or clumsy—a position that Lawrence quarrels with and summarizes in Chapter IX: 'The spirit of Love must always succumb before the blind, stupid, but overwhelming power of the Law.'
  He quarrels with it there because he has seen in Chapter VII how the epoch which produced the over-specialized art of Turner's last phase also produced Sue and her predicament—all arising from a falsification. Again Lawrence picks up the idea from Hardy's fiction and gives it an historical meaning. What are most relevant now are Jude's remarks on Sue as ' "a product of civilization" ', ' "one of the women of some grand old civilization, whom I used to read about in my bygone, wasted, classical days. . . . I almost expect you to say at these times that you have just been . . . listening to Aspasia's eloquence or . . . watching Praxiteles chiselling away at his latest Venus." ' (*Jude the Obscure*,

pp. 145, 280–1.) But Lawrence, in speaking of Sue directly in Chapter IX, will not accept Hardy's view of her as a frustrated figure of Greek-like innocence. He breaks it into mere analogy: just as he sees that the Greeks subordinated woman into a totally virgin idea, so the post-Renaissance Europeans of the north produced by selection and cruel suppression a pure type of 'male' woman: 'What Cassandra and Aspasia became to the Greeks, Sue has become to the northern civilization.' She is a specialized type, perversely bred and then despised by man after he has created her intolerable situation. Lawrence has sympathy for her predicament, because he sees it stored up for her by history. And in coming to this position through a time-perspective, he seems to be doing more than giving an historical explanation to what he has sensed in Helena of *The Trespasser*—'For centuries a certain type of woman has been rejecting the "animal" in humanity. . . .' More importantly, he is offering implicit recompense for his treatment of Emily in *The White Peacock* and Miriam in *Sons and Lovers*, the other spiritual witches. He offers it now from a moral awareness whose ethic is to recognize the special, even if warped being of others.

The defeat of Miriam was a compensation, an exaggerated reaction, just as Hardy's 'light that never was' appeased spiritually. In a sense, Lawrence's consideration of Raphael and Michelangelo is a disguised review of his earlier situation as a novelist, in which he weighted the scales heavily against the poignant yielding to tragedy; the distortions that Lawrence sees in those Italian artists, left behind in the new epoch of Love, have particular relevance to the form of *Sons and Lovers*. Michelangelo, passionately 'female' in a time when the physical is being subordinated to the spirit and mind, reacts upon himself in his art, according to Lawrence, and swings wholly over to the old God of Law: the only salvation is in the flesh. But in order to hold the balance against the prevailing spirituality of his time he must exaggerate the flesh, create huge, physical figures from the Mosaic Law, like his Jewish David. The 'Passion' chapter of *Sons and Lovers*, with its great 'heave' of physicality, is also unsure of the 'true proportion' of its ennobled figures.

If Lawrence's treatment of Michelangelo looks back at previous distortion, his view of Raphael's more abstract, symbolic art looks forward to the dangers with which he contends in *The Rainbow* and *Women in Love*: that is, the temptation to exaggerate and make a false harmonizing of opposing principles by means of a predetermined, theoretical design. In achieving this under-standing, Lawrence glimpses the problem and the hoped-for solution in his own art. His sense of form has a new clarity. He conceives of an art based on the vital relation between man and woman that is capable of admitting the deficiencies, weaknesses, disappointments of human experience without the author's idealism sinking to a tragic ethic or hardening into a defiant assertion of what should be (and isn't) or softening into a vulner-able optimism. It is an art of hazard that he conceives because he has grasped the inherent dangers—the conflict of aspiration with experience that produces human suffering, wild reaction, illusion, and compensation—and because the ultimate prize is clear: the freedom and discipline of reconciliation.

3

By the time that Lawrence comes to discuss *Tess of the d'Urbervilles* and *Jude the Obscure*, he has defined Hardy's position as an artist of the Law who is strong in unconscious and sensuous under-standing but not developed in mind and spirit. Earlier in the *Study*, in Chapter III, Lawrence notes the want of right con-sciousness in the erratic, physical initiatives of Hardy's characters: 'These people of Wessex are always bursting suddenly out of bud and taking a wild flight into flower', acting 'independently, absurdly, without mental knowledge or acquiescence.' Now Lawrence can more clearly understand why Hardy encloses the violent, fatuous movement within a tragic form: the artist of the Law, living in an age of selfless Love yet lacking in himself a confident spiritual consciousness, calls upon the bourgeois morality of his times to reinforce his mind, to give an irrelevant tragic explanation of his own special dilemma.

Lawrence's excursion through religion and art, one sees, enables him to place the 'inelastic' quality of Hardy's energy within a developing, historical process, and also to conclude (in contradiction of his earlier view) that the aristocratic individuals fail, not because they struggle against the community but because they are sufferers from the same developments in time as establish democratic Christianity as the prevailing ethic. The individual who seeks fulfilment has been maimed, over-specialized. The aristocrats' lack of elasticity, 'weak life-flow', is due to a narrowing in the culture. And in coming to see why these figures are historically at odds with their times, Lawrence implicitly retracts his previous dismissal of their fate as not being really tragic, not really offending against the higher morality of life. Now, with Hardy's own tragic form set aside and the characters' self-division inferred from history, Lawrence rescues them from their pathetic toils in the novels, removes them from what he sees as the commonplace grasp of their author, and sets them as partakers in 'real tragedy' of the Shakespearian or Greek pattern. He dramatizes them as sinners and victims on the wider plane of morality which it has been his task to define after his discussion of *The Return of the Native* in Chapter V, with sympathy and with condemnation depending on the extent to which they recognize the laws of their own and others' being.

Tess and *Jude* are reframed in Chapter IX as dramas of over-specialized individuals. In this account, isolated aristocrats seek for aristocratic kin or equals in being, but because their growth has been marred by centuries of democratizing and spiritualizing they are fatally hindered in their natural relations with each other. What is a rotten vice in a Hardy character, what is an ethos of universal blundering and guilt in *Tess*, become, in Lawrence's sympathetic order of thought, merely the ills that arise from the cultivation of one side of the aristocrat at the expense of the other. With Lawrence's earlier, instinctive view of Eustacia's claim on Clym raised into theory, Alec and Arabella persist after Tess and Jude, not as Hardy's coarse seducers and persecutors but as aristocrats seeking noble equals to fulfil them.

Tess, in this reading of the novel, is a victim of her own and others' specialized development. In the epoch of Christian Love, the strong sensual part of her has been so suppressed that she now only recognizes the 'male' spirit in herself and is overbalanced on the side of selfless 'not-being'. She is 'outwearied from the start' in her passive respect for the opinions and actions of others. She needs a physical 'female' complement in the man to right the balance. But Alec, like Arabella, is too strongly 'female': the sensual Law in him has ousted the Christian sense of otherness which Tess has to an extreme. Others are only parts of himself, of his homogeneity, so that he cannot recognize the spiritual part of

Tess's nature, and so he deeply touches the suppressed, sensual part of her being only to betray it. Because the mass and the body are too powerful in him, there is an inertia which prevents Alec transforming the power he receives from Tess into anything creative, in action or speech. Like Arabella he remains arrested in the senses, using Tess as a means of self-gratification, plundering the world with cavalier heedlessness, because he is spiritually impotent. Angel, on the other hand, is sensually impotent. Like Tess he suffers from 'generations of ultra-Christian training'. His body drives him to Tess, but he can only know her body through the mind and spirit, so he labours in deadlock—a plight granted Lawrence's respect: 'One feels that in Manston, and Troy, and Fitzpiers, and Alec d'Urberville, there is good stuff gone wrong. Just as in Angel Clare, there is good stuff gone wrong in the other direction.' (P. 487.) Their playing havoc with the stuff they and others are made of brings on the tragedy—Alec kills the 'male' in himself through Tess (as Clytemnestra kills Agamemnon); Angel kills the 'female' in himself through Tess (as Orestes kills Clytemnestra); and Tess, betrayed and self-condemning, is killed by the community. Lawrence, therefore, sees *Tess* as the tragedy that follows the suppression of one principle, Law or Love.

Jude, however, becomes a tragedy under Lawrence's arrangement because the two principles, Law and Love, are confused. At first it seems like another *Sons and Lovers* with Jude in the place of Paul Morel. A man seeks fulfilment, awakening, in the blood and spirit, but he cannot find a woman who has both qualities in equal measure. He can find a spiritual bride in Sue (or Miriam) and a sensual bride in Arabella (or Clara), but not the two together in one woman. This is the fate of Jude who has Tess's strong 'male' and 'female' qualities; but, because of centuries of Christian teaching, he inherits a physical consciousness stultified by the spirit and the mind. Arabella is good for him, Lawrence thinks, because she scorns the mental form of his desires, the community ideal of book-learning, and diverts him back on the right course. But although she gives him a physical consummation, she is spiritually impotent, self-gratifying, and Jude, with his sensual manhood gained, must pass on to Sue for his spiritual and mental awakening. This she gives him, but she is a greater sufferer from the Christianizing than Jude or Angel Clare, one feels. In Lawrence's interpretation, the division in her nature seems to work more destructively upon her than on the other divided characters. Being so purified into a predominantly 'male' woman, the suppressed 'female' in her demonically urges her against herself. She must know the body through the mind as its food, its stimulus, so she is placed in the predicament of needing a slight physical contact, enough to give her mind life; yet she dare not go as far as involving herself in any deep physical relationship if she is to keep form. So, Lawrence sees, she remains true to her rarefied, special being, in her first marriage to Phillotson and in her spiritual marriage to Jude.

But after Arabella's appearance at Aldbrickham the sins are committed which create for Lawrence the real tragedy. Jude, who has commented that Sue is 'a product of civilization', later reproaches himself at Christminster, ' "You were a distinct type —a refined creature, intended by Nature to be left intact. But I couldn't leave you alone!" ' (*Jude the Obscure*, pp. 354–5.) These remarks are the basis of Lawrence's certainty that as 'one of the supremest products of our civilization', Sue's special form, a creation of Love, is violated when she gives her body to Jude. This confusion, the attempt to marry the spirit *with* the flesh, when a dual marriage for Jude and Sue is impossible, comes about, according to Lawrence, both through Sue's unsure conviction of her special nature—so that she is wrongly jealous of Arabella, and the 'female' in Sue urges her to prove that she also is a physical woman—and through Jude's forcing his senses to follow his mental will into the physical consummation he doesn't deeply want from Sue. It is profanation and pollution to Lawrence because of 'their incapacity to accept the conditions of their own and each other's being'—a condemnation which goes as much against Jude and Sue as against Paul and Miriam in their lovemaking. In Lawrence's novel, with the forcing of the physical love by Paul and Miriam—he impersonally, she sacrificially— there is a similar breaking of form. When Lawrence writes in the *Study* (p. 507) of Jude's exhaustion of himself—'this continuous state of incandescence of the consciousness, when his body, his vital tissues, the very protoplasm in him, was being slowly consumed away'—it is like a review of the meaning of Paul's 'dull pain' after the love-making, a further understanding of the slip into the unfocused mass when Paul's life seems 'smeared away

into the beyond' and he wishes 'to melt out into the darkness and
sway there, identified with the great Being.'

Jude and Sue are seen by Lawrence to be 'overpowered here in
the compound mass the body', but not with Hardy's kind of
fatalism. To Lawrence they are guilty of an inconstancy to their
natures, they have offended both the body and the spirit. Now
they can never be happy because 'in their last and deepest feelings'
they know their own guilt, and their sense of it is communicated
to other people—'Which is why they were, the pair of them, instinctively disliked.' One sees in Lawrence's condemnation how,
having earlier discarded the narrow, social meaning of the
Mosaic Law, he can take Arabella's side with it against the
marriage-sacrilege. The outraged bigots and the conspiring
Arabella of Hardy's novel belong, in Lawrence's interpretation, to
an authoritative outlook, justifiably indignant, not prudish or
hypocritical.

Consistent with Lawrence's raising of the morality, from the
lesser to the greater code, is his view that Arabella's child kills
Sue's children as a rightful judgement of the Law. The children
are Sue's attempted proofs and guarantees of herself as the physical
woman which she cannot be, and so the offended physical in-
stincts rise up against these false creations. (In the same way,
Lawrence interprets Tess's murder of Alec as revenge for his
sinning against her integrity.) Hardy's final mood of supersession
and suicide fits Lawrence's morality: Jude is exhausted through
falsity not work, and Sue's return to the ritual she despised is not
a surrender to a banal, mechanical Christianity but an act of
remorse for her sin against the Holy Ghost.

4

Of course Lawrence is now not interpreting but totally re-
writing Hardy's novel. But while one observes how Lawrence
imposes on *Jude* his own moral ordering, one should also realize
that he is defining the different level of his moral response to the
changing situations of Hardy's fiction. The result is an exploration
of the confused instinct, the self-mistrusting passion, the narrow
metaphysic, the misshaping of growth—indeed, a meditation on
many of the dangers that *The Rainbow* is alert to, as it moves
through the crises of its figures, whose fate and plight is radically

clarified by the kind of understanding which Lawrence in the *Study* brings to Eustacia, Clym, Jude, and Sue.

It is the *Study* which crystallizes further the attitude which Lawrence could only vaguely express a year earlier in a letter of autumn 1913 to Henry Savage:

> As a rule one sees only the intertwining of change and a distortion of half-made combinations, of half resolved movements. But there is behind every woman who walks, and who eats her meal, a Venus of Melos, still, unseeing, unchanging, and inexhaustible. And there is a glimpse of it everywhere, in somebody, at some moment—a glimpse of the eternal and unchangeable that they are. And some people are intrinsically beautiful—most are pathetic, because so rarely they are their own true beauty. And some people are intrinsically fearful, strange forms half-uttered. And all any man can do is to struggle to be true to his own pure type.   (*Collected Letters*, vol. 1, p. 242.)

By the time of the *Study* this intuition has found an emotional balance—an intelligent sympathy that knows the pathos of 'half-uttered' being without denying, by resort to tragic art, that it also knows the possibility of the full utterance. It is in the *Study*, for instance, that one sees Lawrence learning how to place the exact emphasis on Will Brangwen in *The Rainbow*: 'Something undeveloped in him limited him, there was a darkness in him which he *could* not unfold, which would never unfold in him.' When Lawrence intervenes openly to argue against Anton Skrebensky's ethic of community service, he must, nevertheless, qualify his criticism of the man's blindness: 'He could not see, it was not born in him to see. . . .' And when at the end of Ursula's relationship with Anton, she pronounces it a failure, his question—' "Is it my fault?" '—begins to have a reply from Ursula before she breaks down: ' "You couldn't—" '. The weight of suggestion behind her answer, one notes, could only be felt in the kind of art that Lawrence now achieves in *The Rainbow*.

V

The Rainbow

I

THROUGHOUT the *Study* Lawrence is constantly returning to one problem which particularly engages him as the author of *The Rainbow*—how art can truthfully portray the thwarting of mankind's religious desires by the disappointments of actual experience. In Chapter VII of the *Study* he describes the struggle of men and women for a perfect consummation of body and soul, for an absolute within earthly life which is 'Eternal, Infinite, Unchanging', but which can only be attained by mutual endeavour amongst imperfect conditions. The struggle for a timeless, infinite peace must go on within the world of time and space, with its frictions, resistances, dangers, distractions, where either man or woman may lack sufficient stability or movement to keep the whole relationship in balance.

How the balance is kept or lost, how mankind copes with the insufficiencies of experience, are concerns in the *Study* which give rise to the watchful sympathy of *The Rainbow*, its astute sense of measure and proportion, its preparedness. For only by a subtly ranging comprehension of the many levels at which religious desire confronts, transcends, or is distorted by failure, does Lawrence possess a scale of knowledge, a fund of precise response upon which to draw when portraying in the novel all the various, deep attempts of the soul to meet the bargain of God with man, to make real the Covenant of the Rainbow in perfect reconcilement and infinite stillness. Lawrence cannot celebrate the joint victory of man and woman by 'religious art'—indeed, he cannot define human achievement—without envisaging all the pressures against the fulfilment of desire; hence his form knowingly contends with and includes the breakdown in the human struggle, when it loses sight of the over-arching whole in which it is set, and becomes a deadly, personal fight—another movement altogether. Then the map becomes more real than the land, and the novel has to pause and take its bearings again. Yet the infinite purpose is eternally there at the back of the action, signalling and beckoning onwards, to be given its shape and boundaries by the religious human struggle, but not to be circumscribed by its form in time and space, not to be gainsaid when the boundaries break down.

Marriage is the marking of the boundaries, the restriction of possibilities yet a concentration of relevance. Here, where a finite struggle attempts to keep faith with the infinite, there is a joint fate at stake, both wonderful and terrible in the knowledge it includes. It is that double quality, of discipline and freedom, strict limitation and greater meaning, which is felt in Tom Brangwen's review of his marriage with Lydia, still 'like two children camping in the plains', and in the description of the family as 'a small republic set in invisible bounds'. This is close to the call of the *Study* for all to be 'like kindled bonfires on the edge of space, marking out the advance-posts'—the call which remembers Eustacia's blazing signal from the lonely house on the Heath and Hardy's suggestion of the house as 'a fortification upon which had been kindled a beacon fire'. The Vye home is entrenched behind the 'thick square clods' of Egdon earth, forming 'the bank which enclosed the homestead, and protected it from the lawless state of the world without'. The old home of the Brangwens, the Marsh farm, is also sealed off, reprieved for a while from complete contact with an advancing civilization and industry: their lives are protected and enclosed by the 'high rampart' of the canal embankment built across their land, the 'raw bank of earth shutting them off' and keeping their 'homestead . . . just on the safe side of civilisation'. They are both defended and limited by their earth-boundary—the enclosure which might well stand for the self-disciplining art of the novel, as it sets up 'camps' further and further on in the unknown and works through the responsibilities of a marriage till it reaches, defines, and surpasses the boundaries of consciousness beyond which the Brangwens of that moment cannot go.

The novel's spread of time passes on responsibilities that the characters and the novelist accumulate. Riches and problems are inherited. There are the riches of life, strength, inner resources which the inheritors can bring to fertile use in their relationships, or, if thrown back on themselves, render waste and ugly. There are the baffling, half-understood problems—some that have to be faced and others that are often beyond the capacity and need of the individual to understand, since they could hinder and side-track more central purposes. As the novel expands and considers society at large, these problems become more pressing—recognized by Lawrence within his form but still not allowed to deflect the purposefulness. It is a dark 'mass' of unresolved meaning which Ursula moves among, strives against, and which *Women in Love* inherits.

This is not to say that Lawrende ignores all that sidetracks fulfilment. It is an essential concern here, as it could not be in *Sons and Lovers*, to trace divergences, to follow out the consequences of stress and disaster through change, convalescence, recovery, and return. But concern of this kind is carefully balanced against another interest—the need to rediscover where the real growth is to be found, in whose hands the purpose is being kept, and which is the clear thread in the labyrinth that leads in continuity from past to future. The breaking of continuity, the arrest of growth in the individual, is personal tragedy, not the novel's; for where the traveller halts at one of the phases of the journey and is forced to mark time in repetition and reaction, the holy struggle is seen as humanized in egotism and personal wilfulness. When the ideal of the infinite as only mutually attainable between man and woman is given up for the ideal of separate divinity and personal absolutes, then the irony appears that sees the confusion where the real purpose and the egotistic imitation strangely resemble each other. The greater and the lesser purposes are denoted by the same language, with words like 'fate', 'separate', 'absolute'; and the genuine travellers move in error and recoil between the two possible meanings of their journey.

2

The Rainbow, then, deals in growth's danger, in the soul's mistakes and self-retrieval, so that the veering course is constantly under correction. It is as if the reader were led and involved along one direction, only to find that he has missed the forward-moving way, and that the growing purpose has passed into new, unlooked-for courses. At first one sights what *seems* the all-sufficient power, the total expression of life in its sensuous running, the Brangwen life on the land—'So much warmth and generating and pain and death did they know in their blood, earth and sky and beast and green plants, so much exchange and interchange they had with these, that they lived full and surcharged, their senses full fed' (p. 3). With their generations of prosperity and blood-riches, the Brangwen men have inherited an independence from the movement of civilization and a largesse of strength. But the stored wealth, the blood-knowledge, cannot be spent, can go nowhere. The sensuous understanding, so powerful by day in the fields, is by night inert, unleavened, clinging like the earth. In this primal poem the Brangwen man of the ages is heavy and blinded by his work at the source, the earth-mass, with no larger-souled individuality distinct from the vibrant scene which, as Lawrence says of Hardy's great background in the *Study*, 'matters more than the people who move upon it'. Indeed, this life which seems the only possibility, the comprehensive whole, the knowledge which is 'enough', is homogeneous like the *Study*'s Law of the purely physical God the Father which recognizes no separateness of individuality. The Alfred Brangwen of the 1840s, sensuously replete, 'spoilt like a lord of creation', can hardly tell his wife apart from himself: her railings and self-assertions only confirm his 'pride and male triumph', and they exist, 'knowing nothing of each other, yet living in their separate ways from one root.'

Brangwen woman, as she stirs in the 'mass', turns towards the 'consciousness' and 'carefulness' that the discovery of the larks at Cyril's feet signalized in the big field ('something little and dark, moving indefinitely'). The blood and body holds her stable but fixed, and in seeking the omitted leavener, the clarifying consciousness and aware spirit, she looks towards a world of distinct, detached individuals. Through the vicar and aristocrats of Cossethay she half-discerns a subtler, more developed motion and rhythm of life than the heated mould can offer—'lean, eager men with strange movements, men who had command of the further fields, whose lives ranged over a greater extent.' Yet here one sees how Lawrence's defining of his attitudes towards idealism in the *Study* cautions his portrayal of female yearning in the novel, as the Brangwen women look out to what Eustacia Vye calls ' "all the beating and pulsing that is going on in the great arteries of the world." ' In the *Study* such yearning is seen as a religious effort to overcome the dissatisfactions of experience: men or women, finding a lack within the other, seek to make up the missing balance by adding a symbolic weight to the other sex. Mankind comes to 'symbolize and so to possess that which is missing.' It is this desire to equalize and add to her life that makes the Brangwen woman take sights on the want through the vicar and aristocrats as symbolic figures. They deputize for the clearer space of forward-moving activity and articulateness, 'the far-off world of cities and governments . . . the magic land'; the vicar speaks the 'magic language' lacking in the Brangwen woman's life.

It is like a gathering up of the intuitions of Mrs. Yeobright, Eustacia, Clym, and Jude, and directing them towards another Christminster, another 'city of light', another place 'that teachers of men spring from and go to', where the 'tree of knowledge grows'. But his criticism of Hardy's characters and the forms which they take to be representative of their desires has taught Lawrence the novelist how to maintain a careful relationship between ideals and reality: thus his poise of understanding enables him to affirm the genuineness of the Brangwen women's need in symbolic-ally ennobling the 'lean, eager men', while at the same time keep-ing the suggestion of a discrepancy between the desire and the person symbolized, the person who incompletely expresses what is sought. What is referred to later in the novel (p. 285), when the smaller purpose is mistakenly received as the larger—the 'passionate confusion between the vision world and the weekday world'—waits as a dangerous possibility within the generalized want that the Brangwen women symbolize in those aristocrats at the Hall who bear Hardy's name.

The aspiration of the women is kept alive by their romantic idealizing and gossip about the aristocrats—'they had their own Odyssey enacting itself, Penelope and Ulysses before them, and Circe and the swine and the endless web'—but already there is some mysterious ailing in the lives of the higher figures, with the drinking squire, Mrs. Hardy, and her 'scandalous brother'. The problem is beyond the scope of the Brangwen women's under-standing, but not the yearning for the 'more vivid circle of life' which Mrs. Hardy represents and which is imitated by Mrs. Alfred Brangwen. But though she has symbolically added to her life with Brangwen, her conscious knowledge of what she wants is prey to a mere class-interpretation: her wish for fulfilment takes a bourgeois form, the romanticism of social ascendance. She wants her sons to be gentlemen.

The limitations of the dream, at this level of desire, are indicated when young Alfred Brangwen, a mysteriously subdued figure, with something broken and vitiated in him, is admired by the women as a hero 'just because he didn't live at home and was a lace-designer and almost a gentleman. But Alfred was something of a Prometheus Bound, so the women loved him' (p. 13). Here the dream is diverted in failure and illusion, as if the Odyssey myth enacted in the Brangwens' lives is only a partially completed journey. The 'Ulysses' who travels out among the dangers of the world in order to return and redeem the waiting 'Penelope',[1] seems delayed and spellbound by wayward experiences. He cannot break through to his own individual form and consciousness under pressure of the world's established terms of action and speech; he does not know how to grow further, and must let his spirit be cramped under the smaller action and speech, resign himself to the tiny squares of lace-draughtsmanship. His energy is turned back on himself. He reacts in frustration to mistresses as 'a silent, inscrutable follower of forbidden pleasure'. He is trapped among Circe and the swine.

But the Brangwen woman, the 'Penelope', who has now initiated another movement in the household, distinct from the master's conservatism, remains the guardian of the 'endless web', the lifeline of continuity and awaited fulfilment. As the squire's lady marks the direction for her, so Mrs. Brangwen is (p. 13) the measure by which her men know their course: 'The woman was the symbol for that further life which comprised religion and love and morality. The men placed in her hands their own conscience, they said to her "Be my conscience-keeper, be the angel at the doorway guarding my outgoing and my incoming." ' The gentleman-ideal is only a partial expression of the Brangwen woman's rule of law and stability, only an aspect of the moral civilizing: 'She was the anchor and the security, she was the restraining hand of God, at times highly to be execrated.'

---

[1] Cf. Paul Morel's comment when he sees Clara grinding away at the spiral machine in the factory: ' "There is always about you", he said, "a sort of waiting . . . you are waiting—like Penelope when she did her weaving." ' (*Sons and Lovers*, p. 266.)

It is within this guardianship that Tom Brangwen, the youngest son and the more delicate of feelings, is kept safe, despite his unsatisfactory wrestling with the social ambition of his mother, the formal education and gentlemanliness. He is saved from attempting to enact the lesser ideal by his confusion over learning and his healthy power of recovery. He has a resilient span of emotions that moves upon a stability—the rich nature inherited from the Brangwen forefathers: 'one could watch the change in their eyes from laughter to anger, blue, lit-up laughter, to a hard blue-staring anger; through all the irresolute stages of the sky when the weather is changing.' There is an instinct for continuity in him governed by his own resourcefulness and the influence of the women in the household—first his mother, then his sister, then Tilly—who instinctively keep the sights clear, marking out a hidden way. Tom struggles to hold a direction, encouraged onwards by experiences that make up for disaster, that signal an unrealized good. The painful experience of school-learning and the angry scene with the master are somewhat balanced by the David-and-Jonathan relationship that Tom has with the frail, consumptive boy, so that 'Brangwen always remembered his friend that had been, kept him as a sort of light, a fine experience to remember.'

After this—and after the rages at himself, the torments of sex, the shock of seduction at nineteen by a prostitute, the drinking, and the death of his mother—the experience at Matlock is another symbolic encouragement, another 'light' to remember. The meeting with the girl and the strange monkey-faced aristocrat, with his gracious manners and subtlety, who significantly wishes Brangwen 'bon voyage', is the substance of Tom's later dreams—the mixture of desire for a voluptuous satisfaction and something foreign, 'subtle', aristocratic. But the dream begins to fade, unrealizable, it seems, amongst the commonplace life of Cossethay to which Tom feels doomed. It is when the direction seems lost, when Tom's resources are near the end, when the compensatory drinking and the loss of his sister to marriage leave him without support except for the old servant Tilly, that the Polish woman crosses his path. Yet Tom is still within the guardianship, the moral authority of the Brangwen women: he instinctively refers to the counsellors of his old safekeeping when he asks Tilly about Lydia or when, after going with his sister Effie to church and seeing the foreign woman with her child, his purpose is somewhat confirmed by Effie's remark, ' "There's your woman for you. . . . You'd better marry *her*." ' It is the appearance of Lydia, entering upon the safety of this old guardianship, which marks the end of Tom's childhood.

In Chapter II one sees how Lydia herself is brought to this convergence: a new line is traced backward, gathering to it the unresolved meaning of the aristocratic *malaise*, the Hardys at the Hall and the cold, dry-skinned foreigner at Matlock, as it passes to the memory of Lensky's pride, despair, and failed revolution. But looking forward from the disaster of the Lenskys, the line crosses over or swerves past the soul's wound, the pain that would distract Lydia from living to a recovery. Like Tom, she has her guardians in this crisis—the Church and the child. Anna replaces her father as the jealous protector of her mother, constantly straining to watch and call her back to wakefulness when she would let her soul drift off in abstraction to old memories, or relapse in trance-surrender to obscure evil forces. But the child's defence is static because it prevents the inroads of past *and* future experiences. It is the Church which urges Lydia forward, gently summoning her on through a faltering convalescence, when it hurts almost too much to live, issuing her through a winter of relapse and recovery. When she is sent to nurse the dying vicar in the northern vicarage, it is she who is being subtly nursed and guarded, 'as one holds a bee between the palms of the hands, when it is benumbed.' Her weakened spirit would drift out from its stay, yet the vicar recalls her to her living; and though by the spring he is dead, by then, 'with curious equanimity', the snowdrops are out, the sign that her own frail life-line remains unbroken like 'the white, shut flowers, anchored by a thread to the grey-green grass, yet never blown away, not drifting with the wind.' But, though kept, her spirit still seems too weak to flower again, not strong enough to endure the pain of being born anew. The experience at the Cossethay vicarage is a further convalescing, a regathering of strength, with the fragile, humorous joy of feeding the bees in the crocuses and disclosing the thrush's eggs. Therefore, when Lydia meets Brangwen she has regained the will to struggle, like a flower that is trying to open now and needing help. She is ready to recognize Brangwen as the inevitable next step, just as he, because of his experience, is ready to recognize her.

The old guardianships are displaced—the Brangwen women, the Church, the child Anna—but the moral idea survives in the new relationship. After they have fatefully entered upon each other's lives, after Lydia has passed across the threshold of the Brangwen home and Brangwen has sought her from the Church and child at the vicarage, the new independent fold remains under a moral guardianship. When Lydia comes to the door to ask for butter from the Brangwens, she is still seeking help in her recovery, for a nurture and, in a symbolic sense, for a share in the riches of life that the Brangwens have inherited. In this appeal for the tangible fruits, for a hold upon the anchoring permanency, Tom is inevitably forced to shift from his old centre, to assume a protectiveness towards Lydia which puts aside Tilly's chaffing guardianship over himself, just as it must displace Anna's guardianship of her mother. In the world of the body, activity, external work, Tom has to keep a stability for both himself and Lydia, an equanimity to hold up the structure that retains her uncertain, random spirit. He is a guardian for both in the flesh-and-blood sense, just as she, one sees later, is a guardian in the spiritual sense; and both, straining away in fear yet returning to the struggle, toil within the new enclosure, within a newly-recognized sense of fate, a mutual journey. It is this which Lydia realizes at the vicarage, her spirit beckoned on by the 'brilliant stars that she knew of old, from her girlhood. And they flashed so bright, she knew they were victors.'

Tom both recognizes and wants to avoid the paining endeavour of coming to a new birth. He stands afraid, as shepherd *and* sheep:

But during the long February nights with the ewes in labour, looking out from the shelter into the flashing stars, he knew he did not belong to himself. He must admit that he was only fragmentary, something incomplete and subject. There were the stars in the dark heaven travelling, the whole host passing by on some eternal voyage. So he sat small and submissive to the greater ordering. (P. 35.)

This sense of fate is not Hardy's, although it repeats the scale that the *Study* sees—the small figures within the huge, unfathomed background; nor is it the same fate as carries Paul and Clara in their passion, 'grains in the tremendous heave'. Lawrence avoids a blindness, for Tom and Lydia, though moved by the great invisible currents as fragments on the wave, have made a choice in their souls—an acknowledgement of a deep logic which, Lawrence suggests, could only have been prepared for by the experience of their differing pasts. Therefore the undertaking of their fate is neither impulsively careless, pathetic or ironic. Their journey is not through the horror of lonely space which Clym sees in the moon, or Alfred Brangwen in his avowal to Tom at Anna's wedding—' "You've got to go on by yourself, if it's only to perdition. There's nobody going alongside even there." ' In fact, the shepherd-scene, with its fear and submission, is like an artistic verification of the remark in the *Study* (*Phoenix*, p. 485), when Lawrence, with Angel Clare in mind, rejects what he sees as Hardy's Huxleyan-Darwinian idea of evolution: man travelling through time's immense solitudes alone. For 'Space, which so frightened Herbert Spencer, is as a Bride to us. And the cry of Man does not ring out into the Void. It rings out to Woman, whom we know not.' The meaning is in the polarity, the denial of the lonely oneness by another principle in the universe.

But the 'eternal voyage' which Tom undertakes also owes its direction and purpose, perhaps, to Lawrence's view of the strange progress in Chapter II of *Far from the Madding Crowd*, where Gabriel Oak in lambing time gazes up from the fields at the heavenly twinklings—'throbs of one body, timed by a common pulse'—and (like Tess on the road to market) thinks himself completely alone in space, detached from 'human shapes, interferences, troubles, and joys', only to find that one of the apparent 'stars' is the light from a hut where he is to rediscover Bathsheba Everdene, one of the troubles and joys of his life. So, like the entry of the tiny figure on the 'vast dark surface' of Egdon, 'Humanity appears upon the scene, hand in hand with trouble.' But whereas Hardy's imagination must remark on the ironic anomaly and has an uneasy relationship with Gabriel's sense of 'majestic speeding' through the stars—so that Hardy half-sympathizes with the dream yet inevitably undermines the illusions of the 'tiny human frame'—Lawrence's support for the dreaming journey is the reverse of escapism. The conflict is not of sky-flights with earth-humiliation, but between the shifting weights of a joint struggle to keep and touch an infinite purpose within the bounds of time and space.

The mutual struggle of Tom and Lydia creates a circumscription of possibilities for each; but their gradual drawing of the boundaries of the marriage-circle serves to define the moral

choices confronting them, for within the enclosure there persists an
evil which, though not completely understood, can be exposed
and fought. The subtlety in this limited but concentrated vision
contrasts with the crudeness of Hardy's 'morality play' in *The
Return of the Native* in which, as a mere token of a moral ordering,
the devil is called into the circle of light and defeated. For Lawrence, the moral ordering of Tom and Lydia is only one expression
of religious struggle (and *The Rainbow* offers further, more expanded expressions), but this necessary limitation of viewpoint is
not, as in Hardy's art, left inadequately affirmed. It is an evolving
discipline, a fate hard-learned, with its terror and wonder. On
Tom falls the anguish of patient balancing on his side where
Lydia is frail on hers, of restraining his own wants to measure
with her own separate nature and her less powerful physical
needs. Tom's long wait outside the vicarage, as he lets things
slowly take their course, is a foretaste of the equalizing restraint to
come in the marriage, the gradual leavening that forces him to
recognize the different kinds of separateness in Lydia—both the
autonomous, self-willed abstractness, with which he cannot
grapple in its obscure danger, and the richer individualism in her
which admits him, and for which he must wait while she is distant
and abstracted. The self-curbing is bitter, and he would break
from the discipline, but 'a certain grace' in him, 'an instinct of
gratitude and a knowledge that she would receive him back
again . . . prevented his straying very far.' As originally the
Church kept the onward aim clear for Lydia and Anna secured
the life of the moment, so now it is Lydia herself who holds the
future direction in sight, while it is Tom who guards the fabric of
the present.

But when the conditions of the trial harshen and he is cast out
physically while she expects his child, one mainstay is gone from
under him. Lydia on her side has to struggle painfully to bring
the child (and, indeed, herself and husband) to 'birth' in the flesh.
Tom must bear the other responsibility on his side, the burden of
keeping the flesh whole, the fabric unweakened, during its time
of vulnerability and tearing change. He bends to take the weight
and hold the balance, passing through all the phases of his own
temper and resources, from a careless, shrugging-off humour to a
more reckless zest to an unshakeable gloom; and when in the
winter trial his own resources fail, it is to Anna he turns, the dis-

placed support of her mother, now to find a new place in helping to keep the balance, the sane continuity. In the confinement scenes, Lawrence brings the crisis to a divided struggle—outgoing movement counterweighted and allowed for by a backward movement, fightingly aiding its complement. At the very moment that Lydia is in the painful labour of birth, Tom with Anna in the barn is leaning in 'sheer backward resistance'—the new being delivered on the strength of the old. But Tom must go far back to maintain stability, and as he moves through the barn feeding the beasts and balancing Anna carefully on his shoulders, he instinctively sinks into the atmosphere of old boyhood securities, into the remembered warmth of his mother's guardianship, becomes again the person he has been. But he is recalled and held once more by the forward purpose, by a sense of the mutual journeying. That searching 'impersonal look, in the extreme hour, female to male' from his wife, which scalds and pacifies him, is the rectifying stroke which declares a certain victory, the painfully rewon sense of the over-arching whole: 'There was the infinite world, eternal, unchanging, as well as the world of life.'

The birth is the end of Tom's and Lydia's childhood as it is the beginning of Anna's. But still Lydia keeps faith with another purpose to be realized after the birth in the flesh and the torturing settlement of the physical marriage between them. There is a marriage in the spirit, unmade as yet; and this is endangered by Tom's divergence, the backward movement that has been partly traced in the earlier crisis. The energy which in Tom can only partly be given over to Lydia in their physical love finds outlet in the recompensing way already discovered with Anna. It is a necessary diversion which, taken far enough, leads away from the main issue of Brangwen and Lydia. With Anna, in nursery rhymes and reckless, childish play, Tom establishes a new 'centre' apart from Lydia: in joke he is Old King Cole, the lord and father, the physical Godhead, with the suggestion in the jollity of the fictional mood that he is the 'creator' of woman, that he will make Anna into a lady.

In necessarily being set apart from Lydia, Tom veers to the other aspect of separateness—the wilful, absolutist personality. So that when he drives to market with Anna and the girl shares 'a sort of recklessness with her father, a complete, chosen carelessness that had the laugh of ridicule in it,' one sees in such rides and Tom's ambition for Anna's gentility something of the urge to mockery and fantastic pride of the child's forebears—those Polish aristocrats, described by Lydia, riding into Russia and back again, taking a spree on a train filled with naked women, and damned in a kind of perverse, repetitive oscillation. Tom's own compensatory divergence leads naturally away from Lydia, is uplifted by Anna, to the admiration of the kind of separateness embodied in his brother Alfred's mistress at Wirksworth. Here with Mrs. Forbes is the *apparently* larger, superior life, the achieved purpose for which he has always craved—'the atmosphere seemed open and spacious, like a mountain-top to him.' Here, with the 'curious, separate creature', seems the type of what he wants—the ego alone and 'free' in space, not in bondage to a joint discipline.[1] And in measuring the greater purpose by this lesser standard, he wants to break the moral order of which he has been a patient, exasperated guardian: 'He wanted to smash the walls down, and let the night in.'

This Ulysses returns from his foray, the Circe spell still confusing him, but his Penelope is ready to issue her thwarting counter-challenge and make conscious to him the real scale of his dis-content. For while he has veered, Lydia has kept patient hold of the continuous thread, the 'endless web' of morality, religion, and love. As she sits at her sewing and Tom rages silently, the surprise which shocks him from his confusion is her innate know-ledge of his complaint. In attacking him and finding him out for himself, she is separating his main desires from his divergent wants, making the ideal of joint sharing distinct from freelance absolutism. As at the birth of their child, she again recalls him. ' "You are not a baby," ' she challenges, summoning him back from the game that has led from Anna to Mrs. Forbes, and deny-ing the principle of egotistic oneness: ' "I want you to know there is somebody there besides yourself." ' Indeed, he knows this already but not consciously, and Alfred's mistress has seemed the expression of his inarticulate desires; but Lydia's words and touch are the real clarification, the awakening of his body *and* soul: 'her

[1] Cf. the rejection of lonely evolution in the *Study* (quoted on p. 90) with Tom's asking Mrs. Forbes, ' "Does my brother like reading?" ' and the answer, ' "Some things. He has been reading Herbert Spencer. . . ." ' (*The Rainbow*, pp. 85–6.)

hands on him seemed to reveal to him the mould of his own nakedness.' Now they are separate individuals on condition of their mutual bondage, and the enclosure which has seemed so small becomes, with joint discovery, the real mountain-top: 'They had passed through the doorway into the further space, where movement was so big that it contained bonds and constraints and labours, and still was complete liberty.'

With this marriage in the soul completing the marriage in the body, Lawrence is able to voice the kind of artistic reconciliation that the *Study* has shadowily sketched and *Sons and Lovers* was unable to realize. In the *Study* (p. 449) Lawrence pictures man and woman coming towards each other in space from opposite directions, reaching forward with outstretched hands to clasp, part, and separate till they begin the cycle again. The movement of meeting is significantly described: 'Then she draws near, and he is full of delight. She is so close, that they touch, and then there is a joyful utterance of religious art.' In the sacraments of Tom's and Lydia's marriage, desire and experience, aspiration and actuality, finally converge (p. 92) to the victorious affirmation: 'Now He was declared to Brangwen and to Lydia Brangwen, as they stood together. When at last they had joined hands, the house was finished, and the Lord took up His abode. And they were glad.' This on the terms of the *Study* (p. 516) is 'the art which knows the struggle between the two conflicting laws'—Law and Love—'and knows the final reconciliation, where both are equal, two in one, complete.'

3

In making his 'joyful utterance of religious art', in establishing the possibility of achievement between man and woman, Lawrence has achieved an important but restricted 'utterance', a vital measure not an absolute. More experience, fuller consciousness have to enter into the language and relationships of the novel before a victory can be conceived again. More must be accounted for, new and more dangerous conditions reckoned with, before the 'morality play' can be re-expressed to the full. One remembers the *Study* (p. 476): 'every work of art adheres to some system of morality. But if it be really a work of art, it must contain the essential criticism on the morality to which it adheres.' The journey is illimitable, but the human travellers are bounded.

Tom and Lydia are necessarily enclosed for their time and needs; and in portraying how they undertake responsibilities for themselves through their commitment to one another, Lawrence is free to leave aside some of the riddle that Lydia and Anna bring into Tom's life and to place it beyond Tom's capacity, as something he neither understands or needs to, if he is to direct himself to the central issue. The restriction is for the sake of relevance, without it being forgotten that it is a restriction. Therefore the Brangwen harbour 'on the safe side of civilization' is a refuge of economic independence for Tom and Lydia in the modern world, where Tom is saved from a career like his brother Alfred's and where Lydia can recover from her wounding past with Lensky.

As regards the marriage, Tom does not need to understand or look back with Lydia at her paralysing memory of hurt and failure; his stabilizing power does not need to be rocked and confused by Lydia's lapse into moods of communication with a mystic, 'dread' religion. His keeping of faith with an intuitive purpose carries him past the puzzling facts of Lydia's history, placing aside all previous experience that would exclude or obstruct him: 'Nevertheless, beyond all this, there was herself and himself which should meet.' The balking is not allowed to dissuade, and in the marriage-struggle of Tom and Lydia a new pattern establishes itself in place of the tragic, repetitious nostalgia inherited from the Lensky disaster—that hypnotic fixture of the spirit which the *Study* (p.449) conceives as the result of breakdown in the clasp of man and woman, so that 'man, remembering what lies behind him, how the hands met and grasped and tore apart, utters his tragic art.' The 'religious art' of Tom's and Lydia's reconciliation cancels out for this marriage the paralytic remembering: 'Poland, her husband, the war—he understood no more of this in her. . . . But he knew her, he knew her meaning, without understanding. . . . What was memory after all, but the recording of a number of possibilities which had never been fulfilled? What was Paul Lensky to her, but an unfulfilled possibility to which he, Brangwen, was the reality and the fulfilment?' (P. 91.)

The cancelling out is essential to Tom and Lydia, but not for the novel, which in its forward movement must still contend with mankind's endeavour in the larger community, of which Lensky's life and that of the Polish aristocrats are constant reminders. Their failure, their mad pride, their conserving of a once-living motion in repeated, frustrated rhythm, does not mean that they cannot stand as symbolic attempts at higher individuality, the fixed parts that point to an unrealized whole. The continuity with this aspect of their meaning (together with their dangerously rigid aspect) is kept by Anna. She is the necessary criticism of the morality to which Tom and Lydia adhere, the outgrower of the established boundaries which have made her righted childhood safe for its time. But whereas the parents move in gained freedom in what is for them a great space, their 'wordless, intense and close' kind of living is too cramped for the growing child and the ambition of the novelist. Lawrence takes his bearings: Tom and Lydia live by a satisfying, tacit religion, but Anna, though rooted in its stability, needs a clearer voicing of her inarticulate religious sense and a link with action in the world beyond the confined Marsh. Her need to have her spirit awakened and created, clarified and individualized, seems stifled by the implicitness.

She seeks a widening in her cousin Will Brangwen, but, like her, he is only 'half articulate'. With his father, Alfred Brangwen, he shares an immaturity of spiritual consciousness while at the same time lacking Alfred's corrupt despair; for although he follows his father in submitting his external self (as lace-draughts-man) to the industrial world, Will remains under the sway of the deep religious feelings which he has inherited from his mother. Though his passions, like his father's, cannot be made articulate and given scope in the network of conventional consciousness and action, he still keeps his religious instinct at large in the sensuous, unspoken darkness underneath. Anna, therefore, is seeking fulfil-ment from a youth who has separated off his everyday work and thought in the community from his inner passions. This disregard for the outer surface and articulateness is a saving trait when he can go to earth and escape being finally pinioned to an idea he basic-ally disbelieves in. But the insufficient valuing of all consciousness is a danger when he cannot move forward and find individual ex-pression, in words or art, for his inchoate beliefs. As a person whose sensuous emotions are more powerful than his mind or spirit—'some mysterious animal that lived in the darkness under the leaves, and never came out'—he is a rememberer rather than a progressive. Significantly, the art-form of medieval Gothic to which he is attracted belongs to the past and for Lawrence has particular associations.

His view of the conflict inside medieval art, which the *Study* surveyed, has a definite importance here, for by setting the plight of Jude and Sue in this historical period, by freeing it from Hardy's novel into an area where his imagination has leave to work upon it, Lawrence comes to possess the basic terms of Anna's and Will's unsatisfactory struggle. In stylizing Jude's religious absorption and Sue's detached criticism (as the old static Law, the presumptuous absolute, attacked by the raillery of the subordinated spirit), Lawrence has moved Hardy's situation nearly all the way into *The Rainbow*. But in Will the image of Jude is taken further. Both, of course, share the same Victorian culture—Jude with his 'fixed vision' of Christminster, his interests in the Tractarians and the Oxford Movement, Pugin, and Anglo-Catholic church ritualism; Will with his beloved Christian symbols, his delight in illuminated missals in Catholic bookshops, his reading of Ruskin. In Will, however, Lawrence seems to penetrate with a particular emphasis into Jude's portrayal by Hardy as an enthusiast of the Gothic Revival.

Hardy suggests the Revival as an intrinsic part of Jude's contemporary atmosphere, but he is not concerned, in the way that Lawrence reveals himself to be, with the Revival's interest in the idea of a total, descriptive, symbolic language. The Revival's centring on the thirteenth century as the highest point of medieval religious art and its special regard for the church architecture of that period and Fra Angelico's paintings, is an interest which is inferred in *Jude the Obscure* rather than explicitly set out. Lawrence also assumes the background, but from a different bias, for while he was writing or just finishing the *Study*, he read a short guide to ecclesiology by Mrs. Henry Jenner called *Christian Symbolism* ('We have been reading a book on Christian Symbolism, which I liked *very* much, because it puts me more into order').[1] It is this book, in fact, which seems to form the link, to be the clarifying agent in Lawrence's imagination, between the 'medieval' phase of the *Study* and the kind of symbolism that now enters the novel with Will Brangwen.

The Jenner book—several of whose symbols, phrases, and pictorial illustrations are drawn upon in *The Rainbow*—seems the

---

[1] Letter to Gordon Campbell, c. 19 December 1914 (*Collected Letters*, vol. I, p. 304). See *Christian Symbolism* by Mrs. Henry Jenner (Methuen: Little Books on Art series, London, 1910).

final stage in the imaginative process by which Lawrence translates Jude and Sue into Will and Anna, and leaves behind the special spiritual meaning he assigns to Sue in the *Study*. There is, however, a double awareness in Lawrence which governs his 'symbolic' view of the translated Jude-figure, Will. On the one hand, there is the artistic enthusiasm in discovering an emotional language that has at the back of it a great unifying conception. As Lawrence's letter on the subject says, 'The old symbols were each a word in a great attempt at formulating the whole history of the soul of Man.' He is thinking of the ordered hierarchy that Mrs. Jenner describes, descending from God through the choirs of angels to man; together with the symbolic content of the Trinity, the colours, beasts, and plants. On the other hand, there is the critical aspect in Lawrence which is aware, despite sympathy, that the symbols for the modern world are only a vulnerable, obsolete half-language, not quite convincing to his Sue-like Anna, in her desire for individualism and original expression.

The symbols which Will brings with him—both those he handles as an artist and those by which the novel identifies his emotional states—are not completely acceptable to Lawrence in the way that the symbol of the rainbow arch is acceptable. Will's symbols and symbolic art, in their rapt, over-intense perfectedness, serve to chart the phases of dangerously immature emotions, of excesses and potential egotisms. It is a descriptive method which Lawrence does not need when he portrays the emotional movement in Tom's and Lydia's story, with its emphasis on all that comes naturally out of the land and sky, all that grows unhurriedly in its time. In Tom's passage from tenderness to anger there was no marking of 'all the irresolute stages of the sky when the weather is changing' in the way that Lawrence identifies the dark rage of the Lion in Will becoming the Lamb of tenderness and mercy, or Hawks changing into Doves. Tom's realization of his purpose, his submission to 'the greater ordering', gradually evolves from a sense (p. 35) of unspoken fate: 'As he worked alone on the land, or sat up with his ewes at lambing time, the facts and materials of his daily life fell away, leaving the kernel of his purpose clean. And then it came upon him that he would marry her and she would be his life.' Will's realization, as he walks home in the rain (p. 115) after Anna has kissed him, is more charged, trembling, adolescent: 'The veils had ripped and issued him naked into the endless space, and he shuddered. . . . The hand of the Hidden Almighty, burning bright, had thrust out of the darkness and gripped him.' The tearing and thrusting emotions that the symbolism characterizes belong to a younger experience, more oscillating and unstable than one meets in the physical coming together of Tom and Lydia at the beginning (p. 54) of their marriage-struggle: 'And he let himself go from past and future, was reduced to the moment with her. In which he took her and was with her and there was nothing beyond, they were together in an elemental embrace beyond their superficial foreignness.' This is unlike the exalted bliss of Will and Anna in the physical beginning of *their* marriage:

Here was a poised, unflawed stillness that was beyond time. . . . As they lay close together, complete and beyond the touch of time or change, it was as if they were at the very centre . . . where there is utter radiance, and eternal being, and the silence absorbed in praise. . . . Then gradually they were passed away from the supreme centre, down the circles of praise and joy and gladness, further and further out, towards the noise and the friction. (P. 141.)

The language comes directly from *Christian Symbolism*,[1] not betraying with irony the kind of high, angelic experience it celebrates but suggesting all the same that the wonder known here is out of a young, untried experience.

After a battle of particular ferocity, some 'pure love' of their first kind comes again, and once more Will is characterized (p. 167) by the kind of 'half articulate' symbolic speech which thwarts his development: 'Then as if his soul had six wings of bliss he stood absorbed in praise, feeling the radiance from the

---

[1] Cf. *Christian Symbolism*, Chapter IV, 'The World of Spirits'. The author, in describing the nine choirs of angels, speaks (p. 65) of the three nearest God— the Seraphim, Cherubim and Thrones—as 'utterly absorbed in perpetual love and adoration of God'. The Archangels and Angels (of the eighth and ninth choirs respectively) are 'the messengers of God . . . the perpetual guardians of the children of men', and in Christian art 'the cupolas of Greek churches often contain row upon row of these celestial beings absorbed in praise' (p. 69).

Lawrence recounts this to Gordon Campbell in the letter quoted above (c. 19 December 1914): 'He is surrounded by the Hierarchy of the Cherubim and Seraphim, the Great Ones who partake of his being and transmit his glory; and they are *absorbed in praise eternally*. . . . I cannot forget that the Cherubim who are nearest God and palpitate with his brightness are *absorbed in praise* . . . absorbed for ever in fiery praise' (*Collected Letters*, vol. I, pp. 302–4).

Almighty beat through him like a pulse, as he stood in the upright
flame of praise, transmitting the pulse of Creation.' With Tom, in
a similar moment of recovery after a quarrel with Lydia's nature
(p. 57), there is a sturdy exultance, a swing to the physical lordship, the sensuous Godhead, but Lawrence does not formalize
the experience by symbolic identification: 'the passionate flood
broke forward into a tremendous, magnificent rush, so that he
felt he could snap off the trees as he passed, and create the world
afresh.' There is no suggestion of the Seraphim who stand nearest
to God in the traditional ordering. When Tom appears at the
vicarage threshold, he stands like a fearful, momentous presence
to Lydia—dressed in black, elemental, but human: 'She stood
away, at his mercy, snatched out of herself. She did not know him,
only she knew he was a man come for her.' But this fierce, terrifying sense of demand, when given shape in Will's changing moods,
assumes (p. 167) the force of the Archangel Gabriel: 'He appeared
to her as the dread flame of power . . . he seemed like an Annunciation to her. . . . He had a dark, burning being that she dreaded
and resisted. She was subject to him as to the Angel of the
Presence.'

This last characterizing does more than locate a phase; it
partially identifies a danger. One sees why the arch, the Covenant,
the Rainbow, belong to a different order of symbolism, because
they suggest an encompassing whole, not just one phase or mood
asserting itself as the totality. In his states of angelic exaltation,
Will celebrates the ecstasies of the personal self rather than the
impersonal whole, and the symbolic art he creates is an expression
of something fixed and ungrowing in him, of emotions that have
been torn from their healthy place in the span of human feeling
and rapturously exaggerated in isolation. It is a misappropriation
of feeling which is revealed (p. 111) in the phoenix-shaped butter-
stamper given by Will to Anna.[1] One thinks of Tom's gift of
butter, his offering of daffodils to Lydia, and the Brangwen
family's 'old wooden stamper of oak-leaves and acorns' which
the phoenix significantly replaces. Like Will, this is no natural
creature of the earth, but odd and unique. It is mythical and
splendid, but rather fantastic, like its carver. The bird, 'something
like an eagle, rising on symmetrical wings', has been made

---

[1] There is a reproduction of a phoenix from a thirteenth-century bestiary
opposite p. 150 of *Christian Symbolism*.

'mechanically' out of Will's emotional darkness, and the transcendence it symbolizes (if one thinks of Tom and Lydia)—the
sharing of riches, the struggle to resurrect a new, victorious body
and soul out of the flames that consume the old selves—is qualified, held back, by the voluptuous, self-absorbed suggestion that
is seen in the mould's 'curious, thick waverings running inwards
from a smooth rim'. Anna's use of the gift in repeated pressings—
'She loved creating it over and over again'—is a mark of her
tendency to seize the riches offered her by her men for her own
private satisfaction, disallowing the male part; even that other
mechanical thing, the mangle given her by Tom as a wedding
present, is taken up to be turned again and again as if she were a
kind of sole creator.

This is the potential fiction, the denial of the whole, which is the
temptation for both Anna and Will. If Anna cannot be met with
the balancing consciousness she desires, she will fall back on the
half-truth as if it were the total truth—on the belief not that man
and woman help to create each other (as one sees in the joint
endeavour of Tom and Lydia) but that the woman alone with
God creates man according to her will as a dependent, childish
thing. It will be her solitary, self-sufficient victory. On his side,
Will tends to the same emotional disproportion, as if the Law
which holds him back in his inward-turning sensuousness naturally compels him to produce an unbalanced art—the wooden
carving (p. 116) of Adam asleep, while God, 'a dim, large figure',
delivers a 'small vivid, naked' Eve from the man's side. For both
Anna and Will there is the inclination to halt at the phase which
Tom Brangwen passes through in his veerings from Lydia and
which is itself a throwback to the lordly absolutism of *his* father.
With man or woman as potential godheads, each refusing to
recognize the separate nature of the other and patterning the
other according to a fragmented vision, the conditions of Will's
and Anna's battle are already displayed before their marriage.

4

Behind the wedding at the Marsh the suggestion comes again, as
with Tom and Lydia, of a new religious undertaking. Another
'camp' in the unknown is set up and blessed. The old fold is left
behind as the young take on each other's keeping. And still the

guardian ideal remains, the sense of the infinite purpose that has to be worked for amidst the imperfections and frictions of this earthly life: hence the ragged, tipsy chorusing by the elders of the hymn, 'In the fields with their flocks abiding'; the star that 'blazed like a signal at the side of the hill'; the church-clock and the noises of the human world summoning on the newly-married lovers from their first childlike absorption in each other. Even the sprigs of yellow jasmine left with the milk jug are a 'sign' that calls them out to an activity in the larger world.

Characteristically, Anna is more ready to answer the summons than Will. As regards action and consciousness in the world, Will in his flinching must leave too much initiative in Anna's hands. He is over-dependent on her, physically and morally, so that she is dominant in the early days of their privacy, keeping him back from the world in her happy laziness, only to leave him stranded when she ultimately wants to emerge. The actual event by which Anna steps out—'She was going to give a tea-party'— humorously qualifies Will's ennui as something emotionally adolescent. Anna is also immature, but she has the advantage, the ambition in the soul and the consciousness where Will is at his weakest and most vulnerable. In her attraction for and dissatisfaction with Will's inarticulate religion, Anna's sympathies are confused between the child and the would-be adult in her. For her it is not enough for Will to exist in dark absorption as 'an angel or a fabulous beast', and yet, while she irritably wants to shake him from his sensuous sleep, she still does not want to dismiss the possibility of Will offering her an authentic expression of the implicit beliefs that she shares with him. Her challenge to his accepted symbols is a questioning that only demands a better answer, with a destructive intent still in abeyance. So her child's love for the yellow lamb in the ruby-coloured glass of the church window is no longer sufficient: the victory it symbolizes is merely that of the democratized Christ and the selfless love for other members of the community. 'She was never sure that this lamb with a flag did not want to be more than it appeared.' And yet, when she challenges Will on this symbol, one feels that she *does* want the lamb to mean as much as it suggests. By her ridicule Will is forced away from his own unserious attachment to the orthodox interpretation—' "it's the symbol of Christ, of His innocence and sacrifice" '—and made, with difficulty, to offer (p. 158) another answer: ' "It means the triumph of the Resurrection." ' He can clarify no further, and she hesitates unsurely and half-satisfied in the emotional allowance she has granted him, but with an impatient dismissal of his poor offering ready to strike: 'Something dark and powerful seemed to extend before her. Was it wonderful after all? . . . But no—she refused it.'

Her disbelief in his offering overbears his helplessness, and the continuity of the joint purpose begins to suffer. The phoenix points to a mythical, not a real resurrection; and as Anna cannot be prevented from breaking off their life in the body from the purpose that now seems in Will just a mystic extravaganza, the only birds that fly are greedy, proud hawks, hunting each other's game for private satisfaction. The dove-like tenderness lessens with this coarsening and with the steely striking of their sexual life. Because Anna is the first to seek outright victory in separateness from Will, she is the first to violate the moral fabric which she has guarded on her side of the marriage. The sensual ferocity passes into the destructive mastery with which she works at her sewing-machine (p. 160) in defiance of him: 'He hated beyond measure to hear the shriek of calico as she tore the web sharply, as if with pleasure.' The conscience-keeper, the Penelope, is cutting her own link with the forward-moving purpose, unable to grow further.

The friction, noise, and fighting begin to shut off a sense of the infinite, eternal world. Although peace returns intermittently and part of Anna still responds to Will's shadowy religion in the Sunday mood of the tranquil church, he cannot stop her assumption of power as the critical master-consciousness. He is driven back from his token acceptance of the orthodox, literal meaning of the symbols and miracles, into an entrenched self-division: while his mind bows to her destructive criticism, he lives on underneath stubbornly as if the miracles had occurred. She is finally triumphant in the mental consciousness when she forces him to give up his Brangwen man's claim as part of the physical Godhead —both as master of the house and the artist whose wood-carving makes ' "Adam as big as God, and Eve like a doll" '. He burns his Creation panel, and she substitutes *her* disproportionate fiction. When she realizes that she is to be a mother, she feels finally confirmed in her latent belief that woman is the creator of men—

of Will Brangwen according to her shaping of him, of the male-child she hopes for.

The wistful calm of the second half of the 'Anna Victrix' chapter is the peace of Anna's dominating illusion that the child she is soon to bear will prove her conquest as sole creator. Will, sensually beaten down, assents on the surface to the new, absolutist fiction that the 'unflawed stillness' which they touched together in their first days of marriage shall now be attained by one alone. The print he possesses of Fra Angelico's 'Entry of the Blessed into Paradise'[1] is like the offerings of the phoenix-stamp and the Resurrection symbol of the Lamb—an old sign of the infinite purpose which she narrows for her own finite ends. By ignoring the real friction and ferocity present in her relations with Will, by shutting out of her consciousness the fearful 'beast of prey' she has reduced him to, Anna seems to debar all that would spoil her illusory wholeness. For her now, bliss prevails without struggle, passive innocence without the challenge of proud sensuality, lambs without tigers. Fra Angelico sets the seal on her dream-achievement: she believes (p. 177) she has made her journey, come through the 'purifying fire' of passion to 'this peace of golden radiance, when she was with child, and innocent, and in love with her husband and with all the many angels hand in hand.' The map has become more real than the land for Anna: the paradisal entry she makes is a reproduction not an original, just as earlier (p. 161) the 'doorway' by which Will steps alone into 'a marvellous, finely-wrought universe' and celebrates 'his triumphant strength and life and verity', is only a book on Bamberg Cathedral.

It is Lawrence's clear sense of what comprises a real 'entry' into peace and wholeness (as established in Tom's and Lydia's story) which enables him to regard illusory triumphs with a supple, shifting response, and to make the reaction against such dreams so different from the downfall worked by Hardy upon his para-disal aspirers like Clym and Tess in their gazings upon celestial bliss. Body and blood reassert themselves in Will against Anna, not with the Hardyesque inevitability of the reviled snake in the

---

[1] There is a reproduction of this picture opposite p. 74 of *Christian Symbolism*; Mrs. Jenner describes it as 'A flowery meadow with angels and saints hand in hand in sweetest fellowship seeming to circle with rhythmic movement over the flowery grass.'

desired Eden, but with the inevitability of the disfigured part of
the truth which has been provoked to destructive attack by the
regime of fiction. This is the logic of breakdown not to be found
consistently in Hardy, and which now makes Will the sensual
disturber of Anna's spiritual sleep, as she was the would-be
wakener of Will in her more progressive days. In order to defeat
this challenge to her illusion, Anna is forced to draw upon the
wilfulness and cruelty that her 'innocence' refused to acknowledge
in herself and in her husband. The lion in her, one might say, has
to emerge to vanquish the lion in him. In her naked dance 'before
her Creator in exemption from the man', Anna exultantly proclaims the one female Godhead, the arrogant absolute, which
stamps out any rival pretension in Will. The new bout of ferocity
heralded by the dance is to end with her throwing off the clinging
'leopard' or prowling 'tiger' in Will. At last 'the powerful un-
satisfaction in him seemed stilled and tamed, the lion lay down
with the lamb in him' (p. 188).

But like that 'seemed', Anna's victory over Will in the birth of
the child is qualified. The lamb may deny the lion, and Anna may
teach her newly-born to ridicule the fighting blue-tits outside the
window as 'wicked things' who should be stopped, but her disappointment in her moment of final victory—that she has borne a
girl, that she is not the creator of men—releases the child into the
father's influence. Will is an outcast, wounded and weakened,
helpless in the new separate independence Anna has forced him to,
and he must draw away from his wife in order to recover and con-
valesce. Like Tom's divergence with young Anna after Lydia has
borne a child, Will 'adds' the young Ursula to him to make up the
lack in his damaged male sovereignty. While Anna marks time,
her individual growth arrested, producing child after child in a
trance of repetition, Will is gathering a new strength in the reckless games which he plays with Ursula—the contemptuous straining at moral fixture which leads him inevitably, after the diving
off the bridge and the soaring in the swing-boat, from his infant
to the girl at the Nottingham music-hall—'Her childishness
whetted him keenly'—and finally back to his wife. The moral
fabric on his side of the marriage has been destroyed at last, and
he returns as an equal, another absolutist personality to partner
Anna in a new combat of sensual wills. The surrender of the joint
purpose is now complete on both sides with this fragmentation.

There is to be no mutual 'Angel' to be striven for, only separate self-gratification of the senses, a lust to absorb the other. The 'supreme centre' of their first union has moved from a shared heaven to the forced perfection which Anna and Will have as human absolutes, each his own centre.

5

Throughout the lengthy involvement of the novel in Will's and Anna's interior fight, Lawrence is concerned to restrain the artistic impetus from itself falling into the kind of subjective absorption with which it must necessarily deal when depicting the emotional movement of the marriage. The stretch of work which lies between and includes the chapters 'Wedding at the Marsh' and 'The Marsh and the Flood' especially needs the objective reference, the scaling of the experience by another standard; a sense of relativity has to be called upon to keep the novel clear of the absolute, over-total effect which might seem true for Anna and Will in their immature joy, unhappiness, or egotism, but which must not obscure other possibilities. Within the drastic movement of their childish emotional life—'One day it seemed as if everything was shattered. . . . The next day it was all marvellous again, just marvellous'—the old Christian symbols and the sacred art mark out the stress on the marriage of these violent, unstable transitions of mood. They also indicate, by Anna's or Will's domination of their total meaning by insistence on a part-meaning, that a sense of the whole has been lost.

But outside Will's and Anna's marriage there is a living human measure, a faith in the reality of the Covenant, which is embodied in Tom and Lydia. At vital points one renews the link with what they have known and accomplished together, to set it beside the experience of the younger couple. There is inter-reaction in this measuring: the elders and the children reciprocally define each other's limitations. One is aware that Tom Brangwen in his limited capacity has achieved more as an individual than Will Brangwen in his greater limitations, but it is also evident that though the younger generation has failed to develop, it has failed by not fulfilling desires for consciousness which are beyond the scope of the elders. One is not allowed to forget the satisfaction of what *has* been achieved, in measuring the young by the scale of the elders, nor to forget, in seeing how the onwardness of the young sets the old within inescapable limits, what further achievements are possible.

Tom Brangwen shares a conflicting sense, hurt aspiration and graced satisfaction, when young Anna's love for Will makes him know his enclosure as a man. The self-ashamed demand for that something more with Anna, for 'the rapid life of youth', is sealed off by age and the bondage of his 'long, marital embrace'. Like the stained glass picture in the church where Anna and Will are married—with 'little yellow flowers held fast in veins of shadow, in a heavy web of darkness'—the limitations and inadequacies of his life seem enormous to Tom at one level of reflection, and yet, at another level, by virtue of the old sense of grace, the limitations seem nothing compared with the freedom that he has within the enclosure: 'How rich and splendid his own life was . . . sporting itself in the dark meshes of his body.' And when Anna goes to her parents soon after she knows she has conceived and after strife with Will, it is because of such knowledge—the fear and wonder over the marriage-journey, and Tom's gratitude for that 'something . . . eternal' in his bond with Lydia—that Anna receives none of the sympathy she expected: 'they took the tragedy of her young married life with such equanimity.'

The 'Anna Victrix' chapter pauses here (p. 174) in the visit to the Marsh, drawing apart from its heavy involvement in the conflict of the young to sense a calmer air, an atmosphere of spacious reflectiveness. As Anna feels the child within her and asks her mother about Lensky, the remembrance of such 'burning, far-off things' is like the awakening of a forgotten alignment travelling from past to future—the journey that Anna and Will cannot make together, the creative movement onward from which they are soon, inescapably, to diverge. The sense of space, scale, and the unknown which emerges in this peaceful pause is a terrifying leavener: 'In the room, there came a silence and a singleness over all their hearts. They were separate people with separate destinies. Why should they seek each to lay violent hands of claim on the other?'

Sights are retaken by the novel. Anna may renew Lensky's memory in her mother-of-men mood and thereafter dominate Will by the egotistic meaning she gives to 'separateness', but its greater, more fruitful meaning has re-emerged as well. The calming visit to Tom and Lydia—a clarifying pause which is continued in a sharper key by the visit to the Skrebenskys' (in the chapter, 'The Cathedral') and the reference of the young experience to another scale of comparison—sets up a line of purposefulness which is to pass through Anna and Will to Ursula. Anna and Will draw a momentary initiative from it, an influx of energy, but one is now directed along the line to a point beyond them. Their lives become subsidiary to an impetus with which they can no longer keep pace. Yet in this objectivizing of the novel, this re-opening of the distinction between the greater and lesser meanings of 'separate' individuality, there is a certain sympathy for the smaller perspective which is offered, despite the novel's concern not to be confused or beguiled by something that is fixed, ungrowing.

In the visit to the refined air of the Skrebensky home (so like the enchanted 'high' atmosphere surrounding Alfred's mistress), one is made aware not merely of the lesser expression pretending to the greater ideal, but also of the predicament in which the would-be individuals find themselves. They inadequately represent a growth beyond their attainment, but yet, all the same, they point to journeys of the spirit which must be undertaken. Therefore, while the novel traces the destructive effect of thwarted growth, it is strongly aware at the same time of the individualism which Baron Skrebensky, for instance, distortedly symbolizes. This old friend of Lydia, the Polish aristocrat and Anglican vicar, remains in himself a stunted, imperfect sign of the higher individuality which Anna misses in Will; yet through Skrebensky one again glimpses something of the ideal beyond the egotistic pride and social status-seeking at which he is personally arrested. The keen, detached Baron is still a reminder of the onward-travelling purpose, a keeper of the faith—as regards Anna, 'he considered himself in some way her guardian, on Lensky's behalf'—whatever the cruelty and appeased fanaticism of his own limited expression of individuality, and despite the fact that Anna (the Brangwen woman once more dangerously admiring a Prometheus Bound) mistakenly takes Skrebensky's superiority over Will to be not merely a higher form of manhood, but the highest she can imagine.

Because of the new aligning in the novel, the 'Cathedral' chapter is not concerned in the same way as 'Anna Victrix' with the destructive effects of human wilfulness. The return of the novel in 'The Cathedral' to the first year of Anna's and Will's marriage is not solely in order to reiterate the woman's victorious attack and the man's counter-challenge. Nor is it the major interest of 'The Cathedral' to see how Anna's frustrated individuality reaches for a criterion in the clearer atmosphere of the Skrebensky home as an encouragement, only to make her memory of the half-expression a new symbolic ally in her cause against Will, an extra weight on her side which helps to swing the victory to her. Also, it is not Will's later reply, as he emerges from defeat and takes the child he has 'claimed' secretly from Anna to be *his* new ally of restoration, which is the central point in the outlook of 'The Cathedral'. The fight takes its course, but now one is regarding it with an awareness of the problem which Ursula is to inherit and at which her mother balks—that of the man's failure to achieve an individual expression of himself in the larger world, either in fresh, modern consciousness or in creative work.

Again one is made aware of the woman's uneasy toleration of the man's token individualism. The Penelope-like patience is awkwardly strained—attracted towards, yet only half-satisfied with, the man's being; sympathetic to the would-be in him yet ready to round in defensive destruction on his claims to be the arrogant All. The visit to the Skrebenskys' and Lincoln Cathedral stresses the woman's difficult balance of sympathy for what the man falteringly attempts to signify, rather than its aftermath in the vanquishing which Anna deals to Will's inadequacy. In fact, that aftermath is an expected result which 'Anna Victrix' has already taught, and the novel returns, one notices, to the stage in the marriage just before Anna knows she has conceived what she imagines is a male child, just before she has replaced Will's absolute man-God with her own exaggeration, a female Creator. 'The Cathedral' comes back to the point where Anna's ridicule is forcing Will to shed the beautiful yet outmoded language of his symbols and the immature conception of his Adam and Eve carving. But where 'Anna Victrix' carries on to portray the negative effect on Will and Anna in their marriage, 'The Cathedral', by re-stating the conflict with a different emphasis, can see also the positive effect of the shedding to which the previous chapter cannot attend. Where Will's loss in 'Anna Victrix' is considered from the point of view of the marriage—so that he is driven from Anna to learn in independence a new kind of egotism —his loss in 'The Cathedral' is considered from the point of view of Will as a man in the world. Therefore, while Anna's jeering destruction of Will's Adam and Eve carving is cruel when seen from within the marriage-tie, the cruelty of her laughter in his beloved cathedral is not as important as its value and necessity when seen from the viewpoint of male individualism.

She wrests him from a voluptuous complacency in his religious life, denying him refuge in old satisfactions. She cannot offer better, her criticism is inevitably destructive, but she necessarily deals a blow to a greater symbolic expression of the infinite purpose—great for the medieval past, but now an old map with which to chart old spiritual journeys, a tyranny if held to as a modern total, an unreality suppressing newer movement. In Will's decadence, his voluptuous retreading of old paths, there appears Lawrence's opinion of the moon-gazing Clym, but also, more closely, of the Jude of Hardy's novel and the *Study*. It has already been noted that Lawrence particularizes the Gothic Revivalist in Jude as the Christian symbolist in Will. But there is another development which extracts more meaning from Jude and refers it to a particular nineteenth-century interest. One sees it in the mystic devotionalism which Will shares with Jude, the self-absorbed inarticulate fervour without conscious, fitting ethic. In the cathedral-church of a Christminster college Jude is borne along in 'a sustaining atmosphere of ecstasy' as 'great waves of pedal music tumbled round the choir'. At night in Christminster he pores over his Greek Testament (while Sue elsewhere sets up her pagan Greek images), and imbibes 'an indescribable enchantment' from his fervent murmuring of the 'inexplicable sounds'. Will has a similar pleasure from lingering (p. 161) over the reproductions of female statues in his book on Bamberg Cathedral. It partly compensates him for his damaged pretensions to male lordship. 'He liked all the better the unintelligible text of the German. He preferred things he could not understand with the mind. He loved the undiscovered and the undiscoverable.' This non-intellectual fascination which, in his first talk with Anna before their marriage (p. 108), makes the land seem to her 'covered with a vast, mystic church, reserved in gloom, thrilled with an unknown Presence' and which seems to deny the reality of the living flowers 'towering' outside the window of the room, is a fascination which stems partly from a literary source: 'The influence of Ruskin had stimulated him to a pleasure in the medieval forms.'

As Will approaches and enters Lincoln Cathedral with Anna, there is also present, perhaps, a memory of Ruskin's way of seeing and feeling. If this is so, it is a recollection of the younger, un-disillusioned Ruskin—the medieval revivalist who could confidently recommend to the builders of the 1850s that they should take their styles from 'the Northern Gothic of the thirteenth century, as exemplified, in England, pre-eminently by the cathedrals of Lincoln and Wells, and, in France, by those of Paris, Amiens, Chartres, Rheims, and Bourges.'[1] This is the Ruskin who un-wittingly added to the list of models by his admiration for Venetian Gothic, and who in *The Stones of Venice* ecstatically presented St. Mark's as a timeless ideal transcendent above the modern Italian throng and noise surrounding it, above the yells of tradesmen and blare of music—'as if the rugged and irregular houses that pressed together above us in the dark alley had been struck back into sudden obedience and lovely order.'[2] It is like the 'magnificent new order' which Will Brangwen possesses precariously in the early days of his marriage when friction and the outer world of 'Ilkeston, streets, church, people, work, rule-of-the-day' seem 'peeled away into unreality'—a state of angelic absorption into the divine infinite which he wants to repeat at Lincoln.

Like Ruskin before St. Mark's, observing the carved doves on the porches as a reminder of the Covenant of the Holy Ghost, Will sees the distant cathedral as a 'watchful' guardian of an aspiration—but for him it is totally unrelated to the affairs of the world: 'It was the sign in heaven, it was the Spirit hovering like a dove, like an eagle over the earth.' When he comes (pp. 198–9) to swoon in the symbol of infinity, in this 'great, involved seed . . . whose beginning and whose end were the circle of silence', where 'the stone leapt up from the plain of earth' to a perfect resolution, a 'timeless ecstasy', it is comparable to a Ruskinian kind of heightened experience. When Ruskin beholds St Mark's,

---

[1] Preface to the second edition (1855) of *The Seven Lamps of Architecture*, ed. E. T. Cook and Alexander Wedderburn (London, 1903).

[2] *The Stones of Venice* (Dent: Everyman, London, 1907), vol. II, p. 60.

there rises a vision out of the earth, and all the great square seems to
have opened from it in a kind of awe, that we may see it far away;—a
multitude of pillars and white domes, clustered into a long low
pyramid of coloured light . . . hollowed beneath into five great vaulted
porches, ceiled with fair mosaic, and beset with . . . sculpture
fantastic and involved, of palm leaves and lilies, and grapes and
pomegranates, and birds clinging and fluttering among the branches,
all twined together into an endless network of buds and plumes; and,
in the midst of it, the solemn forms of angels, sceptred, and robed to
the feet, and leaning to each other across the gates, their figures indistinct among the gleaming of the golden ground through the leaves
beside them, interrupted and dim, like the morning light as it faded
back among the branches of Eden, when first its gates were angel-
guarded long ago. And round the walls of the porches there are set
pillars . . . their capitals rich with interwoven tracery . . . and
mystical signs, all beginning and ending in the Cross; and above them,
in the broad archivolts, a continuous chain of language and of life—
angels, and the signs of heaven, and the labours of men, each in its
appointed season upon the earth; and above these, another range of
glittering pinnacles, mixed with white arches edged with scarlet
flowers,—a confusion of delight, amidst which the breasts of the Greek
horses are seen blazing in their breadth of golden strength, and the St.
Mark's Lion, lifted on a blue field covered with stars, until at last, as
if in ecstasy, the crests of the arches break into a marble foam, and toss
themselves far into the blue sky in flashes and wreathes of sculptured
spray. . . .   (*The Stones of Venice*, vol. II, pp. 60–1.)

Lincoln also has an 'endless network', 'a continuous chain of
language and of life' as it seems to leap through 'the whole range
of desire' in massive inclusiveness:

Spanned round with the rainbow, the jewelled gloom folded music
upon silence, light upon darkness, fecundity upon death, as a seed folds
leaf upon leaf and silence upon the root and the flower, hushing up the
secrets of all between its parts, the death out of which it fell, the life
into which it has dropped, the immortality it involves, and the death
it will embrace again.   (Pp. 198–9.)

The earthly day has been excluded from Lincoln's 'jewelled
gloom' just as it is from St. Mark's where natural light, Ruskin
says, enters the roof-domes 'only through narrow apertures like
large stars. . . . What else there is of light is from torches, or silver
lamps, burning ceaselessly in the recesses of the chapels.' In the
Baptistery of St. Mark's, he notes: 'The roof of the canopy above

has been blue, filled with stars.' Anna's awe in Lincoln rightly
gives way (p. 200) to resentment at the live, true individualism
denied by this Jude-like or Ruskinian emotion: 'But yet—yet she
remembered that the open sky was no blue vault, no dark dome
hung with many twinkling lamps, but a space where stars were
wheeling in freedom.' And here one realizes that Lawrence has
deeply qualified the conflicting interests of Jude and Sue, so that
more is at stake than one sees in Hardy's novel of ironic inconsistencies, and the upset of Jude's instinctive faith by Sue's modern,
advanced mind.

The preference for railway stations over cathedrals, the buying
of pagan plaster images and the remarking of 'grotesque childishness' underneath the picturesque Norman of Christminster
Cathedral—these are presented by Hardy as evidences of Sue's
passionate individualism in advance of its time. Anna, however,
with only a slight mental advantage over Will, is presented by
Lawrence as an undeveloped soul, resisting the massive sweep of
this old enclosure, but, because she is too weak on her own to
make an underivative expression of her desires, having to fall back
on an inferior, destructive form of challenge. As with her measuring the Baron against Will, her grasp for some aid leads her to
clutch hold of and stand 'arrested' at stunted symbols of progressive individuality—'the wicked, odd little faces carved in stone',
slyly breaking the lines of the Cathedral in their call to egotistic
freedoms. The impish, leering gargoyles, with their expression of
'separate wills, separate motions, separate knowledge', suggest all
that has been omitted from the system. Although what they
intimate is warped in expression, because it is done in destructive
resistance to the Cathedral's leaping to old conclusions, it is still
true: ' "However much there is inside here, there's a good deal
they haven't got in" ' (p. 201).[1]

The great conception has become a presumptuous lie for the

---

[1] Cf. Lawrence's article, 'America, Listen to Your Own' (1920):

Let the beauty of Venice be a sort of zenith to us beyond which there is no seeing.
Let Lincoln Cathedral fan her wings in our highest heaven, like an eagle at our pitch
of flight. We can do no more. We have reached our limits of beauty. But these are not
the limits of all beauty. They are not the limit of all things: only of *us*.
Therefore St. Mark's need be no reproach to an American. It isn't *his* St. Mark's.
It is ours. And we like crabs ramble in the slack waters and gape at the excess of our
own glory. Behold our golden Venice, our Lincoln Cathedral like a dark bird in the

modern sensibility, and even though its ruining is the work of the undeveloped spirit in Anna which can only itself attain the status of a half-truth, Will's attachment to the old form is vitally loosened. It is the necessary if hurtful beginning of a new development in himself. This does not mean that he is completely freed, that he is sure of his next movement onwards, after Anna has retired in personal victory. He must still hang back amongst the fragments of the old expression. The Church ritual and symbols are no longer adequate for the religion still in him, but they are maintained at the moment for want of a better expression: 'He tended it for what it tried to represent, rather than for that which it did represent.'

Again, Will's guardianship of the purpose by means of the broken thing resembles Jude's inevitable stamping of Christminster's worn image on his undefined 'fixed vision'. Jude's work in the stone-mason's yard at Christminster (where only 'copying, patching and imitating' is done for the city's 'decrepit and superseded chambers'), the repair work at Melchester, the making with Sue of the Christminster college model and the Christminster cakes—all have that repetitive handling of inferior materials to which Will is also stuck, as he toils in his woodwork shed to restore things destroyed in the church. The *Study* indicates the plight, when it speaks (p. 433) of the would-be individual retracing past ground in a working effort to redeem himself from the old matrix: 'By re-enacting some old movement of life's, a struggling soul seeks to detach itself, to become pure . . . to receive the stimulus which shall help it to continue to distinguish itself.' Will can no longer re-enact the old journey as if it were still true, but, lacking further stimulus, he re-enacts it from the position of wanting it to be true, of treating what he knows to be dead as a live thing: 'It was the church *building* he cared for; and

---

sky at twilight. And think of our yesterdays! What would you not give, O America, for our yesterdays? Far more than they are worth, I assure you. What would not *I* give for your tomorrows!   (*Phoenix*, p. 89.)

Cf. Hardy's comment on St. Mark's when he visited it in April 1887:

There is surely some conventional ecstasy, exaggeration,—shall I say humbug?—in what Ruskin writes about this, if I remember (though I have not read him lately), when the church is looked at *as a whole*. One architectural defect nothing can get over—its squatness as seen from the natural point of view—the glassy marble pavement of the Grand Piazza.   (*Life*, p. 193.)

yet his soul was passionate for something. He laboured cleaning the stonework, repairing the woodwork, restoring the organ, and making the singing as perfect as possible. . . . The church was false, but he served it the more attentively.' (Pp. 205–6.)

Anna's destructive impetus has only partially awakened him from the old adherence, and he lacks the power to move forward on his own. It takes another impetus—the stirring of the 'unfathomed distances in himself' which his baby Ursula wakes, and the initiative he is urged towards as he reaches an absolute self with Anna—before he can make another step forward, this time breaking more drastically with the ruins of the old expression and the old self. At last he can join with the forwardness of 'purposive mankind' from which the visionary in him has previously shied. The emergence of Will into local public life turns the woodworker who repairs the old church fabric into the woodworker who teaches carpentry to the village boys in the refitted parish room, who eventually becomes handicraft Instructor for the county, rises in social esteem, and moves from rural Cossethay to the suburbs of industrial Beldover. There is, however, a logic which connects Will the handler of superficial fabric with Will the outward, social man, who now deals with real human individuals in the modern world. The destruction which has made his movement possible has cost him his inner coherence and vision. Like Tom's and Lydia's son, young Tom Brangwen, Will emerges into the outer community without the strength to strike out an original direction in it; he has exchanged his allegiance to a ruined concept for allegiance to a newer but more recently jaded idea. Even the parish room of Will's teaching already has a 'stranded obsoleteness' in its meaning, for all its relative freshness.

After all this time, Will has only attained, like Baron Skrebensky, a 'stranded' kind of individualism. His sense of himself as one member of a vast social ordering broadens his artistic purpose: 'It had to do with the establishment of a whole mystical, architectural conception which used the human figure as a unit' (p. 276). But like the Adam and Eve carving of his immaturity, he can never carry his new artistic work or himself beyond the impetus of the first moments of creative energy: whatever he takes up—modelling in clay, water-colours, metalwork, jewellery-making—can never be carried far as genuine expression before it becomes imitation or reproduction. Like himself as a public man and a groping, visionless soul, his water-colour of the church tower (p. 355) is in the modern fashion of 'atmospheric' painting, yet the subject is incongruous with the style: the tower 'really stood and asserted its standing, but was ashamed of its own lack of meaning.'

The novel follows through Will's development—his losses, new bouts of impetus and qualified gains—but Lawrence can afford to trace the lines that lead to man's stranded predicament in the modern community, because he has already renewed the major ideal to which all action here is relative—that of man and woman's fulfilment together. One sees in Will, Baron Skrebensky, and young Tom Brangwen what they try to represent rather than what they actually can or do represent in practice, but for Lawrence there is a need to balance their failure with a sense of what achievement *is* possible for a man. It is done by a blow, a sudden recall of a standard to measure by. At the point in the novel where Will becomes a public, social man and his father-in-law's sons have reached the spiritual impasse which is to be the limit also set for Will and Anton Skrebensky, the death of Tom Brangwen in the flood again affirms the great perspective of wonder and terror, from which the others have shrunk through lack of strength, fear, or perversity, and which Tom has painfully embraced in Lydia.

The bursting of the canal bank and Tom's drowning in half-sober consciousness would seem, from one point of view, the murder and disgrace of man, the denial of meaning to all his purposes. He is suggested as another Noah, revealed in his naked-ness to his stepdaughter as the Biblical Noah lay in shame to his three sons. It is suggested, furthermore, that Tom's death is like Noah betrayed into utter tragedy on earth: the Rainbow Covenant made by God to Noah, with its vow that 'neither shall all flesh be cut off any more by the waters of a flood,' seems broken. It seems that here is fundamental cause for man's cry against the unfair conditions of his existence; for man's dismayed curse upon the flesh in the Hardy style; for the younger Tom's gesture, fists raised against 'the open distance', and his tortured, grimacing fixity. But Lawrence harshly poses the tragic suggestion in order to qualify the apparent betrayal; he admits the blow and the anguished response of Tom's sons in order to turn the force of judgement not against man's existence but against man's lesser vision. Only the outer standing of Tom is brought to indignity; only the public covering is disgraced and shamed. It needs the 'incongruous market-clothes of a well-to-do farmer' to be stripped away before there can be seen in his nakedness the meaning that still coheres, the covenant between two worlds, which Tom once saw in his wife's eyes as she struggled in labour.

The dead man is brought to Anna's house—to the woman who denied the Godhead in man, whether the Godhead was expressed as the stable authority of her stepfather or as the exaggerated claim of her immature husband. Before her lies the revealed body, in all its 'majesty of the inaccessible male', like a great measuring power, against which all her assumptions and arrogant experience as Will's wife seem as diminished as those of her husband. When she first knows of Tom's death (p. 247) 'the shock threatened to break in upon her and sweep away all her intervening life, make her as a girl of eighteen again, loving her father.' The awe seems to flood over the conclusions reached in her marriage with Will, as if what she and her husband have become were subsiding beneath remembrance of what Lydia and Tom became. As in the Marsh visit in 'Anna Victrix', the violence, friction, and frustrated activity of the young are momentarily silenced by a calm beyond their reach or marring; again egotism and the 'violent hands of claim on the other'—those of Will and Anna or those of Tom's stricken sons—are put aside by an overwhelming sense of space, distance, and separateness (in its greater meaning). 'Neither the living nor the dead could claim him, he was both the one and the other.' In death Tom spans the mortal and immortal world: he is the finite symbol and the infinite reality it signifies. Unlike Will's or Baron Skrebensky's manhood, Tom in death *is* as much as he represents, and his wife has the knowledge beyond her daughter: ' "I shared life with you, I belong in my own way to eternity." ' From this recognition the bearings of the journey and the struggle are again made known, as the novel draws back from past and future conflict into the quiet refuge of reflectiveness where Lydia and her grandchild Ursula meet.

Like the dead man and the potent meaning which Lydia keeps alive, the novel is here 'laid in line with the infinite.' The insistencies of the present—'the seethe and rage and passion' of Lydia's sons, or the 'many lives beating against each other' at Ursula's home—are placed in abeyance. In the 'paradisal' refuge of the old woman and the child, Lydia seems to reach across the distractions of this generation to fetch from her past the knowledge and purpose which she delivers, uninterrupted, into the hands of Ursula, the next generation. As Lydia bypasses the threshings of the present, there comes from her talk and memories of her two husbands a renewed sense of sympathetic measurement which the novel at large balances by: she can compare Lensky and Brangwen —one the mistaken overlord, the other the sharer and fulfiller— —and yet, while knowing Tom as her real husband, she is able to honour both in their different ways. From her grandmother Ursula imbibes a sense of the dwarfing background to human endeavour which Tom and Lydia have knowingly toiled under and which Lensky never realized—'loves and births and deaths, tiny units and features within a vast horizon'. Yet there is the other perspective as well—the 'unyielding passion of life', the human desire for a religious, loving fulfilment which makes Lydia say, ' "we have a right to what we want." '

These powerful criteria are passed on to Ursula's imagination with an emphasis which looks towards the rest of the novel. After this there can be no more reference to Tom's and Lydia's scale of wisdom as a living form, and the impetus is here gathered from the past to carry her across the waiting mistakes and confusions of the future. The signal is here explicitly sounded, because after this Ursula (and the novelist) have to outlast failure and tragedy by reliance solely on personal intuition, unguarded by the securities which held Tom and Lydia in safekeeping till their meeting. Lydia was helped by Church and child in her lonely crisis, but Ursula, as she moves in a land where all men seem like Will Brangwen or Lensky, thwarted or maimed at different levels of society, has no human wisdom outside herself which can aid her. *The Rainbow* can keep the covenant of reconciliation for Lydia with Tom after Lensky; but Ursula's Lensky (Skrebensky) cannot be cancelled by *her* Tom (Birkin) within the terms of the novel. The thrust-forward which keeps Ursula clear has to strain amidst perplexities with a force that has no adequate counterbalance to stabilize it. The mood has Tom Brangwen's determination—'Nevertheless, beyond all this, there was herself and himself which should meet.' But that 'nevertheless' in Ursula's later experience is forced into a strident key, brought to a ferocity which no man can mitigate.

6

To Ursula falls a double responsibility. As a would-be individual, she must safeguard her own growing spirit, while it passes through the stages from childhood to womanhood, struggling to emerge distinct and clear 'out of the nothingness and the undifferentiated mass' (p. 281). But she has also to take on a responsibility to the men of her world—those who like her father are too undeveloped in soul and consciousness, driving on in stubbornness and angry puzzlement within the labyrinths of their being. Even as they turn upon her and would dominate from their limited vision, so that she must resist the egotism to which they have been narrowed, Ursula remains a more lasting encourager of their attempt to find a way out than her mother has been. Her sympathy is more resilient: even though she is herself forced into the sterile fight of woman against tyrannical man, she is still defending the man in his wrong while she is defending herself against the onslaught of the wrong. When as a child she is accused by her father of being the wrecker of his beloved church—after the cleaning woman has scathingly railed at Will for the child's untidiness—Ursula instinctively (p. 216) does not join the side of the righteous women against the weaker man, despite Will's slapping her and her mother's attack on his cowardice: 'Still her heart clamoured after her father, for him to be right, in his dark, sensuous underworld.'

Like Lettie in *The White Peacock*, Ursula is placed in a difficult position: wanting her men to be more than they are able to be or believe they can be, without completely assuming the female lead in her disappointment. She is continually urged towards this wilful role of supremacy, but the ideal of joint endeavour, of a man as strong as a woman, still hovers in her faith. It is typical that while her parents have lost the vision of a reconciliation higher than they now have, the Brangwen children remain the guardians of the religious ideal. In the noise and friction of this world, where a sense of the infinite is now confined to the refuge of Sunday, Ursula and her brothers and sisters are 'the wardens of the Sabbath decency'. As Ursula grows up, her girlish daydreams still preserve the desire for high individuality and redemption by a manly equal: the symbolism is immature and romantic, but the desire it speaks for remains intact. So in girl-hood she is another Penelope expecting her Ulysses, as she imagines herself (p. 263) an Elaine the fair guarding the sacred shield of Lancelot till he returns, 'polishing the terrible shield, weaving it a covering with a true device, and waiting, waiting, always remote and high.'

That 'high' quality of separateness in her nature encounters opposition from the community code of commonplaceness, just as it inevitably and awkwardly quarrels with the selfless form of Christianity from which the communal assumptions depend. Ursula's dissatisfaction with Christ's message of love and giving is the same as her mother's. For her also, the conventional interpretation, when applied to actual living, seems inferior or absurd in its meekness. But, whereas Anna breaks away in irreligious impatience and cannot be stopped by Will from rejecting the possibility of a higher meaning for the Christian Word, Ursula reacts against inadequacy with a self-assertiveness which is essentially different from her mother's. Significantly the girl prefers to veer to her father's side—a position which is ethically poor in its non-literal acceptance of the scriptures, but which, despite its arrogance and self-absorbed vision, has the merit of not debasing the integrity of belief in a whole.

In avoiding the danger of reacting into her mother's kind of egotism, Ursula embraces another danger. While she is saved from accepting the impossibility of fulfilment, her idealism is maintained by wilful insistence: ' "If we had a father as he ought to be, he would be Earl William Brangwen, and I should be the Lady Ursula? What right have I to be poor? crawling along the lane like vermin?" ' (P. 283.) In that 'ought to be' one sees how Ursula, impatiently re-creating man in an image to suit her will, contrasts with her mother, for where Anna as creator reduces her man to a subordinate, Ursula in *her* humanizing illusion raises him to match her as an aristocratic equal. Therefore, in this excess of pride which bolsters the self against the extremes of selflessness, Ursula's dream of a Son of God out of the unknown is made to come true by her own arrogance.

But where her own girlish wants dictate the shape of the redeemer to match her, a sense of degradation or disappointment must lie at the back of her pre-determining: she does not completely want, is not totally satisfied with, what she has wilfully created for herself. She cannot help narrowing the meaning of fulfilment while at the same time desiring beyond her knowledge and dictation. The sense of shame that follows after she has humanized Christ in her inflamed sexual imagination as a physical bridegroom is similar to the souring hurt she feels after she has elevated Anton Skrebensky to the arrogant height that she cannot maintain in real stability. Where 'separateness' means only egotism, where aristocracy in the self is merely a cruel flare of pride, the feeling of transcendence is an upthrust of illusion which is inevitably followed by a downswing. So Ursula and Anton must dismount into bathos after their 'aristocratic' ride on the wooden horses of the roundabout (p. 294), when 'it seemed that he and she were riding carelessly over the faces of the crowd . . . moving on a high level, spurning the common mass.'

The vision that Ursula has from Anton when she first meets him (p. 291)—'He seemed more and more to give her a sense of the vast world, a sense of distances and large masses of humanity' —shrinks, when it is anarchically acted out, to degrading proportions. But the intrinsic value of the vision remains, and it becomes clearer than ever how much strategic subtlety in *The Rainbow* comes from Lawrence's critical grasp of Hardy's art. Will Brangwen's dilemma, of having to use inadequate forms to express a genuine, religious instinct, has been perceived in Jude's predicament, but with a discreet wariness that enables Lawrence to avoid the naïveté of Hardy's drama of collision and its ironic overthrow of idealism. As with Lawrence's treatment of Jude in Will, so with his clarifying of the meaning of Eustacia Vye's romanticism in relation to Ursula's adolescent dreams, there is the same ability to portray a soul 'passionate for something' and passing into error, without the wrong choice made automatically discrediting the crude rightness of the instinctive desire.

Hardy's betrayal of his erring individualists offers a cautionary precedent to Lawrence at this stage of *The Rainbow*, where, after the story of Tom's and Lydia's mutual creation, he continues to trace the plight of those who attempt a one-sided creation or ordering out of an undeveloped spirit. It is possible that the entire theme of creation (even as one sees it in *Sons and Lovers* in the shaping wills of Paul and his mother) stems originally from Lawrence's glimpse of its significance in Hardy's presentation of

Eustacia. She ennobles the men of her actual experience to meet the standard of her yearning: Wildeve is inadequate but she looks upon him 'as upon some wondrous thing she had created out of chaos', and then seizes Clym's appearance in her life—'like a man coming from heaven'—as the realization of her dream of the knight in shining armour. Unlike Hardy with Eustacia, Lawrence decisively places Ursula's dreams at an adolescent stage, as she also idealizes her men in Anton—'She laid hold of him at once for her dreams'—so that he is made into the image of the redeeming Son of God, given the rightness and stature which her father in reality could not supply: 'he reminded her of her father, only he was finer, and he seemed to be shining.'

Yet, as in Lawrence's treatment of Clym's and Eustacia's mutual idealizing in the *Study*, the onus of self-deception lies more heavily on Anton than on Ursula. Lawrence, it seems, is led to this over-emphasis because he feels that Anton's conscious beliefs, like Clym's, are a more pernicious illusion, with more to support them, than the female dream: for Anton, like Clym in the *Study*, is a servant of the community, one who hides from responsibility for himself within the larger mass. Therefore, the irony in Ursula's romantic mistaking of Anton's purpose does not apply to her in the way that it works against his social consciousness. His ethics *seem* to share the grand perspective—even the language—of Tom's and Lydia's vision, with its 'loves and births and deaths, tiny units and features within a vast horizon.' As for Anton: 'Who was he, to hold important his personal connection? What did a man matter personally? He was just a brick in the whole great social fabric, the nation, the modern humanity. His personal movements were small, and entirely subsidiary. . . . The Whole mattered—but the unit, the person, had no importance, except as he represented the Whole.' (P. 326.)

For Anton, the map *is* the land: the impersonal, social idea is more real than the great, impersonal, religious idea which it represents, and travesties. Anton cannot say like Lydia, ' "we have a right to what we want." ' Nor is the 'fated' quality of his self-possessedness, his confident rocking upon a narrow compass, more than an intensely restricted expression of the non-egotistic movement, the acknowledged destiny in the soul which brings Tom to Lydia and sets him 'small and submissive to the greater ordering'. Anton's submission is different, because, when Ursula first sees him, his languid 'resting in his own fate' has an ease which reveals him to be the most socially acclimatized figure that the Brangwens have known. Whereas the Brangwens who enter the industrial, commercial world have an inherited passion in the blood which makes them know an innate dissatisfaction, a restless uncertainty and fear, a faltering of direction which turns them perversely back on themselves and their blood, in Anton (at first) there is no wrench between the inner and outer world. Unlike the Brangwens and his father the Baron, Anton seems to have transferred his allegiance entirely to externals. His only real home is the nation.

It is Ursula who, by rousing his latent pride in the recklessly sensual games they play, eventually brings him to the painful knowledge of a division in himself. Her flaunting challenge to him, her kiss in her father's work-shed brings out 'a dare-devilry in him, like a cynicism, a cut at everything he pretended to serve.' The suppressed individual in him can only emerge under these conditions as disfigured, bestial, and voluptuously egotistic. Yet there is a poignancy about the combats of Anton and Ursula, for their games rage now in settings that were once the background for different things—the shed where Will Brangwen worked at his Adam and Eve carving, a place which is a 'descendant' of the barn where Tom soothed Anna in her childhood; and the church, the place of spiritual endeavour which complements the place where man works amongst physical adversities. Ursula and Anton profane the meaning which these places once symbolized, but with a kind of decadent pleasure which goes beyond Anna's mockery and Will's sensuous introspection.

There is the same corrupt thrill in the air in the festivities which follow the marriage of Fred Brangwen to a schoolteacher— a debauchery of the ideals which it is supposedly celebrating. The sense of the married couple as entrants into a hard-won fate, making a new encampment in the unknown, is surrounded by cynicism and dominated by the presence of the 'subtly coarse' young Tom Brangwen. When one remembers the wedding of Anna and Will and the hymn that blesses them on their way, the festivities here (p. 306) seem insistently mock-rural, a self-conscious revival. Uncle Tom 'would have a jolly wedding, a harvest supper and a wedding feast in one', while Fred's 'half-educated' bride 'also must have a great and jolly feast. It appealed to her educated sense. She had been to Salisbury Training College, knew folk-songs and morris-dancing.' There is to be no new embarking, only a Dionysiac celebration of soulless lust, of flesh and earth. The ark of human endeavour is stranded here—like the family of barge-people at their moorings in the lock, with the father looking out reveringly at Ursula from his 'captive soul'.

But Ursula's and Anton's meeting with this family (p. 309), before they go on to the festivities, has the quality of a tender pause, a hushing of the friction to touch upon a possible grace in human relations which the 'violent hands of claim' have shut away. It is a scene which in its relaxed humaneness remembers the calm of another pause, when Anna went to her parents knowing she had conceived the child who was to become Ursula. Now as Ursula momentarily leaves Anton aside in his aloof, sterile disapproval and comes down amongst the dirt of the coal-barge, she seems to stand again with her father in the puzzle of his underground life. As she gives her name to the canal-man's child and he gropes carefully for the necklace in the coal-dust, it is as if her deepest desires were blessed, seen clear of her sensual arrogance and her self-deception in Anton. Again she naturally takes the role of the spiritual encourager to man, offering from the riches in herself a thread of grace, an inference of the covenant between the human world and the infinite. The canal-man in his darkness can grasp and revere this thread, but for Anton it is impossible. The only communion he can have with Ursula is physical, soulless, overbearing.

So the warm knowledge that is ascertained in Ursula's pause with the canal family is an emotional scale to set against the frenzied dance which follows, when Ursula strains madly to be free and clear of Anton's downward-bearing, heavy mass of sensuality. She would instinctively evade capture by his dark absolutism, and like Anna in the Cathedral, she clutches (p. 317) at an ally beyond the terms of the enclosure that is being woven round her. Her guardian is the moon, gradually rising above the red fires of the dance—the signal to the sunken spirit: 'Out of the great distance, and yet imminent, the powerful, overwhelming watch was kept upon her.' But, as with the conflict in the Cathedral, the conditions of the fight are such that the female can only save herself by destructiveness; and so the strength that Ursula draws from her talisman, the moon, becomes in her a deadly, spiritual hardness, 'like some cruel, corrosive salt . . . destroying him in the kiss.' His male pride is murdered even as it attempts to dominate her for his gratification. It is like a strange reversal of the woman's intent in the eclipse scene of *The Return of the Native*. Where for Hardy Eustacia's sensual shadow overwhelms and blights Clym's painful moon-'thoughts', for Lawrence it is now the bitter moonlight in Ursula which gives the fatal eclipse to Anton's darkness.

She is forced to a victory over him which she cannot bear to know and enjoy, like her mother in her crushing of Will's pride by her dance of pregnancy. Ursula has had to destroy what she created or roused in Anton, defensively vanquishing the tyrannical pride she herself has called up. But like her mother, only for a different purpose, Ursula after her victory does not want to know the ferocity in herself, only the innocence and lovingness: the spiritual lamb must pretend that no wounds have been inflicted by the raging lion. In fear of this knowledge, her imagination must bring to life what she has killed, and restore Anton to his status as a romantic partner. But the actual Anton has been nullified, going off to the war in South Africa like a man who gratefully escapes from her wounding contact and knowledge of his deadness. As with Will Brangwen in convalescence apart from Anna, Anton goes away to recover and in the end to add a power to himself, a reinforcement to his will, with which to match her in a further, inevitable trial. He is lost to her, non-existent, but she makes him exist from 'her soul's own creation', revives his memory as 'almost the symbol of her real life. . . . But even her memories were the work of her imagination.' He is a complete hypothesis.

By the time they meet again in a kind of destined appointment, Ursula has waged *her* war and battled on different fields from those of Anton. It is an ordeal of persistence for the growing spirit, a painful shedding and clarifying movement that is won and done out of conflict with all that would drag her down—like the 'heavy cleaving of moist clay' which Winifred Inger's body becomes to Ursula after her infatuation with her schoolmistress turns to nausea. As in her dance against Anton, she is inevitably in a state of battle with all the dark masses of friction in the world, with a corrupt kind of fatalism that she can only sense instinctively: 'Vaguely she knew the huge powers of the world rolling and crashing together, darkly, clumsily, stupidly, yet colossal' (p. 326).

The flood which broke through the Brangwens' embankment, their protection from the civilized outer world, has symbolically let in this wider experience for a Brangwen woman. It is as if Ursula, in her battles with her mother and in the schoolroom, were moving doggedly through an intractable element of tragic forces that are paring away her immature romanticism as the cost of her winning through. She is moving into Anton's world, fighting for her place in it, able to satisfy its mean standards as the essential condition by which she has power and knowledge to reject them. In the schoolroom, one feels, she is taking on (in her decisive fight with Williams) the struggle with a mysterious, sapping evil which the men of her world flinch from. So she endures the test of the working community, and is granted her place as a fellow with man—by Harby at the school, and by her father as she works with his tools in their new house at Beldover: now he has 'a ready belief in his daughter'.

She moves on, leaving behind the men of her experience, the sensuous captives like Harby the headmaster, Uncle Tom, Anthony Schofield, figures with imprisoned souls who are the basis of the disillusioned philosophy to which women like Winifred Inger and Maggie Schofield succumb, bitter at men's loveless egotism. But now Ursula, 'staunch for joy, for happiness, and permanency', goes to seek for herself a conscious expression of the religious desires which she has only known instinctively—the kind of fresh knowledge that Will could not give Anna.

Even though in the college 'the religious virtue of knowledge was become a flunkey to the god of material success,' Ursula still persists in her concern to verify the deep psychic facts known to her. And as she works at Botany, glimpsing 'the strange laws of the vegetable world', her realization becomes gradually clearer, placed on a semi-scientific footing by using the tools of man's nineteenth-century science. Not far behind the realization is Venn's and Wildeve's gambling scene, or Clym labouring in his microscopic work on Egdon:

This lighted area, lit up by man's completest consciousness, she thought was all the world: that here all was disclosed for ever. Yet all the time, within the darkness she had been aware of points of light, like the eyes of wild beasts, gleaming, penetrating, vanishing. . . . This inner circle of light . . . seemed like the area under an arc-lamp, wherein the moths and children played in the security of blinding light, not even knowing there was any darkness. . . . But she could see . . . the eyes of the wild beast gleaming from the darkness, watching the vanity of the camp fire and the sleepers . . . grey shadow-shapes of wild beasts, and also . . . dark shadow-shapes of the angels, whom the light fenced out.   (Pp. 437–8.)

For the moment in her spiritual sanctuary, Ursula forgets the sensual arrogance, the proud savagery, in herself and in the men of her world. As in her meeting with the canal family, such pressures are put aside while she concentrates upon the aspiring 'angel' in her desires—that deep craving for a consummation in the spirit which cannot be satisfied in actual experience. So the dark shape, the 'unicellular shadow' of a tiny organism, which she brings to focus under the light of her microscope, is the basis (p. 441) for a spiritual rather than sensual realization: 'Self was a oneness with the infinite. To be oneself was a supreme, gleaming triumph of infinity.'

The discovery of this eternal purpose by means of consciousness and science marks an advance in Ursula beyond the young girl who gave away her necklace on its 'little golden chain' to the canal man's child. Now the chain, the 'endless web', the thread of continuity and religion are all perceived intellectually as the principle which holds together and gives purpose to the 'conjunction of forces, physical and chemical' in the living organism. But the affirming of this knowledge, the securing of it through man's science, is achieved in reflective isolation, sublimely cloistered from the frictions and pressures of the world. And at this moment one cannot be sure what this kind of knowledge entails, what it will be revealed as when embodied in the finite to-and-fro of human relationship. Almost immediately, however, the quality of Ursula's realization moves towards ampler definition. Just as her parents are called back by the chimes of the church-bell and the world's noises from their 'poised, unflawed stillness', so Ursula is summoned from her 'stillness, like passing away' by the college clock booming the hour of her appointment with Anton.

As in the moonlit, dancing struggle which followed upon the pause with the canal family, it becomes clear from Ursula's new relationship with the returned Anton that her perception of the infinite purpose is and must be one-sided. Anna, in schism with Will, receives a sense of the eternal journey in the peace reigning at her parents', but cannot help turning it into affirmation of her coming victory over the man. Ursula also transfigures what she receives because of the will in her that has been strengthened through man's inadequacy: the form of her realization—'To be oneself was a supreme, gleaming triumph of infinity'—is radically coloured by the language of hard assertiveness. For Ursula 'supreme' cannot help being narrowed to suggest not a joint transcendence but the triumph of the woman as self-sufficient creator, the lone 'angel'; under the conditions in which she toils, she cannot but make a half-truth out of her realization where her grandfather was able (p. 135) to glimpse the sum total (' "If I am to become an Angel, it'll be my married soul, and not my single soul" '). Therefore when Ursula sees the infinite purpose it is gripped by 'an intensely-gleaming light of knowledge', by the same finite will which broke Anton in the past and which now again fixes on his memory as the redeemer to translate her knowledge into reality. If he had stayed with her, she deludes herself, 'He would have been her angel.' Indeed, one sees in Ursula how her will, grown more nakedly savage and raging, is made to serve the wants of her spirit. Despairingly, like her father with the ruined symbols of his church, she is caught in the shame of using Anton sensually, knowing the falsity of this, yet making such experience *represent* a spiritual consummation, an angelic transcendence.

Anton comes back to serve this passion, bringing home new, suggestive material for it to work upon. He has ranged emotionally further than Will Brangwen in *his* outcast years, for if Will returned changed from his sensual practice on the girl picked up at the Empire music-hall in Nottingham, Anton returns from the Empire itself, from Africa with its terrifying sense of blood worship, its 'hot, fecund darkness', its sensual madness. This is his new offering, the basis of his and Ursula's complete rejection of man's conscious, social world. They adventure as wild beasts, sensual aristocrats, 'feeling triumphant as two angels in bliss.' But now Anton has so given himself to complete dependence on the blood connection alone that he is even more vulnerable than before. When he comes down into the external world, he risks disaster because he has rendered himself totally subservient to Ursula's will. He cannot exist, his strength is a fiction, without her support, while she, the creator of him as an equal, still has her resources apart from him. It is as if the sick adventure can only end and the illusion be broken when the weaker falls for the last time, incapable of being revived again; when Anton can be propped up no longer—either by Ursula's fear of standing alone or by her creative will.

Before the end they are together, high above the society they have spurned, but not supreme in the sense of having reached victorious, mutual consummation in body and soul. It is as if on the South Downs they meet (p. 463) upon another Egdon, where the living universe denies the map made by social man or his arrogant enemies: it is 'a high, smooth land under heaven, acknowledging only the heavens in their great, sun-glowing strength, and suffering only a few bushes to trespass on the intercourse between their great, unabateable body and the changeful body of the sky.' From here Ursula tearfully sees the same blind endeavour that Eustacia and Sue look out upon in their men— Clym cutting at his furze, Jude absorbed in his pictures; but Ursula watches a mechanical energy that sums up that labyrinthine toiling—a train gallantly and blindly steaming along in its pettiness, mindlessly tunnelling through the earth-mass. 'Where was it going? It was going nowhere, it was just going.' It is like the Puritan will of *Sons and Lovers* seen from afar: the code of Mrs. Morel's father, the stern engineer and maker of the concrete world, leads to the society which contains Anton Skrebensky the Royal Engineer. The distinction has been emphatically made, the onward purposefulness of *Sons and Lovers* split in two. And one is reminded here of the coherent idea, the disciplining standard, in which Lawrence's sense of religious purpose is lodged and given shape in distinction from merely social purposes: for as Ursula sits to cry 'on an old prehistoric earth-work' one remembers the idea of marriage as an encampment between man and woman— the stable camp which Ursula cannot set up with Anton, the bondage with him that she instinctively shies from. Yet even in her anarchy she wants to be part of a greater ordering, the religious fate which her grandfather saw in the travelling stars; so in her intense unhappiness she is 'grasping at the stars with her hands'. And these are 'the violent hands of claim' which grip Anton to her under the stars, making him a manikin doll, her pathetic intermediary between herself and the stars.

It is a frenzy of illusion which is destroying the last remnant of Anton's manhood, and their only escape from their knowledge of this horror seems to be in falsehood, in marriage, so that they can hide from their now-unbearable nakedness behind social conventionality. Even after Ursula has delivered the final eclipse to Anton, sacrificially killed him in the moonlight, so that he is utterly beyond the recall of her imagination, her mind is still tempted to what seems the inevitability of marriage with him. But her fear is forestalled by the fevered vision (p. 487) of the horses rampaging in the rainy field, blocking her way as she tries to reach 'the high-road and the ordered world of man'. She is forced to change course, impelled to reach the way out of the labyrinth by climbing the oak tree, by taking once more the growing way in herself, the hard lone upward struggle which she was about to relinquish. It is like the harsh measure, the violent renewal of scale, which is brought in by the flood that drowns Tom Brangwen and denies Anna the truth of her victory as female Creator. Ursula may escape from the mad threat of the horses, she may cast off Anton's child in her as a sickness in the flesh, yet, whatever the necessity of this for her own recovery, whatever the need for her spirit to keep clear of sensual domination, the flesh cannot be cursed, only its disease. She escapes and can see the horses from her safety, creatures imprisoned in their sensuality, 'almost pathetic, now'; but even so, Lawrence insists earlier, 'the darkness and wetness of rain could not put out the hard, urgent, massive fire that was locked within these flanks, never, never.' It is with the same insistence, the same qualifying measure which avoids the tragic conclusion, that Lawrence portrays Ursula emerging from illusion about her relation with Anton:

she had created him for the time being. But in the end he had failed and broken down. . . . It was good that he was as he was. Who was she to have a man according to her own desire? It was not for her to create, but to recognise a man created by God. The man should come from the Infinite and she should hail him.   (P. 493.)

The bearings are given, her patience invoked, and Lawrence, in 'sheer backward resistance' like Tom Brangwen, must uphold her faith in the coming of a man who can match and contend with her indomitable spirit. Yet, for all the diffuse hope of the novel's last pages, the values which give *The Rainbow* its sure form are still evident in the incident with the horses as are the form's limitations at this point. *The Rainbow* is the triumph of relevance won in the face of distraction, mistake, and the half-truth. Throughout, the stress comes down on the instinctive ability to know what is immediately relevant to the growing life, the ability not to be dissuaded and caught by the unravelled problem or the mystery that cannot be understood. The novel's overall movement shares something with Ursula confronted by the animals in the field: 'she began to work her way as if making a wide detour round the horse-mass.' The 'mass' of corruption, the demonism, the frictional violence, the threshing backwards and forwards—all this is a gathering perplexity, a dark obstacle, which Lawrence will not allow an exclusive triumph over life. In Ursula's story, Lawrence keeps an appointment with the form and faith which govern the idealism of the novel. Only then can he turn, with a different art, towards all that has been captured in the ground already taken, all that has been included in the form but left unresolved. 'However much there is inside here, there's a good deal they haven't got in,' say the little faces in the Cathedral. *Women in Love* knows more clearly what they mean.

VI

Women in Love

I

IT is not easy or intelligent for *Women in Love*[1] to be guided by *The Rainbow*'s sense of measure. In the intricate conditions, in the newly felt art of the later novel, Lawrence cannot strike out with the broad, clean ampleness which *The Rainbow* allowed. The consciousness he moves through in *Women in Love* is too bedevilling for Lawrence to raise against it the 'magnificent irony . . . the challenge, the contempt' of the kind which he saw in Hardy's fiction and which in *The Rainbow* wrought its grand denial of a narrow human ethic—as in the flood which broke through the embankment; as in the blast of sudden moonlight which caught Ursula and Anton on the shore and made them shrink back; as in the fire of the maddened horses within her life which forced Ursula to veer. The beauty of this movement drew its sureness from all that Lawrence brought to his impression of Hardy and, in particular, *The Return of the Native*. As he looked back through *Jude* at the scenes of the eclipse, the gambling, and the furze-cutting, there seems to have come clear the tension on which the art of *The Rainbow* was founded—the intercourse between absolute and relative knowledge, between the human presumptuousness which claims totality and the honest recognition of something outside such oneness; between the vanity of the camp-fire sleepers who dare not live beyond 'the security of blinding light' and the shapes fenced out by the consciousness.

But *Women in Love* has left behind the mood of the *Study* and the manner which challenges egotism by placing it, surely and boldly, within a great, encircling vision. It is no longer possible to under-estimate with Ursula the lengths which humanity has to go before it has done with its corruption. At the end of *The Rainbow* Ursula could believe in the imminence of the day when mankind 'would

[1] Published in 1920, but completed in 1916.

cast off their horny covering of disintegration, that new, clean, naked bodies would issue to a new germination'. But *Women in Love* reckons with the toughness and imperviousness of a Gerald Crich, and Ursula knows here that mankind 'had a long way to go yet, a long and hideous way'. The 'blinding light' of egotistic, mental consciousness cannot be diminished to a small area of vanity set in the midst of a huge, scornful darkness. It is too pervasive and treacherous, as if it were cast infectiously over the whole world—an optical horror that has raised the visual sense to such an extreme that touch is numbed and even the words of protest against it assume some of its hard will. In Birkin the brilliant light persists fiercely even in his honesty: ' "There's the whole difference in the world . . . between the actual sensual being and the vicious mental-deliberate profligacy our lot goes in for. In our night-time, there's always the electricity switched on, we watch ourselves, we get it all in the head, really." ' (P. 37.)

The confusion and sickness is more cunningly rooted than *The Rainbow* realized, but if Lawrence's form has to change in relation to this and be denied access to a large, clear corrective, he gains for *Women in Love* a discipline, a moral refinement, a profound scrutiny as he answers the desires of the Brangwen women, their striving to see 'the far-off world of cities and governments and the active scope of man.' In their representative way, the dialogues and discussions of *Women in Love* are 'the lips and the mind of the world speaking and giving utterance', heard distantly by the Brangwen women and now brought close to finer appraisal than Ursula's relationship with Anton discovered. Anton is a lame spokesman for his society, lazy in his consciousness and conventionally accepting the delivered standards of morality which he is unaware that his inner being scorns. He can only be challenged by Ursula in sensual contradiction, not through the mind. He does not stand with those who, in *Women in Love*, touch more intimately and articulately the centres of activity and power in the land, in government, advanced thought, education, industry, and art.

Anton is not squarely in the 'blinding light' with the certainty of Gerald Crich whose flesh and hair possess a 'glisten like sunshine refracted through crystals of ice', as if he were the most advanced 'product' of his civilization. With his self-command, poise, and keenness, Gerald seems to be conceived by Lawrence as a uniquely specialized being, and granted the kind of acknow-

ledgement that is given elsewhere to Sue Bridehead. The outlets
for Gerald's pent-up energy may be questionable and one may
ask with Gudrun, ' "Where does his *go* go to?" ', but that does not
prevent Lawrence from also suggesting (p. 74) a certain authoritative fineness in him, when Minette goes back to the 'half men',
because she can deal with them: 'The real men, like Gerald, put
her in her place too much.' For all the moral criticism of Gerald
that stems from the activity he engages himself in, Lawrence is
not quarrelling with the strange *fact* of his specialized form:
Birkin can respect the conditions of the other man's nature,
admitting in him (p. 265) ' "a northern kind of beauty, like
light refracted from snow—and a beautiful, plastic form." '

The acuteness of Gerald's visual poise is heightened by a feeling
that the society which he supremely represents is endangered in
some unconscious way, threatened by something which is literally
out of sight of his mental mastery. The 'strange, guarded look'
which he wears at the wedding seems to be part of a constant
watch for attacks out of the unseen, upsurges of energy that
might overturn the social-visual form. Gerald's fear of murder or
of being bound hand-and-foot is a larger, more abstract appre-
hension than is shared by all the other guarded selves in this
society, also watching or being watched, as they try to estimate
the hostility in the air. Gerald has a mass-personality to guard, a
social philosophy and system: but, in contrast to others who feel
nakedly vulnerable to attack, Gerald's defences are extensive, and
(as Gudrun is to find) one must penetrate a long, exhausting distance into the man before reaching the core. For Hermione and
Gudrun, with a fear that does not touch Gerald—that of being
eyed in one's inmost privacy, devilishness, or insufficiency—the
menace is more immediate, as they easily suffer under the stares
of the miners' wives and ordinary people at the wedding. Ursula
does not fully subscribe to the standards of Hermione or Gudrun,
and so does not suffer like this, but in her class-room she has 'all
her suppressed, subconscious fear' startled in her by the sudden
appearance of Birkin at the door (p. 29) as an inspecting observer
—'the face of a man . . . gleaming like fire, watching her, waiting
for her to be aware.'

Yet for Birkin and Ursula the cautious objectivity, the fear of
letting go because one might be committed to falsehood, to a
trap: all this defensiveness assists the moral subtlety in Lawrence's

handling of their relationship. There is a shrewdness in their caution besides the self-protection of the will; a readiness in each not to be taken in by the other's guile. When Ursula secretly tries on the rings that Birkin has given her (p. 295), she cannot conceal the fact that his theories do not exactly fit her reality, even if she would at this moment pretend, in hidden disbelief. But she is exposed: 'He always saw, if she wanted him not to. It was another of his hateful, watchful characteristics.' On the other hand, it is her watchfulness which earlier in the novel sees him preparing again to enter into his old intimacy with Hermione, like a conspiracy which shuts her out. It is a movement into hostile, exclusive alliances which is typical of the social atmosphere, as Ursula herself closes ranks with Gudrun or even Hermione; as the London bohemians turn against Gerald; as Birkin and Mrs. Crich at Shortlands confer together (p. 18) 'like traitors, like enemies within the camp of the other people.' Here Birkin resembles 'a deer, that throws one ear back upon the trail behind, and one ear forward, to know what is ahead.' With the same cautious distrust he stands later on a railway platform, distancing himself from Gerald ('It was against his instinct to approach anybody'), noting (p. 46) how the other man reads a newspaper intently and how he keeps 'a watchful eye on his external surroundings . . . his eye ran over the surfaces of the life round him, and he missed nothing. . . . Gerald seemed always to be at bay against everybody, in spite of his queer, genial, social manner when roused.'

As he watches his fellow social man, or scans the visual field to ensure that the decencies of dress and behaviour are in order, Gerald really is his brother's keeper. Like Cain, it is suggested, he has 'accidentally' killed his brother in the past, but unlike Cain he has taken on the responsibility of guarding the surface coherence ever after, in consciousness, at least, holding the threatened externals together. His plausible, soldierly air seems to make all the incidents that do occur into unrelated episodes, insignificant, 'accidental'. At the wedding reception when the guests are nonchalant in their taking of places for dinner, Gerald marshals them to order with a sudden 'shattering blast' on a conch-shell. When Minette stabs the jeering young man in the Café Pompadour, Gerald's 'Stop that' comes with 'quick, instinctive command'. Only at the level-crossing with the Arab mare (pp. 102–4) does one first see him more significantly as the strenuous keeper of visual, social form.

There he appears as if the highest figure in a composed, beautifully grouped scene—'picturesque', restrained, calmly gallant,
with a physical ease that contrasts visibly with the ugly noise of
the hidden locomotive on the track and the crippled man staring
out of his signal box in one-legged incapability. But the composure
is menaced, for as the locomotive, with its terrible noise, slowly
moves across the path of Gerald's mare, the horse's spontaneous
fear threatens to topple the poise and equilibrium of the picturesque grouping. Gerald's will, however, can account for this
deep disturbance, ride the gathering upset, and maintain the
elements of the scene unbroken with a masterly suavity. He is at
once 'sun', with the genial, social calm which Birkin has noticed,
and 'ice', with the concentrated will which forces the surface to
cohere when it would fly apart. 'She recoiled like a spring let go.
But a glistening, half-smiling look came into Gerald's face. He
brought her back again, inevitably.'

With the locomotive's maddening return and the mare's frenzy,
there are further threats to surface demeanour, and to match
them Gerald's will is further exposed, degree by degree, enlarged
beyond the casual rocking restraint with which he began and
brought to a more nakedly brutal suppression. And all the time
the formal manner remains weirdly intact: 'Both man and horse
were sweating with violence. Yet he seemed calm as a ray of cold
sunshine.' It is a strange initiation for the Arab mare. She is more
than just acclimatized to Gerald's industrial England, learning
more than 'to stand noises' (as he explains it later). She has her
being 'sensationalized', her alien beauty and sensuality brutally
converted into mechanical terms and absorbed into Gerald's kind
of beauty. Her natural terror reaches a pitch of automatism
where it is equivalent to the machine which frightens her, and so
becomes part of that machine: 'the mare pawed and struck away
mechanically now, her terror fulfilled in her, for now the man
encompassed her; her paws were blind and pathetic as she beat
the air, the man closed round her, and brought her down, almost
as if she were part of his own physique.' The visual trammelling is
wickedly perfected.

Until the events of the 'Water-Party' chapter, Gerald's power
remains as the highest criterion of the will, the most successful
and terrible standard, judged by which certain others seem
flawed, less numbly 'immune and perfect'. Gerald is aloof, at the

top of the scale of wilful being, which reaches from his most
advanced, brilliantly definite form, down through figures whose
wills are faultier, to a chaotic, formless swamp at the bottom. In
Gerald the will has been brought to an efficient finesse far beyond
the attainment of Hermione Roddice, just as Gerald's new England reaches logically and functionally beyond the liberal, older
culture of Hermione and his father. Hermione's is an older vision,
wavering and strangely dream-like, out of which Gerald's energy
launches itself in appalling clarity, as when he dives before Ursula
and Gudrun—'a white figure ran out, frightening in its swift
sharp transit, across the old landing stage.' Hermione's will is
more ponderous, more liable to hitches when it seeks to maintain
her uneasy equilibrium, to 'stop up the terrible gap of insufficiency.' She has a precarious, overladen form, as if she were top-
heavy with emotions that once had a creative life but now are
cumbersome, all gone to the head and mind. At the wedding she
is seen 'balancing an enormous flat hat of pale yellow velvet' on her
head—a picture whose significance enlarges when one comes
(p. 75) to the enervated, static beauty of Breadalby, her home:
'There were small figures on the green lawn, women in lavender
and yellow moving to the shade of the enormous, beautifully
balanced cedar tree.' Gerald's purer will can get the measure of
his horse's turbulence, but Hermione, poised at Breadalby like
her great, looming tree, can encompass only a more trivialized
movement. Gerald physically masters an exotic animal, but
Hermione's culture intellectually encloses the sensual and the
alien, visualizes them to death.

Like Halliday in London with his West Pacific carving and his
tame Arab who haggles over money to buy underclothes, Hermione has her international possessions in her collection of guests,
English, Italian, French, and German. There is here an optical
illusion of 'unbounded' vistas, but only Gerald among the guests
can speak without illusion and from a more advanced experience
of feeling limitless when he says, ' "It's like getting on top of the
mountain and seeing the Pacific." ' For Hermione, however, the
distant horizons have an insidious mental nearness, like theatrical
scenery and properties which she disposes and groups. Under her
sponsoring power, the guests quibble over an American edition of
a Russian novel translated into French; Birkin copies a drawing
of geese which the Chinese ambassador has given Hermione;

Ursula, Gudrun, and the Contessa are clothed for a dance in the style of the Russian Ballet with extravagant, oriental silks, and Ursula is nearly overwhelmed by the 'corrupt gorgeousness' of some Indian silk shirts which Hermione presses upon her.

Yet at any moment Hermione's balance may be shaken by a live word or undesignated emotion, by a hint of something quicker than the resources of her will can encompass. When Birkin dances to Hungarian music with a certain 'irresponsible gaity', she feels shatteringly betrayed because he has momentarily escaped her form and denied its pretension to absoluteness. Ursula's fear when Hermione bears upon her with the shirts is a live response which obstructs Hermione's will and brings on 'a sort of crash, a crashing down' in her. Her will cannot translate her hatred of Birkin into physical terms with the perfection and precision which Gerald summons in order to dominate the mare. She strikes at Birkin's head with a paperweight, but she fumbles the first blow, and gives Birkin time to recover and 'neutralise' her: ' "No you don't, Hermione . . . I don't let you." ' It is as if in her there were a failure to tally, a delayed connection between a destructive unconsciousness and her movement or her mind. She feels 'built over a chasm', the vulnerable will in her only just managing to link the ever-rupturing parts. Her long absorbed pauses before speech and her speech, with its incontrovertible, predesigned quality, seem indicative of the distance that the signal has to travel, much further than in Gerald. Her outer, visual life has to be worked by a kind of remote control. 'There always seemed an interval, a strange split between what she seemed to feel and experience, and what she actually said and thought. She seemed to catch her thoughts at length from off the surface of a maelstrom of chaotic black emotions and reactions.' (P. 131.) It is this darkness which shows through the inevitable flaw in her surface form. When she greets the sisters at Breadalby, there is an incongruity which spoils her colours of prune and coral: 'her dress was both shabby and soiled, even rather dirty.'

Gudrun is another unstable, vulnerable figure, but with devices and ambitions which mitigate the suffering to which she, like Hermione, is liable. She is a nervous but defiant venturer in the world of concrete surfaces, spectacularly fashionable in her colours, with an audacity, a would-be high form, that cannot be kept up confidently for long in the consciousness. Her dress is a blatant gesture of assertiveness, but her loss of nerve beneath the gaze of the miners' wives (p. 6) seems to surrender her surface demeanour, as if all the gaudy flamboyance of her colours were on the point of melting away into the amorphous dirt of the colliery world: 'She was aware of her grass-green stockings, her large grass-green velour hat, her full soft coat, of a strong blue colour. And she felt as if she were treading in the air, quite unstable, her heart was contracted, as if at any minute she might be precipitated to the ground.' It is natural that she should envy the higher form of existence in Gerald as he dives and swims in the lake with the 'liberty, the mobility' she craves and the confident power to act, which he displays at Shortlands, 'without reference to anybody'. Gerald moving in space 'unquestioned and unconditioned' embodies an absolutist ideal, but Gudrun's desire for such wilful certainty is, like Hermione's, hindered by her relatedness to others. She is at the mercy of their questions and contradictions, as if, like Birkin's dancing in independence of Hermione, they withheld assent to her form and denied it by the very power 'to exist, other than she did.' She hates the colliery women's stares just as she hates Ursula's verbal protest against Gerald's victory over the mare at the level-crossing.

In the latter scene, her sister's questioning momentarily denies to Gudrun the power of uninhibited self-abandonment, and the division in Gudrun's nature is revealed. With one part of her she craves an invulnerable form, clothed, socially perfect, free of others' assumptions of intimacy; with another part of her, there is the fascination for the obscene cracks in the surface tightness, a secret readiness to take pleasure in the friction set up by the disparity between her social consciousness and what is nakedly unthinkable. The 'violent sensation' she receives from her first sight of Gerald at the wedding is a paroxysm that is rendered possible by a cutting edge; it is a spark of knowledge struck against the surface of a social event and enjoyed in solitude, 'as if she had made some incredible discovery known to nobody else on earth.' She wants the thrill of the split between surface and subterranean, but she cannot bear to know her desire in explicit thought and speech. The only knowledge she can have is visual, mindless, and the crack must not be widened too far beyond her capacity for anti-organic, 'sensationalized' experience. Gerald's domination of the horse unwittingly gives her a cruel taste for this thrill. Under his heels, he encloses the horse in his form, but the cost of doing so is the gashes in the surface—'on the very wound the bright spurs came down, pressing relentlessly.'

Gudrun cannot go this far with Gerald. She is sated and stupefied through an excess of vision. Her fainting—'she could not know any more'—is the climax of fear. She has experienced with the horse an initiation, and she is broken in to a momentary fit of pride and courage, flinging open the gates of the crossing for Gerald like a challenge, a symbolic abandonment, a licensing of him to which he can only give at this moment a mere 'wondering interest'. But Gudrun has absolved her consciousness from responsibility for the fearless self-exposure in her action, because she has already re-secured her balance after her emotional involvement in the fight. She recovers from her faint to shift her visual focus for her own salvation: by a trick she is travelling away in illusion, uncommitted to the reality of what she has experienced and able, by reducing its meaning, to escape full acknowledgement of its truth:

The guard's-van came up, and passed slowly, the guard staring out in his transition on the spectacle in the road. And through the man in the closed wagon Gudrun could see the whole scene spectacularly, isolated and momentary, like a vision isolated in eternity.   (P. 104.)

Her mocking, objective art has this removed quality—' "animals and birds, sometimes odd small people in everyday dress" '— and her expedient shift of vision at the crossing explains its necessity. It is an art of wish-fulfilment, of illusory unrelatedness, where people are diminished and caricatured with a witch-like absolutism or 'finality'. When Gudrun observes the guests at the wedding or at Breadalby, there is a certain social self-saving in the way that her eye removes the very real pressures upon her: 'She saw each one as a complete figure, like a character in a book, or a subject in a picture, or a marionette in a theatre, a finished creation. She loved to recognize their various characteristics, to place them in their true light, give them their own surroundings, settle them for ever.' (P. 8.) Her art and her transference to the eyes of 'the man in the closed wagon' have the same escapist meaning as her sudden decision to swerve aside from the path she has taken with Ursula all the way from Beldover through the soiled countryside and up the red carpet which leads into the church at Willey Green. She branches off with her sister at the last moment to a detached, unexposed safety. As Birkin says of her to Gerald later (p. 87), ' "I always expect her to sheer off to Damascus or San Francisco; she's a bird of paradise. God knows what she's got to do with Beldover." '

But when the two girls resume their walk in the 'Coal-Dust' chapter, leaving behind the level-crossing where Gerald mastered the horse, Gudrun's painfully real connection with Beldover becomes apparent. Whatever her power to branch off from commitment in illusion, to cut off the sequence of inevitability, she is here continuing her walk down her line of fate, down the scale of wilful being, leaving behind her Gerald's upper level, with its clear, firmly-held structure—the confidently defined status to which Gudrun rose for a moment when, in 'distinct and formed' words, her 'strange, high voice' screamed her ironic challenge and recognition of Gerald: ' "I should think you're proud." ' But now she crosses down into strata which are socially and sensually more formless, disintegrated, grotesque. When the two girls reach a second level-crossing, they pass another frontier, descend another seam, where two labourers by a 'heap of pale grey slag' watch them go by, with an objective lust in their appraisal. Through their eyes one sees the sisters appear, 'small, brilliant figures in the near distance, in the strong light of the late afternoon. . . . The figures of the two women seemed to glitter in progress over the wide bay of the railway crossing, white and orange and yellow and rose glittering in motion across a hot world silted with coal-dust' (pp. 106–7). Through the vision of the labourers the 'amorphous squalor' of the atmosphere begins to disintegrate form and colour into a shifting mirage. Bodies and clothes become like a smear on a mass of soft, black dust: it is a slow destruction of sensual being, akin to the violence that brings trickles of blood on the sides of the beaten mare.

This melting of one's precariously balanced distinctiveness into a black void is a horror that Hermione fears, but Gudrun, in sharing this fear, is equally attracted by her own repulsion for deathly break-down. She has come to the end of her growing life —for her ' "*Nothing materialises!* Everything withers in the bud" ' —and while she waits fearfully for 'the inevitable next step', she returns from her artistic life in London as if unconsciously to measure what form she has achieved against the source from which she has stemmed, to 'test the full effect of this shapeless, barren ugliness upon herself.' But she has won only a frail independence from her origins. The old darkness still has power to claim back her precarious shape. The labourer who salutes her across the distance with his remark, ' "You're first class, you are," ' gives an ironic echo to her recognition of Gerald's proud, comparatively free life at the same time as he delivers a welcome to one returning inescapably from an attempted higher existence.

As Gudrun walks into the mindless, whirlpool existence of the colliers' town, there disappears any semblance of the structured, grouped 'picturesque' scene with which the 'Coal-Dust' chapter began. The sense of development in time and spatial order has been broken. Now as Gudrun is dragged away, spellbound by the powerful undercurrents, there is a generalized movement in command, a sense of many evenings which are the same evening, an abrasive, nerve-hurting atmosphere. It is like the 'heaving, shuddering struggle' of the mud-creatures in *The White Peacock*, as the masses crowd the streets of Beldover in intermingling, vociferous hordes and Gudrun parades up and down like the commonest slut. Yet in this progress down to the bottom of the scale of being, there is still a sense of parallelism, of strata below and above which are analogous. At Breadalby, in the previous chapter, among the niceties of a higher social form and finitely distinct individuals, there played a cerebral type of conversation —'this ruthless mental pressure, this powerful, consuming, destructive mentality.' At Beldover, among the amorphous heaving of the collier masses, Gudrun is caught by the spell of the frictional talk, the 'voluptuous resonance of darkness', with its mechanized vibrations, 'buzzing, jarring, half-secret'.

Breadalby and Beldover differ in degree and development of form, not in kind. The 'high' and the 'low' have the same relationship to one another as the water-plants have to the 'soft, oozy, watery mud' in which they are rooted, and which Gudrun draws (p. 111) in the following 'Sketch-Book' chapter. Like a concentrated image of the whole hierarchy which the 'Coal-Dust' chapter descends with Gudrun, the water-plants stand in their icy element, with the same cold fluid running through their clearly defined strata. It is like a sensual energy rising out of a formless darkness, but socially rigidified, held in, except for outbreaks of display in its odd colours—'thick and cool and fleshy, very straight and turgid, thrusting out their leaves at right angles, and having dark lurid colours, dark green and blotches of black-purple and bronze.' There is an irresistible connection for Gudrun between the origin from which she rises and the conscious-ness, the individual form, which the blackness limits or calls back. Even in her temporary relationship with Palmer, one of Gerald's new scientific men, she cannot get free of the ambivalence which runs from strata above to strata below. All the time the instability is deriding her would-be aristocracy of the will: 'There they were, the two of them: two elegants in one sense: in the other sense, two units, absolutely adhering to the people, teeming with the dis-torted colliers' (p. 110).

Gerald, however, is still able to hold his own as a high individual of the will, too efficient to give way to the subterranean pull. So his car slowly and inexorably cleaves its way like a knife through the solid mass of collier people; his spurs cut into and sink the resistance of the mare; and his new industrial methods gradually push their way into dominance. But he has tied his will and mind to a social philosophy which is to render his apparently 'immune and perfect' freedom vulnerable to attack from a hidden quarter:

What mattered was the great social productive machine. Let that work perfectly, let it produce a sufficiency of everything, let every man be given a rational portion, greater or less according to his functional degree or magnitude, and then, provision made, let the devil supervene, let every man look after his own amusements and appetites, so long as he interfered with nobody.   (P. 219.)

Where differences of being, where 'high' and 'low' forms of life are valued according to social function, Gerald has settled for a confusion, for an advanced expression of the democratic idea which leaves his innate aristocracy unvoiced. The traditional valuing of being according to class has gone, lingering only with the Hermione Roddices, but Gerald's new functional valuing has an uncertainty of balance—tipping one way to democratic pressures, so that he downgrades himself, tipping back the other way in a forceful readjustment which comes from his aristocratic initiative. 'He did not *want* to claim social superiority, yet he *would* not claim intrinsic personal superiority, because he would never base his standard of values on pure being. So he wobbled upon a tacit assumption of social standing.' (P. 201.) He is unable to embrace either standard completely and, passing continually between the two, he is prey to the kind of unease which he feels when visual appearance or behaviour is no clue to another's standing, socially or otherwise: hence the difficulty (p. 66) with Halliday's Arab manservant, dressed so elegantly: 'He made Gerald uncertain, because, being tall and slender and reticent, he looked like a gentleman.'

Gerald feels easier with Minette who plays the game of 'tacit assumption' with 'a rather formal, polite voice, with the distant manner of a woman who accepts her position as a social inferior, yet assumes intimate *camaraderie* with the male she addresses' (p. 56). It is here that one sees clearly the dangerous duality which is built into Gerald's system: once the social toll has been levied and the surface life has been assured of its coherence, one can be free, regardless of rank or order, in the anarchic area left over—'provision made, let the devil supervene.' Applied to the women of the novel, the philosophy invites a surreptitious danger for the man. Because it depends too much on implicit recognition of boundaries in behaviour, it encourages a clever or masked duality. It represses the mind and lets ferocity loose beneath. ' "She is a social being, as far as society is concerned," 'says Gerald about the woman's role, when he is at Breadalby (p. 96). ' "But for her own private self, she is a free agent, it is her own affair, what she does." '

This is the philosophy which delivers Gerald into the grasp of Gudrun, for all their difference in terms of social degree or being. He has gone further in development than she has, but with him she is lifted beyond her own impasse: 'Gerald was her escape from the heavy slough of the pale, underworld, automatic colliers. He started out of the mud. He was master. . . . He seemed to stoop to something.' (P. 112.) And Gudrun's life is what he stoops to, as from the boat upon the lake he reaches down into the water to retrieve her sketch-book, the symbol of her own distinction and knowledge as an individual. He and Gudrun can thwart and ignore Hermione's assumptions of superiority, the old currency of class and fine culture, the disdaining power which lets the sketches drop into the water. With Gerald's help, Gudrun will not be cast back. She instinctively knows the rules of the 'tacit assumption' which Gerald depends on, as one sees in her impersonal, polite deference to Gerald's apologies. On the surface all is trivial, socially intact—the incident with the book ' "doesn't matter in the *least*" '—while under the words, 'her voice ringing with intimacy', the incident matters enormously: 'In her tone, she made the understanding clear—they were of the same kind, he and she, a sort of diabolic freemasonry subsisted between them. Henceforward, she knew, she had her power over him.' (P. 114.)

But Gudrun's later remark to Gerald (p. 162) has a profound significance, even if she cannot fully realize its extent: ' "It's you who make me behave like this, you know." ' All that he represents, the kind of visual prestige, sure mastery, and electrified sensuality which are his, have the power to rouse Gudrun beyond the limits she has reached in personal development. Unconsciously he forces her to draw upon the fund in her, the 'untouched reserve', which she has been unaware of in herself. But he cannot stir anything creative in her: that is finished, and all that remains, as yet not brought into play, is the destructive movement forward. She is stimulated into the 'next step' of her life, nourished now on destructive food, the only unknown left. When she delivers her cruel affront to Gerald in the 'Rabbit' chapter, she can promise him—' "All that, and more." ' When her hands range over his features as they stand later in the darkness of a railway bridge, she is greedy to have his unknown power, his 'uncanny white fire', but she can be sure of 'many days harvesting' yet for herself. As Birkin says (p. 164) of this kind of late, corrupt flowering: ' "Dissolution rolls on, just as production does. . . . It is a progressive process." '

It is not until the 'Industrial Magnate' chapter that Lawrence chooses to suggest the total need in Gerald which brings him to penetrate into Gudrun's private world and seek a stimulus for his own oncoming inertia. He too is approaching the end of his tether. Physically he cannot go forward to complete the destructive, unconscious destiny which his carelessness with his own life urges him towards. He is becoming too insensate, too numb and arrested. He can be aroused only in part by the words of a more alive consciousness like Birkin's, for as Gerald's mind gets colder and more inert, any open, unoblique language becomes less effective in stirring him. He needs a mental insinuation, thought and speech coming in at a slant and cutting: the kind of stimulus by shock which Gudrun can give him. His manly pride is revitalized by the extra knowledge he provokes from her. By her kind of pornography and prostitution, her 'piquancy or ironic suggestion', he is spurred with the cutting-edge of innuendo and the half-explicit.

2

Women in Love opens on to an intensely visualized world with an immediate suggestion, in the atmosphere of guarded watchfulness, of so much that is held in reserve, so much that has been unconsciously kept to the last, so much that is fearfully to come. But below the conscious reckoning there is more than just a cold, black reservoir of violent forces. There is more to come than an extra stir of growth to the corrupt blooms, the water-plants, the 'marsh-flowers'. For when Birkin declares (p. 118) that ' "mankind is a dead tree, covered with fine brilliant galls of people," ' Ursula cannot help knowing that the statement is 'too picturesque and final'. And there is more than facile optimism in Birkin's remark in 'Water-Party', when he relinquishes his Gudrun-like finality to suggest that besides the *fleurs du mal*, ' "there ought to be some roses, warm and flamy." ' There are other growths, but hidden from the established, picturesque light. There are creative resources as well as destructive, and equally as untouched and unreckoned with.

Gerald in 'Sketch-Book' dips down into Gudrun's private underworld, reaching for the egotistic sensuousness, the 'sensationalized' knowledge she has, but Birkin, as he stands at the door of Ursula's class-room, is on the threshold of a warm sensual reality, untouched and asleep. He enters this quiet reserve with its 'soft dim magic' and its 'ruddy, copper-coloured light', to switch on the electric light and bring a 'distinct and hard' quality to the room—both in his assertive lesson on the catkins and his mental fight with Hermione, when she appears in the visual arena. Ursula is roused from her sleep of life, called to attend, and even though her presence seems at moments redundant beside the major quarrellers, their insistent *talk* about sensuality, their electric light, cannot drive out remembrance of its red reality in Ursula, 'that strange brightness of an essential flame', which is observed, in the first chapter of the novel, 'caught, meshed, contravened'. And behind the electric light and the wilfulness in Birkin, Ursula can furtively see (p. 38) 'a great physical attractiveness in him—a curious hidden richness, that came through his thinness and his pallor like another voice, conveying another knowledge of him.'

The 'hidden richness' in Ursula and Birkin shows through in them just as a disintegrated sensuality is revealed in Gerald and Gudrun. But this creative resource does not count as a valid energy; it has not yet produced any fully individual flowers to set against the established plants and their visual attractiveness. Hermione, in welcoming the two sisters at Breadalby, can see the greater womanliness and physicalness of Ursula, but sets her down as 'more ordinary' compared with Gudrun's striking fashionableness. Birkin at the wedding, with his 'innate incongruity' and 'slight ridiculousness' of appearance, is unable to fit into the visual pattern with the same defensive expertise as those who conform so superbly even as they conspire beneath it. Ursula is on the periphery of the bright, conscious world of form, but Birkin is nearer the centre. He is, however, indefinite in his allegiance— neither a sure associate of the more intensely visualized existence nor a complete devotee of the hidden world of sensual richness which he shares with Ursula. He is not fixed to one aspect of life or the other, and there is a duality in him, but without the hard-edged breach between mind and senses, surface and subterranean, which there is in Gudrun, Gerald, and Hermione. Birkin's consciousness moves dexterously between the two levels, and it is with his different ambivalent movement that he is portrayed by Lawrence as a figure of justifiably suspect qualities yet one to whom a certain credit is allowed. In Birkin's shiftiness, there is that which makes for his unsatisfactoriness and perversity, as well as his saving.

Placed beside Gerald's form in a comparison which Lawrence deliberately draws, Birkin is valued in a way which manages to be both to his detriment and in his favour. When he disturbs Ursula's sleeping world of the class-room, he moves to the fore 'almost like a vacancy in the corporate air', with a spiritual, disembodied power which, after it engages in conflict with Hermione, turns him impotent and static, 'fixed and unreal'. Yet he is happily not as fixed as Gerald, not (p. 199) 'limited to one form of existence, one knowledge, one activity, a sort of fatal halfness, which to Gerald] seemed wholeness'; nor, on the other hand, is Birkin's sensual being as fully credible in a physically man-like way as Gerald's when the figure of the diver makes its plunging 'white arc' through the air in the chapter which follows 'Class-Room'. The spring morning through which Gerald dives may signalize a different kind of existence from his, with its fecund quickening, its hedges glowing 'like living shadows, hovering nearer, coming into creation', but in the wet haze of the hour there is nothing yet as sharply developed and sure as Gerald's movement. When in the summer scene of 'Water-Party', Gudrun's boat draws away from the two men on the shore, Birkin's figure appears 'wavering, indistinct, lambent' beside Gerald who is 'so goodlooking and efficient in his white clothes.' Yet it is the lambency, the unsettled quickness in Birkin, which eludes Gudrun's satiric, dismissing finality of judgement in 'Moony', and which causes him to think later (p. 349) of always leaving 'a piece of raw rock unfinished to your figure . . . so that you are never contained, never confined, never dominated from the outside.'

That is his irritating and gladdening quality in the novel's opening chapters, when he has enough in common with the over-visualized life of his artist friends to take his place beside them, without being confined completely by their cerebrality or fixed in attitude within the group-picture. In the Café Pompadour, after Minette has drawn blood, Birkin, 'white and diminished, looked on as if he were displeased'. This is not the substantial, glistening whiteness of Gerald's commanding form, with which Lawrence is suggesting a contrast, but a mute powerlessness, which leaves him in Halliday's flat (p. 71), 'aloof and white, and somehow evanescent'. Round the carving of the West Pacific woman in labour, he stands in a small group which Gerald observes, but visually shading off, as if only hovering in sympathy—'the Russian golden and like a water-plant, Halliday tall and heavily, brokenly beautiful, Birkin very white and indefinite, not to be assigned.' And Gerald knows that whatever the absolute truth of the carving is for *his* existence (a truth which he cannot consciously admit), it is not absolute for Birkin in the way that the latter believes it is, when he hails it for Gerald as a symbol of ' "really ultimate *physical* consciousness, mindless . . . so sensual as to be final, supreme." ' Gerald can truly say of Birkin's mistake: ' "You like the wrong things, Rupert . . . things against yourself." '

Because Birkin's nature is not finally committed, sensually or spiritually, he is distrusted by everyone. Even though the unease to which he gives rise hits on a limitation or fear in the others— and gives good cause for *his* distrust of *them*—their scepticism (with qualifications) is well grounded. Hermione feels betrayed by Birkin's new gaiety in the dance at Breadalby and agrees with the Contessa's observation: ' "He is not a man, he is a chameleon, a creature of change." ' The judgement, like all those on Birkin, works against the standards of the accusers as well. But there remains a case against Birkin's versatility, even though one notices that Gerald's criticism, like Hermione's, is too dismissively patronizing—'Birkin was . . . a wonderful spirit, but after all, not to be taken seriously, not quite to be counted as a man among men'—as if to compensate for the fact that Birkin's independent spontaneity makes him feel all the more fixed in monotonous suffering. One cannot disregard the core of Gerald's complaint to Birkin—' "I'm never sure of you. You can go away and change as easily as if you had no soul" '—nor Gudrun's charge that Birkin is indiscriminate, ' "treating any little fool as if she were his greatest consideration" ', making one feel ' "so awfully sold, oneself" '. This is not, however, to accept the accusers' terms of reference (Gudrun, for instance, feels her wilful social confidence slighted by Birkin's flexibility) but merely to realize that there *is* a stand-point from which Birkin can be accused and which, in the end, only Ursula can genuinely express.

Like Gudrun, she feels let down personally, individually, by Birkin: 'He would behave in the same way, say the same things, give himself as completely to anybody who came along, anybody and everybody who liked to appeal to him. It was despicable, a very insidious form of prostitution' (p. 121). She deeply distrusts a man who can write off humanity with such splendid words of hate and yet be so ready to save it with all his soul and love. But her criticism of him, her sense of 'something diffuse and generalised about him' (which makes Birkin the social preacher into a strange equivalent of another mass-self, Gerald), is more finely focused, less ruined by disguised private pleading, than her sister's accusation. It concentrates on Birkin's instability with more precision because Ursula is evaluating his changeableness by the standard of serious relationship. Only through her does the criticism find its moral bearings and begin to matter. Only when there is a bond with Birkin do his casualness and shiftings assume dangerous or valuable meaning. It is only from within the relationship that the line dare be drawn against his freedoms.

But until something serious is established between Ursula and Birkin, he is, as at the wedding, 'taking the tone of his surroundings, adjusting himself quickly to his interlocutor and his circumstance,' and courting the part of a mere verbal stimulus to others who lack his spontaneity. In the train going to London, Gerald enjoys Birkin's 'rich play of words and quick interchange of feelings', without, of course, having to consider the content seriously. Birkin is aware of this, but he is more unknowingly a prostitute when he is ever-willing to adjust himself to Hermione, submitting himself to her power at the very moment that she provokes him to rebel vindictively against it. When he rises in counter-assertion, she has him then on her wilful terms, and he has strayed into the trap of 'antiphony' which he despairs over in the 'Moony' chapter —' "they lie, and you sing back to them" '. The source of Birkin's beguilement—an underlying cynical toleration of all that he protests against—is sensed in him by Ursula on the island. As she says later, in 'Continental': ' "even fighting the old is belonging to it" '. But this is only after she has suffered the effects of her own duality in relation to Hermione.

Both for Ursula and Birkin, Hermione is a subtle psychological snare, because, in her intellectual consciousness, she presents all the values of sensitivity, spontaneity, wholeness, in a form which exerts an attraction—negatively, with Birkin's rebellious acquiescence; positively, with Ursula's self-deception. Birkin is providing Hermione with the kind of dissecting knowledge of corrupt things which one part of her hates and another part must have—as when at Breadalby she compels him to give up the secret knowledge he has gained from the copying of the geese. Here he yields himself to the appeal of the other person with that openness which Ursula despises, but at this point the effect of his biting, exploratory language—' "the hot, stinging centrality. . . . fire of the cold-burning mud—the lotus mystery" '—makes him more than just the sulky boy, or the unmanly but wonderful spirit, whom Gerald patronizes and over whose illusory freedom Hermione runs her tape-measure as she superintends the furnishing of his place of exile in 'Carpeting'. For at Breadalby Birkin raises the odds of the cynical game he plays with Hermione, giving her more than just stimulus through conflict. Gerald is beyond taking

Birkin seriously, but Birkin's hit in the dark which destroys part of Hermione's being takes on a credibility from which the unclear language cannot detract. It is the same when Gudrun in the Café Pompadour snatches Birkin's letter about the 'Flux of Corruption' from the mockery of the Halliday group. ' "Why does he give himself away to such *canaille*?" ' she asks (p. 377), registering in her own sense of exposure the essential truth of Birkin's intuitions, whatever the wrapping of jargon and the world-saviour preaching voice with which Halliday reads the letter.

But although the wounded responses of the demonists go to confirm the approximate truth of what Birkin says, this does not mean that his wholeness as a man is confirmed as well. In *Women in Love*, rational wisdom or theories are never the total evidence on which a person's being is judged, nor, just because of the vigour of his inquiring intellect, is Birkin's mind allowed to rule the novel. There is his purpose to be accounted for in his searching out of knowledge, and any view of Birkin as superior to other characters, by virtue of his greater honesty, must be set against the query which Lawrence raises. Having discounted the element of self-protectiveness in his accusers, and ignored the hypocrisy, one is left with the charge that has to be faced, and which only Ursula in the end can accurately judge—the charge by Hermione (p. 36) that Birkin is ' "such a *dreadful* satanist" ', or Minette's remark (p. 375) about Birkin's letter on corruption, ' "He must be corrupt himself, to have it so much on his mind." '

The charges overstate the case, but they point up the risk that Birkin takes amongst the company of demonic things. The cost of prying and analysing, even for the supposed sake of knowing corrupt truths in order to be free of their fascination, is always to be counted when Birkin's spirit seems to lose its quick momentum and for a while becomes fixed, as if wickedly and cynically overcome by the dirt he is detachedly exploring. It is then that Birkin wilfully appears no different from Gerald, with the latter's interest in primitive things as food for a sensational curiosity. But Gerald, in 'seeing out' the process of corruption upon himself, physically, has given over his soul to it, while Birkin's soul still responds to the undestroyed, the living. When he does become preoccupied, however, he is static, mechanical, demonic—as when he confronts Hermione with the secrets of 'the lotus mystery' and destroys her 'with some insidious occult potency', staring at

her, 'devilish and unchanging'. His words have found her out and
the mysteries of the geese-drawing cruelly strike at her (just as
the rabbit's scratches in Gudrun's arm are visually used to tear
across Gerald's brain in a later episode). But the cost to the human
tissue is counted, and Birkin suffers on his head the results of his
unholy study. His theorizing does not get away easily from his
skirmish with the 'final' or 'supreme' sensuality which fascinates
him in the West Pacific carving and the drawing of the geese.
Hermione in her murderous state is that sensuality in all its terrible
reality.

Yet, as with Anna and Will in *The Rainbow*, the woman's
destructiveness which the man's absolutism rouses, profits Birkin.
He is freed more quickly than Gerald is to be with Gudrun.
Hermione's attack releases him for other ways of knowledge,
still with his creative life relatively undamaged. He can, therefore,
suffer out and have done with his belief in the 'finality of love'
with one woman, which he expressed on the train with Gerald,
when the evening light 'flooding yellow along the fields' lit up his
face 'with a tense, abstract steadfastness', suggesting a demonic
insistence on having his woman in the image of his ideas. The
experience at Breadalby violently delivers him from such fixity of
belief, with the result that he no longer considers love to be the
supreme value. The belief in a relationship with one woman
persists, but, as he suggests in 'An Island', the tender desires of
soul and body can be no more final than their obverse, the
violently egotistic feelings, the wilful desires. The theory of marriage which Birkin now puts forward in the face of others' ridicule,
is like a continuation of Tom Brangwen's talk about the Angel at
Anna's wedding, under the mockery of the saturnine Alfred. But
unlike Tom, Birkin cannot be content with the marriage of body
with body and soul with soul as the complete criterion: for
him, in his developing theories, the demonic body and soul of
the man needs to be met and countered by the demonism of the
woman—as necessary a struggle as the matching of the angelic
sides.

This is theory, and for Ursula who hears it in its first outlandish sketch in 'Mino' there is the just fear (after her experience
with Skrebensky) that Birkin wants no more than Gerald does in
his tyranny over the mare—the male will as master. She is also
puzzled and hesitant about a man who can make these inter-

changes between demon and angel. Through her, Lawrence trails the suspicion of hypocrisy in Birkin, the feeling that Birkin is having it both ways. For all the theory, the question seems to be: does not any association with deathly things disqualify one's claim to health and life in the other part of oneself? Lawrence lets this doubt hover in 'Water-Party' and 'Sunday Evening' as a question about Birkin which Ursula can only answer from the knowledge to which Birkin rouses her in herself.

At the summer fête, Birkin's lambency of interchange is in full play. When he appears at first as 'the good angel' who makes the Brangwen parents feel at ease, his smile 'full of natural warmth' cannot disguise the kind of incongruity which was revealed at the wedding—the 'affected social grace, that somehow was never *quite* right.' When he picks up the tone of the witchcraft atmosphere on the far shore, and offers Ursula a sardonic, suggestive dance after her song, he appears like another man altogether, to Ursula's bewilderment. All his goodness seems fraudulent, as this demonic figure woos her 'with an incredibly mocking, satiric gleam on his face.' Yet when the chapter returns from the intensely charged scene between Gudrun and Gerald the mockery has passed away into the happy teasing that Birkin is giving Ursula, as he talks about the black river of corruption and the ' "silver river of life . . . flowing into a bright eternal sea, a heaven of angels thronging." ' But as he presses on her his insistence that their reality is only that of the black river, her protests—' "You are a devil, you know, really. . . . You only want us to know death" '—seem confirmed later by the sight he presents at the sluice-gates after the drowning. He has the key of the sluice and, in a sense, the key to all the corrupt secrets. It is as if he is unwinding the gates of hell, disgorging the horror, while he is himself somewhat automatized and beguiled by all the black knowledge he is opening up by his work: 'She could not bear to see him winding heavily and laboriously, bending and rising mechanically like a slave, turning the handle. . . . It occupied the whole of the night, this great steady booming of water, everything was drowned within it, drowned and lost. Ursula seemed to have to struggle for her life.' (P. 177.) She draws him away from the spell of the Siren music, from the vibrating magic which entrances Gudrun in the collier world, and they turn their backs upon the lake. As they walk home he stops to kiss her, 'slowly, gently, with a sort of delicate happiness', but she cannot respond to the return of the strangely angelic, softly spiritual mood in Birkin.

She still remains apart from it the following Sunday evening when he comes to her home. They sit quietly for a moment by the low burning fire and the soft light of the lamp, before Ursula's little brother and sister come, and Birkin kisses the boy good-night. Speaking in a 'strangely soft and smooth' voice and giving 'a faint touch of love', as he lifts his fingers to Billy's face, Birkin seems like 'a tall, grave angel'—an impression which is reversed when Ursula comes down, after putting the children to bed, and finds him sitting (p. 188) 'like some crouching idol, some image of a deathly religion.' His face is 'very pale and unreal . . . white and purely wrought . . . hard and jewel-like . . . a beam of essential enmity, a beam of light that . . . revoked her whole world.' He has become in her eyes like the silently sitting figure rapt in his book at Breadalby, the 'evil obstruction' whom Hermione struck at to save herself. There seems no difference between this 'crouching idol' and Gudrun, as she sits 'like a Buddhist . . . crouched on the shoal', rapt in her study of the water-plants. Birkin seems to gleam with Gerald's phosphorescent light, as when the latter bent forward in his rowing and 'seemed to stoop to something'.

Yet at this point the implication of falsehood in Birkin's duality —that the deathly is master really, the goodness a disguise—is severely qualified. Misgivings about Birkin's changeableness are widened to include Ursula herself. She fears not only morally, that Birkin's studies into corruption neglect life and deny it its chance, but that now his studies will reach and see into her possibilities for demonism. When Birkin bids good-night to the children, Ursula has something of the distrust of her little sister Dora who will not be kissed and edges away 'like some tiny Dryad, that has no soul . . . that will not be touched.' While Ursula hesitates, hiding the demonism in herself, Birkin's goodness must seem, and is made to be, out of key. If she does not meet him on both terms, of open wilfulness as well as open love, there will be no difference between their shifts between angel and demon, and those of evil dualism.

While Birkin and Ursula remain not fully committed to each other, it is clear that the talent to avoid being fixed on any one line which Birkin displays has also its equal share of untrust-

worthiness and virtue in Ursula's changeableness. While she
refuses to meet him on the terms of heaven *and* hell, because she
wants a lone freedom, Birkin cannot be stopped drifting into the
to-and-fro relationship with Hermione, devilishly assailing her one
moment, with pity tolerating her the next, so that the interchange at this level is a vice and the wilful demon the master of
the angel. And while Ursula keeps her option open, she must
succumb to the influence of Gudrun and (in a different way
from Birkin) to that of Hermione, only to be repelled and then
again attracted. The danger of instability to which the 'chameleon' Birkin is liable, as he spiritually adventures among corruption, is the same danger for the wild 'Dryad' in Ursula, as she
runs off from any discipline that would bring out her sensual
knowledge, and all it contains, to further consciousness. In her
there is latent positive and negative knowledge. On the island
with Birkin, she knows that his picture of wholesale rottenness is
untrue and too absolute because of the creative sense in her, but
she also knows, out of her 'subtle, feminine, demoniacal soul',
that his dream of a clean end of the world is too naïve.

There persists the arrogance of the seventeen-year-old Ursula
in *The Rainbow* who listens in church to the Genesis story of the
Covenant, and thinks that she would like to have been a nymph
laughing at Noah and his sons in their ark, at the 'vanity' of the
four men for believing that they were the only survivors of the
world-destruction under God. But in *Women in Love* she cannot
flee far into an illusion of lone freedom without falling prey to the
pressures of Hermione or Gudrun, as when in 'Water-Party' the
two sisters escape into a perfect world of their own, 'like nymphs',
and Gudrun compels her into a mood of a mindless demonism.
Yet the fear which saves Ursula from yielding completely to
Hermione's claiming of her with the oriental silks or Gudrun's
enchantment is the cry of the responsive life in her, which, untutored and too unconscious, makes her the prey of the other
women. The others can only feel in spasms of brutalized emotion;
but the unkilled sensuality and genuine sensitivity in Ursula,
which cannot make itself numb like Gudrun to the coldness of
the water Gerald swims in or the hurt Gerald inflicts upon the
mare, and which urges her to protest at Birkin's and Gerald's
carelessness with their bodies, is the feeling for life which taken
far enough and given a wilful armour to defend it brings Ursula

to exactly the same mental position as Hermione and Gudrun. The values which enabled her to hold on through the experiences of *The Rainbow*, where she was 'staunch for joy, for happiness, and permanency', are here just as essential. But in face of Birkin's challenge, they appear a disadvantage as well.

What keeps Ursula from surrender to the devil is that which hinders her from accepting knowledge of the demonic and deathly in herself; and Lawrence so positions the choices available to her that Ursula's integrity now appears too closed to the risk of an advance as a person. In 'Woman to Woman' she cannot accept suffering with the resignation of Hermione, but the will for life behind her remark—' "I think it is degrading not to be happy" '—is also the will for self-deception and over-conservative optimism, which, refusing to admit her own sense of hurt when faced by Birkin's confession of failure on the island, asserts: ' "But *I'm* happy —I think life is *awfully* jolly." ' It is this unflinchingness, the feeling that to give any quarter to tragedy is a personal humiliation and a denial of all goodness, which arouses Birkin's irony in 'Water-Party' when Ursula calls herself a 'rose of happiness'. He sees her essential position in her dance with the Contessa and Gudrun at Breadalby. She is there the woman at the end of the last novel, no longer sustained in her idealization of Skrebensky, but refusing to sink into the disillusion of the other women about her. 'All her men were dead, it remained to her only to stand alone in indomitable assertion . . . dangerous and indomitable, refuting her grief' (p. 84). She is so near to the others in their hopelessness, sharing so much of their disbelief and treachery against men, yet not quite dragged down.

There seems, however, nothing actual on which to base her refutation of grief. All her resources have to go into upholding herself by the will, so that she is enclosed both against attack and release. In 'Mino' her sensual knowledge, with its belief in love and passion, cannot accept Birkin's spiritual offer of a 'mystic conjunction'; but if Birkin's spiritual richness is too unconnected to his 'frail, unsubstantial body' and the physical reality of the fuchsia tree's 'dangling scarlet and purple flowers', his loss of balance when he passes into spiritual assertiveness against her is due to her own hardening. Her sensual richness feels threatened, she is uncertain of her bearings, and in her distrust of the new consciousness she passes into the sensual wilfulness which is the equivalent of Birkin's spiritual kind of abstraction. So the beautiful light which he saw in her on the island, the 'powerful sweet fire', still present in the 'baffled light' of her nature, here changes. There comes 'a strange flash of yellow light' in her eyes, 'a curious devilish look', as she successfully insists in a submissive-dominant way on the supremacy of love.

Taken far enough, that light of the will brings her into the circle of radiant arrogance, the 'luminousness of supreme repudiation', which she shares with Gudrun in 'Moony'—the terrible female duality: love and goodness above, demonic hatred of man beneath. When, by the will, her mental consciousness denies the savagery in herself, she is momentarily in unison with Hermione at the mill in 'Carpeting'. After the labourer's wife has thrown cloths over the cages of the noisy canaries to make them go to sleep, so, in like manner, Ursula veils her very real sensual differences with Hermione and agrees with her statements of creativity and goodness. While Ursula's consciousness blurs over the subtleties of difference between herself and Hermione, Birkin as he expounds his theory of duality to Gerald must appear—if reason is depended on as the only guide—no different in his being or in his attitude to male mastery than the other man. But though Hermione's values seem Ursula's—the wish ' "to see things in their entirety, with their beauty left to them, and their wholeness, their natural holiness" '—Ursula cannot disguise from herself (p. 135) her feeling of repulsion from Hermione: 'she tried to feel at one with Hermione, and to shut off from Birkin. She was strictly hostile to him. But she was held to him by some bond, some deep principle. This at once irritated her and saved her.' And Birkin later, far off amongst his sickness and spiritual working through of the corrupt knowledge, knows his link with the creative life is not lost: 'He knew that Ursula was referred back to him. He knew his life rested with her' (p. 191).

Ursula's conscious knowledge is inadequate, but, as in *The Rainbow*, the Brangwen woman is still the conscience-keeper. Gudrun, like her mother, would break the meaningful sequence of relationship, 'sheer off' in fantasy. But as Ursula stitches at her embroidery in the opening chapter, there remains about her the sense of the weaver of the endless web, the Penelope who waits, and guards the thread of continuity. Gudrun breaks it as they turn aside at the church door, but Ursula in her waiting feels

strangely troubled, 'as if it rested upon her' that the bridegroom
has not yet come. It is as if there lingers in Lawrence's mind a
remembrance of the knowledge which Ursula reaches in *The
Rainbow*, after Skrebensky has fallen as her symbolic creation: 'It
was not for her to create, but to recognise a man created by God.
The man should come from the Infinite and she should hail him.'
Such language is not at ease in *Women in Love* (as 'Excurse'
shows), but the sense of responsibility given to Ursula persists, as
she watches the hill beyond the church for sight of the bridegroom's carriage. She sees it and turns (p. 13) to warn the wedding party and guests of his imminence: 'But her cry was
inarticulate and inaudible, and she flushed deeply, between her
desire and her wincing confusion.' It is Birkin who comes with the
bridegroom, who *is* the bridegroom whom Ursula cannot as yet
acknowledge in fuller consciousness.

She withholds the new kind of pledge he later seeks from her
because of the demonism it would acknowledge, but though her
moral fear is essential in restraining Birkin's spiritual adventure
(just as his persistence in knowing beyond her love is essential), it
ultimately rests with her to guarantee the integrity of what he
brings her, to ensure a fine precision in his searchings so that he
does not blunder into offering her evil as if it were good. He is
furnishing her with negative realizations, but it depends on her to
place them in proportion to other truths within an inclusive moral
ordering, and to release him (and, hence, herself) from anarchy.
It is, therefore, as an arbiter of man's activity, curious as to his
new ventures, that in her wanderings on a bright spring day by
the lake she comes upon Birkin working noisily away at a punt.
After the trance-like liaison between Gudrun and Gerald in the
preceding 'Sketch-Book' chapter, after the 'perfect', finished
movement by which Gerald controls the boat, Birkin's 'tinkering'
repairs and his awkward steering of the punt, landing himself and
Ursula on the marshy island, have an amateurishly clumsy but
good-humoured enthusiasm. He has recovered from the violence
dealt him by Hermione at Breadalby, and now, having patched
up the craft of the spirit, he is off again to explore into the corrupt
secrets. The humorous life of the episode comes not only from
Birkin's blithe acceptance of Ursula as his partner on his island of
supposed exile from all humanity but from his acknowledgement
of her as the one who sanctions his purpose. ' "You are your

father's daughter," ' he says (p. 115), showing her his handiwork, ' "so you can tell me if it will do." ' Like Miriam hesitating as Paul tries to mend the umbrella or Ursula with her father's blind groping in *The Rainbow*, the woman stands again in the difficult balance of encourager and restraining sceptic.

But for the moment the sceptical judgement forces Birkin back from the evil-smelling plants of the island, returns him to the mainland, the mill, his submission to Hermione and his acceptance of Ursula's plea for love in 'Mino'. The self-protective will of Ursula prevents her from accepting Birkin's offer until the defences begin to wear away, opening her to evil and death. In 'Water-Party' he has the advantage over the demonism which he, 'with sardonic comprehension', has seen her give in to, at the end of 'Mino'. When with Gerald he stumbles on the female circle of enchantment, he has found her out behind her belief in her own Cordelia-like innocence; but his mocking dance, though it awakes an inner response in Ursula, cannot be acknowledged consciously by her. She fails to match it, polarize it, and so make the evil seem less than dominant. It is not until after the deaths in the lake that the belief in her total goodness suffers irretrievably. The consciousness which has temporarily allied her with Hermione's values and protested at Gerald's cruelty, now loses its faith and its defensiveness. She cannot hold on to life much longer as a creative thing, it seems. All the knowledge there is to be had seems (p. 183) to have been exhausted by her: 'She knew all she had to know, she had experienced all she had to experience . . . there remained only to fall from the tree into death.' She comes in 'the ultimate darkness of her own soul', to see death as she has seen life, treating it with joy. The old innocence has gone, and the only innocence left is death.

But Birkin is ahead of her in the death-process of the spirit, forestalling her escape before she disappears altogether as an individual into the generalization of the wish-fulfilment. Without his realizing, she is again found out in her privacy, but this time she is ready to match him with the demonism in herself, nearly at the point of acknowledging it. The hatred which he engenders in her, when he, a 'crouching idol', sits by the fire, is something which seems (p. 190) 'to throw her out of the world into some terrible region where nothing of her old life held good.' She has entered the 'stark and impersonal' plane of which Birkin spoke in

'Mino', where the hatred has an intense, clear-cut purity, and where she has something of the 'good pure-tissued demons' whom Birkin mentions so vaguely on the island. There has been a clarification: she does not know why she hates Birkin, but at least she cannot escape the knowledge that she has been overcome by this hatred. It brings her to a part-equilibrium with him, in which the demonism is pure only if it is kept within the boundaries of serious relationship, where it becomes an essential of the fight for life between them—a fight that neither must win in order that both may win. Yet though Birkin is again the forestaller in knowledge in 'Moony', returning her to the fight, it rests with Ursula in 'Excurse' to free the relationship of the possibilities that her desire for love means only a female domination and that his desire for something beyond love means only male tyranny in disguise. In order to reach the inevitability of this differentiation, however, Lawrence must carefully define the alternatives.

3

In 'Mino' Birkin speaks (p. 143) about commitment in marriage: ' "If you are walking westward . . . you forfeit the northern and eastward and southern direction." ' Because of the responsiveness of each to the discipline of the other—Birkin spiritually exploring ahead, and Ursula's fear guiding him back on course when he strays too far into corrupt territory; Birkin resisting the demonism in her restraint and causing her to swerve with him towards and away again from the corruption—there is moral peril in such navigation, and yet, by it, a chance to avoid what Birkin calls all 'the possibilities of chaos'. Enough of those possibilities have to be known for Birkin and Ursula to earn the right to forgo the choice of an escape into what might seem freedom beyond their relationship. They have to know enough within their boundaries to make those boundaries morally real, but if they know more than is sufficient they will be demonists like Gudrun and Gerald. For Birkin and Ursula there must be a forfeiting of the 'northern' direction, as they define each other and steer a dangerous course, but for Lawrence their definition depends equally on what Gerald and Gudrun know unconsciously beyond the reach of Birkin's probing. Birkin in 'Man to Man' is no longer so naïve as when he pictures to Ursula on the island a clean, humanless world which her 'demoniacal soul' knows is farther off than he realizes; now he has consciously reached her instinctive knowledge, of the 'long and hideous way' corrupt humanity must go, but even as he vaguely expounds his sense of the 'many stages' of 'universal degeneration' yet to come, his knowledge can never be as advanced as Gerald's—nor needs to be. Gerald smiles at the strange talk, 'as if, somewhere, he knew so much better than Birkin, all about this: as if his own knowledge were direct and personal, whereas Birkin's was a matter of observation and inference, not quite hitting the nail on the head:—though aiming near enough at it' (p. 196).

To hit the nail on the head requires Gerald's precise, self-destructive talent, and though Birkin's blind aiming is near enough to arouse Hermione at Breadalby and Ursula in 'Sunday Evening', Birkin stands as far away from Gerald's position as Gerald does from that of Hermione and Gudrun. One realizes the scale of distance, the amount of wilfulness needed, between the thought of universal destruction and its possible achievement, when one moves from Birkin's naïve earlier wish—' "I abhor humanity, I wish it was swept away" '—to Hermione's declaration, with 'a dangerous and convincing humour in her bearing', that if somebody tried to take her away her symbol of social liberty, her 'national old hat', ' "Probably I should kill him." ' But in Hermione's desire (p. 98) to obliterate Birkin—'a thousand deaths mattered nothing now, only the fulfilment of this perfect ecstasy' —the will is faulty. It needs a determination, a straining against one's physical limits, of the kind which Gudrun, with her power for violence, is capable of, given her man-like opportunities. When a collier woman's voice mocks her green stockings, the anger (p. 7) is ruthless: 'She would have liked them all annihilated, cleared away, so that the world was left clear for her.' But in the 'many stages' which Lawrence suggests between Birkin's comparatively trivial wish and its actual carrying out, Gerald is nearest fulfilment, as the man who has killed in the past, who has broken all organic resistance to his systematizing of the mines, and who, after his treatment by Gudrun in 'Water-Party', can say so confidently, ' "I'd have murdered her for two pins." '

Therefore, Birkin's knowledge is detached, but not so inexperienced that he cannot recognize from afar the kind of duality which, in Gudrun's case, gives her the momentary advantage

over Gerald as a murderess. To articulate this to-and-fro movement between violent extremes, Lawrence has needed the experience of his last three novels—the wild passage between vin-
dictiveness and pity in the relationship of Siegmund and Helena;
the recoil by Paul from Miriam's poignant love into the flood of
purely sensual love with Clara; the sickening fluctuation between
intense, egotistic pride and degrading social humility, which the
swing-boat symbolized in *The Rainbow*. Birkin's own capture by
this motion with Hermione does not prevent him analysing explicitly what the other novels only half-realized as a tragic danger.
' "It's the old story—action and reaction, and nothing between," '
says Birkin (p. 88) of Halliday's oscillations of feeling about
Minette—one moment, the reviled harlot; the next, the adored
baby-faced lily of purity. By his own experience, Birkin argues
against the love which Ursula offers as supreme, because of its
treachery. ' "Proud and subservient, then subservient to the
proud—I know you and your love. It is a tick-tack, tick-tack, a
dance of opposites." ' (P. 144.)

As Gudrun enacts this 'tick-tack' motion in 'Water-Party',
there begins the exhaustion of the 'possibilities of chaos' which
Birkin can only guess at in a healthily objective way. Gudrun's
intent makes her more than the 'fluffy sporadic bit of chaos',
which was the wild cat whom Birkin's tom foiled, like a playful
male check on female demonism. Gudrun, in her refusal to be
bounded by anyone and in her pursuit of an absolutist dominance,
with the world 'left clear for her', is no 'pure-tissued' demon.
But as she comes to the summer fête, one sees again how much she
suffers as a half-formed waverer on the rigid up-down route of
wilful, desensitized being. Neither a confidently distinct individual
nor completely one with the undifferentiated crowd, she knows
the lure of the masses yet wishes to be marked out lone, free, and
anarchically fearless above them. As with the people at the wedding, she suffers from an 'apprehensive horror of people in the
mass', but she is repulsed and fascinated at the same time: 'she
seemed to be backing away in antagonism even whilst she was
advancing.'

It is the duality of her position and the ironic equivocalness o
her expression which attract Gerald, especially when she describe
to him (p. 152) her loathing for (and yet suggests her luxuriating
in) a trip she once took on a Thames steamer. In her tale, there i

an inescapable relationship between the 'high' and the 'low', between herself and Gerald, which she insinuates as she tells of the vulgar, pleasure-seeking crowd of trippers on board the steamer and their pursuit for miles along the river-bank by urchins, calling from the mud for money. The children's cry from out of the mud—' 'Ere y'are, sir'—is *her* subtly vulgar appeal to Gerald for a share in his 'lordly' charity. The harlot's scream from 'that *awful* Thames mud' (like her scream at the crossing-gate) is disguised under social submissiveness, and having secured the use of Gerald's own private canoe, she continues the deferential role of 'the childlike, clinging woman' to 'the most important man she knew at the moment.'

The unconscious purpose of Gudrun's inroad upon Gerald's power is to take over his male courage, to forsake her womanly individuality in order to be a man, with a man's liberty. When she seizes the crossing-gate before the keeper can reach it, when she gives her word 'like a man' to Gerald about her safety in the canoe, when she later grasps hold of the rabbit and ignores his concern to 'let one of the men do that for you'—these are the signs of her determination to come up to the standard of mastery which Gerald has unwittingly set her and helps her towards. But to reach the transcendent state she must achieve a release from her self-conscious caution, break her fear by the will, mechanize her being to the point where no qualms, fears, or criticism by another can impede her perfect illusion of absolutism. In compelling a song from Ursula as an accompaniment to her dance against the cattle, Gudrun mechanically works up to a dominance of the will which she can only hold by a mindless trance. Her urge to back away and advance before the crowd is elevated into a ritual of her victory over them, as she approaches the herd of Highland bullocks, challenging in them the world of the collier masses whose watchful master is Gerald. When he appears on the scene, she is so self-bewitched that she is ready to defy master and masses, to wreck all the civilization for which he stands. Just before she rushes upon the animals, she visually brings together the victims of her attack in a typically clinching 'look' (p. 161)— 'She stood a moment, glancing back at Gerald, and then at the cattle.'

She is his sensational match, but though she has been carried to his height of power, where the masses stampede at her will, she has still to reckon with the personal Gerald, now becoming distinct from the functional Gerald who symbolizes his workers. The mood of lone somnambulism takes her far enough to present him with a strange *touché* of power, a mocking retort in her slap which answers to his previous subjugation of the mare. But the imbalance, the victory of one person over the other, which the absolutist purpose demands, has a paradox within it that comes from the illusion central to the desire. To reach the point where Gerald is not only subordinate but non-existent is for Gudrun the victor to see the waning of her success at its peak. Just as earlier when she and Ursula had created a little world of their own and yet by its very 'perfection' Gudrun felt tipped out of life again, so now at the maximum height of control over Gerald, when his mind has been defeated and his will temporarily allayed, Gudrun finds that his definite form is melting away into a shadow, leaving her uneasy in her command. The absolutist needs the agreement of the other to the fiction that she is all-sufficient. And very soon, with Gerald's will awakened again, alerted to the disaster on the lake, she is back where she started, thrust down the power-scale, and losing her trance-gained sureness, 'spontaneity', and magic. She is again her ordinary conscious self, paddling clumsily under Gerald's masterful command, and hurtfully isolated from the knowledge and action he reaches as he dives for the drowning couple. In the hierarchy of will and numbed fearlessness, Gerald clambering back into the boat and absently regarding the bandage round his injured hand is far beyond Gudrun, as she knows: 'he was the final approximation of life to her.' She returns in her dualism to the submissive character she acted previously, and, at the end of the chapter, having run the full circuit of 'tick-tack' action and reaction, she is preparing for the thrill of rushing to play the comforter to the bereaved man.

She backs away, but her advance, her raid upon Gerald' prerogative, has had its destructive effect. Her onslaught against his will changes everything hereafter, because now she has seriously narrowed his scope of assumption. Gerald, however, has allowed this to happen, unconsciously sought for this injury to his power, because of the duality in him which responds to her duality. As Birkin saw of Gerald at Shortlands, the man who fears to be murdered is one who conceals a desire to murder or be mur dered. The man who scans the visual surface watching for disruption, who has 'assumed responsibility for the amusements on the water', is the sentinel whose personal self is so spread across a mass-self that he invites attack upon a wide flank. He asks for it with a kind of subterranean purposefulness when he cautions Gudrun about the loan of the canoe—' "Don't, for *my* sake, have an accident" '—and gives his unconscious blessing to the female demon to wreak her havoc on all he superficially guards. It is a self-indifference, the hint of deliberate choice about a supposed accident, which is suggested by the wording of his explanation about his injured hand—' "I trapped it in some machinery" '—and which is emphasized by Ursula's response: ' "I hate people who hurt themselves." '

Yet to give himself over, as he does to Gudrun's spell, is to profit, to be relieved of his conscious responsibilities, to drift away from the strain of holding the surface together as a social commander. The will relaxes so far that he leaves behind the hurtful game he plays with Gudrun, with the senses cutting against the mind, and nearly lets his consciousness go entirely. But when he returns to the old responsibilities, his will has been irreparably damaged. The drowning 'accident' is a challenge which he cannot surmount. It is as if in their dance on the roof of the steam-launch, Diana and the young doctor had played out to the end the destructive drama which Gerald and Gudrun have only just begun, as if the chaotic oscillation of the other couple had swung them out of existence, down the scale of will into the water and mud. In this disaster, the 'interval' between the mind and the 'maelstrom' unconscious has terribly widened, for Gerald in his aggregate self, the representative of all his masses: 'The colliery people felt as if this catastrophe had happened directly to themselves' (p. 182). The devil has been allowed to supervene, to deny the vision of the social metaphysic, and it is up to Gerald's will to make good the damage and encompass the chaos as he controlled the mare. But the breach that the subterranean makes in the surface is too great to mend. Diving again and again for the bodies, Gerald finds his instrumentality defeated. He is no longer immune and perfect': he has gone out of focus as a distinct figure. All the suaveness of his shape and movement is reduced to an exhausted clumsiness, as he climbs out of the water 'slowly, heavily, with the blind clambering motions of an amphibious beast.'

The disaster in 'Water-Party' is a tragic blow struck at man's social identity, like the 'Marsh and the Flood' chapter of *The Rainbow*. But mention of such a comparison only serves to point the essential difference between the art of the two novels. The drowning in *The Rainbow* is a blow out of the infinite, which turns the novel again to survey the great horizons, the inexhaustible energies, beyond man's dictation. The deaths in *Women in Love* and Gerald's failure are an omen of necessarily exhaustible energies, of uncreative experience that has to be gone through before man is free to realize again the creative resources, to see the great horizons. The deathly mood which overcomes Gerald, Birkin, and Ursula is like a restriction, a cornering by pressure, so that their choice of alternative escapes from the responsibility of themselves becomes drastically reduced. 'Water-Party' marks the beginning of a closing-in on possible freedoms to which the first chapters are still open. In 'Sisters', 'Class-Room', 'Diver', the emergence of spring forms the quickening background to the women as they awake, half-aware, into uncommitted regard for the men, just as 'Shortlands' and 'In the Train' establish the same lack of commitment between the men themselves. Then summer begins to come in at Breadalby, and advances into the melting heat-haze of the 'Coal-Dust' vision. Just before the events on the lake bring the summer phase to a devastating finish, the sisters (in 'Sketch-Book' and 'Mino') make their challenges to the assumptions of the men, to which Gerald and Birkin, now coming seriously nearer, give a certain deference. Therefore, given its opportunity in 'Water-Party', the female demonism runs loose and destructive.

The upsurge is only just contained, but the pressures on Gerald's civilization can no longer be checked in the old way. The flood of corrupt feelings, the rain and mud of the following chapters, mark the onset of an autumn dissolution from which there is no escape. ' "You can't go away," ' says Birkin in 'Moony', strewing the waters, no longer with the daisies of an earlier season but with dead flower-husks. ' "There *is* no away. You only withdraw upon yourself." ' Yet in the new stage of his relationship with Ursula after 'Water-Party', such tightening of choice is essential. What destroys Gerald's social consciousness vitally weakens Ursula's belief in her own total goodness of purpose; and what releases her for a larger knowledge with Birkin by means of despair is the same closure of escape-routes which allows Gerald in 'Gladiatorial' to consider more seriously a relationship with Birkin.

But the new concentration which makes the individual withdraw from exhausted possibilities also turns Gerald more strongly towards Gudrun. As 'The Industrial Magnate' emphasizes, the social escape into work is cut off. Gudrun may have struck deeply at Gerald's mass-self, the man of functional magnitude, but Gerald has already taken the idea to such an extreme, so perfected the system, that personally there is nothing left for him to do. Gudrun's mockery merely liberates him from what he has already exhausted, cutting away at the generalized, social personality he has become, to bare, and, in the end, to free the man inside the casing. His scope narrowing, he fatally turns to her to see out a last chaotic direction, in which, as in his systematizing of industrial relationships, he is to bring the intimacies of the confined 'love'-relationship to destructive perfection. What Birkin knows more quickly in the spirit, Gerald by dreadful thoroughness is to corroborate in the long term, as he physically lays waste the possibilities of licentious escapism.

The 'Industrial Magnate' chapter and after traces the failure of old alternatives to energy. Thomas Crich's Christian spiritual love and compassion, as mineowner and husband, have foundered in contradiction: all the liberal goodness does not square with the sensual power it suppressingly denies. So the old paternalism is stricken—openly by the miners, surreptitiously by the demonic attacks of Crich's wife—and gives way to Gerald's social philosophy of functionalism. Spiritual love as a supreme value is made obsolete, and the sensual energies are leashed to mechanical efficiency, but the system is perfected at the cost of organic chaos. All that remains, after Gerald has taken his father's regime to a logical conclusion and cleared away the sentimentality, is the unashamedly brutal human relationship, the unremitting, demonic fight to the death. It is at this point that Gerald delays his entry upon such final inevitability, where the mind and the senses will break apart, and hesitates, degradingly, like his father. In shirking the issue, Gerald goes back to Thomas Crich's position—that of one whose will refuses to acknowledge the full horror of the sensual chaos he has called up against himself in his wife. As with his community ethic, Thomas Crich will not see the logic of his morality to its last steps. He will not yield up his mental code of goodness, whatever the hidden pressure of his wife's hatred, but his defences are breaking. He needs extra support, and at the moment in which Gerald's retrogression makes him one with his father, Thomas Crich has found in his child Winifred the figure who will help stave off the collapse by pure make-believe. Just before the old man dies he asks about the leakage from the lake which is running into the pits; but Winifred's determined illusion has already saved him from drowning in a complete, knowing death. In her play, she has made a 'proper dam' against the flood.

After Uncle Tom at Fred's wedding feast in *The Rainbow*, after Hermione at Breadalby and Gerald at the fête, Winifred becomes the latest entertainer, creating another temporary but smaller world of 'happiness' to play in. It is significant that she should make her first decisive appearance in the novel (after the 'Short-lands' chapter) as a voice screaming out of the darkness on the night of her sister Diana's drowning, with an ambiguous appeal to Gerald's power—'Di-Di-Di-Di'—which invokes destruction at the same moment as it calls him to save. She is another child from the mud—like Minette, like the urchins pursuing the tossed pennies of the 'paterfamilias' on board the Thames steamer, like Gudrun deferring to Gerald at the fête. Such figures provide a subservient innocence for the benefit of the adults, acting up to preserve them in their roles as proud or compassionate benefactors, like Billy Brangwen who plays a cherub, with 'a great solemnity of being good', to Birkin's angel.

The knowingness in Billy which makes Birkin's love slightly questionable, too loftily bodiless, is the basis on which Winifred is the saviour of the Criches. They need her quick duality between angel and demon: for her father she perfectly pretends that the darkness does not exist, but for Gerald and Gudrun she is the medium by which total nakedness of struggle can just be avoided. In Winifred the will acts more quickly across a smaller compass, keeping the duality safe so that the friction between surface and subterranean can still be enjoyed, so that the demonism can be savoured and fled from with free-ranging ease by reverting to the angelic pretence. But to avoid being caught in tragedy, the faster movement of action-reaction has to minimize its commitments. Life has to be a mocking game lived in insulated moments. If Birkin's changeableness seems slow compared with Gudrun's to-and-fro shifts, Winifred's motion is even more rapid than Gud-run's. In the moral reality of the novel, everyone has suffered in memory, conscience, and consequence, but Winifred, the refine-ment of escapism, 'could never suffer, because she never formed vital connections . . . could lose the dearest things of her life and be just the same the next day . . . in her every motion snapped the threads of serious relationship with blithe, free hands, really nihilistic because never troubled' (p. 212).

In miniature she guards the decencies of form, visually and socially, while at the same time she, like the adults, knows the pretence of it all. She can make her grotesque 'diagram' of Looloo the weary pckinese for her father's sentimental compassion, but knows 'a wicked exultation' together with 'real grief' for the dog behind her picture. She serves Gerald and Gudrun, when in the wilder teasing of the rabbit Bismarck there is a more dangerous tearing of the visual veil—Gudrun's implicit attack as she flaunts her battle-scratches. It is an excess which wounds Gerald's con-sciousness, and which is followed (p. 236) by another blow, the verbal suggestion of more to come: 'He felt again as if she had hit him across the face—or rather, as if she had torn him across the breast, dully, finally. He turned aside.' And there Winifred pre-serves the 'decencies' of the picture, angelically smoothing over the demonism:

'Eat, eat, my darling!' Winifred was softly conjuring the rabbit, and creeping forward to touch it. It hobbled away from her. 'Let its mother stroke its fur then, darling, because it is so mysterious—'

The tormented Bismarck in Gerald, the witch in Gudrun, can shelter behind Winifred's refusal to know the further bestiality ahead. By her make-believe caricature, her father is Looloo, Gerald is the caressed rabbit, and, in the last game of this little interlude, Gudrun is the high aristocrat who enters the house of suffering as a redeemer.

In this latter make-believe, however, Gerald is welcoming in his enemy, preparing for the final combat in the unconscious. The 'Threshold' chapter takes Gerald and Gudrun to the edge of uncommitment, where all the scruples of form have nearly dis-appeared. But Winifred, prompted by her father and brother, keeps the greeting ceremony together by her power for illusion. It is a stiff, ritualistic episode, where Winifred's 'odd, stately for-

mality' gives Gudrun the status she has always craved. There is a
pause on the threshold of hell for Gerald and Gudrun, but
Winifred provides the last disguise of innocence—as when she
insists (p. 280) to the mother dog and her litter: ' "you are as
beautiful as an angel on earth. Angel—angel—don't you think
she's good enough and beautiful enough to go to heaven, Gudrun?
They will be in heaven, won't they—and *especially* my darling
Lady Crich!" '

It is typical of Gudrun, the would-be lady, who is about to enter
on a hellish course with Gerald, that she should scorn Birkin at
his threshold with Ursula. In contrast, he hopes for a 'paradisal
entry into pure, single being', something that is beyond heaven
and hell, but which can only be reached by knowing them both.
'Death and Love' is the passage over the threshold for Gerald and
Gudrun, while 'Excurse' passes Birkin and Ursula into a different
kind of abandonment and, hence, into a different fate.

4

Like the other couple after 'Water-Party', Birkin and Ursula are
reluctant to commit themselves fully to the relationship. There is
a deathly harrowing at work in them, a breaking down of the old
consolations, which can only be endured in separateness. Birkin
goes off in illness and travel, to be away from woman's possessive-
ness, and Ursula turns back to her old life. Even when they
despairingly converge again in 'Moony', after their escapes, they
have not completely relinquished the insistent wilfulness which,
while it holds them safe against complete surrender to deathliness,
sends them apart again into opposing male and female camps.
While Ursula's defences are up Birkin's desire for a 'proud indifference' between them must seem (and, by the rousing of
wills, is made to be) a narrower thing—the male, egotistic desire
for the woman's submission to him, not to something beyond
both of them.

But now when Ursula reverts in consciousness to the exclusively
female positions of Gudrun and Hermione, where Birkin's pretensions are mocked to an extreme that goes beyond Ursula's own
feelings, these old escape-routes are closed. It is Ursula's new
conscious awareness which makes them known to be unsatis-

factory. She rebounds from Gudrun's arrogant satire, which lyingly makes Birkin appear only a bullying preacher who wants to make woman in the image of his ideas. She knows he wants more than this, but even in revulsion from her sister, Ursula still insists to herself (p. 258) on the supremacy of love: 'Man must render himself up to her. He must be quaffed to the dregs by her. Let him be *her man* utterly, and she in return would be his humble slave.' But the duality of this position is taken from her after her encounter with Hermione in 'Woman to Woman'. Again she defines herself consciously against the other woman, for Hermione, she sees, already has achieved the 'love' relationship with Birkin, with all its instability—the code of slavery to man in order to be mistress of him, so that Birkin's rebellion is a form of submission. Therefore, the anarchic demonism which Ursula has shared with Gudrun and the creative truths she has shared with Hermione are no longer acceptable, for if her sister's satire is too final, Hermione's positives are just 'old, withered truths' on the dying tree of knowledge. But to these Birkin clings by his own attack upon them, for here Birkin is to Hermione what the Crich family are to their dying father. Both Thomas Crich and Hermione in their spiritual belief in the absolutism of spiritual love are the last stubborn strongholds of the old beliefs—obsolete but perniciously and cynically tempting as a comfort.

Only after Ursula has defined her purpose and Birkin's as distinct from the vision of others can she have the knowledge to close off Birkin's spiritual retreat to Hermione. He is routed in 'Excurse' in a way that is reminiscent of Lydia's penetration of Tom's desire for the cultured Mrs. Forbes in *The Rainbow*. Hermione the *Kulturträger* is the dead end of the spiritual 'freedom' which runs from Mrs. Forbes and Winifred Inger, but only Ursula's growth in spiritual consciousness fits her to rival Hermione as both the sensual and spiritual bride to Birkin—demonically finding him out in her attack, yet, after she has broken his caring for the old things in Hermione, returning with tender serenity to offer a pledge of peace. It is as if she is sharing some new-found riches with Birkin: ' "See what a flower I found you," she said, wistfully holding a piece of purple-red bell-heather under his face' (p. 302).

After such violence, the paradisal simplicity that now prevails could seem merely a phase in the action-reaction game, but

Lawrence in 'Moony' has already suggested and surpassed the idea of confusion. When Birkin stones the moon's image in the pond, he sets going the clash of the light and dark waves which in one sense are the sinister fluctuations of the chaotic, anti-organic life, the female demonism which male arrogance calls up. As the broken fragments of moonlight work their way back into a whole —'making semblance of fleeting away when they had advanced' —it is Gudrun's deceptive motion that is seen as well as Ursula's. But the 'ragged rose' of the regathered moon which again and again survives the explosions is no childish daydream of perishable innocence, like Ursula's old belief in herself as solely a 'rose of happiness'. Such a rose as that is really a *fleur du mal*, like the beliefs of Winifred Crich or Hermione or Gudrun as she clutches the bouquet of gaudy flowers which confer on her an illusory status. The 'ragged rose' of Ursula and Birkin is a flower of equilibrium, the Rainbow of this experience, which only the two can reach together.

When Birkin shows Ursula the rings in 'Excurse', and so marks out the marriage ground, proclaims the boundaries, it is the 'rose-shaped, beautiful sapphire, with small brilliants' which is for Birkin, and hesitantly for Ursula, the best. But this 'paradise' above the conflict could so easily become an illusion which hides destructive motives, for even as Birkin and Ursula drive along looking at the sapphire, he suddenly swerves to avoid a cart, and she fears that he might kill her by 'making some dreadful accident'. As throughout the novel, Birkin comes perilously close to the kind of accidental-on-purpose indifference which more strongly governs Gerald as a fate. When Birkin arrives late at the wedding because he has been discussing the immortality of the soul with the bridegroom, his explanation—' "I was *really* punctual, only accidentally not so" '—and Ursula's anxious scepticism in the scene are to have their later parallels when Birkin pushes off in his punt (p. 116) to explore the rankness of the island: he 'veered clumsily in the pond. Luckily the punt drifted so that he could catch hold of a willow bough, and pull it to the island.' In his more self-responsible awareness in 'Excurse' he can with greater moral skill condemn luck as 'vulgar', but not before his own carelessness in 'Moony', his leaving it 'to fate and chance to resolve the issues', lets him drift into the quarrel with Brangwen when he comes to propose to Ursula, so that when she confronts them both, they appear to her like bullies of the same order. As at the wedding, the would-be bridegroom has come too late to be acknowledged.

In 'Excurse' the old self-thwarting carelessness still lingers: 'Why strive for a coherent, satisfied life? Why not drift on in a series of accidents—like a picaresque novel? . . . Why form any serious connections at all? Why not be casual, drifting along, taking all for what it was worth?' (Pp. 293–4.) For Birkin to go that far would lead him into submission to the hellish demonism, the reckless licence, which the yellow ring encloses symbolically. It is 'a squarish topaz set in a frame of steel' which he offers to Ursula after the near-accident, but not as a symbol of their total knowledge, for whatever the danger he knowingly includes in their relationship, he is still 'damned and doomed to the old effort at serious living.' So the 'hell' of the topaz ring is complemented by the 'heaven' of the first ring which Birkin offers her—'a round opal, red and fiery, set in a circle of tiny rubies'. Together, the paradisal sapphire, the sensuality of the opal, and the 'pure-tissued' demonism of the topaz form a trinity of knowledge, the three terms of serious fate. The 'carefulness' and 'consciousness' of *The White Peacock* are again demanded. The novel has narrowed the field of choice for everyone, but there is still an essential lati-tude. Just as Lawrence is concerned that Birkin's ideas alone shall not work Ursula into some spurious pattern of theory, so he is concerned that while Ursula still exercises her criticism of Birkin's being, her acceptance of the fate shall be a willing choice, and the fate itself beyond the narrowing dictates of the chooser. When she first feels the bondage implied in the rings, she draws back, but is afterwards overwhelmed by a sense of fate which 'seemed more than herself'. Later, in the aftermath of the quarrel, she again experiences (p. 302) a power which is beyond the in-dividual personality yet is expressed through it: 'His voice was so soft and final, she went very still, as if under a fate which had taken her. Yes, she acquiesced—but it was accomplished without her acquiescence.'

The delicately balancing relationship between choice and lack of choice, captivity and freedom, the acceptance of 'the beauty of fate, fate which one asks for', are factors which are totally absent from Gudrun's experience. The fate which Gerald presses on Gudrun in 'Death and Love' has, by contrast, a terrible exclusive-ness, allowing no sense of choice. It demands what Ursula has feared earlier in Birkin: submission not to something beyond the self, but to the rapacious gratification of one personality at the expense of the other. As in the latter phase of *The Rainbow*, Lawrence is deliberately using the word 'fate' in two differing meanings: for after Gerald's old father has gone—after spiritual love has passed away as the supreme value and only sensual love remains to be falsely asserted as the new supremacy—Gudrun's abandonment to Gerald is a surrender which defines Ursula's other kind of abandonment to Birkin. When Gerald appears in Gudrun's room (p. 335) for his sexual relief, he is 'inevitable as a supernatural being. When she had seen him, she knew. She knew there was something fatal in the situation and she must accept it. . . . She sighed. She was lost now. She had no choice.' As Hermione with Birkin, so Thomas Crich with Gerald: the old dying order hangs on to the living, and begets a pattern of ruthless compensation which brings Gerald to clutch at Gudrun's life as an equalizer. By drawing on her resources he can 'see out' his father, his work, his usual pleasures, and ultimately his own life. She is captured by a tragic rocking motion, a repeated see-saw imbalance, in which weights of individual suffering are continually being shifted and ironic rhythms created, so that power is always turning over into defeat and submission rising into victory.

As the pressure of deathliness increases against Gerald, the vampirism at work in him must seek replenishments, draining 'the wine of her life'. At the death of his father, however, the flood of deathliness is nearly breaking through. Thomas Crich avoids the final knowledge of chaos, his spiritual 'innocence' kept up to the last, even when the 'nurse in white' enters with her cleaning compassion to wipe away all 'the dark blood and mess' on which the old man chokes. But for Gerald, muffled and shapeless, his clothes plastered with dirt from his father's grave, there has to be a more drastic cleansing when he comes (p. 337) to Gudrun's bed. The pressure is shifted obscenely: 'Into her he poured all his pent-up darkness and corrosive death, and he was whole again. . . . And she, subject, received him as a vessel filled with his bitter potion of death.' As Gerald draws 'nearer' into Gudrun, the image of herself as a receiving 'vessel' of subordination widens and deepens, so that inversely her power expands. Gerald sinks to rest 'in the bath of her living strength', and she becomes the Magna Mater with her child. But as on the lake, success unstably passes into failure, and the 'great bath of life' widens still further, becomes a sea where Gerald sleeps and so is lost to her, separate, 'perfected' and unconscious in his own underworld: 'She seemed to look at him as at a pebble far away under clear dark water.' Again she is left out upon the surface, stranded in painful consciousness: 'She seemed to be hearing waves break on a hidden shore, long, slow, gloomy waves, breaking with the rhythm of fate, so monotonously that it seemed eternal.'

Gerald has come through the night to her room, like a 'supernatural being', a ghostly figure who needs to be restored to the physical firmness he has lost, and now, in contrast to his former certainty, shuns the light because he is 'risky in the common world of day'. At the expense of Gudrun, he gains the strength to continue, but such force of will, casting its spell over the gloom, is of another order from the power which Ursula sees in Birkin at Southwell—'one of these strange creatures from the beyond, looking down at her', one of 'the sons of God' who moves later through a 'good darkness' and, by a different power from Gerald, seems to put the world under a 'strange ban'. After the earlier part of 'Excurse', this symmetrizing interest is disappointing. There is here an unfortunate parallelism, a point-for-point measuring of Gerald against Birkin, which Lawrence employs, as if under the belief that he must make Birkin into a mystic lord who presents a new, positive equivalent to Gerald's kind of wilful aristocracy. Where Gerald is insubstantial in the concrete world, Birkin (with all the numbed words like 'dark', 'inscrutable', 'living', 'subtle', gathered round him) has a 'reality' which Lawrence insists on testing (p. 311) against the world: 'Even as he went into the lighted, public place he remained dark and magic, the living silence seemed the body of reality in him, subtle, potent, indiscoverable.'

That Lawrence is here (as in the wrestling scene in 'Gladiatorial') asserting Birkin's serious place as a man among men, regardless of what he is with Ursula, does not conceal what is quite literally a loss of *touch* with sensual certainty, a lack of proportion: Birkin is only entering a post-office to send a telegram and buy food. It is as if his daydream in 'An Island'—'a beautiful clean thought, a world empty of people'—has been allowed sway, because all criticism or mockery has, by nature of the episode, been removed. Instead, the 'mass' generalization, the momentary literary Absolute, provokes the *reader's* resistance or mockery within the 'uninterrupted' flow. When Lawrence can write, 'He sat still like an Egyptian Pharoah, driving the car,' it is not Birkin who is driving dangerously, but the novelist who wants to endorse a new direction for creativeness without being able to verify something that goes beyond the assured limits of the man-woman relationship. And, like Birkin's movement earlier, Lawrence has to swerve awkwardly to avoid the suggestion that Birkin as the 'son of God' is just a static idol of a corrupt religion.

The scene of Ursula's submission in the inn (p. 305) is too close to the old situation, where Gudrun the spurious 'child' submits to Gerald, where slaves quickly turn masters: 'something was tight and unfree in him. He did not like this crouching, this radiance—not altogether.' Ursula's anal touching is meant to be a freeing for them both, a taking of him as he has taken her, 'at the roots of her darkness and shame'. But though her acceptance of the man's 'last physical facts' routs the suggestion of corrupt absorption (the kind of interest which makes Gudrun's art pornographic, which places her at the beginning of the novel 'like a beetle toiling in the dust', and which gives her the significance of the Egyptian, dung-rolling scarab as she moulds her grotesque 'lumps of clay' in the studio at Shortlands), there is, nevertheless, an obscurity, a lack of frankness, which all the welcoming joy of the scene wants to pass over. There is the same obliqueness, and the uneasy correction of a mistaken effect, when Birkin's 'Egyptian' posture in the car and his 'unthinkable' immobility begin to resemble the deadly mindlessness of Gudrun as she intently studies the water-plants. Lawrence has to apply to Birkin's 'pure Egyptian concentration' a touch of flexibility—a 'Greek' kind of 'lambent' and 'free' intelligence, an awareness that chooses the direction for the other consciousness to follow.

Difficulty arises with 'Excurse', after Ursula's and Birkin's battle in the lane, not only because Lawrence wants to distinguish between Birkin's new creative power and Gerald's force, but also because in the Southwell scene, Lawrence wants to be consistent with the form of *The Rainbow* in an overt way when he has already been so throughout *Women in Love* in a progressive, if hidden manner. When Will Brangwen fails to satisfy Anna's consciousness about his mystic beliefs, when the little imps of the Cathedral mockingly point to freedoms beyond the old circumscription, there begins a great circling out into dark knowledge, where the moral consciousness has previously fallen short. The insane, sensual egotism which Will arrives at with Anna is not as extreme, as denying of civilization, as the knowledge which Anton reaches in further fields. But while Anton's soul is lost under the African blood-worship and the mindless demonism, Birkin's exploring soul is able to remain conscious of the corrupt processes, returning the knowledge as part of a new moral order and offering the articulate metaphysic to Ursula which Will vainly has sought to offer Anna.

Therefore, when Ursula and Birkin come down into Southwell they return as visitors to an older religious framework (' "Father came here with mother . . . when they first knew each other" ', Ursula remarks of the Minster) which has been superseded and re-expressed because the 'freedoms' symbolized by the imps have been known and morally incorporated. This is the basis on which Ursula accepts her man as one of the sons of God, and so fulfils the Covenant of *The Rainbow*, the ideal of reconciliation. After all the new conditions have been reckoned with, before Ursula can reach such acceptance, Lawrence feels ready to suggest again the joy of 'religious art' which blesses Tom and Lydia in their coming together ('When at last they had joined hands, the house was finished, and the Lord took up his abode. And they were glad'). Now, after their sacraments, Ursula and Birkin proceed (p. 306) to what is their wedding breakfast: 'They were glad, and they could forget perfectly. They laughed and went to the meal provided.' Yet here Lawrence is too *formally* consistent with *The Rainbow*, and too concerned to ensure the contrast between the couple who have found freedom within the discipline of marriage and Gudrun and Gerald who are terribly imprisoned in their licence. The contrast with the others' tragedy does not need such symmetry because the sense of difference is already more subtly manifest in a way that is especially *Women in Love*'s not *The Rainbow*'s.

Despite the over-emphatic laughter at the inn, where Lawrence invokes the *Rainbow* mood uneasily in a novel whose expectations have advanced beyond it, there is a humorous consciousness round Birkin and Ursula which Gerald and Gudrun can only allow in to their relationship in a tightened mode, as tense

mockery, with the freer awareness taken out of it. However rational
they are, there is no room for real conscious knowledge in the
exclusive intimacy of Gerald and Gudrun, where undestructive
laughter and explanations dare not interfere with the movement
of the absorbed, implicit drama. A polished, stylized superbness,
a magnificently absolute domination of each by the other: these
are the criteria which make any natural misjudgements, hesitations, and fumblings by the will seem peculiarly horrible. To be
exposed at an awkward moment is to give destructive opportunities
to the other.

Birkin and Ursula forfeit such advantages and such kind of
'separateness', just as Lawrence after 'Excurse' is ready not to
insist on Birkin's vitality as something that might redeem mankind
after Gerald's mechanizing has 'seen out' the corruption. It is as
though Lawrence draws back from his absolutist-looking claims
for Birkin's 'potency', from all the uncertainty which lies ahead in
the future, in order to keep unimpaired the integrity of what at
least has been consciously resolved between Birkin and Ursula.
The test that Lawrence would like to make—the proof of Birkin as
a leader or comrade with other men—has here to be subsidiary to
the only truth he can affirm: that of the enduring quality, the
infallibility, of what has been established between him and Ursula.
The frozen, abstract setting of the final chapters is the furthermost
season of proof that Lawrence can envisage, and their journey
through it, their biding by a mutual pledge, is the endurance of
faith in the reality of what they have together, whatever the seeming endlessness of the wintry disillusion. When they pass out from
England they seem 'like one closed seed of life falling through dark,
fathomless space'; and hereafter their course is undetermined.
They are moving but suspended; the creative mystery is alive but
waiting.

The end-of-the-world abstraction through which they pass is
the place of the 'last issues', that extreme state to which Birkin
looked ahead in the 'Mino' chapter, where he foresaw that 'love
gives out'. It is where Gerald's visual civilization, so hurtfully
picturesque, so ravaged by eyes and wills, reaches a brilliant,
snow-blinding climax. The disintegrating psyche goes white.
Yet there is an enticing alternative to these sterile, inhuman heights,
for Ursula suddenly remembers the land of darkness towards the
south, the Italy of 'dark fruitful earth' where she thinks of making

a Romeo and Juliet romance with Birkin, akin to the *Paul et Virginie* life he suggested on his island. But at this extremity such escapes are illusions, with Italy as much an imaginative snare as Hermione, its cultured devotee in 'Woman to Woman'. The Italy of the feelings is retrograde: one reaches it down the old Imperial road, down the old route of action-reaction. As a creative alternative it is an optical illusion of fruitfulness, like the international horizons at Breadalby or Gudrun's visual distancing of herself. It is only from the place in the spirit, where alternatives have been cleared away to reveal the inevitability of 'the eternal closing-in', that one can really see a point beyond this white existence—that something 'more impersonal and harder—and rarer' which Birkin spoke of in 'Mino' and to which the mountain peaks signal—'like the heart petals of an open rose', 'like transcendent, radiant spikes of blossom in the heavenly upper world, so lovely and beyond.' Any other paradise seems personal make-believe, so that when Ursula expands in a wave of conceitful power before the Germans in the guest-house and imaginatively flies like a bird among the stars, the *übermenschlich* freedom is anarchic, not real enough to make her forsake the 'star-equilibrium' which holds her with Birkin. It is a sanity which persists beyond the phase of licentious demonism which sways Birkin after the dance in the guest-house.

For Gudrun the horror is to know only the hell, to be, in a sense, with those envious people who stand looking in at the Crich's summer fête, 'like souls not admitted to paradise'. She is shut out by a 'wall of white finality' because she wants to possess transcendence as an absolute personality, so that coming *alone* into 'a oneness with all, she would be herself the eternal, infinite silence,' not like her sister who 'belonged only to the oneness with Birkin.' But Gudrun is denied her consummation because she is trapped with Gerald in a see-sawing relationship of eternal discrepancy—'one destroyed that the other might exist, one ratified because the other was nulled.' The only way for Gudrun to achieve the equivalent of a paradisal entry into life is by her mechanical usage of Gerald: hence the bursts of wild tobogganing with him, when by a mindless 'ecstasy of physical motion', she gets her moments of absolutist sensation and oblivion—'she seemed to pass altogether into the whiteness of the snow, she became a pure, thoughtless crystal.'

And here (p. 411) the irony of her transcendence by means of Gerald becomes finally intolerable: he *has* been her escape from the mud-life breakdown, but he has only lifted her from a rudimentary dissolution to take her with him many more stages in the long process of disintegration. She is travelling towards her fate along a more wilfully developed track, but, in the flights in the snow, travelling towards it, nevertheless: 'Then there was a great swerve at the bottom when they swung, as it were, in a fall to earth in the diminishing motion.' If Birkin steers near danger, though 'not quite hitting the nail on the head', Gerald here is perfecting his precision of aim to a hair's-breadth, all his energy reduced to this last burning up of the will. He is indifferently relentless with Gudrun, taking her with him along his line of destructive fate in order to go through all the stages of dissolution which are possible. He is now so far from what Birkin calls 'pure integral being', so far from an 'organic hold' on life, that he seems to be passing out of human shape into mechanical force, into the abstract physics of 'velocity and weight', flying onward to his end 'more like some powerful, fateful sigh than a man.'

Gudrun feeds his will to carry on the logical working out of his fate, but she lacks his blind, insane courage. She must extract herself from knowledge of the tragic momentum, and again by illusion cut herself off from the reality of the sequence. Like Anna in the Cathedral, she must clutch at anything which says that Gerald's way is not the final expression, that there are freedoms he cannot know. There are, as Lawrence suggests in the knowledge that Birkin and Ursula hold together, but Gudrun herself cannot believe in these. Along her direction, her only hope of staving off the inevitable is to break away in desperate self-delusion. Winifred Crich delayed the process earlier, softening the blows with her pretended goodness, but at this point of the 'last issues' where belief in the supremacy of sensual love 'gives out' for Gudrun and Gerald, such assumptions are obsolete, too sentimental. To avoid suffering, conscience, and consequence at this extreme stage, commitment to reality has to be reduced to an even smaller minimum than Winifred's; which is why Loerke is the saviour at the place of the 'eternal closing-in', like an irreducible molecule of vision—'distinct and objective, as if seen through field glasses'—who has eradicated any pretence of good feeling. 'In the last issue he cared about nothing, he was troubled about nothing, he made not the slightest attempt to be at one with anything. He existed a pure, unconnected will, stoical and momentaneous.' (P. 417.)

In Loerke Gudrun meets at last her real partner, for keeping up with Gerald's extremeness is a strain, too ultimately dangerous. As Minette reverts to Halliday after Gerald, so Gudrun draws back to the half-man she can deal with, back to 'the little wastrel', the 'street arab', the 'mud-child', for in Loerke, the man of the ordinary masses and the modern artist, she has the true complement to herself. Gerald is the genuine *avant-garde* of experience, taking civilization to a pitch of chaos where everything shall be mechanically destroyed, 'seen out' with visual thoroughness; but Loerke ebbs in clever postponement of that end. It is no longer enough just to retreat from chaos into the carefully lit fantasy world of the little art-studio—as did Gerald, Gudrun, and Winifred at Shortlands. Escape from the end has to be bolder, as Loerke sees, by bringing art to the place of work itself before civilization is destroyed because industrial work becomes intolerable to the senses. In this degrading stop-gap, art's duty is to make ugly labour beautiful, 'maddeningly beautiful'. Gerald may pass on in scorn at Loerke's intent, but the masses and their artist will not follow him, for Loerke, the 'final craftsman' of the novel and the last entertainer, keeps things diverted. His granite frieze for the German factory (p. 414) is a mad, mocking picture of mass entertainment in the twentieth century—a fairground scene of ecstatic restriction, channelled frenzy, with peasants and artisans 'drunk and absurd in their modern dress, whirling ridiculously in roundabouts, gaping at shows, kissing and staggering and rolling in knots, swinging in swing-boats, and firing down shooting-galleries.' This is the 'side-show' existence, the maelstrom of the heaving mud-life cynically contained, which puts the seal on the other fairground scenes of compensation in *The White Peacock* and *The Rainbow*.

But Loerke himself is never the physical partaker of the wildness he sets in motion, as when in the guest-house he stands aside from the licentious gaiety he has provoked, for his detachment serves his other style of art, something which is safe for a higher level of chaotic response. In his bronze statuette of the rampantly phallic stallion, stretched in a frozen transcendence, with its naked girl rider pathetically trying to hide her nakedness, Loerke provides another insulated effect, like his frieze, but for a more refined decadence. The statuette has suggestions of pity and arch-cruelty, both of which the demonists can enjoy dualistically, safe from the reality of suffering because Loerke has disconnected the work from past and future (just as he has ruthlessly cast aside the girl model he used for the rider). If the black races, in Birkin's theories, leave behind their Pacific carving of the pregnant woman as the sum of so much experience after their 'organic hold' has broken, so Loerke's absolutist art seems the white contribution. The statuette is an icon from a perverse religion, with Loerke as the saviour of the world in a way that Birkin can never be.

Halliday in the Pompadour has mocked Birkin's earnestness as religious mania by assuming a priestly voice to utter Birkin's theories, but Loerke is a more grotesque caricature of saviour-hood—both in his art and in the relationship which he takes up with Gudrun. When he saves Gudrun from Gerald, and proposes a relationship of purely mental consciousness, devoid of love and sensuality, it is like a further distorted imitation of Birkin—as when in 'Mino' he offered to Ursula something beyond love. Now Loerke, disregarding Gudrun's looks in the same way that Birkin ignored Ursula's, offers a 'singleness', but not for the purpose of a moral freedom together. It is just a pact of security so that their separate wills can function in anarchic illusion, knowing how to avoid answering the real questions which have threatened absolu-tist behaviour throughout the novel:—as in Winifred's sorrowful question to the dog she has teased—' "My beautiful, why did they?" '; or in Gerald's fruitless query—' "Why do you want to drive them mad?" '—when Gudrun menaces his cattle; or in Gudrun's own unanswerable question to herself when she chal-lenges Gerald over the cattle—' "Why *are* you behaving in this *impossible* and ridiculous fashion—?" '

Because Gudrun and Gerald cannot answer these questions in their consciousness, they are committed to a destructive, implicit fate. By his mindless drive to his end, Gerald has put himself beyond the reach of questions, but Gudrun, delaying, is still at the mercy of taunts such as 'What next?', 'What for?', 'Why don't I love you?', 'Whither?' Loerke, with his confused mixture of European languages, his 'suggestive vagueness', has to let the future peter out in abrupt blankness:

'Do you know,' he said, suddenly looking at her with dark, self-important, prophetic eyes, 'your fate and mine, they will run together till—' and he broke off in a little grimace.

'Till when?' she asked, blanched, her lips going white. She was terribly susceptible to these evil prognostications, but he only shook his head.

'I don't know,' he said, 'I don't know.' (P. 451.)

They are immune from the next step in the related sequence, while they nervously relive the lives and art of the past centuries. Gudrun's next move from here—like her shift of vision by the level-crossing—will be another absolutist illusion, a whimsically picaresque digression: 'One might take a ticket, so as not to travel to the destination it indicated. One might break off, and avoid the destination.' (P. 462.)

5

Gerald, however, goes the whole distance, so far that in his last fights with Gudrun his consciousness is destroyed and briefly he is loosed into a sense of the real heights of existence, beyond his old knowledge. The female demon tears at him, yet, like all her blows, she is releasing him, one by one, from the attachments which have held him prisoner: 'Why should he close up and become impervious, immune, like a partial thing in a sheath, when he had broken forth, like a seed that has germinated, to issue forth into being, embracing the unrealised heavens' (p. 437). It has taken a long, cruel effort to deliver him from the 'horny covering of disintegration' which Ursula saw enclosing the human world at the end of *The Rainbow*. If Gudrun's first blow symbolized the death of his social responsibilities, her last—struck in the fight between herself, Gerald, and Loerke—severs him finally from her power. He can stagger away from the sordid embroilment, leaving Gudrun to her fictitious nobility with Loerke, and knowing at last, ' "I didn't want it really." '

Only now has he had enough, when he has physically exhausted the desires of the will, when he is so wounded that his new freedom for creative possibilities must be tragically brief. For the blow which delivers him into birth, whose impetus sends him blindly climbing towards the peaks and the 'unrealised heavens' in himself, is also the blow which breaks the frayed connection between the mind and the senses, so that at last he falls down into the full death of the psyche which his father avoided. Gerald has carried the process so far beyond the worn, compassionate values of his England, so far beyond the social sense of his father and the liberal nationalism of Hermione, that his death assumes a racial, Western significance. By seeking his own murder unconsciously when he most fears it, he has finally killed all pitying love and its treachery as an absolute: 'Gerald's father had looked wistful, to break the heart: but not this last terrible look of cold, mute Matter' (p. 472). So love gives out in these 'last issues': there can be no feeling which can claim Gerald in death, fallen out of individual distinctness into an inert mass, a stiff block of ice that chills Birkin's heart.

Gerald in his destructive seeing-out has physically taken the long way round, too thorough in his persistence to live after he has exhausted all the lesser opportunities which engaged his aristocratic kind of energy. It is appropriate that Birkin, who has more quickly taken the shorter route of the spirit, should lament Gerald as an 'Imperial Caesar dead and turned to clay', for the idea of Gerald's ruined nobility belongs especially at this moment to Lawrence's sense of tragedy, as one sees it in the Hardy *Study*. It is as if Gerald takes his place among those who for Lawrence actively transgress against life, the great darers like Oedipus, Hamlet, Macbeth, Lear, or Orestes, who sin transcendently and perish under stress of all the forces they have wreaked upon themselves. But Lawrence cannot rest Gerald easily among such thoroughgoing, uncowardly adventurers of negation, for Birkin's sorrow—' "I didn't want it to be like this" '—admits a scruple which cannot completely accept the need for Gerald's unremitting hold on his fate, even though, in the strategy of the novel, Gerald's experience is necessary to substantiate the cause of the living, of Birkin and Ursula. Still Lawrence ponders, in Birkin, all that might have been different, if Gerald in his last wanderings had found the 'great rope' of knowledge by which he could have hauled himself up to the summit of the pass, and thence to the peaks and the heavens. If he had caught on to the life-line which Birkin offered in would-be comradeship, the tragic fate might have been relinquished, and the 'unfinished meaning' of the wrestling in 'Gladiatorial' furthered into something less abortive: 'Birkin remembered how once Gerald had clutched his hand with a warm, momentaneous grip of final love. For one second—then let go again, let go for ever. If he had kept true to that clasp, death would not have mattered. . . . Gerald might still have been living in the spirit with Birkin, even after death.' (P. 471.) It is a speculation which applies Lawrence's sense of 'tragic art' in the *Study*—'man, remembering what lies behind him, how the hands met and grasped and tore apart . . . '—to a situation beyond man's and woman's breaking of the sequence.

At the same time one is reminded that Gerald's distrust of the other man's love has kept Birkin's feeling in the state of being a suspect thing: if Gerald could have been conceived as accepting the relationship—as Lawrence more easily conceives Ursula's acceptance—then, like Birkin's feeling for her, his love for Gerald might have been changed into something less 'final' and been given its placing, its stable reality. But Gerald cannot be the arbiter for Birkin in the way that Ursula is. While Gerald renews his single-minded pursuit of his fate, Birkin must look like, and is not allowed to be more than, an unsatisfactory saviour. When Gerald decisively, in his last moments, avoids the 'little Christ' sticking from the snow on its pole, he not only flees the touch of the Loerkes, the poor people who are to inherit the earth, but also the Jesus spirit in Birkin, the 'good angel' in him which Ursula can only trust when he and she are able to get beyond it.

Her caution now, in drawing him back from the dead and the unfulfilled idea, in suspecting that the desired love is mere wilful theorizing, puts up the novel's guard against Birkin's rule by programme. She is placed in the same position as Gerald's disbelief. Looking from within his tragic limitations, Gerald has been right, according to his narrow law, to disdain interference in his fate by good. Despite hesitations, he has remained true to the conscious form he has, working it out to fulfilment and breaking it. Yet, within another part of himself, Lawrence finds such destructive continuity too final, too damnably and gloriously complete. Tragedy at the end of the world may need a hard courage to interpret in its stages, but Lawrence, in mastering an entire span of tragic experience, is concerned to relieve it of its perverse grandeur. Where Gerald runs to a perfect closure, Birkin and Ursula do not forsake the novel's right to knowledge beyond the superb, absolutist drama; and where Lawrence risks Birkin on an unascertained positive, Ursula's scepticism does not disable the notion, but adds a sane, guarded edge to the idea, which at this moment is precisely what it deserves. In these last pages—so consummate and abstract in one way, so pressingly immediate in another—there is a poise which comes from the interchanging life of the novel as a whole. Here is its greatness. Between suffering all, in tragic, futuristic insight, and knowing enough—enough to be free to keep the sane life true—there goes the consciousness which wins the unique reality of *Women in Love*. On these terms it is durable.

PART TWO

Four Americans and the
Adversities of Morality

MIRANDA. O! wonder!
How many goodly creatures are there here!
How beauteous mankind is! O brave new world,
That has such people in't!

PROSPERO. 'Tis new to thee.

Consider the character of the persons concerning whom Miranda says
this—then Prospero's quiet words in comment—how terrible!

—Herman Melville, writing in his copy of Shakespeare's *Works*, 1849

The slow, smouldering, corrosive obedience to the old master Europe,
the unwilling subject, the unremitting opposition.

Whatever else you are, be masterless.

'Ca Ca Caliban
Get a new master, be a new man.'

—D. H. Lawrence in *Studies in Classic American Literature*, 1923

I

Waste and Idealism in the *Tales* of
Edgar Allan Poe

THE endeavour of *Women in Love* is remarkable in its scope. It is as if here, in gathering to his vision the corrupt potentiality of man that he may yet reach beyond it, Lawrence has earned the right to say with Gudrun, but in a very different sense, '—All that, and more.' His understanding of tragedy has been carried beyond the immediate culture of his own experience, beyond the England of *The Rainbow*, and one realizes anew the extensiveness and continuity of this forward movement. As in the *Study* and *The Rainbow* Lawrence's moral intelligence manifests itself in *Women in Love* as a vital historical sense, a power of envisaging and tracing the further phases of spiritual life. Without this historical sense as an extension of his organic understanding, Lawrence would not have been able to refine and advance his intuitive perceptions by means of the past experience revealed to him by American literature of the nineteenth century. For here, among the Americans where the will is taken to its furthermost reaches, Lawrence comes into possession of the insights which ultimately comprise the great moral analysis of *Women in Love*.

The American experience affects *The Rainbow* as well, but not with the crystallizing force that it exerts upon the later novel, for by the time of *Women in Love* Lawrence's imagination has entered a new period of development. And even after the completion of *Women in Love* Lawrence continues to evolve and alter in his imaginative relationship with American literature, so that his first essays on the Americans (1917–18) reveal him at a level of engagement which in some ways is markedly different from that at which he works as a novelist.[1] The shift of interest warns us that Lawrence's view of the Americans as a critic is not necessarily the same thing as his novelistic understanding of them. But despite his changes, Lawrence offers a consistency of theme as a

[1] See below p. 302 ff.

critic. What has concerned him in Hardy's novels continues to engage him in the work of Poe, Hawthorne, Melville, and Cooper: that is, the problem of the conscious moralist at odds with the unconscious artist.

Certainly the problem exists but as part of a larger American dilemma. One can see, as Lawrence points out in his criticism, that to rise to the experience, to meet it with the consciousness it requires, is not easy for the American writer. Often the latter places false or inappropriate constructions upon experience, and he can be his own enemy, wilfully paralysing the power of genuine evaluation, killing a theme before it can become meaningful or original. But if one wants to understand the importance of American literature for Lawrence the novelist it is necessary to lay aside for the moment his preoccupations as a critic, and to make clear some of the larger difficulties to which the Americans are forced to respond. For it is the quality of their response and struggle which is crucial to Lawrence's art. The assertive extremes in their work which are so valuable to Lawrence are reactions to pressure, strange definitions of individualism which the American writers are compelled to present in defiance of all that intimidates the coherence of the self. In this situation fantasy is produced, and there is the constant temptation for the American artist to order life according to an idealism of the perverse will. His opportunity for searching out the sources of authority in the self—and so finding the centre of stability from which proportion and reality in art take their reference—is continually being eroded by distractions, by the hurly-burly of a democratic consciousness, by an external crowding and distortion of spiritual feeling.

The *Tales* of Poe are especially relevant at this point of discussion. Not only are they significant to Lawrence in *Women in Love*, but it is Poe, above all, who takes us directly to the psychological and artistic dilemmas which, in less obvious ways, hinder the attempts of Hawthorne, Melville, and Cooper to sustain an authentic moral stability in their differing arts. With Poe their problems become more brazenly, desperately visible, because the *Tales* in themselves are public assertions of the author's self-defined eminence. In his magazine tales in the 1830s and 1840s, Poe is continually striving to transcend the relationship between himself and his readers, as if driven to elevate himself above the fear that he is a mere purveyor of sensations to a crowd whose insatiable tyranny demands ever-new and astonishing thrills, excitements to the mind and nerves which are teased out of the writer's own dissolution and pain.

Poe's position resembles that of the crippled court-jester in his tale 'Hop-Frog' who is forced by the King to provide 'something novel—out of the way'. And notably this is a tale which turns into a fantasy of revenge upon the despised crowd, for after Hop-Frog has invented his novel amusement (whereby the King and his ministers terrify the trapped courtiers in the guise of orang-outangs), the King is cornered in turn by the jester whom he has cruelly exploited. The 'last jest'—a vengeful burning to death—reverses the roles of master and fool. In 'The Cask of Amontillado' those who mock superior individuality are represented by Fortunato, dressed for a masquerade in fool's cap and bells. His former butt, Montresor, outdoes his enemy's previous jests and insults by walling up Fortunato as a last, overwhelming joke.

But these assertions of individualism lack the ambitiousness seen in tales like 'William Wilson', 'The Domain of Arnheim', or 'The Assignation' in which Poe creates a type of ideal genius, the superb poet-materialist whose driving imagination (and money) exalts him above the grovelling masses, so that he can organize his décor, landscape, or life exactly as he wills. He differs from the other kind of individualist, like Legrand in 'The Gold-Bug' or the hero of the Dupin tales, who has no wealth and has to earn his way to superior status by organization of material facts, by a display of analytical methods which allows Poe to offer his most detailed and elaborate justification of superior individualism.

The prestige of Dupin, for instance, depends on the detective's talent for extracting significance out of a limited sum of information. Thus he moves beyond the herd, beyond the confinement of factualness in which he triumphantly toils, and into the freedom of supreme, untouchable privacy. In 'The Murders in the Rue Morgue' one sees Poe's essential concern to redeem and differentiate his hero from the vulgar desires of the reading public, the Parisian crowd of the tale, and the criminal material in which he deals. After the murders a crowd gathers outside the house where the crimes have taken place, 'persons gazing up at the closed shutters, with an objectless curiosity', excluded from the inner sanctum of sensational knowledge. It needs Dupin, with his scientific methods, to discover a superior 'amusement' by opening those significantly closed shutters on to the solution of the murders, and his ascendance is carefully prepared. Even before he has solved his first crime Dupin methodically works back along the sequence of his companion's thoughts and deduces that his friend originally began by thinking about a stage-struck cobbler who attempted the role of Xerxes in a Crébillon tragedy and was beaten for his pretensions. Dupin's comment on the unsuccessful actor—' "He is a very little fellow, that's true, and would do better for the *Théâtre des Variétés*" '—scornfully waylays fear of comparison with a similar absurdity of pretension in the detective himself, for by his skill in eliciting his friend's thought he has instantly raised himself above the subject of that thought and cleared the way for his later elevation as the successful actor of the scene. When Dupin has finally outwitted the minister in 'The Purloined Letter', it is fitting that the token he leaves behind him as a mark of his superior up-staging should be a quotation from another Crébillon drama.

For all the extravagance, there is, however, a peculiarly American difficulty here: that of affirming the value of the special individual without giving an impression of fraudulent aids or the methods of the stunt.[1] Hans Pfaall, in another tale, is transformed, under similar difficulties, from the buffoon to the mastermind. He shows that he is more than a freak entertainer who astounds

---

[1] One sees Poe's difficult shift—from the would-be, discreditable eminence to the supposedly real talent which does not need theatrical costume—in certain episodes of Twain's *Huckleberry Finn*. In the hoggish backwoods slum, the travelling frauds, the 'king' and the 'duke', offer their 'thrilling, masterly, and blood-curdling Broad-sword conflict' of *Richard III*. This is a hoax to get the money from their paying audience, and turns out to be a crude satire on them, with the 'king' prancing out to the footlights in the insulting image of his watchers—as the naked, painted, human animal in all his disgusting grossness. But there runs an implied contrast between this deceitful attack and the genuine mastery of Colonel Sherburn, the Southern gentleman, who does not flinch to shoot down the drunken braggart who calls him a swindler, and who later cows a whole lynching mob by the deadly scorn of his presence, his unmitigated contempt for the 'average man'.

Lawrence's comment on the later Mark Twain is related also to Swift and Gogol but could equally apply to Poe: Twain's hatred, according to Lawrence, is a 'bitter, almost mad-dog aversion from humanity'. (Preface to *Max Havelaar*, *Phoenix*, p. 238.)

the Dutch burghers when he appears in a balloon made of dirty newspapers. For the balloon has the shape of an *inverted* fool's cap, and the significance of this is soon quite clear, because after Poe has invented and arranged his scientific facts, he is shown to have taken his hero to the moon, scientifically transcended his journalistic self.

But the dream of superiority can never detach itself completely from the public's ultimate ownership: the crowd's awe grants the 'aristocrat' his privilege at the same time as it coarsens the quality of the individualism won. Indeed, without their disguise of privilege, Poe's heroes are men of the American crowd, representatives who despise their association with it while sharing the intense personal assertiveness of its members and, prophetically, its fate. 'Mellonta Tauta' pictures a dreaded future where Poe's vision of ultimate democracy is of world-wide anarchic individualism, where the 'laws of gradation' by which Poe redeems his hero in the Dupin tales count for nothing under the feverish press of an 'every-man-for-himself confederacy'. No longer are the masses down below while a superior joker taunts and astounds them from his airship, for they themselves have crowded into the skies, and Poe's heroine finds herself 'cooped up in a dirty balloon, with some one or two hundred of the *canaille*, all bound on a *pleasure* excursion'. The voice of superior individualism cannot make itself heard in the rush of the Gadarene swine when 'the air is resonant with the hum of so many millions of human voices'. It is the feared immersion in a last compulsive anonymity which is expressed by Bedloe's dream of death amongst the rabble in 'A Tale of the Ragged Mountains' and in 'The Premature Burial' by the narrator's terror that despite all his careful precautions he has been taken for dead and buried by strangers 'as a dog—nailed up in some common coffin—and thrust, deep, deep, and for ever, into some ordinary and nameless *grave*.'

It seems that the ultimate degradation for the Poe hero is not in suffering physical death but in being deprived of those materials, human or otherwise, out of which he extracts his sense of spiritual distinctiveness. When the supplies of mental excitement are exhausted, when they are too devitalized to be re-used, the result is the paralytic apathy or stupor which is the common hazard for men and women in the *Tales*. Therefore, when the traveller arrives at the house of Usher, the decay and vacancy of the scene

have a specially depressing quality for Poe because there is little
for the mind to work upon, merely 'an unredeemed dreariness of
thought which no goading of the imagination could torture into
aught of the sublime'. One can see why Poe, in other tales, needs
to create fantasies of plenitude, where the mind awards itself an
immense stock of speculative material to feed upon and venture
among. In this way the individualist seems no longer at the mercy
of flattening exterior forces, with his interior reality crushed out
of him, because his spirit has achieved a sense of volume and
density. He can enjoy, like the observer in 'The Man of the
Crowd' who feeds analytically on the passing throng, 'one of
those happy moods which are so precisely the converse of *ennui*—
moods of the keenest appetency, when the film from the mental
vision departs . . . and the intellect, electrified, surpasses . . . its
everyday condition.'

The vistas created by the millionaire 'genius' in 'The Domain
of Arnheim' or the winding stream in 'The Elk', which provides
the idea of 'an endless succession of infinitely varied small lakes',
are channels by which the mind mystifies and loses itself—
bending and confusing the straight lines of its predetermining,
unvariable logic in order to contrive its own forgetfulness, a
sensation of spontaneous movement. The mind soothingly heaps
up for itself a mass of confusion and profusion which must never
be disentangled or counted, like the 'innumerable' desks and
benches of William Wilson's old school, 'crossing and recrossing
in endless irregularity', and the 'innumerable' streets of the
Arabian dream city in 'A Tale of the Ragged Mountains', crossing
each other 'irregularly in all directions'. A treasure of 'general
intricacy and confusion' welcomes the imagination in this city,
with its swarming multitudes who must (of necessity) remain
'countless' and with all its immeasurable, pinnacled complexity.

'William Wilson', in particular, indicates how the illusion of
plenitude is induced. The living, organic self has to be compressed
and tortured, its wholeness reduced to myriad particles, so that
the mind can excite itself on the infinite riches of decomposition:
the greater the material limits imposed, the greater the sense of
spiritual endlessness. The harsh discipline of William Wilson's
school is essential if he is to extract by a 'mental sorcery' such 'a
wilderness of sensation, a world of rich incident, an universe of
varied emotion.' The imprisoning walls of the school provoke the

multum in parvo delight, the 'interest', which Wilson finds in the school gate: 'in every creak of its mighty hinges, we found a plenitude of mystery—a world of matter for solemn remark.' There is 'spirit-soothing' comfort in contemplating the 'incomprehensible subdivisions' of a passageway in the school.

The taste for 'variety in uniformity' shown in 'William Wilson' or in the ideal landscaping of 'The Domain of Arnheim' and 'Landor's Cottage' is also revealed in tales which comprise adventurous writhings inside labyrinths, ingenious activities stimulated by bondage, escapes from almost-certain disaster by the employment of mental audacity. The victim of the Inquisition in 'The Pit and the Pendulum' and the sailor in 'A Descent into the Maelström', suffer in predicaments which force them to extract sensation or speculation out of a diminishing area of personal movement. When the hero of *The Narrative of Arthur Gordon Pym* is 'buried alive' in the hold of a whaling ship, he finds that to be able to move only an inch or so is to inherit a vast territory of mental sensation to explore. The painfully scrupulous step-by-step account of Pym's receipt and deciphering of his friend's letter, with all the mishaps, losses, and recoveries of the operation thoroughly recorded, is followed by a further account of how his friend Augustus, his bonds only slightly loosened, managed to write the letter painstakingly in his own blood.

In finding a solution or escape when all seems perfectly enclosed, the mind achieves in fantasy a kind of synthetic well-being which substitutes patterns of arabesque deadness in place of the real mysteries of life and spontaneity. But then Poe's sense of positiveness—the power of arranging chaos into some significant order—can never be more than an inverted form of the negativity which originally produces the chaos: one finds health by traversing the pathways of disintegration. Legrand in 'The Gold-Bug' recovers from the paralysis which overtakes him when his mind is unable 'to establish a connection—a sequence of cause and effect.' Reversing the sequence of time, he establishes a back-to-front connectedness for the mind: instead of proceeding from cause to effect, he goes from effect to cause, and exercises his ingenuity in retracing the steps of others backward into the past. 'It may well be doubted', he says, 'whether human ingenuity can construct an enigma of the kind which human ingenuity may not, by proper application, resolve.'

Such an arrangement explains why the other analytical hero is regarded as 'a double Dupin—the creative and the resolvent'. It also deepens understanding of the deceivers and compulsive confessors in 'William Wilson', 'The Tell-Tale Heart', 'The Imp of the Perverse', and 'The Black Cat' who reserve the right to be their own detectives for the crimes they have committed, creating and resolving in terrible futility. By the same fantasy-logic, loss can be turned into gain, so that although the student of corrupt knowledge in 'Ligeia' and 'Morella' loses his female material by the physical death of his subject, he manages to retrieve it by substituting an empty vessel to contain it. Thus the eyes of Ligeia are regained for further exploration by giving the dead woman's spirit the body of a second wife to inhabit. Having processed Morella out of life, the husband gets her back through the person of her daughter. Thus 'in the phrases and expressions of the dead on the lips of the loved and living, I found food for consuming thought and horror.'

The detective or solver of puzzles is, therefore, the inverted image of the criminal, the cheat who squanders life and kills organic being in order to make enigmas from the wreckage. But the criminal and the detective are rarely acknowledged as one. When the narrator in 'The Man of the Crowd' subdividingly analyses the crowd sweeping past him, he notices one particular individual of fascination, an old man with a secret. The narrator's 'craving desire . . . to know more of him' takes him on a laborious pursuit of his prey back and forth through winding streets and passages until he comes face to face with the keeper of the mystery himself. But the old man will not reveal his secret—indeed, must not, if the detective narrator is not to know that he is confronting the criminal half of his double self. The tale halts just this side of not-knowing, and only a hair's-breadth distinction remains between the 'creative' and the 'resolvent'.

It is a distinction which Poe insists upon in order to assert the 'rich ideality' of Dupin whose success as a detective depends on his power of reversing sequences of thought and action. As with Legrand, a retreat from the future is made as if it were an advance forward. So Dupin and his friend live in their decayed Parisian mansion, shutting out the day and wandering through the city at night to feed upon an 'infinity of mental excitement'. Dreariness is thwarted: 'we gave the Future to the winds, and slumbered tranquilly in the Present, weaving the dull world around us into dreams.' Poe, however, wishes to give the illusion of transcendence a plausible basis. The same degree of care is employed in differentiating Dupin from a *poseur* like the cobbling actor as in rescuing him from the suspicion that the world of arranged reality in which his investigations triumphantly proceed is a mechanical folly.

The motto to 'The Mystery of Marie Roget' partly suggests the distinctions which Poe is to make carefully in the tale: 'There are ideal series of events which run parallel with the real ones. They rarely coincide.' They must not, since the account given of the murdered girl's clothing—placed about the bushes by the criminal to give the impression of natural disorder—is closely reminiscent of the cunning staging, the imitation spontaneity, which Poe admires in 'Landor's Cottage', where dead branches, withered leaves, and stray pebbles are swept out of sight or pleasingly arranged: 'Not a single impediment lay in the wheel-route—not even a chip or a dead twig. The stones that once obstructed the way had been carefully *placed*—not thrown—along the sides of the lane, so as to define its boundaries at bottom with a kind of half-precise, half-negligent, and wholly picturesque definition.' But in 'Marie Roget' Poe finds it essential to draw an almost invisible distinction between the murderer's version of nature and the detective's by having Dupin assert his sense of 'ideality' above inferior imitations: ' "Here is just such an arrangement as would *naturally* be made by a not-over-acute person wishing to dispose the articles *naturally*. But it is by no means a *really* natural arrangement." '

But the advantage of insisting on distinctions and of accentuating the boundaries of the mental enclosure is that Dupin is able to make an illusory escape from the idea of limitation altogether. His most vital discovery in 'The Murders in the Rue Morgue' concerns the windows which the police assume to be perpetually closed but which, Dupin realizes, can in fact be opened. He finds a way out when the perceptions of the crowd are 'hermetically sealed against the possibility of the windows having ever been opened at all.' At this moment of intellectual triumph for the 'resolvent' power it is as if all the 'well-contrived securities' prepared by the narrator of 'The Premature Burial' were absolutely guaranteed—the comfortable padded coffin and the survival ·ations—while the lever is working perfectly that will cause the iron portals of the vault to fly back. The windows, portals of the mental tomb, are opened for a fantasy escape from materialism, and Dupin's imagination escapes along the track of the outgoing killer.

There is safety for the mind in such exploits, but only so long as the game is played within strict psychological bounds. When the analytical force of the detective mind goes too far and eats up all the supplies of knowledge amassed, there is no effective moral discipline to stop the collapse of the distinctions between the *poseur* and the success, the fraudulent and the authentic. The fate of wastrels like the aesthete in 'The Assignation' and Aegeus in 'Berenice' is to run through too quickly their provisions of 'interest' —living beings or arranged matter—and reach the void unresisted. The dreaded end, the barren future of the mind, has been staved off by illusions of endlessness. Now when it does come it seems like a bizarre intrusion upon the idealized world of the present— hence the premature burials of the *Tales:* the confusions of the time-sequence are suddenly righted, and the future seems to happen grotesquely out of turn before the deceptive consciousness can stop it.

But then, destruction of one's mental safety is the next beckoning move after idealism. When life has been too perfectly possessed and materialized, there is after that little else to be done with all that has been laid waste except to destroy oneself and get some final new sensation in the downfall. The 'unfathomable longing of the soul *to vex itself*—to offer violence to its own nature' which is felt by the narrator of 'The Black Cat' results from his own cutting away of all living possibilities in himself. He has hanged his pet and pushed himself into damnation 'with the tears streaming from my eyes . . . hung it *because* I knew that it had loved me, and *because* I felt it had given me no reason of offence—hung it *because* I knew that in so doing I was committing a sin.' He gets a kind of black glory from the garrulous display of his own wickedness, but he is not tragic on the terms that he would like. Beneath the theatricalism there lies the dreary impotence of one who has not known what to do with the life and love he had.

This incapacity before life runs through the tales of sensational 'love' between men and women, and nowhere more revealingly than in 'The Fall of the House of Usher'. Here the cheating imagination can no longer confuse the sequence of inevitability, and the future is about to appear. The female victim has already been paralysed into a living death before the tale starts, and Usher the idealist lies in *ennui*, nearly bankrupt of dreams and the energy for 'amusement', amongst the remnants of used-up enchantment: 'The general furniture was profuse, comfortless, antique, and tattered. Many books and musical instruments lay scattered about, but failed to give any vitality to the scene.' Usher is the most far-gone of Poe's figures of unrestraint, given over to 'the grim phantasm, FEAR' with an avaricious fatalism, and, like the killer in 'The Black Cat', inflating the drama of his own damnation: ' "I shall perish," said he, "I *must* perish in this deplorable folly. Thus, thus, and not otherwise, shall I be lost." ' But still he holds back from the overthrow by clinging to his last fragments of harmonic idealism—the music of his guitar and the abstractness of art. In the latter he pictures, with 'utter simplicity' and 'nakedness', a chamber voided of all mental furnishings, cleaned out of all ideal accretions, intricate bric-à-brac and profusions. With the consciousness seemingly emptied, all that remains are the walls of materialism, the hard bone as white and irreducibly dead as Ahab's false leg:

A small picture presented the interior of an immensely long and rectangular vault or tunnel, with low walls, smooth, white, and without interruption or device. . . . No outlet was observed in any portion of its vast extent, and no torch, or other artificial source of light was discernible; yet a flood of intense rays rolled throughout, and bathed the whole in a ghastly and inappropriate splendour.

But it is only a picture of the end: Usher's dying mind still beautifies its state with an intensely-lit perfection. After this comes the real end when all the 'arranged' matter can no longer cohere or stand up in the form of the walls of Usher's 'lofty and spiritual ideality'. When Usher's sister returns from the tomb, the ideal matrix is broken with a rough, grating sound which destroys Usher's remnant of 'creative' power, his artistic coherence through music. In a final collapse (and Poe's most truthful moment of American horror) Lady Madeline's grasping crowds in on her brother in a falling motion, clumsily mechanical, the ultimate gesture in a world of completed materialism—the inert hugging the inert, matter adhering to matter and sunken into oneness. So the idealist gets his material back, but too disastrously for Usher to enjoy it. It is left to Poe to make his Usher-like picture and extract sensational profit from this exhibition of his own mental ruin: the narrator escapes to tell his secrets to an avid audience.

He cannot escape to do more, because genuine moral realization is beyond the capacity of Poe's art. Even so, the fantasy of the *Tales* continually points to fundamental connections which Poe wishes to evade. The analyser of sin is the creator of sin, and therefore the conditions by which individualism exists are essentially criminal, murderous. A sense of inner coherence, of richness and equanimity in the self (what Poe calls 'variety in uniformity'), can only be induced by destruction in the living organism. This, in fact, is the small area of paradoxical, spiritual knowledge which Poe unconsciously defines without seizing its larger, American implications. For that kind of perceptiveness one must turn to Hawthorne.

II

Three Novels of Hawthorne and the
Difficulties of Moral Thrift

HAWTHORNE'S spiritual material is to serve a greater purpose than sensationalism. The kind of experience misused by Poe becomes in Hawthorne's art the basis for a distinctly Americanized moral awareness. But there are difficulties, since Hawthorne's kind of moral consciousness tends to remain a consciousness of the *need* to make formal, articulate sense of his discoveries, even if it means using old-fashioned patterns of intelligibility to express private experience in terms of its public meaning. He does not venture by the confident workings of a really felt ethic and re-create his values on the way, because he is a knowing borrower of old standards. This restricts him as a moralist, yet his sense of responsibility towards his material is an important discipline in his art. Therefore he prizes the value of 'sympathy' and the feelings of the 'heart', not because they are powerfully present in him but because they are necessary (even as abstract notions) to check his own potential one-sidedness as an artist—the tendency to analytical destructiveness or to Poe-like petrifaction of living people into 'snow-images'. He moves with only slight moral advantage in artistic situations which are potentially wasteful—opportunities for sensationalism rather than meaning—and which can beguile the would-be moralist as he attempts to interpret the destructive event. Hawthorne's sense of creative good, stemming as it does from his greater sense of evil, is so frailly close to its origin that it risks being drawn in and consumed. And when that happens, we are offered exegetical activity that avoids true meaning.

But in the sustained balance of *The Scarlet Letter* (1850) Hawthorne displays a sternness of control over his material which Poe, for instance, cannot command: there is a firmer, less indulgent attitude towards the evasions and the flights, the illusions of freedom in infinite mental spaces, the temptations to waste the abundance of life. At his American best, one sees in Hawthorne the austere wish to halt the shifting consciousness, pin down the evasion and fix his concentration on the psychological reality which he actually, rather than wishfully, possesses. Then, in actuality, he finds himself like Poe inside a miniature, even crowded area of the psyche. He comes upon that 'fund of suggestion' which Henry James felt that Hawthorne only fully realized later in 'the denser, richer, warmer European spectacle.' James's word 'density' is exact when he contrasts Hawthorne's artistic needs with 'the coldness, the thinness, the blankness'[1] of his American surroundings, but exact in a deeper sense than James probably intended, because it describes the undispersed, hard-packed core of spiritual experience on which Hawthorne founds his best art. It is the 'European spectacle' compacted and foreshortened to a minimum in the American mind. Poe hems it in for concentration, crushes it to a brutal narrowness by the prison walls of his art, but the very ground which Poe wastes Hawthorne is concerned to cultivate. With moral and artistic thrift he is attempting to nurture a genuine inner America of the spirit, to make a home out of that rather than in the idea of diffuse, *physical* space.

In this endeavour, Hawthorne's own introspective habits and the lack of an experience comparable to Melville's are an advantage. He begins where Poe's art comes to an exhausted finish, in a vacuum of impoverished feelings and paralysis. Then he attempts to broaden the work to a point where his immobilized, isolated individuals are delivered from the custody of mental sins and punishments, and freed into the ampler circle of human feelings and relationships. Three of his novels begin with a consideration of the dead, stiffened thing, the disregarded object or the neglected idea—a rag of scarlet cloth embroidered with the letter 'A'; an old New England house and its inmates whom life has strangely bypassed; a vanished experiment in communal living. It is not merely nervous sensations he extracts, for he is gradually teasing out a treasury of significances. The *multum in parvo* expediency of Poe is converted to moral purposes.

---

[1] *Hawthorne* (London, 1887), p. 43.

I

Hawthorne often prefers to regard meaning as a kind of texture to be savoured more for its beauty than for its knowledge. He needs the *thought* of a treasury of significance in waiting before his imagination can begin to stir, and amongst the early Boston Puritans of his first novel he discovers the texture and treasury lacking in the diffuse, unconcentrated, external America of his modern mind, 'where there is no shadow, no antiquity, no mystery, no picturesque and gloomy wrong, nor anything but a commonplace prosperity, in broad and simple daylight.'[1]

The historical setting of *The Scarlet Letter* was to give Hawthorne the artistic tautness which eludes his command in his later work. Because in that novel the past and immediate future are assured and known, he can govern his chosen piece of territory. Placing its period at a particular point in American life—at the interval when the settlers have just left behind the 'sunny richness' of Elizabethan and Jacobean England and before the 'blackest shade' of later New England Puritanism overcomes the scene— Hawthorne can immediately see behind and in front of this 'gray' moment. In the location of the novel, he is certain of his marked limits, of an identified peninsular colony within a greater flux. Ahead is the forest, the 'moral wilderness' of the unexplored continent, with its heathen savages, witches, and devils; behind is another vast space unregulated by human law, the ocean which leads back to Europe. And set literally between the devil and the deep sea is the new colony and its grave Puritan elders, defending the state against the pressures of the imperilling flux 'like a line of cliffs against a tempestuous tide.' Hawthorne aligns himself with their authoritative firmness, although not constricted by their actual moral code, as if the sound and feeling, the texture of their presence, proclaim the colony as a point of concentration among diffusion and chaos, a plot of moral land defined for the ordered cultivation of meaning.

With the Puritan community as the mental base to which all the discoveries must ultimately be delivered up, the novelist can

---

[1] Preface to *The Marble Faun* (New American Library, New York, 1961), p. vi.

venture to consider the moral predicaments which belong to his
own nineteenth-century unconscious rather than to Puritan
history. He has set a ring round those who have lost their way in
this inner America when they slip from European securities.
There are those 'bringing all the learning of the age into our wild
forestland' such as Chillingworth and Dimmesdale—the minister
'astray and at a loss in the pathway of human existence', the
scientist exchanging old European secrets for the new, savage
knowledge of the Indians. There is Hester Prynne, with her taste
for the gorgeously luxuriant, the fantastic and the proud, as if she
were part of the American wild flora. In the illegitimate child
Pearl, the New World has most nearly discontinued its relationship
with the values of the Old, for (p. 132) she skips over the graves of
the Puritan dead 'like a creature that had nothing in common
with a bygone and buried generation, nor owned herself akin to it.
It was as if she had been made afresh out of new elements.' She
and the 'sin' which creates her have a peculiarly native, elusive
quality which are, perhaps, Hawthorne's most daunting challenge.

So, in one defined area of history and civilization, Hawthorne
discovers the atmosphere where he can range between suggestions
of devilish encirclement and divine portents, between corrupt
obsessions and transfiguring miracles. He can be eclectic amongst
his varying textures. He is able to preserve his demeanour as the
nineteenth-century modern man, open to imaginativeness yet
rationally hedging, picking from vulgar and mature opinions
alike, employing the common people's superstitious fear of the
devil together with the elders' defensive wisdom and ceremonial
dignity. Yet the picking and choosing are not for the sake of theatricalism, so that Hawthorne can escape into ambivalence: the
beliefs are scenery which catch between them the difficult,
modern play on which the novelist's concentration is fully engaged.
In this 'little town on the edge of the Western wilderness', all the
unendorsed suggestions of the community exert a pressure which
keeps continual attention on the closeness of concepts to one
another, of individuals, levels of thought, opposing values,
crowded up against each other. The Boston morality and government, citizens and legislators, are the force which narrows the
margin between good and evil, constricts spiritual purity into
tight neighbourship with the grossest filth. A witch lodges with
her brother the Governor, and, initially at the people's bidding, a

Satanist takes up residence with their most revered theologian. And Hawthorne's new moral art is hemmed in by the historical morality of these people to the discipline of the few public stages like the prison, the scaffold, the meeting-house, the graveyard, and the Governor's mansion. The private drama of the sinners, the American spiritual crowding, is pushed into being and activated by the rigid narrowing from the outside.

It is that sparse and concentrated suggestion in the first chapter of the novel which makes Hawthorne a profound American poet, singling out two symbolic ideas. On the virgin soil of America stands a prison, a 'black flower' of civilization which has been transplanted from overseas but easily takes root here. In the young void of America the prison is a crude mental enclosure of meaning, assigning reality and ratification to this blank Eden. 'The rust on the ponderous iron-work of its oaken door looked more antique than anything else in the New World' (p. 55). It is an old, persistent, and necessary symbol of moral law, its agedness peculiarly enhanced because of the wild rose-bush which grows next to it like a live bordering to a stern frame. This home of sinners and prisoners has a reality of feeling which Hawthorne shares with Poe, but the rose-bush by the prison door, denying the prison's completeness, is a flower of extra consciousness that does not grow in Poe's region. Like the figure of Pearl later in the novel, the rose points to what has been disregarded, to what, unless brought in and acknowledged, will invalidate the wholeness of any moral vision. Hawthorne would like to see the flower as a token of gentle feelings, a treasure of pity and kindness with its 'delicate gems', but the wild growth suggests rather the untamed feelings which he cannot order as a novelist. The wildness is nearly controlled, the rose almost abstracted and imprisoned, but not quite. There are still in equipoise here the two impulses which make up the interplay of Hawthorne's literature.

On the one hand, with the prison, there is Hawthorne's interest as a specifically American artist in the Poe manner—mechanizing the life of the living, mentally abstracting the flesh into manageable objects, symbols, and pictures. It is here that the vulnerable side of his moral interest, the side which criticizes from spiritual gentleness or pity, surreptitiously goes under and gives in to the wilfulness it is officially chastening. The 'grim rigidity that petrified the bearded physiognomies' of the Puritans in front of the prison

door is due not merely to their coldness of heart as human beings
but to the artist's own petrifying technique in moral depiction.
Even when (p. 63) Hawthorne imagines a Papist's view of Hester
standing with Pearl on the scaffold, his impulse is to convert the
rich and living into a stilled posture which the mind can grasp at
leisure: 'he might have seen in this beautiful woman, so picturesque
in her attire and mien, and with the infant at her bosom, an
object to remind him of the image of Divine Maternity, which so
many illustrious painters have vied with one another to represent.'
There is here an ironic passage of thought between public and
private vision, when Hawthorne suggests, through the hypotheti-
cal Catholic, a rich emotional value which is on full display, an
open secret of the Puritan consciousness which the Puritans do
not have the eyes to see. But Hawthorne's control of suggestion
does not arise entirely from an interest in morally qualifying the
scene. In winning this idea from under the stern, unrealizing
gaze of the Puritan public, he is savouring the *thought* of an ex-
tracted meaning, enjoying the secret colour and grain of the idea
—the more precious because discovered where only cold austerity
seemed to exist.

On the other hand, there is a correcting impulse to this artistic
tendency, something that seeks unironic connections, an urge to
play a light of fancy or uncaught life in and about the dense
texture of enclosed meaning; to vivify the categorized with a
quicker, brighter feeling than gentleness. It is this vigour which
goes into and comes out of the strict enclosure, carrying away
material for moral assessment from aesthetic sources. By a quick,
audacious clarity, Hawthorne's sense of sin is yielded from observation of his own predicament. It is the 'artists' of the novel who
commit artists' crimes and gather artists' punishments.

2

The sinners come out of England and go straying in the New
World. With this, the unity of the allegorical family of mankind is
broken into unrelated parts. There is no father, on earth or in
heaven, for the illegitimate child, nor a revealed husband for the
adulterous mother. Hawthorne has dispensed with the first pro-
voking sin before the novel opens and is free to consider a
secondary area of sinning quite distinct from the conventional

area of moral judgement on sexual misdemeanour. Therefore, Hester, Dimmesdale, and Chillingworth are caught in secondary sins and torments in a strange, inverted existence where the values of the open human family—'home', 'sympathy', love, intuition—take on, with this secret, dislocated family, destructive meanings.

Sin in America creates for Hester and Chillingworth what a contemplation of 'picturesque and gloomy wrong' imparts to Hawthorne's mind: a cohering of the imagination, a new rallying point in the consciousness, and a needed sense of identification. Hester lingers in the Puritan settlement, haunting the spot where the 'great and marked event' of her crime has given the meaningful 'color' to her life. 'Her sin, her ignominy, were the roots which she had struck into the soil. It was as if a new birth, with stronger assimilations than the first, had converted the forestland, still so uncongenial to every other pilgrim and wanderer, into Hester Prynne's wild and dreary but lifelong home' (pp. 83-4). Like the 'black flower' of the prison-house and like Hester, the roots of sin anchor and give a real 'home' to Chillingworth the predator: ' "Here, on this wild outskirt of the earth, I shall pitch my tent; for elsewhere a wanderer, and isolated from human interests, I find here a woman, a man, a child, amongst whom and myself there exist the closest ligaments. No matter whether of love or hate; no matter whether of right or wrong! Thou and thine, Hester Prynne, belong to me. My home is where thou art, and where he is" ' (p. 80). The outer chain of human goodness, the ties of organic respect, no longer bind the three together. Having shaken off the now-unreal coherence of past values, they find in secrecy a more close-fitting kinship, in which each is harshly defined as a wilful individual. Yet, by the cutting away of creative good, each has delivered himself or herself to a relationship of pure power and ever-possible interference. The new separateness means, as Chillingworth shows, a denial of separateness. So they are pioneers, not into American land space, but into an American sense of evil which impinges upon and hurtfully makes the land an inner reality for the soul to live in.

Just as Hawthorne's art flourishes most readily in an atmosphere of moral decay, so Hester, Dimmesdale, and Chillingworth—'artists' of mind and body, speculators among the ruins of the old moral codes—practise the sins which emerge from Hawthorne's knowledge of his own literary technique and tendencies. The novelist's petrification of the living, and his scrutiny of material to make the dead scrap live and give up its secrets, are transmuted into Chillingworth's obsession with grasping the physical into his mind, there to know and possess it. He must keep Dimmesdale alive and parasitically extract his secrets, not as the outraged cuckold but as one who presses for further knowledge among disintegration. He is a practiser of secondary sins, not for conventional morality's but 'for the art's sake'. Hawthorne's habitual ironic use of paradox and ambiguity becomes, at another level, Dimmesdale's tormented ambivalence, as the minister shifts between truth and falsehood, pretending to reveal while still he conceals, playing with values and redemption in a manner which is only one stage removed from his author's uncertain commitment to the positives he presents. To Hester the novelist contributes the American artist's special sense of isolation in the democratic atmosphere of the day—the proud awareness of aristocratic individuality among the herd, an innate feeling of riches and creative power that must be suppressed below a dull surface, because Hawthorne will not go to Poe's defiant lengths. To be an open aristocrat, without assertiveness or apologies, is too difficult or impossible; and the only role left, that of the secret pariah, is so extreme for Hawthorne that the idea of communal solidarity seems the preferable good, the ultimate alternative, even if individualism loses in the preference.

Although the Puritan state, with its authoritarian dignity and ordered levels, allows a better alternative than the egalitarian insistencies of the version of contemporary America in his next two novels, Hawthorne is still impoverished in choice: he has to equate what he values at one moment—the privacy of an inner life, personal integrity—with what he disdains at another—self-festering introspection, the aggressive will, and unbearable solitude. It is an artistic hell on earth, and the greatest sinner, perhaps (the old physician), is the one closest to Hawthorne's own situation as a novelist—the leech feeding on the rich material of another's decay, who, when his food is gone, is left 'uprooted' (from his inner 'home' in America) like a weed in the sun, or, like one of Poe's wastrel geniuses, deprived of the subject which he himself has exhausted.

But Hawthorne has brought consciousness to the Poe situation.

He plays a flexible thoughtfulness across the artistically-derived dilemmas, persistently calling the reader's attention to a readiness. One is asked to see in two directions at once, to note the inconsistencies within the community's mind, first in its harsh judgement on Hester, then later in its over-just leniency towards her as a Sister of Mercy; to see the discrepancies in treatment given to Hester and Dimmesdale by the people, whereby each is isolated in a separate prison of the self. She is dashed too low, he is raised too high, so that both are coerced into abstraction, unable to speak their way into the communal reality—she with her one scarlet letter, he with his many eloquent words. Yet Hawthorne's control of sympathy demands recognition of more than the people's share in spiritually exiling its hero and its one discovered adulteress, for after the first public arraignment, it is Hester's and Dimmesdale's continuation of the ironic lie on their private initiative which matters. As they withdraw into self-isolation, the difference between appearance and reality increases. Hester with her marble-like, statuesque strength and her hidden defiance, makes pride in the end look the very facsimile of humility. Dimmesdale, weak and haggard, agonizingly unable to tell dream from reality, unable to emerge from fraud even if he tries, makes the truth hidden in his generalized confession to the people into yet more falsehood.

And while the outer pressure is kept up, a secret transformation is coming about. The Puritan discipline is indulgent within the bulwarks of its sternness, sufficiently permissive and corrective to nurture and train plants from the old life into a new fruitfulness. Under the severity of Pastor Wilson's appearance one has the suggestion (p. 108) 'that pears and peaches might yet be naturalized in the New England climate, and that purple grapes might possibly be compelled to flourish against the sunny garden wall.' Hester, Dimmesdale, and Chillingworth are making an inner community within the Puritan bounds. Theirs is the inner American experience which is gradually being realized inside the imported European framework. Dimmesdale and Hester are becoming representatives of the community more than the community consciously acknowledges. Hester's fantastic embroidery for the colony's great ceremonials of birth and death can now be seen more as an American flourish than as a persisting Jacobean tradition. Just as her needlework gives the new native edging to the meaning of birth and death, so her scarlet letter of shame takes on the moral reality of America, glowing no longer in mark of old offended codes. If Hester gives the native decoration, in all its involuted beauty, Dimmesdale provides the new moral voice of the community.

But Hawthorne is not insisting on the mere irony of the situation, for as they deepen their duplicity inside the old formal values, they are destroying the validity of the traditional vision and language and entering a new reality that has no language of its own. It is, therefore, not just the growing falsehood of Dimmesdale's state which is relevant here but also his advance in moral decay which gives him new power to speak to the sin in others, to recognize a fellowship amongst a hidden community of the anguished. In the same way Hester's afflictions prove her a 'Sister of Mercy', false in one context, true in another. So when Dimmesdale gives the official sermon on Election Day towards the close of the novel, it is an unconscious *American* cry of anguish and solitude which is heard filtering through the church walls and the imprisoning old matrix of language. It comes through to the other 'American', Hester, as she listens outside. As she catches (pp. 227-8) Dimmesdale's 'profound and continual undertone' of plaintiveness, pain and guilt, while it shrieks and sighs 'amid a desolate silence', the sermon has 'throughout a meaning for her entirely apart from its indistinguishable words'. It is surely from this passage that Lawrence gains one of the insights of his first essays on American literature: 'We read the English utterance without getting the alien American implication. We listen to our own speech in American mouths, but our ears have been shut to the strange reverberation of that speech. We have not wanted to hear the undertone, the curious foreign, uncouth suggestion, which is in the over-cultured Hawthorne or Poe or Whitman.'[1]

Hawthorne's purpose, if not his achievement, is to centre the novel on 'the alien American implication' and try to hold down the elusiveness within his total patterning of experience. Most aptly he focuses on scenes of wasted experience; on temptations to flee from conscious responsibility; on moral sleight-of-hand which pretends to resolve in encompassment what, in fact, remains disordered. That Hawthorne himself fails to master the

[1] *The Symbolic Meaning* (the uncollected versions of *Studies in Classic American Literature*), ed. Armin Arnold (1962), p. 16.

latter problem is not to deny his attempt upon it when he presents throughout the novel a series of false wholes, spurious entries into a fuller, redeemed life, which are deliberately incomplete. These pseudo-revelations take the form of scenes whose essential incongruity, or absence of complete honesty, offend an aesthetic sense of wholeness at the same time as they call up a moral attack on subterfuge, ambivalence, and self-deception. It is an exhibition of pictures, with vital elements consciously omitted or unwittingly disregarded, which begins with the arraignment of Hester and Pearl, as the exposed sinner and the fruit of sin, upon the public scaffold in the market-place, before the eyes of the whole community, at the sun's zenith. Two unrevealed elements in the picture, Hester's lover and her husband, keep the public show morally unreal, unsanctioned by their secrecy. In their refusal to be assimilated, they hold out for a darker experience, and the novel has to wait until their experience is worth assimilating.

In the minister's chamber, another scene of apparent revelation takes place. Again it is noon, as Dimmesdale lies drugged by the leech and Chillingworth steals in to glimpse the secret mark of guilt on the flesh which the minister has been at pains to hide. Yet this scene which is so Poe-like in its parasitism, this private disclosure in a private room, emerges as a moment of utter wastefulness, its show diverted from moral purposes on to a selfish, personal track. Hawthorne inveighs (p. 136) against the greed in Chillingworth which snatches possible moral material for self-delight: 'All that dark treasure to be lavished on the very man to whom nothing else could so adequately pay the debt of vengeance!' Later still, Dimmesdale joins Hester and Pearl in the darkness of the market-place scaffold to stand for a moment as a secret family. But Pearl's questions emphasize, and Dimmesdale's maintained secrecy suggests, that this is another 'vain show of expiation'. It is a false noon here at midnight. The appearance of the meteor in the cloudy sky of their veiled hearts —aptly 'burning out to waste' and luridly lighting up the street 'with the distinctness of midday'—stresses again the incompleteness of the offered picture. At the equivalent moment in Poe's work, the narrator of 'The Black Cat' exults in confessional grandeur over his evil and Usher shows his picture of a brilliantly-lit vault, bathed 'in a ghastly and inappropriate splendour'.

But Hawthorne's art is not satisfied with meretricious penitence.

His moral discipline avoids Poe's dramatizing just as it holds back from spacious excitements when the forest outside the settlement seems to offer Hester a genuine openness, a breath of 'the whole wide world' when she urges Dimmesdale to fly with her beyond the seas into apparently safe anonymity. In throwing off her scarlet symbol, however, as a gesture of liberation, Hester estranges Pearl from the group, so that the child is left out, hovering between image and reality, not happy until the embroidered letter is back on her mother's breast. The forest offers only a momentary and fitful sunshine. It is not until all the theatrical sensationalism has been exhausted in Dimmesdale that the novel is ready to fit the experience of the hidden family into the consciousness of the everyday community. Then it is noon, in the market-place, in front of the people, with Dimmesdale publicly declaring his link with Hester and Pearl, and even Chillingworth following him up on the scaffold. They are a cast of 'actors' but the sinister lighting has gone from their drama and thus finished it. There is no drama when the full sun shines on a completed picture, a mended chain of community with new links.

Pearl is the continual seeker of the sun, yet at the same time the one who denies Hawthorne the satisfaction of a genuine communal finish to the picture, for it is she who throughout the novel and even at the end—when she has become an aristocrat far from America—is an alert check on the petrifying, static quality in his art, on his artist-sinners and his grim, solid Puritans. Her figure aerates the density of the material, leading a dance of untrapped meaning in and out of the fixed scenes or picturesque groupings which her elders construct, as a perpetual reminder of the life they omit. Her name appropriately indicates value: she is the vital link in the circle of full humanity, the elusive knowledge whose moral capture and piecing into the chain depends utterly on the right response of her elders' hearts. And yet while Dimmesdale and Hester slide between good and evil, truth and falsehood, joy and torture, she must represent a treasure which is perpetually cast before swine. As 'the scarlet letter endowed with life', she is their unstabilized spirit at large, an unsteady light, a physical paradox who flits between the possibilities of hell-fire and heavenly sunbeams, yet cannot be either. Unlike her parents, hers is a quirkish, open duplicity; yet as a 'living hieroglyphic' she is also the tantalizingly open clue, if it can be used, to a way out of the labyrinth. Hawthorne wants to solve the problem, to bring the 'alien American implication' at its most alive in Pearl, into a native, psychological wholeness. It is in her that one sees the restrictiveness of Hawthorne's art at its closest, for not only does he find rooted American meaning in the material of crime and punishment, but that same ground which provides the weeds of guilt also must nurture a flower of innocence, growing the more fruitfully, it seems, the greater the enforced moral decay of the soil. But when Hawthorne restores the native findings to the communal consciousness, they will not easily rest there, for Pearl at the end is still, for all her transfiguration into a stable child, a reminder not only of the 'incomplete morality' of sinners and judges, but also of the novelist's form.

And, indeed, Hawthorne has to work the final harmony too abstractly and symbolically. The motto on Hester's grave to which the novel leads up—'On a field, sable, the letter A, gules' —resembles a succinct thought stretched tight over the unresolved and unreconciled. It is as though in presenting this heraldic device as a harmonic reply to the prison-house and the rose-bush which stand in separation in the first chapter, Hawthorne cannot resist savouring the cross-hatched texture of the meaning without respecting the conscious meaning itself—the blazoning of the American individual on a dark background. As an American poet he catches again in image alone the significance of the 'undertone', but misses as an American novelist the wildness which fights his particular formalizing. He must petrify the meaning for his art to weld, and yet as soon as he has done so he has lost the sense of the meaning's power.

3

But the limitations of *The Scarlet Letter* do not alter substantially the quality of its achievement—the artistic tension exercised on a carefully-defined area, the dignified pressure, and the controlled relationship in which, at the novel's best, an alert moral subtlety watches and co-operates with the artistic tendency. These qualities seem more valuable still when one comes to consider *The House of the Seven Gables* (1851), where the balance of elements is becoming upset, and the moral intelligence of the author is gradually unfastening itself from its orbital movement round his artistic interests. As it grows more diffuse in effect, the morality becomes less assured of itself. The result is a strange diversion of energy, whereby immense creative effort is concentrated on a few areas, while others suffer neglect. Detail, outline, structure, symbolism: all are firmly over-presented with density and careful shaping, and yet the life-giving tone is gradually disappearing, together with the brisk integrity, the watchfulness of 'morality' from which it derives.

The difficulty here is that Hawthorne is stretching his resources in a task which, for his kind of art, is especially difficult. He is attempting to embrace more psychological territory over time and physical space; to repair relationships broken with outer life not just over seven years—in a small community on the edge of the wilderness, firmly in the author's surveying scope—but over two centuries in a house on the threshold of an America which is jostling, modern, and fiercely democratic, where the author's command of tone and grasped significance must proceed with greater caution. In now seeking to link up the reality of the secret, inner America of the past with the present America, to make, as in the previous novel, a continuity of the private realization with its public significance and so look towards the future, Hawthorne cannot avail himself of the ordered authoritativeness of the Puritan state. Here the temptations of diffuseness lie when Hawthorne attempts to make a pact of communal wholeness with democracy. It is this danger which undermines Hester's hope (and Hawthorne's theme for the second novel intimated at the end of the first) 'that, at some brighter period, when the world should have grown ripe for it, in Heaven's own time, a new truth would be revealed, in order to establish the whole relation between man and woman on a surer ground of mutual happiness' (*The Scarlet Letter*, p. 245).

New emphases now claim attention. Hester, the voluptuous, defiant aristocrat, shrinks into old Hepzibah, the 'gaunt, sallow, rusty-jointed maiden', wizened, blighted, and self-imprisoned by the repugnance of a scowl which nullifies all attempts to smile in human sympathy; condescending in her attitudes, but in the face of these hard, democratic times, lacking the financial substance to back up her lady's airs. Dimmesdale's spirituality, sensitivity and ghostly effeteness go into Hepzibah's brother, Clifford, the abortive 'lover of the Beautiful' who has suffered the degradation to his spirit of wrongful imprisonment. But if the Hester in his sister has been humbled by time to the point where she must bargain openly with the world, the vicious involutions of a Dimmesdale in Clifford have been lessened into a passive introspection. Chillingworth's predatory role in *The Scarlet Letter* was that of the destructive representative of the Puritans inside the hidden drama which existed, unrealized, in the midst of their conscious code. As the cuckold who leaves behind the outer morality once he has come upon 'artistic' opportunities; as the physician who inverts the conventional meaning of his role, Chillingworth has a parasitism which Hawthorne now translates in terms of two contemporary figures: Judge Pyncheon, a massive creation of double-dealing, the invading brute male force entering upon a house of women and effeminacy; and Holgrave the daguerreotypist, the modern scientific artist of the truth, the non-intuitional spectator lodging in the old New England house and dispassionately savouring the situation as if it were a fascinating private drama enacted for his benefit. The Pearl element, the dance of vigour through the deadening scene, is allotted to Phoebe, another figure of untempered joy and light.

It is when one considers the artistic presentation of Phoebe and the Judge, the two extremes in Hawthorne's spectrum, that one realizes how alarmingly disproportionate an art can become when its tutoring is done by an ineffectual moral interest. In Phoebe and the Judge there is, respectively, an under-focus and over-focus of artistic concentration. With the Judge, Puritanism has run its forceful course into materialism, and Hawthorne pinpoints in him (p. 201) the state of those whose marauding wills organize an external, physical territory yet leave no room for spiritual freedom: 'They possess vast ability in grasping, and arranging, and appropriating to themselves the big, heavy, solid unrealities, such as gold, landed estate, offices of trust and emolument, and public honors.' But whatever the show of moral criticism which Hawthorne exercises on the Poe-like movement of 'big, heavy, solid' matter, he cannot prevent his values being lost under the stress of his own 'arranging, and appropriating' when he indicts the Judge. The artist tends to freeze the bulk of the public man of action into a stilled object, whose hypocrisies and crimes can be inspected and turned over at leisure, whose every aspect can be known, seen behind and in front, and appropriated into the mind. The Judge is not so much an intricate sinner as a summarized weight of circumstantial evidence, a generalized effect made up of manifold detail, with 'the snowy whiteness of his linen, the polish of his boots, the handsomeness of his gold-headed cane, the square and roomy fashion of his coat . . . the studied propriety of his dress and equipment' (p. 203), with his continual shifts between a scowl and an infernal smile of overpowering heat.

Passing from the immense effort bestowed by Hawthorne on the presentation of this ponderous burden of guilt, and looking from the stiffened density of the Judge's character to the redeeming figure of Phoebe, one sees that she is not completely able to bear the moral light of transfiguration expected of her by the author. This time Hawthorne has no alert, enigmatic Pearl to save him from working the action by a morality at low-pressure, by values so enfeebled that in enforcing them Hawthorne's will makes them redundant. Just as guilt is now less subtly evoked (and most of it is eventually moved on to the Judge), so the concept of good and innocence blurs into the simplified meaning of Phoebe. As Hawthorne views the disposing of the parts in the picture, it is 'the stern old stuff of Puritanism with a gold thread in the web' (p. 73). Like Pearl, Phoebe grows into maturity in the course of the novel, from a girl to a tempered woman who is filled out with knowledge of sadness and thoughtfulness. But she is not a problem figure like Pearl, and because Hawthorne can circumscribe Phoebe he settles early on for a received rather than an earned positive. She is a New England practical girl, bringing light into the house where her stern counterpart, the Judge, intrudes with menace. She touches the ghosts and dreams of the gloom with the warmth of the 'Actual' and 'sympathy', bustling in with a conventional world of thinking, an everyday homeliness, which gradually disperses the mystery—a dispersal which means dilution. For the light that Phoebe brings 'as a gleam of sunshine falling on the floor through a shadow of twinkling leaves' (p. 76) is not the sun which accepts the strange realities brought to view in the small Boston settlement of an earlier period. It is the diffuse sun of a vast, patchwork democracy, the 'broad and simple daylight' of Hawthorne's contemporary America.

The rigour of the author's stance is weakened when the outer consciousness tends to mean the extremely superficial, when relaxation brings exaggeration, so that a cruder sense of guilt demands greater innocence and purer redemption. Here the ironic paradoxes of *The Scarlet Letter* are dampened into pity. So, when Hepzibah opens her little shop and makes her timid first step into modern America, the reader is taught to observe (p. 42) no 'tragic dignity' (in a situation which resembles Hester's first exposure on the scaffold) but is asked instead to feel the 'purest pathos' in his contemplation of the decayed aristocrat as she attempts to come to terms with a hustling democracy. When Hawthorne now notes the incongruous and the insufficient, he more readily calls for a response which allows the playfulness of gentle humour or the forgiving smile of pity than a shrewd to-and-fro assessment of the intricacies involved in the full judgement of a situation. One remembers the moral attention he exacted in his picture of the diseased relationship between Chillingworth and Dimmesdale: these two figures disintegrating further and further into damnation—the man of medicine who keeps his patient sick and the man of exalted spiritual purity so self-befouling—in a crazed reversal of values, whereby the priest encourages as curative treatment the destructiveness of his worst enemy. But when two shrivelled ghosts meet in *The House of the Seven Gables*, and the wizened Hepzibah, with smiles of love that cannot help turning perversely into scowls, attempts to entertain her painfully sensitive brother on his return from prison (p. 120), a different attitude is sought:

There could be few more tearful sights—and heaven forgive us if a smile insist on mingling with our conception of it!—few sights with truer pathos in them than Hepzibah presented on that first afternoon. . . . How patiently did she endeavor to wrap Clifford up in her great, warm love, and make it all the world to him, so that he should retain no torturing sense of the coldness and dreariness without! Her little efforts to amuse him! How pitiful, yet magnanimous, they were!

As it ponders the awkward gropings of the two old people in the prison of themselves, as it smilingly delights in the tears called up by the incongruities of the scene, the pathos that watches here is a weakened moral eye. Hawthorne yields easily to an over-release of forgiveness, because although it is allowed that Hepzibah, Clifford, and Holgrave transgress in different ways against the bond of human sympathy—Hepzibah with her anomalous delusions of power and vain glory, Clifford with his super-refined aestheticism, Holgrave with his over-detached appraisal of the spectacle—their total fund of offence hardly amounts to sin, just as the pathos hardly rises to a judgement.

Where Hawthorne attempts to come to a more acute indictment, as with the Judge, it can be seen that his art's activity now pretends to serve moral purposes while it is really serving its own self-delighting ends. On the verge of discovering the material treasure which he believes is hidden in the house, the Judge suffers a fatal fit of apoplexy and dies in a chair, stilled by his author for denial of the real worth, the spiritual treasure. But the play of mockery which Hawthorne casts round the dead figure suggests not a moralizing effort but an exhibition of artistic power. The author becomes an unimpeded Chillingworth feeding on an unaware victim. The moral watchfulness has disappeared into pathos which lets the art loose into a kind of raw power. It is a pushing, mocking note which is at large for most of the novel—a pervasive sense of controlling forces crudely jerking the manipulated to nervous attention: as with Judge Pyncheon's menace working on Clifford, the shop-bell of urgent America behind Hepzibah, the Italian boy behind his barrel-organ figures, and time behind everybody.

There is a cynical sense of control which Hawthorne cannot exorcise from the atmosphere because it is supplanting moral control. When, with a frenzy equalling that of the frustrated crowd of Pyncheon ghosts round the hidden secret, or the busy Judge, or manifold America on the move, the Italian's barrel-organ figures suddenly start to play at the turn of their gold-hungry master's crank, the cynical point emerges (pp. 145–6) that 'all dance to one identical tune, and, in spite of our ridiculous activity, bring nothing finally to pass. For the most remarkable aspect of the affair was that, at the cessation of the music, everybody was petrified, at once, from the most extravagant life into a dead torpor.' It is like a Poe masquerade in miniature—so like it, in fact, that the cynical idea threatens the spiritual positives that Hawthorne wants to launch in resolution at the end of the novel: for 'Saddest of all, moreover', among the dolls, 'the lover was none the happier for the maiden's granted kiss! But, rather than swallow this last too acid ingredient, we reject the whole moral of the show.' The rejection is only in principle, however, for Hawthorne's art has, by its mockery, let in the journalistic, exploiting interest, the opportunities for Poe's kind of 'exposé'. It is inevitable that where Hawthorne fixes the dead Judge into a static, literary photograph, there Holgrave comes later, to take his daguerreotype.

The treatment of the Judge eats up possibilities with a thoroughness, a ridiculing effectiveness, which in the end diminishes the value of the freedom which his death brings about. It is as though here Hawthorne is caught between an American author's sense of limitless possibility, as a man made larger by his inclusion in the world's business, and the smaller, cynical sense of utter poverty and spiritual restriction. There is a terrible discrepancy between all the huge physical, material spaces he can cover and the actual spiritual distance he can go. It is a particular American irony which produces Clifford's unhappy poise at the window of the house, as if he would throw himself out extravagantly to merge with the bustle of a passing political procession, yet is held back by his introspective self. In the two chapters, 'The Flight of Two Owls' and 'Governor Pyncheon', Hawthorne has pared the choices down harshly: intense, exaggerated activity or petrification.

At last Hepzibah and Clifford break out from drab containment into the American day which, like the forest and the ocean to Hester and Dimmesdale, offers an escape into freedom and endless horizons. As their train flies on, Clifford comes to life, spiritualizing with idealism the world of material inventions, conjuring up possibilities, and seeming to enact Holgrave's bright American hope (p. 159) that ' "the moss-grown and rotten Past is to be torn down, and lifeless institutions to be thrust out of the way, and their dead corpses buried, and everything to begin anew." ' But one corpse remains unburied and unreckoned with: Hawthorne has not yet finished with the full meaning of the Judge's corruption. There is still a cloud in the open sky, and Hepzibah looks back regretfully at the 'home', the reality, from which she and Clifford have uprooted themselves too soon. The escape into the outer world remains a flight into superficial, heady materialism because Hawthorne has still not done with the inner drabness of its representative, the Judge. The author is delayed in the postmortem, and it is this spiritual slowing of Hepzibah's and Clifford's flight which checks their over-hasty release into life.

But it is not a moral caution which Hawthorne is exercising, rather the power of the organ-grinder to stop the action at will. While Clifford on the train rushes on, toying with glamorous future possibilities, Hawthorne supplies these unfulfilled possibilities for the Judge, runs over the packed time-table which the Judge can no longer undertake, taunts in the chapter-heading, 'Governor Pyncheon', at the office which the Judge can now never occupy, and mockingly hints at the treasure just beyond the dead man's reach. The stream of external life and time goes on without the Judge's participation, and the train goes its way, leaving behind its two old passengers. The two chapters of outer flight and leisurely investigation neutralize each other, as if Hawthorne still has his earlier image in mind—that of the cab and omnibus trade which flits (p. 143) across the end of the street, 'typifying that vast rolling vehicle the world, the end of whose journey is everywhere and nowhere.' The barrel-organ figures start into ludicrous energy, and then stop; the Judge, like one of Hepzibah's gingerbread figures, has his meaning devoured; and all returns to a dead stillness.

It is in this stillness, as Phoebe comes back to the silent house where the dead man sits, that Hawthorne seeks to present a golden, youthful dawning on the basis of all the previous dark workings-out—the coming together of Phoebe with her twinkling sunshine life and Holgrave, the objective assessor, who makes 'pictures out of sunshine'. But the 'flower of Eden', the new relationship, which springs out of the black, rich soil of long decay and ancient sins, after the American ground has been despoiled by the wilful and the wicked, is too sudden a growth, too fabulously forgetful of all that nourishes its resurrection: 'The bliss which makes all things true, beautiful, and holy shone around this youth and maiden. They were conscious of nothing sad nor old. They transfigured the earth, and made it Eden again, and themselves the first two dwellers in it' (p. 267). Hawthorne conjures up a new Eden out of the first, bad American beginning, and yet because of the rough will which lies under the idealism, it remains unratified.

4

It is ratification that the socialist community, the new Eden of *The Blithedale Romance* (1852), so urgently requires. Even when

Hawthorne re-creates the society of the Brook Farm experiment as a literary successor to the Puritan colony and the diffuse, busy democracy of his previous novels, to be the one community where the inner life and culture might link up with the reality of physical action in the world, the Hester-like need remains to make a psychological entrance into the land, to impinge upon the blankness, weather it in the mind. ' "This spick-and-span novelty does not quite suit my taste," ' says one of the more hesitant Utopians (p. 162). ' "It is time, too, for children to be born among us. . . . And I shall never feel as if this were a real, practical, as well as poetical, system of human life, until somebody has sanctified it by death." ' It is the corpse of the wild will which is needed, and although its death *seems* to occur, Hawthorne can neither realize its persistence nor use its apparent downfall for moral purposes. The art is now alone with itself and the author at last: the pathos and the pity have been consumed. Left untaught and unmitigated, the art fastens upon itself and its dilemmas with an effect of self-strangulation.

Significantly, a literary artist, Coverdale, occupies the very front of the picture while, at the same time, a controlling wizard-showman stands dimly at the back. It is the 'creative'–'resolvent' situation of pursuer and pursued in Poe's 'Man of the Crowd'. The curiosity of the foreground narrator, the idealistic poet, is employed in making out the connections, the correspondences, the secret significances which link together the three main characters. Through his eyes the figures of Zenobia, Hollingsworth, and Priscilla are confused and inflated into phantasmagoria, waiting for the theme which the artist believes to be there if he can but tease it out. But in the activity of Coverdale's other self, the devilish background figure, Westerwelt, one sees why there is no unifying meaning other than a sensational, deathly one. For in the showman-artist the main interest is materialistic, as he instigates pseudo-mysteries, groups relationships, and sets up the apparatus of a tragic moral drama while suppressing the chance for any real moral explanation to take place.

It is inevitable that the figure of moral redemption in the novel, the pallid Priscilla, should now, after Phoebe, be a mere ghost in the imagination—an idea for Westerwelt, the hurdy-gurdy man of the novel, to exploit for psychic thrills. There is a self-defeating quality that comes from this control: what is supposedly opened up is at the same moment being shut down. No matter how many veils of consciousness Coverdale or Hollingsworth take off the Veiled Lady, Priscilla, the secret rottenness, the masculine spiritualizing of the woman, have many more layers in reserve. As with Dimmesdale, there is a sickness working in inverse proportions: the more daring the supposed exposure, the worse becomes the secrecy; the greater the mental confession, the falser becomes the consciousness to itself. Between them, Coverdale and Westerwelt are the detective and the criminal, immorally tightening the psychological compass of the novel till the strong living figures are forced into violent, lavish action to break out of the network.

Coverdale himself supplies a symbol which epitomizes the peculiar quality of the novel, its desire to squeeze out the life of the vigorous and have it in the mind as a spectacular hallucination. After the poet's first experience with the Blithedale community, he retires self-protectively for periods into a wood where he makes himself a 'hermitage' among the branches of a pine-tree. For all the socialism, he is not risking his detachment as the spectator on life. He then observes (p. 128) a huge wild grape-vine which has twisted itself up the tree, caught hold of several neighbouring trees, 'and married the whole clump with a perfectly inextricable knot of polygamy.' A hollow chamber has been formed by the decay of some pine branches, 'which the vine had lovingly strangled with its embrace, burying them from the light of day in an aërial sepulchre of its own leaves.' Here sits the spy on the drama in a nook of cross-purposes, a place of deadly artistic paradoxes. As in the previous novels, the flower of eventual innocence is nurtured on the shadow and humus of decay, but, as the 'loving' strangulations of the image suggest, the fruit to come in Priscilla has to feed on a disintegrated vitality. At Blithedale it is idealistic, brotherly love which is squeezed out of existence. Coverdale finds (pp. 172–3) that the special 'closeness of relationship' operating in the Blithedale community as a 'species of nervous sympathy', 'betokening an actual bond of love among us', is impractical, 'mortal tempers being so infirm and variable as they are. If one of us happened to give his neighbor a box on the ear, the tingle was immediately felt on the same side of everybody's head.'

Hollingsworth and Zenobia withdraw from this network of communal good work, as individuals of undiminished exclusiveness. But they withdraw to be re-established in a closer power-struggle. It is as if the two are heightened, by the hidden sensuality in Coverdale, into an over-vivid, almost caricatured life, so large and powerful that Hawthorne cannot expand the novel's awareness to fit them. Therefore, in the background a considerable fictional apparatus is being assembled all the while to fix their meaning in a static moral tragedy; and in the foreground, with Coverdale, their modifying is prepared for. He is hard at work, assigning sensational captions in the Blithedale episodes—so that Zenobia's 'passionate force' and Hollingsworth's 'dark, self-delusive egotism' enable Coverdale to look forward to 'some sufficiently tragic catastrophe'. Hollingsworth has a male power, the persisting Puritan in him making him a would-be reformer of criminals. With 'his great shaggy head, his heavy brow, his dark complexion, his abundant beard, and the rude strength with which his features seem to have been hammered out of iron' (pp. 51–2), he is presented as the contestant against a similar indomitableness in Zenobia. She in her female grandeur is a modern, blatant Hester, an Oriental queen set in a democratic landscape, with no scarlet letter of shame but (with theatrical dash) her tropical flower of passion. They are carried towards the sham morality-struggle of the novel, by which Hollingsworth is designated a moral hero when he rescues Priscilla from the arms of the magician and Zenobia is incriminated as Wester-welt's accomplice in the suppression of Priscilla and her 'innocent' love.

But the morality play which Hawthorne stages in the New England village hall does not stand up even with the lax conviction which Hardy displays in his similar picturings in *The Return of the Native*. The innocence which is later asserted in Thomasin Yeobright is already at a sick, transcendental extreme in Priscilla; and the passionateness in Eustacia, which accepts its condemnation out of bewilderment, still resists its fate in Zenobia's attack on her judges. Like her Egdon counterpart, Zenobia goes under, as when she begins (p. 259) to sink beneath Hollingsworth's judgement at the old Puritan rock in the forest: 'It was as if a great, invisible, irresistible weight were pressing her to the earth.' But before she has gone she replies, in defiant astuteness, to the implicit assumptions and the 'invisible' mechanism which wants to make her fall *appear* irresistible. She will not accept the cunning slur upon her sensuality, the hidden nineteenth-century verdict by which Fenimore Cooper, for instance, casts a stain on Judith Hutter in *The Deerslayer*. Zenobia knows the situation: ' "What strange beings you men are, Mr. Coverdale!—is it not so? It is the simplest thing in the world with you to bring a woman before your secret tribunals, and judge and condemn her unheard, and then tell her to go free without a sentence." ' (P. 253.) She has enough insight to realize that Hollingsworth's Puritanism has led him to accept his part in this dubiously moral identification of values. His purpose has 'stifled down [his] inmost consciousness', making him the criminal, not the reformer of criminals or the judge—' "A cold, heartless, self-beginning and self-ending piece of mechanism!" ' (p. 257).

Hawthorne's intelligence, therefore, suggests the falseness of the moral denouement, without being prepared to reject the methods by which the values are finally assigned. He accepts the way in which Hollingsworth survives as the champion of gentle values in Priscilla, at the expense of Zenobia's survival and his own masculine vitality. The important effect sought, it seems, is the humbling of the proud Americans, a lessening of the magnetism and power in relationships so that a new, more tolerable reality may emerge. The morality-method is a faulty, if useful means of seeing into the future with Priscilla's clairvoyance. So the proud go down under the enfeebling morality which she represents: Hollingsworth is sapped of his strength and Zenobia is drowned. But when her drowned body is recovered (p. 275), the attempted moral effect is derided still:

She knelt, as if in prayer. With the last, choking consciousness, her soul, bubbling out through her lips, it may be, had given herself up to the Father, reconciled and penitent. But her arms! They were bent before her, as if she struggled against Providence in never-ending hostility. Her hands! They were clenched in immitigable defiance.

It is a defiance which one sees again in Ahab and in Magua, the Indian of *The Last of the Mohicans*. In them, as with Zenobia, a native force breaks out of the inadequate morality which attempts to encase it. It is like Usher's sister cracking the 'beautiful' vision which hems her in.

But the surprising volte-face of the description belongs in manner to a novel where the holy and the vile may become interchangeable at the command of an artistic demon. One remembers the spiritual materialism of the man whom Coverdale listens to at the village hall (pp. 234–5) before Westerwelt's show: 'Human character was but soft wax in his hands; and guilt, or virtue, only the forms into which he should see fit to mould it. The religious sentiment was a flame which he could blow up with his breath, or a spark which he could utterly extinguish.' Coverdale does not consciously want to believe the depraved idealism which this represents, but it is only a short step from Westerwelt's show to Coverdale's discovery (pp. 248–9) of the Blithedalers playing at a masque in the forest, seen in a kind of artistic delirium. A mixture of figures from American colonial history and Hawthorne's short stories—Puritans and witches, cavaliers and revolutionaries, pastoral shepherds of idealism and rough woodsmen of actuality —are all dancing to the devil's tune, intertwined in meaning and individuality with vine-like horror. Whirling round so fast, 'their separate incongruities were blended all together, and they became a kind of entanglement.' Suddenly they stop and start to pursue Coverdale at their masquer-devil's bidding. The narrator is 'like a mad poet hunted by chimeras' of his own seeking. So in one moment all the links are made everywhere in a terrible homogeneity, and yet at the same all the moral consciousness has vanished into nowhere. The artistic will has fastened on itself, making a tight mental circle and prison. As the author moves so does his subject, reflecting back his own image.

III

Moby Dick and the 'All Stretchable Philosophy'

IN *The Scarlet Letter* it is not a question of the profundity or truth in the Puritan ethic which matters to Hawthorne. Instead, he warms to the Puritans' authoritative stand, their enduring *conviction* of their rightness, their unparalysed power of action, their capacity for including (even unconsciously) within their communal vision strange states of being which might otherwise remain undefined. The Puritan fathers could endure against diffuseness, for they 'had fortitude and self-reliance, and, in time of difficulty or peril, stood up for the welfare of the state like a line of cliffs against a tempestuous tide'. But in Hollingsworth's later phase, the Puritan firmness and the masculine decisiveness it represents, have reached bankruptcy. The old rigour has become an instrumental force that spends itself in a last attack on the vanities of the flesh before it falls away enfeebled. The patriarchal power has gone and a new virgin-mother love has grown out of its disintegration when Coverdale meets Hollingsworth and Priscilla towards the end (pp. 282–3) of *The Blithedale Romance*: 'the powerfully-built man showed a self-distrustful weakness, and a childlike or childish tendency to press close, and closer still, to the side of the slender woman whose arm was within his.'

It is a position implied by Melville when (p. 424) Ishmael gives his vain, Pearl-like appeal in *Moby Dick* (1851)—'Where is the foundling's father hidden?'—but the cry comes from a greater extreme of disintegration than Hawthorne envisaged and is answered by Melville with a coherence that is equally extreme, as he gathers in the castaway fragments of the human (and especially American) family to merge them in a stranger body of love than that signified by Priscilla. The Puritans of *The Scarlet Letter* are rock-like but their authoritativeness is transformed as Father Mapple mounts his 'self-containing stronghold' of a pulpit in the New Bedford chapel to deliver his sermon on Jonah and the Whale (p. 47) while the Atlantic storm howls outside: ' "But oh! shipmates! on the starboard hand of every woe, there is a sure delight; and higher the top of that delight, than the bottom of the woe is deep." ' One remembers the consolation of the new, futuristic morality for Hawthorne—the fruits disclosed when the vine in the Blithedale wood strangles the clump of separate pines, marrying them 'with a perfectly inextricable knot of polygamy'. Out of the ruins of the old, proud faith, the patriarchal wilfulness, Hawthorne extracts an invalid's humility and nourishes Priscilla. But Melville's compressions of sensuous being are more intensive: he produces Queequeg and the dead nurture to feed the spread of an all-embracing, inorganic network of hope and devoutness: 'Life folded Death; Death trellised Life; the grim god wived with youthful Life, and begat him curly-headed glories' (p. 390).

Ishmael is here describing the carpet of verdure being woven over the bones of a shipwrecked Sperm whale on the shore of a Pacific island, and this 'Bower in the Arsacides' is a long, decomposing way from the Blithedale wood. More violently than Hawthorne could intimate—when, in *The Scarlet Letter*, he suggested a new fruitfulness emerging under the Puritan pastor's stern dominion—Melville has trained and naturalized the consciousness in his own way; awareness of mind and body is 'compelled to flourish' along new pathways, but only after it has been wrenched again and again from its old Christian inclinings. When scruples have been killed in the consciousness by such crippling education, the reward is a bizarre calm for the feelings, a kind of distended, illimitable beatitude.

I

In contrast with Melville, Hawthorne's method in *The Scarlet Letter* appears slow, as he sets up pictures of supposed moral good or honest confession, and then ironically dismantles them. No sooner has a film of secure consciousness settled in *Moby Dick*, than it is violently and rapidly dispatched. Peace is not to be had until Melville's restlessness has gone through layer after layer of thought and feeling—letting a tranquil veil cover the scene, then tearing it away, consigning it to its place among the other desensitized layers, all heaped up in a great myriad mass by the ruthless drive. Supersession follows supersession as Melville frets at the civilized inclination to accept 'all the horrors of the half-known life' in an ethical sleep of familiarity.

It is the disruptiveness in *Moby Dick's* opening chapter which brings all those *habitués*, 'tied to counters, nailed to benches, clinched to desks', to look out beyond their weekday life of work and habit to a religious calm, far away through the disintegrative experience they refrain from undertaking. The old, vulnerable sense of kinship with one's fellow human beings has to be fragmented irrevocably before Melville can again tolerate the idea of community, and the sea-experience is the great breaker. That the sea encloses the land, the infinite the finite, Sunday the weekdays, seems to be part of the strange pall of realization which hangs over the crowds of New York 'water-gazers' as they stand in their hypnotized thousands upon the 'insular city of the Manhattoes'. These Sabbath-worshippers gaze out to the Atlantic not as Manhattan Christians, but as aboriginal islanders, with the weekday land-consciousness reduced to a sharply-defined minimum by the greater watery blankness. Indeed, as Melville subdivides further (p. 106), the whole earth is only an island, and the ships that voyage from it are islands, carrying men who are unattached islands: 'They were nearly all Islanders in the *Pequod*, *Isolatos* too, I call such, not acknowledging the common continent of men, but each *Isolato* living on a separate continent of his own.' And the nationality of the ship which carries these fragments—dismembered from the 'joint-stock' body of mankind's hearth and home, and held together by a greater human fragment—is significantly (p. 491) that of the world's orphan: 'its wood could only be American!'

But even on the sea the consciousness has a chance to settle and make an external, ideal beauty from it, so that the water becomes secure American land again, ready to be pioneered, and the distant ship, with only the tops of its masts visible above the high waves, appears (p. 423) to be struggling 'through the tall grass of a rolling prairie: as when the western emigrants' horses only show their erected ears, while their hidden bodies widely wade through the amazing verdure.' Melville, however, forces the consciousness back from the familiar expansiveness, making it revert inwards to the narrower, violent quarters of the spirit known to Poe and Hawthorne. Sleep is impossible and the American ethic deceptive until Melville has mentally inured himself to the savagery and wilfulness packed under the surface. It is as if he is hurtfully re-creating for himself the feeling of 'the full awfulness of the sea which aboriginally belongs to it' when he contemplates (p. 245) the 'magical, sometimes horrible' whale-line surrounding each of the *Pequod's* boats: 'Thus the whale-line folds the whole boat in its complicated coils, twisting and writhing around it in almost every direction. All the oarsmen are involved in its perilous contortions; so that to the timid eye of the landsman, they seem as Indian jugglers, with the deadliest snakes sportively festooning their limbs.' The human flesh is webbed and riddled by this poisonous decoration of mental complexity, exactly like one of Poe's self-confusing arabesques, but Melville brings the mind out of clear judgement into dilemma, to make a different dream-soothing out of the forgetfulness. There is a cold, hysterical audacity in the suggestion of the unthinking sailors as 'Indian jugglers'—those whose art inures them to the dangerous writhing, to the terror electrifying the mildest calm, as if their feelings were immunized by the horror and there were a ghastly joy ensuing.

To get that curious amnesia Melville must break distinctions that the moral, 'land' consciousness makes between familiar good and evil, between beginning and end, person and person, storm and calm. There is a confused inter-reaction: Melville turns back and forth, so that one cannot determine whether it is the calm that contains the storm it supersedes or the storm that contains the superseded calm. There is a nervous insistence on reaching a poised, nerveless non-judgement by making it thrillingly uncertain whether it is the mild purity of whiteness which intensifies the latent horror beneath it, or the horror which heightens and justifies the whiteness. Constantly Melville is shocking the mind out of its drift into ordinary sleep and returning it to a poise. 'Over Descartian vortices you hover' is the sudden caution given the Pantheist dreamer at the mast-head (p. 139) when he is lulled by the sea into a reverie of sympathy. Backwards and forwards goes Ishmael at the helm when, after watching the hellish try-works fire, he falls into a hypnotized drowse. When he awakes, the picture has turned round: he is morally and literally reversed, so that the ship appears (p. 368) to be 'not so much bound to any haven ahead as rushing from all havens astern'. Other sleepers are forced to awake and climb to a stark poise of knowledge

—like the drowsy seaman who rises from his bed to mount the first watch for Moby Dick in the Whale's own ground, only to fall and drown; like the crew of sleepers awakened at dawn on the first day of the Chase by the knocking of the aboriginal Daggoo.

This constant start into perilous awareness, back and forth, is of the mind circling within circles it has already drawn, making smaller and smaller the vortex spiral. When the memory looks back at the previous circles gone round it is with a tired horror of dismay. As Ishmael sails out of New Bedford, he sees (p. 56) berthed side by side those ships which have just returned and those about to embark, the beginning and the end of a world-experience brought together and foreshortened in a weary tele-scoping of time: 'one most perilous and long voyage ended, only begins a second; and a second ended, only begins a third, and so on, for ever and for aye. Such is the endlessness, yea, the intoler-ableness of all earthly effort.' Time contracts 'before' and 'behind' into one when all the immense circumnavigations of humanity lead 'only through numberless perils to the very point whence we started, where those that we left behind secure, were all the time before us' (p. 207).

Yet the voyage of the *Pequod* discovers more: the circling of mankind inside the coffin of time reaches a point where physical death and life have their distinctions erased. Melville is more persistent than Poe in realizing that the consciousness can feed for what seems eternity on dead matter, once the physical life has been devoured and digested. The organic quality is killed, but the material is indestructible, and it has a further, horrible exist-ence. So when the sharks are massacred at midnight round the *Pequod*, murdered in their turn as they feed upon the lashed body of the whale murdered by its hunters, the mind contracts the savage meaning even further, forcing it to revert upon itself, making (p. 263) an endless, mad circle: the sharks 'viciously snap-ped, not only at each other's disembowelments, but like flexible bows, bent round, and bit their own; till those entrails seemed swallowed over and over again by the same mouth, to be op-positely voided by the gaping wound.' When Ahab is first seen (p. 107) he looks 'like a man cut away from the stake, when the fire has overrunningly wasted all the limbs without consuming them', and the torment of endless material existence is felt again when Starbuck's boat finds itself (p. 197) in the midst of a squall 'like a white fire upon the prairie, in which, unconsumed, we were burning; immortal in these jaws of death!'

Hawthorne in *The Scarlet Letter* inverts moral values, bringing cause and effect, the holy appearance and the demonic reality, so close that they share the same tight space. But Melville inverts values not to set up an ironic reaction between the moral pose and its distorted image, but to press the two together with such force that the irony and discrepancy disappear, and a complete circulation has been set up, with good flowing continuously into evil, evil into good, all digested to become the same fluent material. Melville seeks no irony of moral reference when the *Pequod* sails out on the whale-hunt, owned by Christians— Quakers 'with a vengeance'—whose mission is to kill the creatures of God in order that their sperm oil may light the churches and houses of Christendom. The sleeping inattentiveness of men to their own world-hypocrisy is too hysterically obvious for an ordinary ironic edge to be inserted. Brutal actuality runs on, without a flaw in the joint which connects it with its civilized, initiating principles.

Beginning and end, cause and effect, swallow each other's tails, when Melville considers the *Pequod*, persistent on the blind circuit of cannibalism, with the dismembered parts of her previous victims supplying the ship with equipment for its purpose—the dead whales aligned to pursue the living. The whales' teeth make pins for the 'one continuous jaw' of the bulwarks; the jawbone is the source of the tiller, the captain's false leg, and his ivory stool. The ship altogether 'was a thing of trophies—a cannibal of a craft, tricking herself forth in the chased bones of her enemies' (p. 65). In this destructive circuit of continuity, the whale-chasers are themselves followed. The ship pursues the Grand Armada of whales through the Sunda Straits into the China seas, and yet is itself hunted by the Malays. Ahab wheels back and forth to grasp (p. 332) the two situations as one: 'in his forward turn beholding the monsters he chased, and in the after one the bloodthirsty pirates chasing *him*.' So the circling continues, right to the last moments of the novel, to the final round of reckless intensity, when the sharks are ravenously chopping away at the oars of the boat that is driving Ahab to his prey, Moby Dick. At this mad hour, judgement is stunned by the cannibalism: who can tell, asks the captain, ' "whether these sharks swim to feast on a whale or on Ahab?" ' (p. 489).

But by then Christian feeling has been so crippled under pressure, so madly crowded upon, so twisted round and round upon itself by the inward-spiralling mind, that it is ready for release. The coiled spring is unwound but it leaps back beyond its old position to a height where it oversees all previous consciousness. Religious feeling has been stretched to assimilate everything by the wicked tension to which Melville has subjected it. It becomes a kind of radiant, superior, carrion-like faith which lives off the murders and cannibalism under its vision.

One sees this expanding movement in the 'Stubb's Supper' chapter and immediately after, in the 'Try-Works' and in the 'Doubloon' chapters, where attitude rises upon attitude till a poise is reached, an inclusive, multiple sight. With the sharks gorging at midnight on the dead whale, one is present at the mindless, savage, inner core—the evil blatant and noisy. Then there is Stubb, the second mate, eating the same whale-meat as the sharks, but finding the sharks too noisy. So the negro Fleece, the cooker of Stubb's whale-steak, is cynically urged by the mate to muffle the sharks with a layer of good Christian words; and the black Lamb of God obliges by preaching a sermon on the virtues of silence and Christian brotherhood to the oblivious fish (thus providing a parody of Starbuck's uneasy faith in which the knowledge of evil in the world undermines his wish to believe in the absoluteness of good). The whole scene of eating and fraudulent preaching is lit by the whale-oil burning in the ship's lanterns, supplying a strange light of understanding over the morally blind. Out of the murdered flesh a liquid is distilled, burning with an infinite, 'holy' silence in the noise of the world. It is an impassive, poised benevolence whose light allows sharks and man-sharks to proceed with their business and yet includes all the layers of consciousness below it. In this expansiveness, the whale becomes an ever-philanthropic martyr, giving eternally that ungrateful man shall take.

Only by building out from disintegration to an abstract immanence can Melville here conceive a blessedness. It is not a source of active good, however, for this new comprehensive sanity is martyred and tortured into existence by turning insanity inside out. When in the 'Doubloon' chapter, the spiralling consciousness is released, and all the interpretations of the coin nailed on the mast build up into one large brotherhood of truth, for Pip the cabin boy the condition of having this multiple sight is intolerable madness. The verb is declined (p. 376) to make a meaningless sum—' "I look, you look, he looks; we look, ye look, they look." ' A strange kind of hope is fashioned out of the assimilated material of despair, yet it needs Queequeg the cannibal to make the poised truth bearable.

2

Queequeg is the positive figure of the novel created out of disintegration. Therefore the values and health which he implies are ideal wish-fulfilments made out of the breakage of Christian sensibility. In him the consciousness spins back from its perverse wrenching round and imagines now (without innately knowing, because it has lost touch with a living wholeness) that Queequeg's way is the direction that the positive should go. As in a dream, he is what the sick negative imagines that sanity, love, the spontaneous life, the creative unconscious, should be like.

Because Queequeg is created under such conditions, it is not surprising that he can only contribute as a momentary saviour, an interceding mirage from a dream state, rather than as a long-term remedial influence for good. But he is more important as a receiver of broken feeling, a strange trustee of the faith lodged in him by the unfaithful. At the first lowering for a whale, when the hazards of chance turn the first mate's wisdom into folly, when his boat is lost and coffined in the white squall, Starbuck's Christian faith cannot stretch across the pitiless, blank immensities. He lights a candle as a beacon, but hardly believes in the promise of salvation. It is Queequeg the pagan who is handed the lantern (p. 197) and who thus becomes the repository of decayed Christian consciousness, 'the standard-bearer of this forlorn hope.' The situation not only parallels Stubb's eating scene, but it is also a reminder of Ishmael's thoughts (pp. 36–7) on the plaques (those 'bitter blanks') commemorating the sailors lost at sea, in the Whaleman's Chapel: 'What deadly voids and unbidden infidelities in the lines that seem to gnaw upon all Faith, and refuse resurrections to the beings who have placelessly perished without a grave.'

But then, if one can bite on enough, one can move outwards, encompass those encompassers, open oneself wide enough to admit the widest voids. So containment turns destruction into creation, and 'Faith, like a jackal, feeds among the tombs, and even from these dead doubts she gathers her most vital hope.' It is this 'jackal' faith which sustains Ishmael after the bad experience of the squall, in the chapter appropriately named 'The Hyena'. Only the laughing hyena in Ishmael can find food in despair, and only Queequeg can sanctify this sub-Christian exultance. So with Queequeg as the trustee, Ishmael is able to resign himself and make his will, with the realization that he is committed to other men's folly and chance destructions. Having settled up with death through Queequeg as the lawyer and legatee, Ishmael manages (p. 200) a tranquil resurrection of the spirit, 'like a quiet ghost with a clean conscience sitting inside the bars of a snug family vault'.

In such feeling there is a controlled, hysterical bravado which smiles at the reader and dares him to fault the emotional skill of this posture. As Ishmael re-enters the human family under new conditions, the self-aware glibness of his contentment develops later into the strange, exaggerated ease with which he works the dead lumps of whale sperm and returns them to fluid by the squeeze of the human hand: 'I squeezed that sperm till I myself almost melted into it . . . and I found myself unwittingly squeezing my co-labourers' hands in it, mistaking their hands for the gentle globules' (pp. 361–2). Out of the compression comes an indiscriminate love which for Melville is no longer Christian, because it has lost its right to moral criticism. It has been broken into a wide, loose tolerance, so that Ishmael realizes that men squeezing sperm together may flowingly meet in 'the very milk and sperm of kindness'. In the same way, with equal accidental ease, the man who stands on the slippery sheet of blubber may, with a slice of his spade, cut off his own toes or those of his assistants. But, asks the Ishmael who is bizarrely adjusted to the indifference of it all, to the soft squeeze of the hand, or the chopping off of toes, if the mutilation should occur, 'would you'—he dares us with poised nonchalance—'be very much astonished?' The capacity to be neither astonished nor afraid is the very height of attainment desired here, and Queequeg's figure makes it possible. The sharp edges of the mind's bleak materialism, the world of shark-like cannibalism, tooth and cutlass, are all mollified, once Ishmael can accept through Queequeg's poise the full savour of indifference: 'No more my splintered heart and maddened hand were turned against the wolfish world. This soothing savage had redeemed it. There he sat, his very indifference speaking a nature in which there lurked no civilized hypocrisies and bland deceits.' (P. 49.)

Queequeg is the 'Indian juggler' *par excellence*. Amongst the intricate mental patterns cast upon the savage body, the white man's moral consciousness loses itself in order to find a love which includes in one all the other kinds of loves—parental, marital, brotherly. It is a democracy of feeling which is initiated at the New Bedford inn before the start of the voyage, when Ishmael shares his bed with the savage and remembers a childhood experience. He had tried to climb the chimney of his home, but was dragged out of it, legs first, by his stepmother, and packed off to bed for sixteen dreary hours on the longest day of the year, an exile from the sunlit outer world. Then he was horrified to wake from sleep to feel in the dark an unknown, supernatural hand placed in his as it lay on the counterpane. But now, when the affectionate arm of Queequeg is casually thrown over him in the bed at the Spouter-Inn, Ishmael wakes (p. 27) to find himself embraced by a strange consoler and his fearful scruples gone. The pagan arm, 'tattooed all over with an interminable Cretan labyrinth of a figure', merges with the squares and triangles of the patchwork quilt, and dissolves the hard distinction between the American 'Isolato' and the Polynesian islander. They cannot be told apart in feeling. Melville does not seek to lessen the oddness of the marriage he implies, but with the characteristic audacity with which he attacks the white consciousness throughout, he puts forward Queequeg's axe as the 'hatchet-faced baby' of the union, the symbol of war become also that of peace and fecundity. So the American child who sought to escape his sense of alienation in the cruel 'stepmother world' of time and endless consciousness, finds his way back into the womb's eternity through the medium of a Queequeg. In fantasy, Queequeg is the bridge that has to be there for the American mind to pass outwards from itself, from the turnings of mental asphyxia which are Melville's dread and fascination—'calms crossed by storms, a storm for every calm.'

Again, in the 'Mat-Maker' chapter, the unknown hand is placed, so to speak, within that of the trapped materialist. To the narrow fixed pattern of mental determining, where human free will and fate move mechanically, 'subject to but one single, ever returning, unchanging vibration', Queequeg casually adds a latitude, another dimension. As he stands by the woof, poised and 'idly looking off upon the water, carelessly and unthinkingly' his sword at random weaves into the strictness the unconsciousness of chance: 'chance, though restrained in its play within the right lines of necessity, and sideways in its motions modified by freewill, though thus prescribed to by both, chance by turns rules either, and has the last featuring blow at events' (pp. 187–8). But in the creation of this variegated, 'counterpane' consciousness, where all the terrors and weariness are melted into one huge inconsistent consistency, one sees that Melville's introduction of chance resembles Poe's belief that spontaneous life is the image in reverse of his arranging mind: if he is a regularizer and an ordainer life must be irregular, haphazard, the accounted-for impulsiveness within the deadly neatness. The *Pequod* has inverted life, and that inversion is itself spun back. Queequeg ministers to this second correction, active only as an energetic attendant, the midwife who is continually delivering man from his living grave. The sword which intervenes in the mat-making is the same as that which rescues Tashtego when the Indian harpooner falls into the whale's head and begins to sink with it below water. The trapped man is delivered and born out of the world of dead time and the old mental consciousness (literally out of a corpse's head) in 'the good old way', head first. In disdaining the leg which the Indian thrusts out at first from the sinking prison, Queequeg is the opposite of the cruel stepmother who dragged young Ishmael by his legs back to dreary time. In this dream enactment below the water-line, where the finite consciousness goes fluid, the child is rescued from the chimney, and Tashtego and Ishmael survive the ruin of the civilized mind.

Once outside the constriction and pressure of the narrow quarters where the mind and body suffer together, the human being is delivered not, as with Hawthorne, back into the specific community but into a world-wide expanding heaven. Falling ill on board ship, Queequeg thins away as a physical personality, while inversely his eyes seem (p. 412) to grow fuller—'a wondrous testimony to that immortal health in him which could not die, or be weakened. And like circles on the water, which, as they grow fainter, expand; so his eyes seemed rounding and rounding, like the rings of Eternity.' With Queequeg, the dissecting, analysing, subdividing, and reducing are all set in reverse: the separate islands and islanders of life spread out to merge into a vast, infinite island; and what is merely a coffin to the Nantucketers, symbolizing man's limits inside the walls of the material universe, becomes to Queequeg a canoe, which, in the traditions of his Pacific people, is to bear its dead warrior to the starry archipelagoes: 'for not only do they believe that the stars are isles, but that far beyond all visible horizons, their own mild, uncontinented seas interflow with the blue heavens; and so form the white breakers of the milky way' (p. 413). With the death of the old feelings, there arises the kind of religious eroticism which views the 'milky way' of life—the generative sperm and mother's milk —as one thin, soft fecundity, and which makes Queequeg a way of accepting that other native of the Pacific, Moby Dick. The mind has overrun the body, bemusing sex with its analytical puzzles, till it finds itself placidly forgetful amongst the maze. Then the hieroglyphic tattoos on the body of Queequeg assume (p. 416) the nature of some incomprehensible scripture—'a complete theory of the heavens and the earth, and a mystical treatise on the art of attaining truth'—a network which the imagination must superimpose on the blank surface of the White Whale. It is this dream of enigmatic wholeness, this faithless trust in faith, which sets Moby Dick for Melville on the course which the *Pequod* intercepts on the last day of the Chase, towards a tranquil leeward destination. The Whale is swimming away from the old lee shore of the finite and insular, passing towards Queequeg's heaven, 'to something else than common land, more palmy than the palms' (p. 485).

But when Queequeg implicitly refers to an outlet from man's coffined world-confinement, the heaven looked for, one remembers, is that of reversed negativity. The positive is regarded as another way (more successful than moral) of having what the negative wants but which the latter is debarred from grasping by the restrictive conditions under which it operates. A difference in the *method* of attaining the heavenly, not a difference in values, separates Queequeg from Ahab. In the mat-making scene, as Queequeg stands poised between sea and ship, between heaven and earth, he possesses with ease the double vision which Ahab craves, clumsily and madly stretching, with self-destroying effort. Queequeg has the vision of the whale whose eyes are placed on either side of its head so that, without any conscious exertion, it can 'at the same moment of time attentively examine two distinct prospects, one on one side of him, and the other in an exactly opposite direction' (p. 287). Queequeg sees with the calm indifference noted of the new-born whale calf when the sailors attain the blessed inner ring of the Grand Armada of whales, as the ship enters the Pacific: the whale baby looks out (p. 337) 'as human infants while suckling will calmly and fixedly gaze away from the breast, as if leading two different lives at the time.'

So the earthly desire to have things both ways is translated into the dream of semi-divine ease, with the materialists' limited vision enlisting the extra help of the aboriginal prophets. If Westerwelt has Priscilla for clairvoyant, Ishmael has Queequeg and Ahab has his fire-worshipping Parsee, Fedallah. With the other pagans (Tashtego, Dagoo, and the rest of the Parsees), Queequeg and Fedallah see beyond the white man's consciousness and view of time. All are seers of their mysterious religions, lookouts and pilots who, like Fedallah in his prophecy to Ahab, go 'before'. But Fedallah can foretell to his master no more than the shadowy details of disaster, while Queequeg's activity is to prepare safeguards for the white consciousness to live beyond its disaster. His holy significance is soothing rather than ethical in its relevance. Through him the unconscious can swallow what the intellect refuses. For the unredeemed intellect, the universe is one narrow material channel along which man's being struggles and pushes, constantly suffering hurt and friction against the hard edges and angles. But in dream-fashion, with Queequeg, the unconscious fluently and sinuously passes through, beyond the constrictions and compressions to a new, charmed space where the spirit opens out.

3

Queequeg's home belongs to a dream territory of desire: 'It is not down in any map; true places never are.' But the Nantucket home of Ahab can be exactly charted with the mental eye: 'Take out your map and look at it. See what a real corner of the world it occupies; how it stands there, away off shore, more lonely than the Eddystone Lighthouse.' (Pp. 58–9.) It is a 'real corner' of angular, barbed materialism, and the impulse of the Nantucket people is not to yield over their insular consciousness to some all-sweeping infinite. The infinite shall come to them. Since they are so encompassed, 'shut up, belted about, every way enclosed, surrounded, and made an utter island of by the ocean', their obsession is to encompass their encompasser, to make within the terms of materialism an island of that which makes an island of them, to 'put an incessant belt of circumnavigation' round the world. Ahab sees in Moby Dick the everlasting, elusive physical life which makes him know his own limits. The Whale is the encircler inside whom Ahab rotates in the exasperating superficies of death-in-life. It is the Whale who has taken away his leg in the last encounter, but Ahab has got beyond physical caring. His course now is to outcircle his encircler, ' "dismember my dismemberer." ' Ishmael stops short of the full destructive intent, extracting vague love from the fragments, but Ahab's insane mental ambition drives him further—to escape and enclose his surrounder, to get beyond the physical limits by amassing them inside himself, to get outside by making the external come in: ' "How can the prisoner reach outside except by thrusting through the wall? To me, the white whale is that wall, shoved near to me." ' (P. 143.)

Ishmael knows a different answer to Ahab's question, but the problem is the same for both: like Ishmael, climbing the chimney, Ahab's wish is to reach outside this stepmother world, and he also is pulled back by the legs. For him, taking the hard, frictional way, without benefit of dreams, there is to be no pacifying birth into an acquiescing consciousness. After the mutilation by the Whale, Ahab's mind burns on the fuel of his physical disintegration in 'a kind of self-assumed, independent being of its own', as if, diabolically, an 'unbidden and unfeathered birth' had taken place. It stands in contrast with Melville's conception of the 'natural' or 'good old way', the coming anew into the world, head-first, with a consciousness changed for the better. Instead, Ahab's emergence is perverse, a tail-end backward motion, wilfully retrogressive. It is tortuous in its liberties with the flesh, as if he would gradually kill the tissue and replace it with mechanical parts—like that pseudo growth, his bone leg, the stake on which he turns in fixed, perpetual self-martyrdom, with himself as both Prometheus and vulture. To 'reach outside' he must transform all life into externalities. He is a mechanizer and a converger. His 'island' of the self refuses to lose any of its identity by merging outwards; instead, all other 'islands', human or animal, must merge into his, to be crammed into one large, definite mass, with his mind electrically supreme above all the additions to himself. His mental awareness encompasses the frail beliefs and secular oblivion of the Starbucks and Stubbs of mankind, collecting the Quaker wish for fixity and the Yankee assertiveness, to carry them inward in an arrogant, mechanical surpassal: ' "my one cogged circle fits into all their various wheels, and they revolve" ' (p. 147).

Thus the general purposes of the ship are narrowed down from hunting whales to hunting one White Whale, and all the world-variety of the crew is 'overmanned' into one tight assimilation: 'They were one man, not thirty. . . . This man's valour, that man's fear; guilt and guiltiness, all varieties were welded into oneness, and were all directed to that fatal goal which Ahab their one lord and keel did point to' (p. 477). Yet, as with Dimmesdale and Hester in their secret life to which the Puritan judgement has prompted them, Ahab's converging of the nations and the ships' purpose is not an act which ultimately betrays the interests of the American owners and initiators, the Quaker Christians. Rather, it extends those interests to a point of destructive logic, where mankind gathered together under the American flag is further concentrated through Ahab's supreme hatred. All men's woes merge inwards upon him to make one monstrous, mad super-personality, the leader of mankind's delegation of complaint against life in the flesh. On him lie all the contracting spirals of human experience and suffering, all the age-old layers of mental awareness: ' "I feel deadly faint, bowed, and humped, as though I were Adam, staggering beneath the piled centuries since Paradise" ' (p. 465). It is as though in 'upholding on his frozen brow the piled entablatures of ages' Ahab unforgetfully carries all the crowded anger of the race, now stratified into a mass of dead, coffin-like knowledge, like those 'huge hills and mountains of casks on casks' which are 'piled' in futile accumulations on the New Bedford wharves. Hardy's Jude cries out a tragic complaint from Job against the quandary of the physical life which man is born to, but it is beyond Hardy to conceive the extravagant American purpose which curses Job's whale in Moby Dick. Ishmael can accept the physicality and suffering only when he has passed into an erotic wash of feeling, so that the white surface is adorned with the ciphers of the Pacific religion, but Ahab's impulse is to bear the entire load of mental involutions and agonies of man, adorning the white surface with *that* superimposition: 'He piled upon the whale's white hump the sum of all the general rage and hate felt by his whole race from Adam down' (p. 160).

Sheer weight and numbers comprise the stature which Melville imparts to Ahab. The very quantity of the 'hills and mountains' of human pain builds up to a massed height from which the ego of fallen Adam proudly reaches for the heaven which thrust him down; and the totalized agony which Ahab bears also glorifies him for the author who speaks (p. 109) of 'the clouds that layer upon layer were piled upon his brow, as ever all clouds choose the loftiest peaks to pile themselves upon.' Reaching this far, Ahab has the 'royal mantle of humanity' lain upon him by the extent of his democratic effort. Poe's masterminds had to be protected from the scrambles of other American wills, but Ahab leads the crowd's ambition, demanding god-like status, with his 'royalty' of aim celebrated by Melville: 'Thou shalt see it shining in the arm that wields a pick or drives a spike; that democratic dignity which, on all hands, radiates without end from God Himself!' (p. 102). This is the strenuous way of transcendence, the attempt to win it by material work, to actualize it by missing out none of the steps along the path to infinite space.

The spike-driving Ishmael also goes this destructive way, staked and martyred to this terrible humanism, but he is still able to share in the laxer strain of democratic feeling. The fierce claims then pall for him, the picks and mountain-peaks lose their hurtful edge, and with Queequeg he melts in redemption, as if the sharp-cleaving aggressiveness had never been: 'No more my splintered heart and maddened hand were turned against the wolfish world.' In adapting to existence with Queequeg or refusing its conditions with Ahab, Ishmael turns between two wish-fulfilment extremes within the democratic principle. He is loosed for either, circulating freely without any moral interruption. As he slips between affiliations, compacted with Ahab in hard defiance or melting away in bland surrender of self-responsibility, there is nothing to impede the easy flow. One moment he is implicated to the full in his captain's mad quest—'Ahab's quenchless feud seemed mine' (p. 155)—and then, in another moment, the mind, the memory of centuries-old hatred, and the conscience disappear as Ishmael flows out of the friction into a lubricated bliss: 'I forgot all about our horrible oath; in that inexpressible sperm, I washed my hands and my heart of it' (p. 361).

Ishmael's 'clean conscience' is not the result of inner purgation. It is, rather, an act of life-insurance, by which he attempts to keep the democratic spirit at a level of tolerable feeling. Queequeg shows Ishmael how man can be 'equal to himself'—a state of strange contentment which the democrat in Ahab cannot enjoy because he, demanding godship at such an extreme, takes democracy to a point of contradiction and denial. Ahab wants to have in his mind and pin down with the spike, the mysterious knowledge of the universe which is only available—according to Melville's conception of the unconscious—through the equable, impassive state of the feelings. Ahab wants to have in harshly material, non-mystic terms the double vision which is naturally possessed by Queequeg, the whales, and the sun which shines so equably over a Pacific that contains both Ahab and his prey, Moby Dick. ' "This instant thou must be eyeing him," ' Ahab remarks of the sun (p. 430), tantalized with frustration. ' "These eyes of mine look into the very eye that is even now beholding him; aye, and into the eye that is even now equally beholding the objects on the unknown, thither side of thee, thou sun!" '

In effect, Ahab must see round the corner of his angular materialism. In his desire to nail Moby Dick, he claims the lead of an instant in time before anyone else, insisting on being the first to sight the Whale, tugging always at his place in the sequence of time and degree in Creation. To this end, he strains 'before' and 'behind' himself, his mind during the Chase turning (p. 482) into some aberrant clock-mechanism, 'his hid heliotrope glance anticipatingly gone backward on its dial' during the hours of darkness and 'set due eastward for the earliest sun.' His intent is to catch the ubiquitous Whale at the intersecting moment when, like Queequeg's sword entering the woof, the creature touches his material vision, comes into view between the fabric of free will and fate, at the coinciding point in the Pacific, the 'set time and place' of the Season-on-the-Line. Just as he kills other Sperm whales, because the creature is bound every hour by the necessity to surface, breathing only 'one-seventh or Sunday of his time,' so Ahab intends to kill Moby Dick as he swims out of eternity into time. Yet in order for the 'weekday' Ahab to kill the holy Whale at this 'Sunday' moment, an immense effort must be made to overcome the limits of consciousness and materialism, which place him with those who are 'tied to counters, nailed to benches, clinched to desks.' In surpassing these human restrictions, he suffers the effects of the constant turning. Like his bone-leg which swivels in its pivot too violently and breaks into splinters, Ahab is broken again and again by his revolving awareness. His brow is left 'gaunt and ribbed' after his wrenching round of the consciousness in order to see himself being hunted by pirates even as he hunts whales. New gloom is added after the first encounter with Moby Dick, as, turning back and forth past his wrecked boat, Ahab contemplates its 'reversed' position, where, 'broken bow to shattered stern', beginning and end insanely point in on each other.

Before that, however, the Promethean intent in Ahab has freed him from some of the physical restraints which have thwarted his progress. The quadrant, the pilot-guide which is both Ahab's link with heaven and the indicator of his location in time, is smashed, so that a wilful licence for his psyche prevails. Now, with his own will as the guide, Ahab follows out his own creations and resurrections. After the quadrant's rejection, he takes his bearings by the compass. The electrical storm reverses the polarity, and unknowingly he sails away from his prey, in the direction of health, flowing along with the fair wind. But, in a movement that is exactly opposite to Ishmael's readjustment at the helm after the try-works scene, Ahab realizes the mistake, turns the ship round to face the wind again, frictionally revolving inward upon himself, and renewing the compasses filled by the diabolic magnetism he now possesses. The log and line breaks with natural rot, but ' "Ahab can mend all" ', out to substitute for the creativity of nature and the lost link with human feelings his mechanical replacements. His bone leg is fractured, and the ever-renewing Prometheus commands the making of another. His slouched hat, symbol of his self-consuming woe, is stolen by a hawk, and this too, but without comment, is replaced. He cannot bear the other kind of resurrection, with its equally strange replacement for feeling that has gone dead in human relations. He turns aside from the lifebuoy which Queequeg has converted into his own canoe-coffin, and which is now a substitute for the rotted cask which failed to save a lost sailor and was itself lost. The human life-lines which Pip and Starbuck hold out to him are now too frail or incredible to be taken. He starts the *Pequod* away from the area in which the captain of the *Delight* is conducting the burial of Moby Dick's victims and beginning his prayer (p. 463) with the words, ' "may the resurrection and the life—" '.

The rejection of 'mortal interindebtedness' is perversely thorough. As the greatest, most compendious 'Isolato', as the self-reliant hero of mankind, Ahab presents in his agony and fragmenting a philosophic challenge to Creation. He believes he has the truth which outrivals all others when he thinks (p. 401) that 'equally with every felicity, all miserable events do naturally beget their like. Yea, more than equally . . . since both the ancestry and posterity of Grief go further than the ancestry and posterity of Joy.' He begins as a democrat (almost like Queequeg 'equal to himself') and ends overreachingly as he demands a 'more than equal' kingly status and lineage in time for his woe. He is 'before' and 'behind' with the woe, and also 'below' and 'above' in profundity and height; so that 'while even the highest earthly felicities ever have a certain unsignifying pettiness lurking in them, but at bottom, all heart-woes, a mystic significance, and, in some men, an archangelic grandeur.' The American Satan claws at heaven, his unholy claims paralleled by Melville's challenge (p. 129) to his own literary powers: 'Oh, Ahab, what shall be grand in thee, it must needs be plucked at from the skies, and dived for in the deep, and featured in the unbodied air!'

For Melville in this competition between insanity and an expansive form of sanity, Ahab's 'grand' woe outleaps the weak 'felicities' of the Stubbs and the Starbucks, yet it must be set against the 'self-containing' ethic of Father Mapple—' "on the starboard hand of every woe, there is a sure delight; and higher the top of that delight, than the bottom of the woe is deep." ' Therefore, the Ahab in Melville forces the abstract positive to such an extreme that in order to contain the madness the envelope has to be infinitely elastic, stretched beyond ethical reference into the super-agility of 'top-gallant delight':

And there is a Catskill eagle in some souls that can alike dive down into the blackest gorges, and soar out of them again and become invisible in the sunny spaces. And even if he for ever flies within the gorge, that gorge is in the mountains; so that even in his lowest swoop the mountain eagle is still higher than other birds upon the plain, even though they soar.   (P. 369.)

It is a contest of flexing and reflexing between rival assimilators; between the mental hell and the mental heaven which is its image; between different capacities for fantastic adjustment, which makes up the terms of the final fight between Ahab and the Whale.

4

The last pages of the novel give astounding contraction and release for the mind, as Ahab and Moby Dick meet again in the Pacific. The Whale is first sighted (p. 468) in a setting of calm, magnificent expansiveness and interflowing ease. Moby Dick proceeds as at the centre of a religious procession, whose significance radiates out to infinity like Queequeg's healthful soul amongst sickness. The Whale's hump is in a 'revolving ring' of foam, blue waters interchanging with his white wake; at his side, bubbles arise and dance, to be broken—yet the breach softly feathered—by the attendant sea fowl, rising and falling about him. It is a scene of 'mortal interindebtedness', of solemnity and reposeful play, of softly palpitating peace, which the hunters disturb. After they have made their first contact with the Whale, the radiation goes into reverse, and the spiral of consciousness turns more madly than ever before in Ahab. He scans the place where the Whale disappeared, seeking out the 'before' and the 'behind' in exasperation: 'his eyes seemed whirling round in his head as he swept the watery circle.' He is forced to swivel upon himself yet again as the Whale rises beneath him, 'timely spinning round the boat upon its axis.' With the boat chopped in half by Moby Dick and with Ahab in the water, the Whale begins a spiralling movement of 'revolvingly appalling . . . ever-contracting circles' in the 'direful zone whose centre had now become the old man's head.'

Saved from this first encounter, when his boat's bows are actually inside the Whale's mouth, Ahab attempts another 'head-and-head' meeting on the second day (p. 478). Again one sees even more amazing compressions of thought-experience upon the mind of Ahab: awareness so closely tightens upon itself that bizarre paradoxes are compelled, buckled into being. The Whale so entangles the slack of the three lines fast to him 'that they foreshortened, and, of themselves, warped the devoted boats towards the planted irons in him.' In one instant, the defiant, profane hunters have been transformed into devout worshippers. And for Ahab, trying to disentangle the line, there is the horror of seeing his own flung weapons returning upon himself, all 'caught and twisted—corkscrewed in the mazes of the line.'

Contraction on the third day of the Chase reaches strangling point. 'Forehead to forehead,' Ahab faces the Whale again, but without his Parsee who has been lost the day before. In a moment of astonishing revelation (p. 488), Fedallah is found, fastened to the Whale's back in a mesh of insoluble complexity, as if he were bound there by the knots of Ahab's weary mental inwardness: 'Lashed round and round to the fish's back; pinioned in the turns upon turns in which, during the past night, the whale had reeled the involutions of the line around him. . . .' The aboriginal knowledge of Ahab's priest and prophet has been used up, materialized, and now the dead eyes look back at Ahab, presenting another blunt stop, another reversal upon the self. One remembers the piled heaps of 'casks on casks', like coffins of deadened knowledge on the New Bedford wharves.

Yet the Parsee rides on a natural hearse, one that is, according to his prophecy, 'not made by mortal hands.' The unnatural hearse is the vessel of Prometheus, the American ship, the carrier of mechanized, heroic mankind. But as the Whale heads towards the ship, the sound of repairing hammers—heard at the beginning of voyages in New Bedford harbour and heard throughout this voyage—is stilled. The Promethean, self-renewing labour freezes, the substitutions stop, as the seamen hang inactive at the ship's bows, 'hammers, bits of plank, lances, and harpoons, mechanically retained in their hands, just as they had darted from their various employments,' their eyes spellbound by the oncoming of Moby Dick.

Now the final moments of intense poise are reached, in which the last scales of judgement weigh Prometheus and the God he defies. Although seeing that his ship is doomed, Ahab will not yield. Earlier in the Chase his heart had risen in destructive anguish to be 'fixed at the top of a shudder', and still his unsurrendering mind is ready to pursue the Whale into hell, into further torment of the physical life, in mythic self-splendourizing. He heaves himself to a last poise—' "Oh, now I feel my topmost greatness lies in my topmost grief" '—and, before flinging his last

harpoon at the Whale, calls upon all the billows of his foregone life
to ' "top this one piled comber of my death." ' But a further enclosure curls over this strenuous reaching by the age-old layers of
mental hatred; for, as Father Mapple asked, ' "what is man that he
should live out the lifetime of his God?" ' The solitary democrat
whose island stands off the American shore 'more lonely than the
Eddystone Lighthouse' is topped even as he attempts to top: 'So,
in a gale, the but half baffled Channel billows only recoil from the
base of the Eddystone, triumphantly to overleap its summit
with their scud.' The criminal is hanged by his own noose, the
whale-line; strangled in a final suffocation of compressed consciousness.

But Ahab's destructive impetus is still not spent even after he
personally has vanished. He is whipped away in an impassive,
'holy' silence, and the ship begins to sink after the Whale has
stove it in, but Ahab's last Promethean order, to renew the flag
stolen by the sky-diving hawk, is being carried out by Tashtego
the Indian in a frenzy of faithful, desperate mechanism. Above
the waves drowning the *Pequod* (p. 492) 'a red arm and a hammer
hovered backwardly uplifted in the open air, in the act of nailing
the flag faster and yet faster to the subsiding spar.' It is Ahab's
'fine-hammered steel of woe', battering out defiance, knocking
the last nail in mankind's sinking coffin, and, with creativity
reversed in the backward posture, fixing up the Promethean
liver in insane self-renewal and punishment.

Yet, like one of Hawthorne's deliberately incomplete groupings
in *The Scarlet Letter*, the stance is denied its perfection. With only a
few moments to spare, a strange qualification is slipped into the
narrow space between the warp of fatal necessity and the woof of
human free will. Again comes a sky-hawk (pp. 492–3) to peck at
the Promethean flag of defiance, at the mechanical fabric, at the
pennons on the unnatural hearse:

the bird now chanced to intercept its broad fluttering wing between
the hammer and the wood, and simultaneously feeling that ethereal
thrill, the submerged savage beneath, in his death-gasp, kept his
hammer frozen there; and so the bird of heaven, with unearthly
shrieks, and his imperial beak thrust upwards, and his whole captive
form folded in the flag of Ahab, went down with his ship, which, like
Satan, would not sink to hell till she had dragged a living part of
heaven along with her, and helmeted herself with it.

Like the heraldic finish to Hawthorne's novel—'On a field sable, the letter A, gules'—the simultaneity, which compresses hammer wing, and wood in one multiple American banner, suddenly rams the novel's universe together as an inclusive abstraction. Chance 'has the last featuring blow' when, like Queequeg's sword out of the blue, the wing intersperses itself between the strictures of the materialism. The Catskill eagle reaches down from the stars, as Satan reaches up, and in one instant the driving nail becomes the bridge between earth and heaven. The bird goes down, but in the elasticity of the consolation, even if the eagle 'for ever flies within the gorge, that gorge is in the mountains; so that even in his lowest swoop the mountain eagle is still higher than other birds upon the plain.'

The *Pequod* sinks and the whole voyage contracts to a last tiny spiral, all the varieties of mankind spinning into one black vortex. Ishmael revolves towards it, and yet the tightness and immense foreshortening is suddenly relaxed. Like one of Hawthorne's flowers of innocence springing up in expiated youth out of the old, sinful ground, the coffin-lifebuoy leaps out of the very place where the ship went down. But Melville has pressed for more destruction than Hawthorne, leaving himself the airy, philosophic afflatus, the hollowness which buoys up Queequeg's coffin and saves Ishmael. In the relaxation of the dream after exhaustion, the rebounding American imperturbable comes up, just as Bulkington the helmsman arises in the memory (p. 95)—'Up from the spray of thy ocean-perishing—straight up, leaps thy apotheosis'; just as the irrepressible Stubb 'leaped up' fish-like (p. 424) in the golden light of the Pacific. But it is the resurrective energy of the recoil, the slack aftermath of compression. Ishmael is picked up by 'the devious-cruising *Rachel*, that in her retracing search after her missing children, only found another orphan,' but the peculiar bitterness of that 'only' is not to be explicitly realized till later in Melville's art, in the weary unwindings of *Pierre* (1852):

With the soul of an Atheist, he wrote down the godliest things; with the feeling of misery and death in him, he created forms of gladness and life. . . . And everything else he disguised under the so conveniently adjustable drapery of all stretchable Philosophy.   (P. 380.)

IV

The Leatherstocking Novels and Moral Adaptation

AN irony lingers in American fiction. As Hawthorne saw, there is often not the explanatory power nor sufficient moral intelligence in the spirit, to keep up with all the physical and mental adventuring. Because the moral field is often so confined, undeveloped, or inapplicable, the world of physical space and external human effort refuses to be brought into proportion, made to square with human realities and limitations. While any other standard of reference is lame or too small, the physical world seems titanic, abundant, and energetic. Where individuals expand so wilfully and infringe upon others' being, it is difficult for the spirit to legislate inwardly for its own self or for its neighbours, thus to establish full freedom of movement in the world in which the body has won its superficial rights. A leavening is wanted and an authoritativeness is sought to ensure that some moral space is guaranteed, that some inner reality should be defined and lived with.

It is, therefore, natural that Hawthorne and Melville look back to a patriarchal power to be for them at least a past standard of reference. The Puritans of *The Scarlet Letter* and Father Mapple are invoked as the shadows of authority. For their authors, they cannot be the thing itself, but the idea is borrowed and the principle of authority is extended hopefully to sanction the new findings of American experience, to fit them into a useful realization. But, as Melville's novel reveals, if the idea of authority is not developed in living awareness, and is merely stretched to cover all contingencies, one has an indiscriminating embrace instead of a moral grasp. These American authors find it difficult to pursue the meaning of the experience without losing some honesty of consciousness in the attempt. They are outstripped by their own ability to shed guilt and memory, slipping out of an old age of sinful travail into an elusive youthful innocence—a state enjoyed by Pearl skipping over the graves and by Ishmael when he is resurrected from Ahab's fiendish cause, but which seems beyond the critical range of any morality yet known to their authors. Pearl may be reborn as an adult figure through the tempering of 'joy' with sorrow, and so Ishmael through the experience of 'Woe' and 'Delight', yet it cannot be said that their authors have brought an adequate realization to bear on the break in consciousness which absolves the reborn characters from the claims of any moral authority.

False, abstract harmonizing of unreconciled disorder occurs when inadequate attitudes are made to fit specifically American experience. And then what one is seeing is the wish for moral rule replaced by the powerful, organizing capacity of the artist's will, operating in morality's name. The folklore and the literature reflect this tendency to deduce innate power and authority from external achievement. The physical space of America, its profuse natural wealth, are met and matched not by men who are morally as great as the land but by mythic heroes, like Ahab or Paul Bunyan, whose achievements or ambitions are as 'tall' in their stories as the experience they subdue. In the same place as brute force and physical power, the authority-seeking author tends to discover his model of lawmaking, and then carefully differentiate and qualify if he can. Morality must be competitive to outmatch the land and its people; it must have the power to deal on the physical plane before it can be granted authority for the moral. One sees this competitiveness in *Moby Dick*, but the odds of the conflict are raised so high by the Ahab in Melville that the worth of the nerveless, mystical love which matches him is seriously diminished. At Cooper's more restrained level in the Leatherstocking novels, the need is the same: to assume in full, unborrowed confidence a power to counter the experience with moral sufficiency—an intelligence that will keep pace, adapting and adhering with precision to the elusive surfaces of land and people.

I

The first novel of the Leatherstocking series, *The Pioneers* (1823), discloses an American village of 1793, still self-consciously new and transitional, and its settlers not yet fully incorporated into a society that can be recognized as a distinct American community.

The new, national consciousness is only just appearing, but with 'half the nations in the north of Europe' represented here, with the religious sectarianism and vivid memories of their origins still potent, the people are foreigners yet, intruders on the wilderness. The adolescent stage of the new enterprise, which Cooper portrays in the make-shift, temporary oddness of the dwellings, is partly forgiven with a charmed smile for the unfinished, the crudely imitative, and the imported notion. But the adolescent beginnings are not completely forgiven, because the dangers of the future can be divined even in these early, enthusiastic moments in America. The description of Judge Temple's mansion or 'castle', with its reminding background of fired trees and blackened pine-stumps set off glaringly by the snow, points some of the cost of the intrusion. Built with untutored enthusiasm and rough measurement, the Squire's house is oddly unadapted to a place where the action of frost causes the platform and outside steps to come adrift from the imitation classical pillars which support the roof, leaving the pillars suspended. Inside the house, where imported ideas of cultural grace are forced to share the room with more homespun, basic comforts, the incongruity of the temporary moment is quietly reflected. Chandeliers hang from the ceiling in which the pipe from an enormous stove finds its outlet; tables of wild cherry wood reside with an imported mahogany sideboard, the native product having been fashioned to imitate the foreign pieces of furniture; and the natural undulations of grain in 'the wavy lines of the curled maple', which are observed in a small table, seem no happy neighbours of the 'black lines . . . drawn by no very steady hand' which are seen in some yellow-painted chairs. Unreconciled as yet to its setting, almost humorously confused in its intentions, and crassly copied by others as a semi-European model, the Judge's 'castle' seems to epitomize the mixed feelings, the good-humoured tolerance and wary disapproval, with which Cooper views its builders, its chief inhabitant, and its imitators.

Temple's relative, Richard Jones, who has superintended the construction of the house, is the pulse of this energetic hour, the leader of the games amidst the great bounty of the forest or the Christmas table. In him is centred much of the lawless optimism of the prevailing mood: the hearty taking what the land so profusely offers, the careless consumption of apparently never-ending abundance. As a character of the American dawn, oblivious of an end to the spree, Jones is also something of a Benjamin Franklin, with his rigidly-kept notebook of every day's happenings in the settlement, with his bustling projects and his vow on becoming Sheriff to sit down and 'systematize the county'. It is in the latter role, of law officer, that Jones, so comically vain in his arrogance, appears as incongruous and cross-purposed as the house he has built.

Billy Kirby, whose physical labour with the axe provides the wood for the settlement to build such houses, is a stage nearer to the land than Jones, closer by the virtue of his muscular power and expertise. In this big, vagrant figure, in the 'noisy, boisterous, reckless lad, whose good-natured eye contradicted the bluntness and bullying tenor of his speech', who would rather be idle than lose one particle of independence in a fixed job, there is a glamour that Cooper's American feeling finds it hard to resist. While Billy clears the way for the oncoming nation, 'with an ardor that evinced his native spirit', Cooper's compatriot admiration extends with a thrill to Billy's professional exercise of his frontier craft, as the human giant measures up the great trees, approaches listlessly, flourishes the axe, administers the light blow of pure precision, and brings the tree down, threshing and tearing, in earthquaking shock. With this combination of simplicity and professionalism, Kirby is placed in a tableau of nostalgic pioneer feeling as he, the giant with the few modest tools of his craft, is viewed among the stately trees, a 'picture of human life in its first stages of civilization'. When he sings his song at the drawing of the maple-sugar (p. 214), Cooper's feelings are yielded up for the moment to the romance of the tune 'that no American ever hears . . . without feeling a thrill at his heart.'

Although Billy is idealized into another Paul Bunyan as he stands in the forest—a figure of 'dexterity and Herculean strength' measured to his credit against the tall trunks 'towering apparently into the very clouds'—Cooper's ultimate attitude is less acquiescing, for Billy's song is given a dangerous accompaniment when Richard Jones taps his whip in time to the beat. The association of Billy and the Sheriff in the pioneer glamour implicitly counts the cost of the romance. Jones's boyish exclamation of triumph after the pigeon-shooting (p. 239)—' "Victory . . . victory! We have driven the enemy from the field" '—complements the picture of Billy after a similar mass-destruction, that of the forest, when the darker implications of the apparently innocent energy become harshly visible. Billy marches away (p. 182) from the scene of his hewing 'under the blaze of the prostrate forest, like the conqueror of some city, who, having first prevailed over his adversary, applies the torch as the finishing blow to his conquest.' So the oblivious waster moves off and away from the past act in a state of perpetual transience, of unindictable forgetfulness. He is the advance guard of civilization, but he does not stay to be implicated in the results of his clearance of the forests: as another of his songs indicates, the would-be purchasers of land can choose what sites they will, for ' "It matters but little to me." ' He is a legend for the community he leaves behind, but Cooper can see that the legend is dependent on eternal, destructive motion, on the assumption of a never-ending supply of forests for him to work his power on.

Judge Temple, the inhabitant of the house built from trees felled by the Kirbys of the scene, looks beyond the present moment, beyond the axe-wielding forerunners and village Franklins, to a modern, industrial America. Deploring the needless waste about him, Temple wants ' "to protect the sources of this great mine of comfort and wealth from the extravagance of the people themselves." ' The word 'mine' suggests the non-rural direction of his mind, but his forethought still has a European rather than American complexion: 'To his eye, where others saw nothing but a wilderness, towns, manufactories, bridges, canals, mines, and all the other resources of an old country were constantly presenting themselves' (p. 306). The word 'comfort' suggests another aspect of his ordering purpose. As his daughter feels, lying in the safe warmth of bed and listening to the wolves howling outside in the night: ' "The enterprise of Judge Temple is taming the very forests! . . . How rapidly is civilization treading on the footsteps of nature!" ' (p. 202).

However, as the novel gradually makes clear, Temple's importation of law to protect the resources is inadequate in accounting for the native situation. Like the mansion, the design of his law is founded on unsure assumptions: it cannot stretch over the scene, it cracks on the physical facts of men and land. Even the actual right to build a dwelling, let alone a metaphorical house of laws, cannot be assumed with full, righteous comfort, for an uncertainty is trailed within the novel: perhaps the land belongs to others with prior rights, like the Effinghams, or before them to the Indians. There is also another misgiving, this time arising from the law's application and its appliers. Temple's ideal of justice is inevitably contravened and distorted in practice by its local, human executors: Temple's European sense of needful order is maintained at the cost of incongruity and self-contradiction in the house built by Sheriff Jones, out of materials supplied by men such as Billy Kirby.

It is the figure of Natty Bumppo (together with his companion of the woods, Indian John, and in a lesser way, Oliver Effingham) whose presence and behaviour in the novel point out the incongruities, the confused purposes and mixed feelings. When Natty at different moments is associated with the purposes of the Judge and Billy Kirby, Cooper takes the opportunity of distinguishing him from the Judge's meaning of order and from Billy's implicit ideal of pioneer independence. A new, hard refinement can then come about. Natty, like Pearl, brings in the element of the incalculable or sceptical, disqualifying the attempted pattern in its claim to comprehensiveness, making it, if he is omitted, an 'incomplete morality'. He occupies the space of moral understanding left vacant and unaccounted for by the other schemes of justice.

At first Natty seems associated with the Judge in a common hatred of excess and waste, but it is an alliance which, on closer inspection, is seen to be as superficial as Richard Jones is in believing it when he remarks: ' "A very pretty confederacy, indeed! Judge Temple, the landlord and owner of a township, with Nathaniel Bumppo, a lawless squatter and professed deer killer, in order to preserve the game of the county!" ' The association does not go far because, as the night-fishing sequence shows, the Judge and Natty differ radically on the reasons for preservation. Temple's ethic of thrift is to save the fish for civilization's sake: ' "A net of half the size of this would supply the whole village with fish for a week at one haul." ' But for Natty thrift is employed in a cause independent of Temple's kind of civilized ideals, evoking values of honour and fairness of odds in the necessarily lone, spare duel between man and beast. Wastage of game or ammunition is a betrayal of the craft, a superfluous amateurism; for the old hunter, man must earn his satisfaction

' "the flesh is sweeter where the creater has some chance for its life; for that reason, I always use a single ball. . . . Besides, it saves lead; for, when a body knows how to shoot, one piece of lead is enough for all" ' (p. 254).

That this is not independence for anarchy's sake is made clear when Billy Kirby is sent as a deputy to arrest Leatherstocking for breaking the Judge's new game-laws. Billy is closer to Natty in frontier feeling than the higher law-makers, admiring Natty's superior skill with the rifle as one expert respecting the professionalism of another. He sympathetically understands the single man's defence of his property and freedom. And as frontier professionals of different crafts, the two men make the formalities of the eventual legal proceedings against Natty appear makeshift and unreal beside their frank, vivid presences. Yet Billy's scorn for the civilizing and legal processes he serves and his belief that rough justice is superior to any court methods—' "take it out like men, while Jotham and I see fair play," ' he suggests to Natty and another deputy at the attempted arrest—ultimately set him apart from Natty's purposes, as Judge Temple is set apart in another direction. With his gun at the turkey-shoot, with his spear on the lake, Natty is granted the admiration given elsewhere to Billy's feats. But the feeling with which Cooper invests Natty is more defined than the author's mixed sympathies for Temple and Kirby—the Judge whose gentlemanly ideal of law grates on the sense of human practicality, and the woodsman whose blind practicality does without law entirely. Cooper in Natty moves beyond the amateur or the incongruous muddling, and strives for a moral clarity of definition.

The supernatural effect of Natty's appearance on the dark lake (p. 251) is like an image of his growth as a legendary figure throughout the sequence of the Leatherstocking novels. At first, as Natty with his boat and lantern emerges from the darkness of the far shore, the phenomenon is presented of 'a small and uncertain light . . . occasionally lost to the eye, it seemed struggling for existence.' Then as it moves across the water it expands and brightens to a focus, 'until it became of the size of a man's head, when it continued to shine a steady ball of fire.' Approaching the group of settlement people who include Temple, Jones, and Kirby, as they fish on the lake, the light is brought against them in direct moral contrast: 'It did not at all resemble the large and unsteady light of their own fire, being much more clear and bright, and retaining its size and shape with perfect uniformity.' Compared with the whale-light in *Moby Dick* which oversees the gorgings of Stubb and the sharks with impassive, compendious awareness, or the burning of the St. Elmo's fire on the *Pequod* in the storm, the illumination is not taken by Cooper as far as complete abstract consciousness. Moral awareness is not yet so crippled and impassive that it cannot still move in human proportions, 'the size of a man's head', and arrive to confront the spoilers as the active impeder of their easy forgetfulness—'the red glare fell on the weatherbeaten features of the Leatherstocking.' The 'steady ball of fire' and the 'large and unsteady light' resemble the contrast seen already in Temple's house between the natural lines in the maple-wood table and those amateurishly painted lines 'drawn by no very steady hand', on some chairs. The diffuseness, the unsteadiness, the unsure assumptions into which Temple's kind of law is mixed along with Jones's and Kirby's lawlessness, are like the larger fire which, through human carelessness, eventually destroys much of the woods round the settlement.

Natty's 'steady ball of fire' is a harbinger of the setting sun, the westward retreat from the pioneer advance, towards which he goes at the end of the novel. Nevertheless, Cooper holds by the ideal of a constancy in the flux: Natty's fire can retain its moral shape while Temple's ethic, as seen at the pigeon-shooting, can be swallowed up in the powerful pressures of the moment, in the mass delight in killing, oblivious of past precepts and future consequences, which grips the assembled settlers (p. 238): in Ishmael style, flowing between Ahab and Queequeg, 'Even Marmaduke forgot the morality of Leatherstocking as [the pigeon-flock] approached, and, in common with the rest, brought his musket to a poise.' As a semi-legendary figure on the lake, Natty replaces the other pioneer legend, Billy, in sparer, more tight-cut fashion—not a physical giant battling against a multitude of trees, but a single man who duels with single prey. The myth of American power here shifts its bearings slightly: the prestige of professional precision and skill is carried over into moral precision and skill. It is not the size or mystical world-spread of Natty's light which differentiates it from the larger fire, but its hard clarity.

Temple's law fails to adhere and contain the American nature with which it deals, as is made evident at the close of the novel by the uncontrolled forest fire. Indian John, whose people were disinherited long ago from the despoiled land, dies resignedly in the fire but in his last moments his tainted honour is re-glorified, vindicated in newly-disclosed authority above the inconsistencies of the white vision of justice. The conflicting purposes of white civilization which have made Chingachgook into the lesser figure of Indian John—the white man's drink which has degenerated him, the Christianity which has clothed him—are transcended in death and he reassumes his former glory as the Great Serpent of the Delawares. Just as Cooper makes over to Natty in full the admiration which he can only give partially to Billy Kirby, so also Natty is granted something of Chingachgook's dying grandeur and his Indian vision to 'the land of the just'. Acting as an interpreter—literally for the clergyman attending the dying man and metaphorically as a careful guide finding his way along a path between two cultures—Natty converts the weight of the Indian's vision of the after-life into an authoritative lesson taught to the whites. Chingachgook goes now to be judged ' "by a righteous Judge, and by no laws that's made to suit times, and new ways" ' (p. 403).

In the moment of 'silent awe' which follows the death of the Indian, with thunder and lightning signalizing the heavenly sanction for his spirit's reposeful departure, one sees again, as in the 'ball of fire' upon the lake, Cooper's method of asserting transcendent authority, his imaginative need to exhibit grand seconds of clear moral power that will work upon the beholders and let them know their place in the scheme of Creation. The conservatism does not stretch to Melville's kind of elastic consolation. When Natty gives an account (p. 279) of his climbing the Catskill mountains to see 'the carryings on of the world', he is like Melville's Catskill eagle, a figure of adjustment to American experience, but with an important difference. When he stands 'the best part of a mile in the air' and looks down at the world spread out below, it is as if the dream of power which made the myth of Paul Bunyan had transferred its affection to a figure of moral height.

2

In *The Last of the Mohicans* (1826) the confusion of feeling prevents Cooper from turning physical power, practicality, and expertise into moral worth. He is delayed by violent, deathly interests, and like Hawthorne in the 'Governor Pyncheon' chapter, the name of morality is invoked to cover half-understood attitudes, feelings that he cannot make clear.

What is clear, however, is the attitude to European *naïveté* of mind. As in *The Pioneers*, Cooper displays the inadequacy and inherent contradictions of a code which has been imported into American conditions. Just as Temple's law breaks up on native ground, so in this earlier period of the Seven Years War, the European ideals of military chivalry and gentlemanly honour come to grief. In the forests are heard the laughter of 'gallant and reckless youth', but their 'long night' of death is close at hand. Armies march through the wilderness, their bands sounding with an arrogant lack of caution, only to retire in terrible confusion. The song of Romance sung by a French sentry ends with an Indian knife-thrust. There is an effete disarray within the spirit of the opposing commanders (those pledged 'to uphold the cold and selfish policy of the distant monarchs of Europe') which the Continent seems to provoke. Munro, the British commander at Fort William Edward on Lake Horican, is abandoned by his colleague, Webb, and, left without reinforcements, surrenders to the French. After this he is a broken man, crying for his lost daughters in an agony of 'apathy'. Montcalm, the French commander to whom Munro surrenders, seems hardly possessed of a sure Christian ethic on American soil when he allows his Indian allies to break the honourable settlement which has been concluded between the Europeans, and massacre the emerging British. The chivalric code's failure to contain the savage forces it employs beneath its banner provides, as with Temple and the settlers, another example of 'the danger of setting in motion an engine which it exceeds human power to control.' The forest fire of *The Pioneers* is here (p. 211) a bloody massacre, 'while the armed columns of the Christian king stood fast in an apathy which has never been explained.'

Cooper is not interested in explaining the 'apathy' but in

ensuring that once the stiff, chivalric gestures of honour and duty have come to military disaster on American ground, they are supplanted, through the agency of Natty as Hawk-eye, by a behaviour more cunningly adapted to the environment and Indian enemies; by an expertise which though it carries over in weakened state the moral dubiousness of the discarded code, is more capable of practical survival. After the massacre, Major Heyward and Munro become pupils in Hawk-eye's school of the woods, learning disguise, caution, trust in the confidence of their teacher and Chingachgook, and a new idea of moral law: ' "Remember" ', says Hawk-eye (p. 272), ' "that to outwit the knaves it is lawful to practice things that may not be naturally the gift of a white skin." ' The terrain and its native inhabitants are matched with a cunning which leaves moral cries far behind and makes the Leatherstocking of this novel into a kind of Billy Kirby, exercising his destructive skill on Mingo Indians not on forests, as if they were objects that he must ruthlessly track down and eliminate. After a victory over the Mingoes, 'the honest but implacable scout' is described (p. 134) making his round of the dead Indians 'into whose senseless bosoms he thrust his long knife with as much coolness as though they had been so many brute carcasses.'

The bloodiness outpaces the moral explanation, despite the fact that Cooper is concerned to justify the 'stern and unyielding morality' of Hawk-eye's acts as hard lessons in practicality. The protestations by Hawk-eye about his uncontaminated white blood and his Christian difference from the barbarism of his Indian foes, appear as aggressive attempts to make up for a missing moral attitude of real value. When he surveys the massacred dead at the fort and wants revenge, he eludes the taint of barbarism by force of rationalization: ' "Revenge is an Indian feeling, and all who know me know that there is no cross in my veins." ' Dissociated on the surface from savagery, he has leave to urge it by carefully apportioning separate roles to himself and his Indian companions: *he* will act with white rifle power, while he allows ' "the tomahawk and knife to such as have a natural gift to use them" ' (p. 216).

It is a combination of explicit, very deliberate moralizing and implicit toughness which produces the precarious attitude of the novel, displayed nowhere more strongly than in the presentation of Magua, the Mingo chief, and Cora, the dark-haired daughter of Munro. The Indian 'Prince of Darkness' and the dark child of Munro's marriage with a Creole, belong to an area of thought in Cooper—the suggestion of mingled blood—which he refuses to resolve consciously. The question is therefore obliterated. Hawk-eye's feud with Magua is the surface aspect of the cruelty, but while the death-blow given to Cora partakes of the same feeling, in her case the blow has gone subterranean, under cover of senti-mental melancholy. It is as if Magua and Cora ask something in themselves which the novel cannot answer except by brutality.

Neither the obsolescent European code nor the supplanting forest code of Hawk-eye can tolerate Magua's complaint of white hypocrisy and cross-purposes, that the whites give whisky to the Indians and then (as Munro does with Magua) have them whipped for being drunk or enraged. ' "Is it justice," ' asks Magua (p. 120), ' "to make evil, and then punish for it?" ' But when Magua takes over Natty's role in *The Pioneers*, of one who pinpoints incongruities and the unstable moral pose, he receives no justice because there is none available on the terms by which the novel works. Magua's sins are to bring out into the open much of the cruelty and fear that lies hidden in the white attitudes; his mocking of the white's racial and moral impeccability in his suggestion to Cora is an outward expression of the mingling idea which Hawk-eye is at continual pains to deny with regard to himself. Magua is un-bearable, the evil force of the novel which Cooper must root out and silence. Magua and his Indians are the persisting, defiling thoughts which taint the psychological rather than the natural scene, but in the latter background they can be hunted out with the appearance of moral demeanour once they have been reduced to the level of things—' "See!" ' says Hawk-eye at a fountain used by the Mingoes, ' "the knaves have trodden in the clay, and de-formed the cleanliness of the place, as though they were brute beasts instead of human men" ' (p. 140). But when Hawk-eye's allies, Chingachgook and his son Uncas, kill a French sentry and stain a pond with his blood, the affair is justified (p. 162) by Hawk-eye's moral partitioning: ' "'Twould have been a cruel and an unhuman act for a whiteskin; but 'tis the gift and natur' of an Indian, and I suppose it should not be denied." ' Power answers power, all in the same mingled turmoil. The reaction to Magua's sexual suggestion towards Cora as he lays upon her dress hands soiled by the blood of her massacred compatriots, or the reaction to the fouled purity of Lake Horican when similarly stained by their blood is in the same violent currency. The torment of the Lake in response to defilement is almost that of Hawk-eye and Cooper: 'the green and angry waters lashed the shores, as if indignantly casting back its impurities to the polluted strand' (p. 213).

Like an image of the novel's moral confusion, an ethical attitude struggles to assert itself in the very place ravaged by evil. There is an attempt to cleanse by foul materials, but the stain is hard to erase, appearing again when it seems to have been wiped out. Like the wounded sharks in *Moby Dick* and their posthumous activity, the Indians are so hard to kill and nail once and for all because of their slippery elusiveness: ' "These knavish Maquas cling to life like so many cats-o'-the-mountain." ' Refusing to loose his hold upon a branch, a wounded Indian sways in the wind over a river before finally being brought down by Hawk-eye's bullet. Magua is harder to kill, slipping away from Chingachgook's grasp, eluding Hawk-eye's rifle, and only at the end is he caught like a mountain lion among the high rocks, shot by his white enemy who significantly is 'crouched like a beast' to take aim. But Magua goes down the side of the precipice with a last shake of the hand in 'grim defiance'—as unresolved in his author's feelings as those other defiers, Zenobia and Ahab. The American wildness and elusiveness of spirit is sentenced to death by a brutish 'morality', but it does not go without a fight. It refuses to be accounted for so easily, and even after physical death there seems an uncertainty which Hawk-eye's insistence on killing the Indians over again with his knife is meant to quash. When an Indian passes a knife round the 'exquisitely molded head' of Cora, 'with a taunting and exulting laugh', the impure thought is responded to with a bludgeoning excess that seems designed to crush the idea rather than the man—'The tomahawk of Heyward and the rifle of Hawk-eye descended on the skull of the Huron, at the same moment that the knife of Uncas reached his heart' (p. 132).

The devious treatment of Cora Munro touches on another aspect of Cooper's sensibility which is equally confused: the idealization of women or the unprotected weak which he retains in the form of a cruel sentimentality from the European code of genteelness when he has openly dispensed with the old masculine chivalry as treacherous, military futility. The attitude which

makes poignant, sacred pictures of Alice the weaker and fairer
swooning into Cora's motherly, stronger arms, or of the sisters
singing and praying together, is a literary piety which stems from
a tough knowingness allowing itself to be forgetful and naïve for
an interlude. The reverence afforded to Cora merely hides the
insidious workings of repulsion and contempt, so that when Munro
tells Cora's suitor, Major Heyward, of the particular circumstances
of the girl's birth, she is suddenly tainted, and Munro (p. 188)
senses Heyward's horror: ' "You scorn to mingle the blood of the
Heywards with one so degraded—lovely and virtuous though she
be?" ' Heyward denies this, but hereafter the animus goes underground. Magua's lust for mingling blood with Cora helps to
confirm the implicit hardening of attitude towards her, enabling
Heyward to turn (without comment and without the author's
disapproval) to Alice as a possible wife instead. Nothing is said,
but all is assumed, with a doom-accepting satisfaction at the drift
of events. Cora herself is so placed that she actually makes her
own condemnation easier, giving up Alice to Heyward and then
consenting to her fate as a proud, Christian gentlewoman at the
hands of Magua.

Hawk-eye's protestations of moral intent in no way make the
harsh acts of the novel acceptable, but a bolder attempt at author-
ization is made through the characters of Chingachgook, Uncas,
and (at the end) Tamenund. The Indian codes of honour, courage,
and stoic control nearly become a proven replacement for the
damaged attitudes to feelings which result from the downfall of
the European chevaliers. There is an inuring, a paring down to
the essential, in the lesson in adaptation which the Delaware
nobles represent. Like the Puritans for Hawthorne in *The Scarlet
Letter*, they stand against the flux with a defensive, stiffening
fibre. They take the pain and the horrors full-faced, unflinchingly.
Yet they are sufficiently Protean to have practical flexibility,
melting with superb rapidity into the scene, becoming in one
moment a rock, a post, or a shadow. Just as suddenly they start
from an inert composure to run and kill, and then revert to their
statuesque calm. Their abstract stoicism, their superhuman control, is the only plausible force for order capable of grasping the
toughness, the contempt, and the cruelty—the real, dominant
feelings of the novel—and giving them an authorized dignity.
Only Indian control can give realization to an overriding wish to

be beyond the effect of pain, beyond the humiliation and awk-
wardness of creative feelings that have become unclean and
embarrassing.

The behaviour of Chingachgook, Wiss-en-tush, and Tamenund
has a meaning for Cooper which is to enlarge beyond the immediate interests of this novel. Each is a father, always a figure of
special vulnerability in Cooper's feelings, and so intensely susceptible to loss or hurt. And each of these Indian fathers, losing his
natural or adopted son, is able to confront his agony with a surface of restrained indifference, which decisively contrasts with
Munro's open cries of grief for his lost daughters and his breakdown. Wiss-en-tush, the Mingo father whose son is convicted of
cowardice and executed by the tribe, is naturally anguished, but
in obedience to the stern Indian code he formally rejects his son
(p. 293) as an impurity—' "his blood was pale, and it came not
from the veins of a Huron." ' But although Cooper admires the
Indian capacity for indifference, he will not go to Melville's
lengths to break himself down to it. The condition of such freedom and cleansing is the loss of caste; and it is perhaps because
Cooper is so near to it in this novel that the noise of protestation,
the refusal to mingle blood, is heard so indignantly. Therefore
Cooper admires with some caution when he later concedes
Chingachgook, mourning the slain Uncas, a picturesque grandeur
and solemn awe in his amazing self-control: the father's gaze
upon the son is 'So riveted and intense . . . and so changeless his
attitude, that a stranger might not have told the living from the
dead, but for the occasional gleamings of a troubled spirit that
shot athwart the dark visage of one, and the deathlike calm that
had forever settled on the lineaments of the other' (p. 403). With
Tamenund, the patriarch and sage, Cooper rises to the idea of
fatherhood which appears at the end of *The Pioneers*: that of the
godhead represented by the grand, aged figure of wisdom whose
authority is granted by divine right and is a secret communicant
with the all-enveloping 'Great Spirit' who rules over both white
and red. One sees it in Tamenund's appearance (p. 348) to hold
court with Magua—supported in the assembly up to the 'high
place of the multitude, where he seated himself in the center of
his nation with the dignity of a monarch and the air of a father.'

But the moral authority invested in the sage rides upon the
cruel poignancy with which Cooper finds it necessary to instruct

the events. It is typical that in a novel in which moral innocents are either weak swooners or righteous fools, Tamenund should never be free from the slight suspicion of senile imbecility in his judgements. Under him Uncas can be rediscovered as the lost son of the Delawares, leading his braves for an hour of saddened glory, and, with a melancholy that is equally cruel, Cora can be awarded to Magua. So Uncas, by his hint of love for Cora; Magua, by his lust for her; and Cora, by her birth, are all dismissed, and the suggestion of mingled blood to which each contributes is disguised by the mood of ritual order which prevails from Tamenund's appearance till the end of the novel. But beneath the staged awe of the funeral scene and the mask of grand solemnity, a hint of unresolved impurity still looks out from the ordering attempted over it. The Indian girls who attend the dead Cora think she is superior to her sister and imagine that she and Uncas are united in death. Only Hawk-eye among the whites knows the Red idea, hidden among Indian language and imagery, but he keeps it secret from Munro and Heyward. As in *The Pioneers*, Natty is the interpreter to the whites of a higher authority, but this time the duplicity of his office is more noticeable than his accurate powers of translation.

3

In the next three Leatherstocking novels, Cooper develops with gathering rigour the idea of moral definition—the attack on incongruities and the spacing out of individuals—which, seen in *The Pioneers*, nearly disappeared from view in the minglings of *The Last of the Mohicans*. As if looking deliberately away from the confusion of the latter novel and the profuse, natural background of the former, the setting of *The Prairie* (1827) is sparse and clean-swept, with the prairie as a metaphor of time. On the one hand, it is an omen of that future which *The Pioneers* guessed at. As Natty sees it (p. 24), ' "I often think the Lord has placed this barren belt of prairie behind the States to warn men to what their folly may yet bring the land!" ' It is a moral exhibit of the future visible in the present, a divine surprise in the offing which will unerringly pin guilt to the elusive and the oblivious, for when the 'Yankee choppers' have cut their way to this point, these Billy Kirbys will find that God's hand has 'swept the country in very mockery of their wickedness.' Almost like the ghastly reversals on the self in *Moby Dick*, the spoilers ' "will turn on their tracks like a fox that doubles, and then the rank smell of their own footsteps will show them the madness of their waste" ' (p. 79). On the other hand, the prairie intimates an immense, unknown past, where many civilizations have been engulfed because 'Time has lasted too long for them.' Furthermore, the prairie is the place of the present, the new territory that stands in the way of the expanding American nation and consciousness. It is Cooper's 'White Whale' that in its greatness marks the ultimate limit to the adventuring of the American Prometheus who ' "would mount into the heavens with all his deformities about him if he only knew the road" ' (p. 249).

Pushing across that land and matching against the huge wastes the stamina of his own physical bulk is Ishmael Bush with his 'tribe' of wife, relatives, and 'seven sledgehammer sons'. As the wagons of the pioneer move slowly across the prairie, the sluggish, dull unwieldiness of the father—the 'overfatted beast'—symbolizes the massive, seemingly irresistible movement west of America as a whole. Ishmael's tribe resemble (p. 68) 'those distant and ever-receding borders which mark the skirts and announce the approach of the nation as moving mists precede the signs of the day.' The family are seen as bees from the hive of the republic, 'the numerous and vigorous swarms that are culling the fresher sweets of a virgin world.' Like the 'large and unsteady light' of the settlers in *The Pioneers* these 'moving mists' are moral hazes and these 'vigorous swarms' denote the crude, overweighted spread of obtuse power for which Cooper shows so much distaste, in his love of the essential, the stripped down, and the keen. It is the diffuseness in Ishmael's mind which is so pronounced when, having left behind him the jurisdiction of the east, he comes upon the space of the prairie where (p. 96) it seems that no moral code he has known can apply, only the rule of power: ' "When the law of the land is weak, it is right the law of nature should be strong." '

'Nature' is to have an ambiguous value, as Ishmael discovers, but Cooper's main interest at the beginning of the novel is to pursue the contradictions and discrepancies which result when Ishmael attempts to legislate out of an untutored sense of judgement. He has fled from the encroachments of eastern civilization as they are heard in the sound of the forest-clearing axes, and, in rejection of settlement law, he asserts (p. 82) his ethic of property and the rights of physical space: ' "The air, the water, and the ground are free gifts to man, and no one has the power to portion them out in parcels." ' Because he believes ' "the rule that 'arth is common property" ', his sons are not to be stopped from wastefully cutting down the prairie trees, just as the settlers they have left destroyed the Kentucky forests. When his son Asa strikes Ishmael's brother-in-law, Abiram, and Ishmael declares, working by the 'law of nature', that ' "justice shall be done" ', the statement has little further meaning. He regrets Abiram's killing of a Kentucky law-officer and is uneasy about his implication in his relative's kid-napping activity, but he can bring no steady moral authority to bear on the situation. Like Temple with the settlers, like Mont-calm with the Indians, Ishmael discovers (p. 97) that his family are 'a set of beings who were restrained by no obligations more powerful than the frail web of authority' with which he has en-veloped them. In fact, Ishmael's power ethic rebounds on him in the way that the woodsmen, in Natty's vision, are turned round upon their own footsteps. 'United to their parents by ties no stronger than those which use had created, there had been great danger, as Ishmael had foreseen, that the overloaded hive would swarm and leave him saddled with the difficulties of a young and helpless brood.' The squatter is made painfully to remember (p. 149) how 'in the wantonness of his youth' he him-self had 'cast off his own aged and failing parents to enter into the world unshackled and free.'

Also occupying the prairie is an aboriginal parallel to the squatter's problem of power and anarchy, for the Sioux Indians, like the white 'tribe of wandering Ishmael', are equally greedy in asserting their monopoly of the land. But despite the arrogant assumptions of these 'Ishmaelites of the American deserts', Cooper as always is able to extract a raw ideal of discipline and authority from them to be set against white flounderings, even if later he checks and refines the ideal more thoroughly through Natty and Hard-Heart the Pawnee. Unlike Ishmael in his un-certain mastery, the Sioux chief Mahtoree, with his 'rare com-bination of moral and physical influence', can back his outer capacity with the fulness of inner wisdom: 'Courage and cunning had established his ascendancy, and it had been rendered in some degree sacred by time' (p. 284). The attack he directs on

Ishmael's camp—'with an order that would have done credit to more enlightened beings' (p. 49)—is prepared for by his silent reconnoitre, made with an attentiveness and self-control which suavely contrasts with the dull incuriousness of his enemies. While the Ishmael group seem like alien usurpers, stuck in the jutting assertion of their 'single naked and ragged rock' on the prairie, the Sioux, as they melt into the scene, appear to run with the grain of the land. Mahtoree can sink into the shadow of a tree and become 'as dark, as motionless, and apparently as insensible as the wood itself' (p. 53).

Following on behind the author's theme, but never quite catching up with his imaginative needs, is that part of the plot represented by Middleton, the American army officer, and Paul Hover, the bee-hunter. Both men belong to the pursuing forces of the settlement law which the Ishmael group has transgressed. Middleton, descendant of the Major Heyward of *The Last of the Mohicans*, is out to recover Inez, his newly married Spanish bride and the victim of Abiram's kidnapping; Hover is on the trail of Ellen Wade, a relative of Ishmael attached to his party. It is significant that settlement law should only be carried over and allowed to persist as useful with regard to the protection of women—to that area of thought and feeling where Cooper is muddled, in contrast to the direct confidence with which he tackles masculine power. The uncertainty of attitude towards women and their embarrassing of the clarity of moral schemes are displayed (p. 28) in Natty's musing, with a hint of the impending sentimentality to come: ' "The law—'tis bad to have it, but I sometimes think it is worse to be entirely without it. Age and weakness has brought me to feel such weakness at times. Yes—yes, the law is needed when such as have not the gifts of strength and wisdom are to be taken care of." ' If the genteel side of law, the settlement variety, is retained to look after the 'weakness', Cooper's surer imaginative interest is given to the sterner ideal of law which is promulgated through Natty.

Battius, the naturalist who accompanies the Ishmael party, finds that in terms of age the prairie's 'moral existence is not coequal with its physical or geological formation', but in Natty, now an old trapper whose age and wisdom seem akin to the prairie's span of time, Cooper is concerned to adjust the inequality between the moral and physical worlds. In a novel in which physical space and energy are so central, Natty has moved on from youthful impulsiveness to a natural decay, to a reflective stage where only his guiding wisdom is left. Close to death, with the honest disinterestedness of an old man, he is the Tamenund, the Father of the novel, but without the hint of senility which betrayed the former creation, as he adapts instinct to prudence, 'reason' to 'nature' and restraint to action. After the dubiousness of the previous Leatherstocking novel, he is once again (pp. 119–20) the careful treader of the path between white and red: 'Unlike most of those who live a border life, he united the better instead of the worst qualities of the two people. He was a man endowed with the choicest and perhaps rarest gift of nature, that of distinguishing good from evil.' What this is to mean for Cooper is the ability to assert the indissoluble differences between the races, and then within those larger distinctions, to delimit the 'gifts' and 'nature' of individuals. If diverse, conflicting energies can be given their due and kept apart, the spirit will have some moral space to breathe in, and all the proclaimed liberties of external movement will take on the real meaning of freedom. To this end Cooper stresses the recognizable differences between individuals rather than their similarities or special qualities of being which it is beyond his art's capacity to show.

The stress on the need to recognize the other man's skill or trade is Cooper's inadequate way of portraying respect for the other's individuality—a way of keeping standards by making them socially visible, at low pressure. Superficiality is to come from this temperateness, but also the value of a certain refining and paring. Cooper's preference for contrast over similarity sets Natty's purposes apart from Ishmael's. Just as Natty's demand for independence seemed allied on a superficial level with Billy Kirby's, so here Natty's choosing to exile himself in the freedom of the prairies, away from eastern depredation, appears to share Ishmael's urge. But Natty's challenge to Mahtoree's assumption of Indian monopoly on the prairie (and, by implication, Ishmael's) together with his welcome (p. 191) to Hard Heart—' "there is room on the prairie for another warrior" '—only point out the different ideas of freedom enjoyed by the trapper and the two groups. The 'room' is only really there as a complete fact when men are willing not to overflow the inner rights of others, when warring individualities are not crowded against each other.

Cooper's American need is to sharpen the faculties, so that the physical spread retracts, consolidates itself, becomes more aware, and makes room for some spiritual acuteness. To bring clarity out of the haze of muddled ethics demands a special, even exaggerated sharpness. Therefore, as the listless tribe of Ishmael push their incurious way through a prairie whose vastness makes the eye 'fatigued with the sameness and chilling dreariness of the landscape', they are confronted (p. 15) with a strange spectacle:

The sun had fallen below the crest of the nearest wave of the prairie, leaving the usual rich and glowing train on its track. In the center of this flood of fiery light a human form appeared, drawn against the gilded background as distinctly, and seemingly as palpable, as though it would come within the grasp of any extended hand. The figure was colossal, the attitude was musing and melancholy, and the situation directly in the route of the travelers.

The effect of the vision on the halted travellers—'a dull interest that soon quickened into superstitious awe'—is to bring a possible moral ideal directly 'within the grasp' of the now 'silent and wondering' group of Americans. Poe heightens the interest of the dreary wastes by finding a cerebral, sensational tonic, but Cooper's power of criticism is still at work in the torpor. Like his appearance to the fishermen in *The Pioneers*, Natty's monumental presence here acts as a miraculous pause which brings the unconsidering 'mist' to a stop. It appeals as a sanctified yet credible human form to the beast-like spoilers it awes, yet at the same time it is able to suggest the 'colossal' standard of law and nature in which their passions may find moral reference.

As with the sun which shines on Arthur Dimmesdale, which finds and gives shape to the lost and wavering father before it loses him again, the sun here is part of a moral appeal to the authoritative father in Ishmael, to the higher 'nature', to the lost judge inside the deep, parental feelings. Unlike Hawthorne, Cooper is sufficiently conservative to feel he can re-awaken the moral decisiveness. For him it is not dead but dormant, ready to emerge if the right appeal is made. Other scenes through the novel repeat the assumption that if 'nature' can be unlocked fully, a spiritual good will be surprised into the open. When Natty weeps over his memories, those with him experience (p. 120) an awe which turns into sympathy—'Nature could endure no more.'

During the siege of Ishmael's rock, Ellen Wade is asked (p. 157) to respond to the claims of her best feelings and so admit the law-bringers. ' "Natur' *will* work in the bosom of the child," ' says Natty confidently, ' "and we shall gain our object in good time." ' And Ishmael is appealed to again by the appearance (p. 95) of another visionary sight—the 'extraordinary . . . spectacle' of Inez, standing on the rock as the 'beau ideal of female loveliness', the unprotected child, piously inviting Ishmael's violence against her and thereby calling upon his pity. Inez is soon to be restored to the safety of settlement law, returned to her husband and her distressed parent, and one sees, as in *The Last of the Mohicans*, that Cooper's art is most confidently and unequivocally engaged not in the cause of the lost child but in that of the lost father.

The appearance of Inez is really important for the way that it begins the resurgence of the father in Ishmael. She again presents the problem of law over which Ishmael's son, Asa, quarrels with her kidnapper, Abiram, and her appearance indirectly provokes the murder of Asa by Abiram. The finding of the dead boy is the signal for another moment when moral appeal and wonder can intervene and transfigure. With the family gathered apprehensively round a thicket, 'clustered together in an amazement with which awe was singularly mingled', and the prairie wind rising as the vultures circle, the mood is set for the discovery of the lost child, and through that, the lost father. Awakening from his moral haze, Ishmael directly experiences the hurt consequent upon his own ethic, and another 'nature' begins (p. 148) to emerge, quite distinct from the 'law of nature' and the brute power it implied: 'Nature was then stirring powerfully within him, and the muscles of his stern visage began to work perceptibly. His children fastened their eyes on his as if to seek a direction to the strange emotions which were moving their own heavy natures.' In this crisis of 'direction', Ishmael becomes established as the authoritative leader he never was before, confidently guided by his deepest 'nature' to the justice for which he has fumbled.

It is a slow-moving but logical progression from here to the eventual arrest of Abiram by Ishmael's deep, 'awful' voice. The fair trial which Ishmael gives to the other whites (including Natty, whom he has suspected of the murder) raises Ishmael above the prejudices and animal behaviour of Mahtoree's court of judgement immediately before; and the arrest of Abiram places

Ishmael and the case beyond the reach of the settlement law which merely looks after the Inez affair. Middleton has no brief to interfere in these matters, and on seeing the revelation of Abiram's guilt, departs for home (p. 367), 'awestruck by what he believed a manifest judgement of heaven.' Searching in his Bible for precepts, Ishmael condemns the murderer with a certain Old Testament gravity: ' "You have slain my firstborn, and according to the laws of God and man must you die!" ' The execution of Abiram is carried out, endorsed by the full 'solemnity and majesty of nature', and Ishmael's family go back to the east, swallowed up into anonymity once more. The pioneer legend of unlimited expansion is put into reverse.

The re-awakening of the father ideal, and the kind of justice-giving which ensues from it, are framed by Natty's visionary appearance at the beginning of the novel and his figure discovered at the end, seated in composure in the midst of the Pawnees, waiting for his death, like a white Indian John. As the setting sun again lights the grand ordering moment of which Cooper's imagination is particularly fond—'The hour, the calm beauty of the season, the occasion—all conspired to fill the spectators with solemn awe' (p. 401)—Natty, seated in peace and dignity, is the childless Father set carefully in the middle between white and red conceptions of death, and partaking of both.

4

The strong moral ordering which Cooper gradually fosters in the Leatherstocking novels is brought about by the collapse of naïve laws into irrelevance, but it is done at great expense to the generous, shrewd art which made *The Pioneers*. As *The Pathfinder* and *The Deerslayer* take Natty towards a mythic abstraction of youthful, virgin purity, one realizes more clearly the cost at which Cooper exercises his moral ordering, just as one understands that the implications of static imperturbability were already there in the law delivered in *The Pioneers*—one that refuses 'to suit times, and new ways'—but were then still undeveloped.

In *The Pathfinder* (1840) Cooper's special conservatism becomes painstakingly firm. Now he deals centrally with the theme which the arguments over physical space in the previous Leatherstocking books tended to confuse—that of the problem of the moral room allowed each man. Yet in clarifying his interests and separating individuals—so that their differences and the distances between them are far more important than their relationships—Cooper orders his art only to impoverish it. There is a new, cool facility. Morality now has the character of self-erasing social conduct, treading carefully and genteelly, like the 'propriety of thought, fitness of language, and decorum of manner' which Mabel Dunham displays and which pervades Natty's behaviour as the Pathfinder in 'his rebuked manner of thinking of himself, and all that habitual deference for the rights and feelings of others, which appeared to be inbred in his very nature' (p. 408). For Cooper, he is now a continual declarer of differences, an exemplary master of considerateness: ' "each color has its gifts, and its laws, and its traditions, and one is not to condemn another because he does not exactly comprehend it" ' (p. 396). Strictly practising what he preaches, Natty allows that ' "as Providence rules all things, no gift is bestowed without some wise and reasonable end' ", and finds (p. 74) that the Indians, even the wicked Mingoes, ' "were produced for some rational and proper purpose, though I confess it surpasses my means to say what it is." '

Unlike Melville, Cooper does not have to expand his consciousness to include all the horrors. His Christianity is not taken to the limit and destroyed; instead it stops, while Cooper brings to it the strange variety of existence to be rationalized upon and ordered. As Natty remarks to Captain Cap, the salt-water sailor, he thinks ' "Christianity and the compass both pretty stationary" ', and he finds God's works and words unchanged, despite the flux and instabilities of America's development. The compass does not have to take account of so many possible courses as with Melville in *Moby Dick*, because Cooper does not intend to voyage so far. When Chingachgook scalps an Indian, Jasper, the fresh-water sailor and friend to Pathfinder, turns his head away in disgust, but Natty can survey the bloody work with philosophical indifference, because he accommodates the natural savagery in a system of order, control, and courtesy. Indian honour must be seen as very different from the European conception: Chingachgook ' "is a lone man in this world, and yet he stands true to his training and his gifts!" ' (p. 74). By insisting scrupulously on the different backgrounds of men and the various skills adapted to their diverse milieus and traditions, Natty creates a mental order as he gives credit (p. 89) to the range of 'gifts' in the world: ' "In my judgement, every man is to be esteemed or condemned according to his gifts; and if Master Cap is useless in running the Oswego falls, I try to remember that he is useful when out of sight of land; and if Jasper be useless when out of sight of land, I do not forget that he has a true eye and steady hand when running the falls." ' By reference to this ideal of constancy to one's special skill, Natty differentiates himself (p. 105) from Jasper: ' "The gifts of the lad are for the water, while mine are for the hunt and the trail." '

Cooper's 'Isolatos' are given space and set apart in respectful propriety, but there can be no enlargement or deepening of individual natures on the terms of the ordering scheme, only a series of consolidations, as each figure steps outside his limits and is rebukingly set back inside them. Men expand too far and become confused when they deny their own skill, or refuse to respect or crave another's 'gift'. Cap, the dogmatic and prejudiced salt-water sailor, acting on another person's jealousy of Jasper, obstinately refuses to acknowledge the special 'gift' needed to sail on fresh water, and having taken over the British vessel from Jasper's guidance, nearly brings it to grief on Lake Ontario. Cooper can recognize the good seaman in Cap at the same time as he teaches him a lesson, through Jasper's skill, and later in the death of Sergeant Dunham, by placing him beneath an awe which will make him acknowledge something different or greater than himself. It is a tempering method, similar to the effect which Cooper describes (p. 220) in the storm on the lake, where the noise of wind and water is checked by a thin mist 'softening and rendering mysterious the images it revealed, while the genial feeling that is apt to accompany a gale of wind on water contributed to aid the milder influences of the moment.'

But where awe means decorum and deference, the checking of Captain Cap is a static, uninteresting procedure. Because of the equation which makes *The Pathfinder* so dull in spirit—different 'gifts', but apparent sameness of feeling—Cooper is not ultimately concerned with the value of Cap's feelings, nor, as he was with Ishmael Bush, in a moral change awakening the better, authoritative man. When 'Nature' and feeling are so standardized, one cannot expect a psychological progress, as the response of Cap to Mabel's prayers (p. 404) indicates: 'Cap was surprised as well as awed, though the effects on his mind were not very deep or very lasting. He wondered a little at his own sensations . . . but he was far too sensible of the influence of truth, humility, religious submission, and human dependency to think of interposing with any of his crude objections.' Ishmael's sons find in their father a guide to the new course of their emotions, but Cap is left without any, and only expected to conform to the standard of 'proper' feeling which Cooper's heroine embodies in her 'sublime' and 'supremely touching' act of 'filial pity'.

In the infringements of the code which occur during the shooting-match at the fort, it is now more clear than ever that the rights of moral rather than land space are being contested. Jasper, wishing to do well in front of Mabel, 'overlooks his own gifts and craves them of another'—Pathfinder's skill with the rifle; and Pathfinder, deferring as usual to another's 'feeling', finds that in letting Jasper win the match, he has gone against himself and denied his own 'gift'. He quickly expiates with a display of precision shooting in front of Mabel, but again he betrays himself when he comes to woo Mabel at her father's instigation. This is a confusion which he tries to clarify; the feelings he has for the Delawares, he explains to her, ' "are not the same as them I got from the sergeant for you." ' The 'feelings' seem like an awkward load, externally handled, and in the end it is false for the scout to have relationships with women, because ' "they seem to me to lessen the love of enterprise and turn the feelings away from their gifts and natural occupations" ' (pp. 175–6). It is not quality of 'feeling' which decides which of the rival suitors, Natty or Jasper, shall have Mabel, for both 'feel' the same for her. But, says Pathfinder (p. 419), awarding her to Jasper, and stepping back from wooing to become an impartial judge, a Father, ' "I do believe you'll make her happier than I could, for your gifts are better suited to do so." '

It is evident that by the time Cooper has reached the stage in the Leatherstocking novels of ordering wholesale respect for others' feelings, those feelings have lost their worth in the new clarity. After the deference and the considerateness, after the impartial generosity worked out in tortuous fairness, Pathfinder is left alone, unmarked, clear and single. The moral definition once achieved, however, no feeling can pass even between man and man in Cooper's developed ethic. The only exchange across the distance is one of mutual deference. The meeting (p. 411) between Pathfinder, the unmingling white, and Captain Sanglier, the blood-thirsty French officer who has lost caste and forgotten his white 'gifts' among the Indians, is, perhaps, the notable moment of deference and incomprehension that sums up the mood of the whole novel: 'The two separated like those who respect one another, while each felt that the other was an enigma to himself.'

5

The Deerslayer (1841) is the last refinement of segregation, where the spiritual room has so contracted the individual personality that even respect and deference cannot carry across the enormous distance. Lake Glimmerglass, the central area of the novel's action, possesses the same mythic remoteness—uncharted and undefiled by the white man's consciousness—as Queequeg's native island, which 'is not down in any map; true places never are.' But the Polynesian island and the American lake answer to different wishes from their different creators. Melville's dream island, like the savage tattooed with the variegated mystery of existence, is the expression of a sensuous wish to flow beyond the isolation of the individual and mingle in undefined communion with all the other human islanders. But the grasp of the hand between Chingachgook and Hawk-eye in *The Last of the Mohicans* is over an unbridgeable distance, and Cooper's essentially spiritual dream in *The Deerslayer* has made isolation a bearable principle, by removing intimacy of any kind from human relations. The individual is here not allowed to grasp others into himself and his power, nor is he allowed to forsake his identity by adding himself to others.

The scene is no longer Lake Otsego of Cooper's childhood where the 'large and unsteady light' of Temple's law and Jones's lawlessness were associated in a moral haze; it is no longer Lake Horican of *The Last of the Mohicans* whose purity is polluted by bloody deeds and whose attempted moral response is a backlashing of revenge; it is no longer Lake Ontario of *The Pathfinder* where one feeling politely deferred to another in an atmosphere of spaced-out decorum. Lake Glimmerglass goes beyond all these: it is the idea of the blank prairie transferred from the realm of physical space to the moral space of the imagination, and, after all the impurity and confusion of mists and lights, made simple, clear, transparent, and utterly inviolable. It answers to a wish for acute clarity—'the moment when the senses seem to recover their powers in the simplest and most accurate forms, like the mind emerging from the obscurity of doubts into the tranquillity and peace of demonstration' (p. 319). The unchanging sameness of 'nature' and 'feeling' is given shape in a surface of limpid water whose placid simplicity and 'holy calm' nothing can permanently mar. After years of desertion, it remains the same. The violent happenings of yesterday mean nothing today: 'When the sun rose on the following morning, every sign of hostility and alarm had vanished from the basin of the Glimmerglass. The frightful event of the preceding evening had left no impression on the placid sheet, and the untiring hours pursued their course in the placid order prescribed by the powerful hand that set them in motion' (p. 509).

For men in the wilderness, the Lake is the fixed moral compass by which they may take their bearings and know the truth or error of their individual courses. As Hurry Harry remarks (pp. 11–12) when he, Deerslayer's blond giant of a friend, emerges with his companion out of the forest into a clearing by the Lake: ' "Now we have got the p'ints of the compass in our minds once more, and 'twill be our own faults if we let anything turn them topsy-turvy ag'in." ' From this moment onwards, the differences between the two young men are to be known, because, unlike Harry, Natty as Deerslayer steers by the compass with undeviating rigour. He is Glimmerglass in human form—the unadorned, unattached figure of honesty who is like the moment of 'liquid lucidity' after dawn on Glimmerglass (p. 319) when the perspective resembles 'moral truths that are presented in their simplicity without the meretricious aids of ornament or glitter.' Deerslayer is like the surface of a mirror which shows the bloodthirsty and the revenge-seeking the exact reflection of their deeds. But they cannot see the personality behind the glass. There is no man to engage with behind the 'placid sheet' of garrulous, explicit morality. With Deerslayer and Glimmerglass, the moral order has reached its most strict and scrupulous level in the Leatherstocking novels. Infringements of the code have harsher repercussions and quicker expiations. There is a rigour of selflessness in the way Natty demonstrates his firing precision by bringing down an eagle with his new rifle, and then, with exact moral precision, immediately repents that he has abused his powers. Despite all protests by the whites, he keeps his vow to the Indians with unswerving purpose that he shall return to them to risk punishment under their justice. All is accounted for with a detachment and fairness which puts the personal self in abeyance behind the impartial surface, as when he fatally wounds his first Indian by the shore and receives the name of Hawk-eye. While he nurses the dying man (p. 116), he sums up the action: ' "Each party acted according to his gifts, I suppose, and blame can light on neither. You were treacherous, according to your natur' in war, and I was a little oversightful, as I'm apt to be in trusting others." ' The reconciling harmony of this over-lucid assessment (p. 79)—' "Revenge is an Injin gift, and forgiveness a white man's" '—is possible only through the disappearance of human personality, when the ethics can be heard and seen in action but the man cannot be reached.

Such extremes of considerateness can only be regarded by Cooper as a moral standard when actual generous feeling has gone, as one sees in the attitude towards Hurry Harry. Together with Floating Tom Hutter, Harry belongs to the tradition of Billy Kirby and Ishmael Bush—'a set of men who dreaded the approaches of civilization as a curtailment of their own lawless empire', men who are really the advance-guard of the rear forces but who disown the relationship. Cooper can concede to Harry some virtues with the appearance (p. 12) of authorial generosity: 'His air was free, and though his manner necessarily partook of the rudeness of a border life, the grandeur that pervaded so noble a physique prevented it from becoming altogether vulgar.' But— as the word 'vulgar' suggests, with its hint of propriety—Cooper will not allow his feelings to be implicated in Harry with the same mixture of tolerance and wariness which he showed in Billy. The lawless wasters have become more flat in conception, more pre- judged. As the treatment of Cap revealed, they must respond to what has become an awesome, dispassionate standard of morality. If they do not, they continue helplessly unredeemed, or they perish. No half-way stage is allowed: there is the beastly life in its ferment or there is the fixed spiritual morality with its propriety and 'poetical' sublimity. The coming of darkness on the Lake is witnessed by Tom and Harry (p. 311) 'without experiencing any of that calm delight which the spectacle is wont to bring when the thoughts are just and the aspirations pure.' Because of Cooper's unimaginative sternness over men 'who knew no feelings of poetry, had lost their sense of natural devotion in lives of obdurate and narrow selfishness, and had little other sympathy with nature than that which originated with her lowest wants', he is less interested in their moral haze than in their humiliation.

When the men-beasts cannot conform to the static standard expected, a divine revenge is worked on their rough, physical power. The body is harrowed and awed when their crimes—the scalping for money which the French and British codes of law approve—rebound upon them brutally. Hutter knows what it feels like to be scalped alive, and Harry is considerably humbled, both by his partner's death and by the realization of his own bodily helplessness, when, after a fight with the Indians on Hutter's stronghold in the middle of the Lake, he is towed through the water by Chingachgook on the barge. He is further awed by Judith Hutter's rejection of him and his physique. His physical power is brought to heel and set under Deerslayer's spiritual power, but Cooper will not attempt to enact anything further within the figure he has checked. Consolidation of knowledge, retraction of previous claims—these are Cooper's purposes, not personal inner discovery. Harry is awed and 'troubled' by Hutter's funeral, 'though he hardly knew why.' After the death of an Indian girl whom Harry accidentally kills while on a scalping foray, it is related (p. 308) that 'for a minute the mind of this creature, equally of civilization and barbarism, was a sort of chaos as to feeling, not knowing what to think of its own act.' As with Cap, he is to be given no guidance in the dilemma. Even if he gives up scalping, he is to learn nothing from the puzzlement and he blusters back to his old American defiance. All that he can be told at the end, by Hetty Hutter as she dies, is to be more like Deerslayer.

Hetty herself—being in the tradition of the weak, pure figures of endangered innocence which begins in the Leatherstocking novels with Louisa Grant of *The Pioneers* and continues through Alice Munro and Inez—is the feeble, mad ghost of moral ideals that have faded in Cooper's mind to the point of being incredible and charmingly impractical, to be viewed with sentimental pity and a touch of hidden malice. As 'one of those mysterious links between the material and immaterial world', she is like that other ghost of effete virtue, Hawthorne's Priscilla. But though, like

Priscilla, she may tutor the strong man, Harry, in his humbling, her morality has no chance to be dominant while Cooper is affirming Natty as an ideal of spiritual excellence. Hetty in her imbecile way is attempting to adhere to the course set by the moral compass: she is, as Harry remarks, ' "compass meant us" ', meaning that she has the intention if not the precision. In contrast to Harry and her father whose ethic is of the violent response— 'Do as you're done by'—Hetty abandons all thought of personal safety in carrying Christianity to the savages. The Indians, though they may smile on her *naïveté* and traditionally revere a mad person, remember the hypocrisies of white behaviour which Hetty's Christian preaching cannot account for. Cooper eventually winds up his indulgence in Hetty and counters with Deerslayer whose preventive ethic reads, 'Do, lest you should be done by.' When Hetty comes a second time to the Indians, in order to save Deerslayer, her missionary fervour is thanked, but her moral intentions—like Harry's physical violence—are set firmly in their place (as she is later by her death): ' "Ah, Hetty," ' says Deerslayer (p. 472) from his bondage, ' "that may do among the missionaries, but 'twould make an onsartain life in the woods." '

Lawrence rightly saw that Hetty's sister Judith is the Zenobia of the novel—as unresolved in Cooper's mind as that other 'strong' figure, Cora Munro, and as unforgiven by the static code of ungenerous generosity in *The Deerslayer*. Judith is the vivacious, colourful girl who has been slightly besmirched—a taint by association, never to be pardoned—in her former relations with the officers at the distant fort. And her pride, like Harry's physical conceit and Hetty's madness, is judged (p. 214) within an unbending context of 'proper' rules: 'she had been too much accustomed to live for self and for the indulgence of her own vanities. . . . It required extraordinary circumstances to awaken a proper sense of her situation and to stimulate the better feelings of this beautiful but misguided girl.' However, she is not so worldly as to be unable to throw off her old desires and vanities, reject Harry's advances, and want Natty as an honest man of the woods. But, like the others, she is to be allowed no new direction. She falters on Deerslayer's placid, seemingly transparent character; the virgin surface is too smooth for any grip or attachment to it. The idea of marrying Judith briefly crosses his mind, but (p. 408) it is quickly dismissed: 'he soon recovered his reason and smiled at his own weakness, as the fancied picture faded from his mental sight and left him the simple, untaught, but highly moral being he was.' His heart, like the unimpressionable Lake, 'isn't touched', either by Judith's desire for him or by the claims made for him by the Indian squaw whose husband he killed. None shall have him.

When Judith appears at the Indian camp to save Deerslayer, it is in complete contrast to the simplicity of her sister's appearance on the same mission: she comes dressed in her father's looted treasures of gorgeous finery, a proud Zenobia or Hester Prynne, attempting to awe the savages as a queen of the woods. But, just as he puts Hetty's *naïveté* in its place, so Deerslayer settles Judith's ruse, and she is rejected (p. 500) according to the code of order and natural authority: ' "It will not do, Judith . . . it will not do. 'Twas a bold idee, and fit for a general's lady; but yonder Mingo . . . is an oncommon man, and not to be deceived by any unnat'ral sarcumventions. Things must come afore him in their right order to draw a cloud afore *his* eyes!" ' Judith is damned as passionately inappropriate in the scheme. She is stained from the beginning by what Harry has said of her to Deerslayer, stained even by Harry's desire for her. Characterized rigidly to the end as 'that lovely but misguided creature', Judith returns eventually to the English officer whom she had spurned, and goes to reside in shame as a mistress on his English estate. She is left without a father and, as the plot discovers, without even a proper name. But Cooper's blank end enjoys the obliteration of personality. Nothing is changed on Glimmerglass, as if nothing had humanly happened there. The moral space is absolutely inviolable, just as the virgin Deerslayer, the unmarked *tabula rasa*, is absolutely untouchable.

PART THREE

Lawrence and the American Fiction

I

Studies in Classic American Literature, 1917–1918

I

W HEN Lawrence had nearly finished the first versions[1] of his American essays, he could look back at his previous critical writings—the *Study of Thomas Hardy*, 'The Crown', *Twilight in Italy*, 'The Reality of Peace'—and believe, with unknowing irony, that he had at last settled an issue. In the American essays, 'I have got it all off my chest. I shall never write another page of philosophy—or whatever it is—when these are done. ... Yet it is absolutely necessary to get it out, fix it, and have a definite foothold, to be *sure*.'[2] The Foreword to his later essays on the unconscious only extends the statement when it tells how 'the absolute need which one has for some sort of satisfactory mental attitude towards oneself and things in general makes one try to abstract some definite conclusions from one's experiences as a writer and as a man.'[3]

In such phrases—'as a writer and as a man', 'some definite conclusions', 'a definite foothold', 'to be *sure*'—one sees Lawrence

---

[1] Lawrence wrote thirteen essays on American literature between the summers of 1917 and 1918. Eight of the essays, including work on Franklin, Crèvecœur, Cooper, Poe, and Hawthorne, were published in consecutive numbers of the *English Review* from November 1918 to June 1919. Nearly all these published essays, together with unpublished material on Dana, Melville, Whitman (and additional work on Hawthorne), were almost certainly revised at least twice before they were brought together in 1922–3 as *Studies in Classic American Literature*. The original versions of the essays (except for those on Dana and Whitman, only later versions of which are available at the moment) have been published as *The Symbolic Meaning*, edited by Armin Arnold (1962). I am quoting from this collection when I refer to the 'first versions' of the American essays, and from *Studies in Classic American Literature* when I cite the 'final versions'. (Page references in the present chapter, unless otherwise indicated, are to *The Symbolic Meaning*.)

[2] Letter to Cecil Gray, 12 March 1918 (*Collected Letters*, vol. 1, pp. 545–6).

[3] *Fantasia of the Unconscious* (1961), p. 9.

concerned to extricate himself from the limited role assigned him as a novelist: that of a man credited with a great imaginative understanding inside the confines of his art but whose truth is immediately disqualified the moment he attempts to extend its relevance into the living world, where people tell him that his intuitive knowledge is incredible or impossible, that it speaks of non-existent states of being. To have his seriousness betrayed and patronized by others' lesser knowledge deeply angers him—'they say I, D.H.L., am wonderful, I am an exceedingly valuable personality, and that the things I say are extravaganzas, illusions. They say I cannot think.'[1] To be a unique but irrelevant phenomenon in the eyes of the disbelieving world is a position that he will not permit others to rest him in. 'Don't think of me as a raving impractical vain individual,' he pleads to Cynthia Asquith,[2] and to Bertrand Russell, with his philosophical and mathematical eminence, he suggests a more mutual respect for each other's kind of knowledge, because his, Lawrence's, 'world is real, it is a true world.' He feels 'quite sad, as if I talked a little vulgar language of my own which nobody understood.'[3] His difficulty is that in attempting to place his intuitive knowledge beyond the mercy of others' rational disbelief he must work outside the very medium, the novel, where that knowledge is most fully itself—as an experience, felt through all its shifts and phases. He tries to make it stand up by some system or language that will not betray the quality of its truth.

Finding the right abstract language is the problem—hence his avowed hesitation in calling such attempts 'philosophizing'. He needs an articulate discipline but not a new mental prison. Therefore, Lawrence finds himself in the position of reaching for justification on the terms of established science when what he really wants is the prestige of scientific assent. It is relevant to think of Ursula seeking confirmation of her instinctive beliefs among the laws of biology in *The Rainbow*, when one finds Lawrence writing to Russell: 'I have been reading Frazer's *Golden Bough* and *Totemism and Exogamy*. Now I am convinced of what I believed when I was about twenty—that there is another seat of consciousness than the brain and the nerve system.' After dis-

---

[1] Letter to Cynthia Asquith, 16 August 1915 (*Collected Letters*, vol. 1, p. 362).
[2] Letter of 25 November 1916 (ibid., p. 487).
[3] Letter to Bertrand Russell, 26 February 1915 (ibid., p. 324).

cussing blood-consciousness, he ends by asking Russell: 'Do you know what science says about these things?'[1] But although he looks towards science to help his knowledge out of vagueness into an undeniable, more locatable truth, he refuses science the opportunity to kill the quality of the truth he knows as an artist by banalizing it into a formula: thus his lament over the *Psychoanalysis Review*'s discussion of what it calls the 'mother-complex' in *Sons and Lovers*: 'My poor book: it was, as art, a fairly complete truth: so they carve a half lie out of it, and say "*Voilà!*" '[2]

It is not surprising that when he claims in a letter of 1919 that his American essays contain 'a new science of psychology' he adds immediately, 'pure science'[3]—a qualification of the claim, which suggests that he is steering between a wish to organize his knowledge in justification and a fear of limitation by his own method, by the over-systematic or the eccentric exposition. The result is seen in the first essay, 'The Spirit of Place', where Lawrence conceives the hypothesis which runs through the later discussion of the literature. He propounds the occult belief that before the Flood there existed a universal, mystic language of cosmology and sensual expression which was known to all the priesthoods of that time—Asiatic, African, European, American, and Polynesian —and which is now lost, destroyed in the triumphant onset of Christian spirituality. For Lawrence, the symbolic wholeness of speech was ruined when the sensual mind was rendered subordinate to the spiritual, when the primary world of being and 'life-plasm' was put second to the world of matter, mechanism, and 'dynamic-physical' forces. (At this point one feels the influence of Melville's faith in the hieroglyphic scripture tattooed on Queequeg —'a complete theory of the heavens and the earth, and a mystical treatise on the art of attaining truth'.) In accordance with this thinking, Lawrence invests characters in *The Scarlet Letter* with a significance which carries them beyond that novel's terms of reference. Chillingworth is seen as a medieval magician, a descendant from the old order of sensual knowledge, will, and power, even though now, crippled symbolically beneath Christian spirituality, he deals in his alchemy only with the decayed fragments of the old knowledge. And Hester Prynne was rightly called

[1] Letter of 8 December 1915 (ibid., pp. 393–4).
[2] Letter to Barbara Low, 16 September 1916 (ibid., p. 475).
[3] Letter to B. W. Huebsch, 30 September 1919 (ibid., p. 596).

a witch, says Lawrence, calling upon modern science to attend and respect, for 'The ancients were not altogether fools in their belief in witchcraft.' He also quarrels with modern science, in the form of the new psychoanalysis, when in the essay on Poe he attacks it for limiting the larger meaning of humanity's perverse 'self-less desire for merging' to the smaller concept of mother-incest. In that essay, Poe becomes a kind of opposite to what Lawrence makes Chillingworth: Poe is 'hardly an artist' but 'rather a supreme scientist' of cause and effect—a latter-day cripple of the dying spiritual age, dealing with the ruins of purely mental knowledge, just as Chillingworth, the survivor of the more ancient sensual age, deals in fragments of passionate knowledge.

But the presence of 'myth' throughout the essays reveals Lawrence's incomplete satisfaction with his 'pure science'. Myth here, like a tentative but useful structure of thought, allows him to delay full acceptance of the mental explanation for the deeply felt desires. Ultimately this is insufficient, and in the end, as Lawrence indicates in the first of the two essays on Hawthorne, a fuller account must be rendered, one that goes beyond, one feels, any private 'little vulgar language':

The monstrosity of myth is most repugnant to reason. In the same way, the monstrosity of scientific cosmogony and cosmogenesis is most repugnant to the passional psyche. But the progress of religion is to remove all that is repugnant to reason, and the progress of science is towards a reconciliation with the personal, passional soul. The last steps remain to be taken, and then man can really begin to be free, really to live his whole self, his whole life, in fulness. (P. 138.)

The 'religion' and 'science' of the essays progress towards this ideal of a joint, reconciled reality (aided by the 'Two Principles' chapter on symbology, which attempts to piece together some of the old passionate knowledge), and come together in the essay on *Moby Dick*. The last chapter, on Whitman, forms the post-reconciliation state.

2

In the first myth of the essays, Lawrence tries to account for the desires in men which originally brought them to America. He has behind him Celtic and Norse myths when he speaks of the shifting Spirit of Place. All peoples, he sees, are creatively centred on particular parts of the earth; all nations are held by and draw their vitality from the native magnetism inherent in the ground they occupy. But, Lawrence continues, when this vital connection breaks, as he feels that the European polarity broke at the time of the Renaissance, then a new Spirit of Place is established elsewhere and draws men to a new connection, as America hypnotically called its peoples to it across the Atlantic. Lawrence then thinks of the first emigrants, those whom he calls Celts and Iberians, whom he regards as isolated, anti-social peoples, cut off even in their original homeland from the more general warmth of European Christendom. As the English Puritans in North America and as the Spanish in South America, the Celts and Iberians came to fulfil a fate, a murderous purpose. As haters of life—so the account continues—they enforced a cruel imbalance in the psyche: the Spanish repressed the spirit and exalted the flesh, while the Puritans, imposing their version of the Inquisition, set spirit and mind over flesh and spontaneous life.

The account of the Puritan career in North America carries on logically from the *Study* of Hardy and *Twilight in Italy*. The *Study* had dealt with the effect on artistic history which man's changing religious emphases brought about in Europe, and had traced the growing ascendance of a spiritual-mental extremism after the Renaissance. *Twilight in Italy* speaks of the same extremism but in broader terms, seeing it as acting not merely on the artistic but on the political and scientific aspects of man as well. Therefore, Hamlet's killing of the King seems to Lawrence the destruction in art of the flesh that has become so loathsome in the old, sensual Father (the body of the Law, as the *Study* might say); but the Puritans do the killing in political reality by the execution of Charles I, and since the Puritans express so perfectly the advancing rationalism of their age, mankind is led into the establishing of the abstract, selfless community as an ideal and to worshipping mental knowledge and mechanized force. For Lawrence it is a movement towards mental, wilful idealism, and he adds a dimension to artistic history in the *Study* where Shelley had been pictured as the spiritual poet who is tempted to deny the reality of his skylark's body. In the *Twilight* sketches Shelley is the political idealist who believes, with Godwin and the Revolutionaries, in the ultimate perfectibility of man. It is but a short step from this view to the ethic of Benjamin Franklin which Lawrence examines in the essays—all the inheritance of spiritual absolutism of which Puritanism is the adventurous spearhead.

In the first versions of the American essays, the Puritan ego is said to have replaced the idea of a living community with a deadly machine-state, made men into social units and regarded the universe and God as the one great Will admired by Franklin and Poe. These northerners of the 'white' psyche, among them Poe's human vampires, are the killers and criminals in the essays, stirred by the old Puritan lust to possess life by murdering it: as Lawrence remarks (p. 130), with 'The Pit and the Pendulum' inferred but not specified, 'Inquisition and torture are akin to murder . . . a combat between conqueror and victim for the possession of the soul after death.' In Hawthorne's work, there is the self-torturing, over-spiritual Dimmesdale—'He is the Inquisition unto himself' —and Hollingsworth, the 'dark, black-bearded monomaniac', whose obsession, Lawrence notes, is with criminals. In Cooper's novels there is the family of Ishmael Bush rolling forward across the prairie—'shadowed with a sense and a reality of crime. Huge, violent, barbarous figures . . .'—and there is Leatherstocking, although for Lawrence he is a killer with a difference. The last of the criminals is 'the northern monomaniac', Ahab.

Together with this criminal action, the essays describe the unseen, terrible reaction which is provoked. Life—which here Lawrence associates with the repressed, aboriginal sensuality of America—insidiously turns back upon its triumphant torturers, the mind and spirit, and secretly undermines the criminal ego. These treacherous revengers sapping the open, spiritual murderers are restless in their attack on the falsity of man's divided psyche. The sensual side which was unconsummated passionately in life and thought to be dead rises again and again upon spiritual, idealistic man like the ghost of an unsettled score. In the essay on 'Fenimore Cooper's Anglo-American Novels', Lawrence depicts them (p. 79) as 'the angry, unappeased shades that come darkly home to us, thronging home to us from over the seas, entering our souls and filling us with madness . . . unless we, by our active living, shall give them the life that they demand, the living motions that were frustrated in them now liberated and made free.' In the story of haunting revenge which runs through Lawrence's interpretation of Poe and Hawthorne, the ghosts persistently return to torture their former torturers until, in the essay on Melville, the spiritual ego is seen to be broken so finally from its presumptions that in its ruin it can at last admit its unappeased enemies and be reconciled.

But Lawrence sees a spiritual obstinacy in Poe and Hawthorne which keeps the battle going. When the man of mental lust destroys the life in Ligeia, she returns to destroy her husband's second wife: 'it is the ghostly Ligeia who pours poison into Rowena's cup. It is Ligeia, active and unsatisfied within the soul of her husband. . . .' Usher kills his sister with consuming love: 'she died at last, like Ligeia, unwilling and unappeased. So, she rose again upon him.' The line of prostituted souls continues into *The Scarlet Letter*: 'Hester Prynne is the successor of Ligeia.' As the embodiment of the maimed, sensual Spirit of Place—'the aboriginal American principle working in her, the Aztec principle' —Hester secretly turns upon Dimmesdale under cover of the spiritual surface which his Christian era has imposed, and in league with the other 'aboriginal', Chillingworth, surreptitiously destroys the spiritual saint. To Lawrence, Eve's surrender to temptation in the Bible means the fatal disruption whereby mind is set over physical being; in Hester's revenge on Dimmesdale, and its 'extreme serpent subtlety', Lawrence pictures the reversal of the Eve myth, a second Fall, and the collapse of the 'white' consciousness of the human race. 'Once she has destroyed him, her dreadful spirit is more or less appeased'—but, as 'more or less' suggests, Lawrence realizes that the haunting question has not been finally settled even now. So, 'She is appeased, but her spirit lives on in Pearl', and 'Pearl is the continuing of her terrible revenge on all life.' The tradition of secret back-biting is maintained in *The Blithedale Romance*, where Priscilla, the 'mystic prostitute', the 'degenerate descendant of Ligeia', obscenely submits to Hollingsworth in order to drain the male completely of his power.

There is little doubt that Lawrence was driven to these realizations by the oppressiveness of the War atmosphere in which he was writing. It is a terrible stimulus which brings him so directly to his insights and which makes him see enacted in the American literature a drama of pressures felt more painfully nearer Europe. He does not have to imagine vicariously the destructiveness of the 'angry, unappeased shades that come darkly home to us . . . from over the seas.' They are felt, not from aboriginal America, but from European battlefields: 'I cannot bear it much longer, to let the madness get stronger and stronger possession,' Lawrence writes to Ottoline Morrell in 1915. 'Soon we in England shall go fully mad, with hate. I too hate the Germans so much, I could kill every one of them. Why should they goad us to this frenzy of hatred, why should we be tortured to bloody madness, when we are only grieved in our souls, and heavy?'[1] Soon after this letter, he writes to Russell: '*Never* expose yourself to the pack. Be careful of them. Be rather their secret enemy, the secret enemy working to split up and dismember the pack from inside, not from outside.'[2] The 'pack' are the 'Christian democracies', Germany and England, whom Lawrence feels are fast disintegrating in their fight to the death.

But the most galling aspect for him is that though the divided Christian psyche seems to have been reduced to its last obscene phase and is, like Dimmesdale in Lawrence's view, befouling what its spiritual consciousness calls most holy, the psyche is nevertheless hanging on with stubborn indefiniteness. Lawrence sees the dilemma in the second essay on Hawthorne: 'The world is like Dimmesdale, it has its Chillingworth in the dark races. It has had its Hester in Germany. . . . But like Dimmesdale, it persists even after it has fallen' (p. 167). This 'post-mortem' existence of spirituality and its refusal to appease by acknowledging its secret, repetitive attackers denies revenge its satisfaction—and its end. The line of broken, spiritual imbeciles which Lawrence projects from Hetty Hutter in *The Deerslayer* to Roderick Usher should rightly end in the proclaimed Fall of Dimmesdale. But it lingers, seemingly endless like the World War: as Mrs. Crich is thwarted by the spiritual escape of her dying husband, so is Lawrence over Dimmesdale.

It is, perhaps, the attempt to see beyond the deadlock which brings Lawrence, in the discussion of Cooper, Dana, and Melville, to conceive the 'myth of the atonement'. Here there does not have to be a secret wearing down of the resistant spiritual consciousness, for this time the spirit helps towards its own destruction. It actively participates in the liberation of itself from the old presumptions. The purpose is hopefully expressed in the essay on Franklin (pp. 48–9): 'When the great Greek-Christian will-to-knowledge is fulfilled; and when the great barbaric will-to-power

---

[1] Letter of 14 May 1915 (ibid., p. 340).
[2] Letter of 2 June 1915 (ibid., p. 347).

is also satisfied; then, perhaps, man can recognise that neither power nor knowledge is the ultimate man's attainment, but only *being*. . . . We shall at last learn the pure lesson of knowing not-to-know.' In Lawrence's interpretation of American literature, if the will is pushed far enough man is freed from the mechanical responsibility of more criminal conquering and hatred.

But to reach such freedom man has to destroy the arrogant spiritual consciousness, and in doing so he cannot help killing the spontaneous, passionate life as well. In the last, disintegrating phases of both mind and body, the 'white' consciousness and the destroyed sensuality are prepared to embrace each other and become reunited in death, ready for a new creation to come from their fusion in decay. Thus Natty, for Lawrence a spiritual hunter, killing the American Indian and his violent, aboriginal sensuality, ultimately arrives at a communion of souls with Chingachgook. The races recognize each other in an exchange of love before Natty dies in peace and harmony among the Indians of *The Prairie*. The spiritual white man, 'at the end of his race-journey', reaches a state of appeasement during his 'slow, perfect, sensual consummation . . . into death.' He dies among Indians who have 'some sensuous, soft, Asiatic or Polynesian quality'—a remark which is to expand, several essays later, into Lawrence's vision of the Pacific as the great ocean melting-pot which receives all the race-destinies. Already here are the remains of the old sensual order, now decayed into mere repetitious, mechanical dreams. And here the dying white races come as well, disintegrating into a final madness and dead tissue. The two ruined races meet for a last reconciliation—Dana with his love for the dying Kanaka boy, Hope, 'the bright-eyed man of the Pacific' in *Two Years before the Mast*; Ishmael with his love for Queequeg; and Ahab, the fanatical hunter of the 'sacral-sexual consciousness' of man in the Whale, reconciled with the mad negro boy, Pip: 'the imbecile child of the sun hand in hand with the northern monomaniac.'

The love in extremity which Lawrence sees has to be dearly bought. Appeasement, reconciliation, future wholeness, a new era of male comradeship: none can be conceived in the essays except at the price of death and destruction. 'In its beauty, the ultimate comradeship flowers on the brink of death,' writes Lawrence in the essay on Whitman. 'But', he adds with caution (p. 263), 'it flowers from the root of all life upon the blossoming tree of life.' The myth of loving atonement is precarious because it takes its final justification, in the Whitman essay, from the idealism which it uncritically accepts in the preceding Melville essay. In reaching out so far for an eventual wholeness, Lawrence has yielded to some of the dubious harmonizing in the American fiction. He is aware of the American predilection for universalizing personal experience, as the essays on Melville and Whitman show, but this does not prevent him from taking up the position he accuses Crèvecœur (p. 63) of holding, as regards the story of the bees who rise in resurrection from the craw of a slain king-bird— that of spuriously forcing the issue like a Herodotus fable: 'He assumes a victory in sensual cognition which he has not actually won.'

3

As Lawrence is to find, the conditions by which a 'victory' is actually to be won in the flesh and blood ask for more than he is willing to give. To make an imaginative transfer to America in which his whole soul can participate, he needs to be rid of the discriminating European sensibility which he has. And that, the essays suggest, stubbornly persists, not only in the consciousness which he vilifies in his judgements on the spiritual Dimmesdale, but also in the more valuable judgements of the essays. In fact, Dimmesdale represents more than Lawrence concedes, something which the later *Studies* reveal that Lawrence, despite his efforts, could never dispose of: a sensibility which persists in the larger pattern of feelings in the essays. For the mythic framework, of action, reaction, and atonement, does not completely indicate the shifts of desires, nor the symbols which carry and argue for the desires. Sometimes emerging from the American fiction, sometimes Lawrence's own, often a synthesis of the two, the symbols are the real language and logic of the essays, as if only through them can Lawrence attempt to feel his way from European preoccupations to America. The symbols reveal the texture and changing quality of the emotional argument.

At this period, in *The Rainbow*, *Women in Love*, and in the letters, it is Lawrence's sense of the past as containing a latent future which finds expression through the symbol of the dying tree with nascent buds, or the symbol of the buried seed, patiently waiting for spring in winter darkness. In one way, the symbols are a common, everyday language to express Lawrence's private crises, as each winter he suffers his illness and waits for what really seems like a coming again out of the tomb. But the dying tree also symbolizes a larger endurance, the effect of 'winter' upon the human soul and civilization in these War years. 'War is a great and necessary disintegrating autumnal process,' Lawrence writes in a letter of 1915, trying to adjust to the fact that he has been born into a doomed, collapsing era. Soon, he feels, the deathly process will reduce everything to an indistinguishable 'mass', to 'an amorphous heap, like sand, sterile, hopeless, useless, like a dead tree.' However, one can 'let the leaves perish, but let the tree stand, living and bare.' The 'quick of the tree must not perish', for that contains the 'unrevealed buds' of love and creativity for a new epoch of civilization.'[1]

Another letter of the same year takes the thought further: 'life which is still fertile must take its departure, like seeds from a dead plant. I want to transplant my life. I think there is hope of a future, in America. I want if possible to grow towards that future.'[2] The new beginning is nearer there, Lawrence believes, because the death-process is nearer completion, while Europe still has many stages to go in disintegration. At the beginning of the essay on Poe, following the Leatherstocking essay, Lawrence has imaginatively leaped a step with the Americans. In the death of Chingachgook and Natty and their mystic 'conjunction', there is a potent embryo buried with them, expressing beliefs which have yet to be fulfilled: 'we see the passing out into the darkness of the interim, as a seed falls into the dark interval of winter. What remains is the old tree withering and seething down to the crisis of winter-death' (p. 116). But the necessary decay in Europe does not go fast enough for Lawrence. The 'interim' is too long drawn out and tortuous; the 'seed' of patience and subdued desire demands a quicker result. It wants to take wing. 'I wish there were miracles,' Lawrence writes in a letter, early in 1916, '—I am tired of the old laborious way of working things to their conclusions. The seagulls here are so wonderful, large and white, with strong bent shoulders in the light of the sun. Why should one care, or *will*.'[3]

[1] Letter to Cynthia Asquith, 2 November 1915 (ibid., p. 375).
[2] Letter to Cynthia Asquith, c. 16 November 1915 (ibid., p. 382).
[3] Letter to Cynthia Asquith, 7 February 1916 (ibid., p. 423).

The letter hints at the intervention of a mood where conscious control and personal responsibility slip into abeyance, and desire carries one away without the cavilling mind. One sees the transformation in the 'Spirit of Place' essay, when the 'seed' of the patient mood becomes bird-like: the first comers to America are 'borne helplessly as birds migrate, without knowing or willing, down the great magnetic wind towards America.' On the American ground of the Crèvecœur essay, the spirit spreads itself in extravagant assertion after its confinement, and Lawrence praises Crèvecœur's vision of the blood-consciousness in the native birds and beasts—the 'winged hostility and pride, the swinging of the dark wings of the sensual ascendancy.' Then the bird-symbolism takes over-hasty flight into myth. The wish-fulfilment which sought a blind relief now hardens and demands a more violent satisfaction. In his reading of *The Prairie*, Lawrence sees (p. 99) the white criminals rebutted by the Spirit of Place: 'Great wings of vengeful doom seem spread over the western prairie, vengeful against the white men.' Yet the birds carry on the wing the old spiritual consciousness as well as the aboriginal mind, and Natty, the 'mystic destroyer', in killing the native blood is killing the immigrant spirit as well. Therefore, in *The Last of the Mohicans* he brings down the sensual, bird-like Indians—'It is strange and appalling in this book that twice the hostile Indians are shot from overhead, and plunge down almost as from the skies into death' (p. 102)—but in *The Deerslayer* he is equally the killer of the Christian, spiritual principle: 'He brings the highest bird dead from mid-heaven.' The birds die, Chingachgook and Natty embrace across their distance in deathly communion, 'And out of this embrace arises the strange wing-covered seraph of new race-being.'

The winged idea, when repeated in the essay, 'The Two Principles', is more meticulously examined, to be treated with elaborate cosmological significance: the duality of fire and water in the universe is envisaged in a symbol 'like the body of a four-winged bird'. In the Dana and Melville essays, however, the wings belong to storm-birds, to albatrosses of the white consciousness, flying to soul-extinction. In the Dana essay, Lawrence, with his cosmology now informing the symbol, says (p. 197) of the author's 'mystic' vision of the albatross: 'He sees the last light-loving incarnation of life exposed upon the eternal waters: a speck, solitary upon the verge of the two naked principles, aerial and watery.' In the end, the spirit and the flesh are destroyed in the sinking of the *Pequod* with simultaneous effect: 'The bird of heaven, the eagle, St. John's bird, goes down with the ship, nailed by Tashtego's hammer, the hammer of the American Indian' (p. 250). The nailing of the spirit by the aborigine seems to Lawrence an act of destruction complementary to Natty's killing of the sensual Indians. It is also another reversal for former Christian triumphs, although Lawrence does not make this explicit. Just as for him the first Fall of mankind in Genesis is reversed by the second Fall of *The Scarlet Letter*, so St. John's account in Revelation (to Lawrence a symbolic story of the spirit's triumph over the sensual) has its brutal rebuke in the nailing of the saint's bird.

For Lawrence the pinning of the bird has, perhaps, an especially personal significance. When he quotes Melville on the albatross—'it uttered cries, as some king's ghost in supernatural distress'—he says (p. 241): 'We must remember that Melville's albatross is a prisoner, caught by a bait on a hook.' He is thinking of the footnote in the 'Whiteness of the Whale' chapter in *Moby Dick*, in which Melville relates how the captain of one of Ishmael's ships had 'made a postman' of the albatross, 'tying a lettered, leathern tally round its neck, with the ship's time and place; and then letting it escape.' Yet there is an uneasiness in Lawrence's accusation against the 'white' European mind which the essays do not show. Melville's sensibility is not Lawrence's when he writes, in 'The Whiteness of the Whale', of the albatross:

From my forenoon watch below, I ascended to the overclouded deck; and there, dashed upon the main hatches, I saw a regal, feathery thing of unspotted whiteness, and with a hooked, Roman bill sublime. At intervals, it arched forth its vast archangel wings, as if to embrace some holy ark. Wondrous flutterings and throbbings shook it. Though bodily unharmed, it uttered cries, as some king's ghost in supernatural distress. Through its inexpressible, strange eyes, methought I peeped to secrets not below the heavens. As Abraham before the angels, I bowed myself; the white thing was so white, its wings so wide, and in those for ever exiled waters, I had lost the miserable warping memories of traditions and of towns.   (*Moby Dick*, p. 165.)

These are the 'memories' which are blamed for intruding, with their consciousness, upon Lawrence's homage in his later poem, 'Snake': here the observer, in wondering arrest before the creature, is broken in upon by a sense of horror, and a 'clumsy log' is thrown at the departing snake:

> And immediately I regretted it.
> I thought how paltry, how vulgar, what a mean act!
> I despised myself and the voices of my accursed human
>   education.
>
> And I thought of the albatross,
> And I wished he would come back, my snake.
>
> For he seemed to me again like a king,
> Like a king in exile, uncrowned in the underworld,
> Now due to be crowned again.[1]

'Education' here is a cowardly, self-preserving thing, and yet one may well feel that the word conceals a more precious kind of caution in the sensibility than Lawrence will admit to. In these first versions of the American essays, the European mind can be seen as no more than utterly imprisoning. Melville's albatross is caught by it, and so for Lawrence is Eve Effingham in *Homeward Bound*, discussed in 'Fenimore Cooper's Anglo-American Novels'. Eve is the patrician who imprisons herself among the democrats, impaling her 'haughty, winged soul' on her social beliefs: 'There it writhes and flaps ignominious. All her loves and adventures move us not at all.' Something of the same frustration is concealed by all of Lawrence's 'loves and adventures' among the American books. When one remembers the sorrow which overwhelms Cyril in *The White Peacock*, as he gazes out at the battling crows and sees them carried away 'like souls hunting for a body to inhabit', one can sense Lawrence's personal understanding (p. 222) of Melville's predicament in the Pacific: 'Among these islands he wanders like an uneasy ghost seeking its rest, and never finding it. For he cannot yet identify himself with the great sea, he cannot yet escape his European self, ideal and ethical as it is, chainbound.' Nor can Lawrence escape the wider implications of being European, although the value of so being disappears under his hampering word 'ethical'. In the same essay on *Typee*, his accusations against Melville tend to reflect back on the Lawrence who interprets the Leatherstocking novels: 'He could never let be. He

---

[1] *The Complete Poems* (1964), vol. I, p. 351.

could never really let go. His will was always clinched, forcing life in some direction or other, the direction of ideal transcendence' (p. 225).

As a self-description, of course, it is too narrow, for Lawrence's sanity has always the wit to retrieve itself from the exploring and the far-off embattlement with understanding. The onward striving to the very limits of this storm-bird kind of consciousness must have been a strain which Lawrence realized while forcing the issue of these vicarious voyages among the Americans. He was still writing the first versions of the American essays when the authorities compelled the Lawrences to leave Cornwall and the Atlantic coast where *Women in Love* had been written. Staying for a short while in Berkshire, he describes it as 'Hardy country—like *Woodlanders*—all woods and hazel-copses',[1] and in the changed surroundings, admits a lapse from the previous strained mood: 'I no longer want the sea, the space, the abstraction.'[2] Among these woods he seems to move under a quiet spell: 'I believe I could go into a soft sort of Hardy-sleep, hearing the church chime from hour to hour, watching the horses at the farm drink at the pond, writing pages that *seemed* beautifully important.'[3] The still dreaminess of this mood is like a return, without the bitter poignancy, of the mood in which he came to see downfall three years earlier. Then—in his 'vision of a drowning man, the vision of all that I am, all I have become . . . me, generations and generations of me'[4]—the national and personal past, the English land and the Englishman, seemed to crystallize together as an era slowly closed. 'When I drive across this country,' he writes in 1915, 'with autumn falling and rustling to pieces, I am so sad, for my country, for this great wave of civilisation, 2000 years, which is now collapsing, that it is hard to live. So much beauty and pathos of old things passing away and no new things coming: this house of the Ottoline's—it is England—my God, it breaks my soul. . . . No, I can't bear it, I can't let it go.'[5] But, as he insists in the 'Spirit of Place' essay, he must: 'It is time for us now to see that our great race experience is surpassed and exceeded. Our race

---

[1] Letter to W. E. Hopkin, 12 March 1918 (*Collected Letters,* vol. 1, p. 547).
[2] Letter to Cecil Gray, c. 7 February 1918 (ibid., p. 539).
[3] Letter to Cecil Gray, 12 March 1918 (ibid., p. 546).
[4] Letter to Ottoline Morrell 1 December 1915 (ibid., p. 391).
[5] Letter to Cynthia Asquith, c. 9 November 1915 (ibid., p. 378).

idea may apparently hold good in the American mind. What we have to realise is that our way of feeling is superseded. . . . Life itself takes on a new reality, a new motion.'(P. 17.) These are the bold, stern terms with which Lawrence's actual feelings find it difficult to keep pace. To transplant himself beyond his English experience and sense of tragedy he instinctively needs a continuous bridge of feeling by which to cross over.

It is Hardy, as he appears in the letters and the essays on Cooper, who seems to symbolize old feeling in the process of change. In Hardy, Lawrence seems to concentrate his vision of all that is most fine, valuable, and deep in the English sensibility—but set in America and intrinsically transformed. As a symbol of 'all that I am, all that I have become and ceased to be', Hardy seems to offer a way for Lawrence's feelings to run on and envisage what he wants to be. Significantly, Lawrence associates Hardy with Cooper in the letters. Both belong to the reading of his youth and maturity. Lawrence's later essay, 'Indians and an Englishman', speaks of his 'heart, born in England and kindled with Fenimore Cooper.' And as *English* artists Lawrence brings Hardy and Cooper together in his letters of 1916. The art of the continentals— Tolstoy, Dostoevsky, Maupassant, Flaubert—seems to Lawrence at this particular time 'so very *obvious* and coarse' when set 'beside the lovely, mature and sensitive art of Fenimore Cooper or Hardy. It seems to me that our English art, at its best, is by far the subtlest and loveliest and most perfect in the world.'[1] The sweep of praise continues in another letter, where Cooper is ranged triumphantly against Verga: 'I have just read *Deerslayer*. What an exquisite novel. Oh, English novels, at their best, are the best in the world.'[2]

His sense of exultance possibly stems from the chance which he sees in the Leatherstocking novels of applying a pressure to nostalgia, enforcing a change from the 'pathos of old things passing away and no new things coming' to a fearful, positive movement forward. His description of the first chapters of *The Pioneers* carries on the heightened 'English' feeling with which he identifies Cooper in the letters, but he takes it further in an attempt to lose the pathos and remembrance amongst this new 'beauty and magnificence unsurpassable'. The settlement 'is England—but England lost on the edge of the unknown; England more English

---

[1] Letter to Catherine Carswell, 27 November 1916 (ibid., p. 488).
[2] Letter to S. S. Koteliansky, c. 15 December 1916 (ibid., p. 492).

and characteristic than England ever was, asserting itself in the toils of the great dark spirit of the continent' (p. 97). There is a strange overstatement in the glamour with which he invests the scene, a sense of pain trangressed by the over-wrought gladness, surmounted by the 'almost unbearable leap of enchantment', as if Lawrence were urging his feelings on to a pitch where they will break beyond the English 'idea' and enter upon the 'new motion' and the 'new reality'—'astounding Christmas abundance of the tables, that groaned as English tables never groaned, with weight of good things, splendid things to eat.'

Lawrence's whole enthusiasm for the wintry opening of Cooper's novel and the exaggerated sense of American plenty seem to bear him beyond remembrance of the 'Riot of Christmas' chapter in *The White Peacock*, or the tranter's Christmas in *Under the Greenwood Tree* or Ursula's childhood Christmases in *The Rainbow*, where the Midlands wakes and mummers belong to the same England as those who call on the Yeobrights' Christmas party in *The Return of the Native*. Ursula's Christmas 'perished like a nipped thing, like a bud in a false spring' as the religious year passed into an Easter of death. To Lawrence, however, these American classics carry the miracle onwards, beyond wintry death to new creation. The 'leap of enchantment' at the beginning of *The Pioneers* is a leap from Europe across the old consciousness, developing beyond nostalgia 'as the sledge drives over the snow . . . the Judge and his daughter folding themselves in furs as the twilight advances over the pine-dusky winter.' Something of this implicit conception still touches Lawrence in the final version of the Hawthorne essay on *The Blithedale Romance* with its 'beautiful, wintry-evening farm-kitchen sort of opening'. It also prevails in the early version of the essay on *Moby Dick*, as the *Pequod* sails out on a freezing Christmas Day: 'The voyage begins, like Dana's, in the winter-time, strange and dark at first.'

As a touchstone of past feeling, Hardy is left behind. His social 'pioneers', according to Lawrence's *Study*, die in the wilderness after leaving the safe fold of convention; they perish, it is said, because the sensuous understanding of their author is greater than any genuine mental consciousness he can give them, 'and his people move in his landscape almost insignificantly, somewhat like tame animals wandering in the wild' (*Phoenix*, p. 480). But Cooper's racial pioneers move out boldly for Lawrence, suffering none of the sensuous dilemmas which afflict Hardy's characters. Lawrence admires 'a glamour and an extravagance about the white men as they move, so very English, on this strange landscape', 'the insuperable glamour [in *The Pathfinder*] of sailing the sweet-water seas in the early days when the continent was still virgin to white man.' Hardy's characters in the *Study* are fatally bedevilled by their hesitations between fold and wild, but here the courage of the 'outpost souls' is sterner, and (like another 'leap of enchant-ment') the Indian canoe goes over the falls, 'venturing so fearlessly into space.' For Lawrence, Cooper's major pioneer, Natty, is not to be daunted by any Hardyesque confusion in the spirit and the flesh. Discussing the split in the psyche which causes the creation of the separate 'fair' and 'dark' women of Cooper's novels, Lawrence contrasts the two writers: 'This division into duality, and the conflict in dualism in the self, and the inevitable ensuing tragedy, is Hardy's theme as well as Cooper's. Hardy had no way out. . . . Cooper has the same division, the same tragedy. But he has two ways out: either the material-social successfulness into which his admirable Mabels betake themselves, or the strange, blank reality of Deerslayer.' (Pp. 107–8.)

In the Hardy *Study*, Sue Bridehead may have been seen as blundering into tragedy by betraying her special spiritual form when she physically married Jude, but in Lawrence's interpretation of the Leatherstocking novels, Natty avoids any such mistake. He is here a voyager out of the conditions which created the tragic one-sidedness of his race, and he is to surpass them only by de-struction. A woman would be wrong for him, not because of his specially spiritual type but because she would hinder the fulfil-ment of his purpose. For a moment, when Lawrence considers Natty and Mabel Dunham in *The Pathfinder*, his race-voyager flinches back in fear from his destiny beyond—'He trembles on the edge of space'—and is tempted to consider marriage, a home, and children as his real needs: 'It is a shrinking from the sheer communion in isolation, which lies ahead, the mystic consum-mating of the White Soul with the Red. It is the inevitable denial of the extreme mystic impulse.' But Natty after his lapse gets 'back to the right track'. For Lawrence, it cannot have been genuine love that Natty felt for Mabel; the only love that is clean and positive in the essays is that between male comrades, and then only on the edge of death. In Poe and Hawthorne, the essays describe man and woman love as totally diseased and destructive. Because of this sternness, Lawrence does not subject the deaths of Magua, Uncas, and Cora in *The Last of the Mohicans* to the kind of analysis we might expect from one who understood in Hardy how dualism created and removed 'stained' characters. Instead, Lawrence regards the deaths as a justification of Natty's voyage into mystic communion, such being his exclusively confined interest in the character: 'There is to be no marriage between the last fiery slips of the Red and the White race—no marriage in the flesh.'

The race-voyaging is partially completed in Lawrence's account of *The Deerslayer*, the exquisite 'English' novel of his enthusiastic letter. By this time Cooper has shed the Englishness which Lawrence saw in the opening of *The Pioneers*, and Hardy's English art drops back in significance, ranked now with the general European vision from which it had previously been distinguished. Savage, heaving Egdon has been outgone when Lawrence writes (p. 106): 'The world—the pristine world of Glimmerglass—is, perhaps, lovelier than any place created in language: lovelier than Hardy or Turgenev, lovelier than the lands in ancient poetry or in Irish verse.' In arriving at Glimmerglass, Lawrence completes another stage in his imaginative transfer from one stretch of water to another, from the Atlantic desire of the Celts and the Iberians in 'The Spirit of Place'—'Their heaven was the land under the western wave, the Celtic Tir na Og'—to Cooper's 'pristine' lake. In his discussion of *The Deerslayer*, Lawrence's imagery and phrasing suggest that his feelings have arrived at one stage of an arduous process: '*Deerslayer* is, indeed, one of the most beautiful books and most perfect books in the world: flawless as a jewel and of gem-like concentration. From the first words we pass straight into the world of sheer creation, with so perfect a transit that we are unconscious of our translation.'

The 'perfect transit' has been effected by Lawrence's own pressure. The duress of 'gem-like concentration' comes after the sequence of nervous strain which has symbolically asserted itself at the beginning of the book of essays, in 'The Spirit of Place'. There, speaking of the process of purification leading to perfection, Lawrence regards the Spirit of Place as something that is first of all expressed in its birds, beasts, and flowers, and lastly in its men and their works. The mountains are expressed in the blue gentians and the edelweiss, and in the earth-strata which 'come to a point of perfect, unutterable concentration in the inherent sapphires and emeralds.' Then Lawrence sees how Crèvecœur reveals the expression of the place in the birds and beasts—'the pride, the recoil, the jewel-like isolation of the vivid self.' From Crèvecœur's own description of the humming-bird, with its razor-bill and its eyes 'like diamonds, reflecting light on every side', Lawrence gains (p. 64) 'a curiously sharp, hard bit of realisation, something surely intrinsic, a jewel-sharpness and refraction inherent in the little soul of the creature.' In the next essay, on Cooper's 'Anglo-American novels', Lawrence derives from the example of the beasts the idea of quivering polarity and 'singleness', so that opposing creatures, like the deer and the wolf, the rabbit and the stoat, mutually concentrate each other within a charged field of fear, keeping life rich, electric, and magically bright. 'As jewels are crushed between the valves of the earth, and driven, through unutterable resistance, into their own clear perfection . . . so must the human soul be purified in unspeakable resistance to the mass. We wear the ruby and the sapphire as symbols of our splendid pride in singleness, our jewel-like self.' (P. 87.) And so, after stern race-voyaging, Deerslayer and the 'gem-like' world of Glimmerglass are the perfect expression for Lawrence of the Spirit of Place in men.

But having found his satisfaction in passing on from the 'winged hostility and pride' of the native birds to the jewelled poise in men, Lawrence can conceive further development for man only in deathly mitigation of the tautness. The assertive extravagance is not to be betrayed by any relaxing; it is to be slowly burnt down of its own will. If the spiritual and sensual birds are shot from the skies, the 'jewels' must be dissolved in a corrosive. Natty's mystic consummation in death—among the 'sensuous, soft' Indians, according to Lawrence's account of *The Prairie*—is, in the account of *The Deerslayer* (p. 111), like the lowering of Lawrence's own tension: 'Ecstasy after ecstasy of keen peril and terrible death-dealing passes through his frame, gradually, mystically reducing him, dissolving out his animate tissue, the tissue of his oldness, into death as a pearl dissolves in wine.' Yet in the narrowing of these American essays to a concern with the extremes of male comradeship, Lawrence has removed the real, human resistance which sharpens the individual and alerts the meaning in the novels. Here no bearings can be taken, no comparison of experience can be established, in the way that *Women in Love* is able to do when it presents Ursula's checking response in the 'Sunday Evening' chapter. There Birkin comes from his searches into corruption. The demonism has left its visible marks on this 'strange gem-like being', who like 'some image of a deathly religion' is matched and perfectly known for what he is by Ursula: 'He was the enemy, fine as a diamond, and as hard and jewel-like, the quintessence of all that was inimical.' But one sees in *Women in Love* what the American *Studies* do not attempt to admit: that such hardness, in Birkin or Ursula, is one among a range of feelings, and not the absolute expression of selfhood. In the wedding-rings, the topaz takes its place among the opal and the sapphire. 'We wear the ruby and the sapphire as symbols of our splendid pride in singleness', but only in the novel do we know the different values which they hold and the rich, difficult experience by which they have been won.

In his criticism of Cooper's novels, Lawrence encounters no resistance of the kind which is inevitably set up in his own art; and he finds no difficulty in turning the Leatherstocking novels to his purpose, because, like the fiction of Hawthorne and Melville, they offer a way open for his imagination to enter. One remembers his letter of 1916 to Ottoline Morrell where (mentioning that he is reading *Moby Dick* and wishing that he 'were going on a long voyage, far into the Pacific') he asks for the loan of a history book —'not too big, because I like to fill it in myself.'[1] It is not just his own will which enables him to 'fill in' on Cooper but also Cooper's careful ordering and definition of a distance between his races which gives Lawrence leave to take possession of the space. Where in the actual novel a sparseness of feeling creates a blank, the vacancy invites the strained arrival of Lawrence's 'mystic' feeling: bonds are projected across the space and separateness is charged with the value of exchangeable, intuitive knowledge. At the close of *The Last of the Mohicans*, Natty and Chingachgook seem to Lawrence (p. 103) 'Two mature, silent, expressionless men' who 'stand on opposite shores of being, and their love, the inexpressible conjunction between them, is the bridge over the chasm.'

If Cooper awkwardly expresses individuality by reference to

[1] Letter of 7 February 1916 (ibid., p. 425).

'gifts', social proprieties, and mutual respect, Lawrence expresses it by reference to 'the extreme mystic impulse': therefore, in Cooper's novel, Natty's love for Mabel is an aberration because it is a denial of his hunter's 'gifts' and the natural order, but in Lawrence's essay Natty is avoiding the issue of his racial fate. And because Cooper has so carefully segregated races, Lawrence is able to speak (p. 110) of the twin race-destinies: 'This is the beauty of Deerslayer, that he knows at last that there are two ways, two mysteries—the Red Man's and his own. He must remain true to his own way, his own mystery.' But even Lawrence, in his usurpation of Cooper's characters, seems to make an inadvertent confession that the feeling between White and Red has to be 'a love so profound, or so abstract, that it is unexpressed', because it might not really be there—as adjectives like 'unutterable' and 'unspeakable' often seem to say. They belong to the heavygoing language of the 'Excurse' chapter in *Women in Love*, as if the true victory in 'sensual cognition' cannot be proclaimed with the confidence which Lawrence would wish.

Cooper's art gives him enough space to enter and ignore the actual morality found there, unlike that which he finds in *The Scarlet Letter*. The entry into Hawthorne's art is more difficult, because Lawrence comes in through the discrepancy which he sees between the wakeful moralist and the unconscious, perverse artist. Yet he is able to treat Hawthorne's situation as he has treated Hardy in the *Study* because he rightly sees the gap between the elusive disorder of the material and the unifying account of it which Hawthorne is trying, if inadequately, to give. What Lawrence concludes from his insight is less valuable, as if Hawthorne were marred for him because he seems to be cheating, like Poe. Lawrence has no patience with 'the way the ethical Hawthorne embroiders over the artist Hawthorne. The deepest joy is the pride of sin: and all the preaching is so lugubrious and moral.' (P. 168.) And, in this reading, the ironic design of the scaffold scene at the beginning of *The Scarlet Letter*, where Hester and Pearl are suggested as the Virgin and Child whom the Puritans cannot see, reveals only an underhand homage to the Magna Mater— 'the almost insane malice of the situation, the malicious duplicity which exalts in shame that which it worships in lust' (p. 140). It is as if Lawrence distrusts Hawthorne's consciousness because it seems like the obsolete English 'idea' at its most corrupt and persistent. Cooper's Leatherstocking finds a way out from Hardy's tragedy, but Hawthorne's Dimmesdale will not go much further, once he has been intensified beyond the English spirituality in Hardy: 'Arthur Dimmesdale is the very asphodel of spiritual perfection, refined till he is almost translucent and glassy. He is far more refined than Angel Clare in *Tess*, perfect as a moonstone emitting the white and sacred beam of the spirit and the holy mind.' (P. 142.) Yet this 'moonstone', unlike his jewelled counterpart, Deerslayer, refuses to dissolve as a pearl in the wine.

4

'After Hawthorne come the books of the sea.' The opening sentence of the 'Two Principles' essay eventually leads Lawrence, with another 'leap of enchantment', to the Pacific of Dana and Melville: 'The Atlantic is again superseded.' The lakes of Cooper replaced the Atlantic as the longed-for heaven, and they in their turn are replaced by the greatest ocean, 'the first of all the waters', 'the great bourne, the heaven under the wave, like the Celtic Tir-na-Og.'

Myth and reason, religion and science, are still divided in Hawthorne's art, according to Lawrence—'There is a discrepancy between his conscious understanding and his passional understanding'—but the Pacific of Melville's novel is the great meeting-place for the divided psyche, for the symbol and its reality. The *Pequod*'s hunt for the last, free 'passional body' of the White Whale in men 'is a mythical, mystical voyage, as any Argonaut voyage ever was. Sometimes its forced fantasy is irritating. And yet, after all, it is curiously *actual*. This is the beauty—the identity of daily experience with profound mystic experience.' (P. 239.) He likes the interchange which Melville seems to manage between the myth and its everyday substance, and is glad when Melville is not tied too closely to one particular level, when he stops speculating about symbols and 'moves into pure actuality. It is curious how actuality, of itself, in deep issues, becomes symbolic.'

As Melville moves from symbol into actuality, for Lawrence he takes the essays' themes to a point of justification. From Lawrence's standpoint, it is love on the verge of death which Melville actualizes out of symbol. Throughout the essays, fire has been the symbol of the reducing process in the tissue of the white and red races. In the

Franklin essay, Lawrence notes the hellish fire and the drunken Indians which Franklin reports, and it is into fire that Indian John returns elementally in Lawrence's account of *The Pioneers*. Now in the essay on *Moby Dick* the low-burning fire in the bedroom where Queequeg and Ishmael embrace has an added significance, which Lawrence confirms to himself when he notes that Ishmael 'says he loved the savage's "large, deep eyes, fiery black and bold."' In the same vein, Melville's symbolism is seen to incorporate and give reality to the symbolism of water which Lawrence thinks of initially in the Franklin essay. The symbol of the dying tree or plant, whose buds or seeds lie in forced dormancy seems here too inactive an expression of the 'new reality' which Lawrence sees as immanent in the decaying world. His feelings run to a more pulsating symbol of the dead and the unborn, together in the same concept—the symbol of water and waves, with a central point as the 'Godhead', the 'Now', through which past and future come and go, in and away, from death to rebirth: 'ripples of futurity running towards the Now, out of the infinite, and ripples of age and the autumn, glimmering back towards the infinite. And rocking at all times on the shimmer are the perfect lotus flowers of immanent Now, the lovely beings of consummation.' No fixity or persistence are allowed: 'the whole of wholeness lies in the ebbing haste of child-faced futurity, the consummation of presence, and the lapse of sunset-colored old age.' (Pp. 39–40.) The Leatherstocking novels enact the symbolic wish, as old ghosts are appeased, 'sunset-colored old age' gives way to the newly born, and Natty as young Deerslayer is the future latent in the dying present: 'racially, he is an old man. Sensually he is an infant.' Glimmerglass is one form of the immanence, with its 'luminous futurity which glimmers as a plasm in all the landscape', but Melville's Pacific makes the futurity actual for Lawrence, as he quotes the description of Queequeg's illness, with the savage's eyes 'like circles on the water, which, as they grow fainter, expand; so his eyes seemed rounding and rounding, like the rings of Eternity.'

The 'Grand Armada' chapter of *Moby Dick* is significantly acclaimed by Lawrence as 'perhaps the most stupendous chapter'. Here, one remembers, Melville presents a vision of inner calm at the centre of a whale-herd, while outside concentric circles of whales rush round in confusion and terror. It is apt that Lawrence

should quote Melville's description of this 'serene valley lake' or
'enchanted pond' where Starbuck, Ishmael, and Queequeg see
'Leviathan amours' in the deep, and mothers with calves. As if
through a further Glimmerglass, the suckling young look up
through the transparent water, indifferent to the whale-hunters
above them. In this strange scene of adoration—so far removed
from, yet so closely related to the first scaffold scene in *The
Scarlet Letter*—Melville compares the young whales (*Moby Dick*,
p. 337) to human infants who 'will calmly and fixedly gaze away
from the breast, as if leading two different lives at the time; and
while yet drawing mortal nourishment, be still spiritually feasting
upon some unearthly reminiscence.' Because Hawthorne's
scaffold scene maintains an edge of ironic duality, Lawrence
regards him as a malicious double-dealer, hiding under an outward consciousness he does not believe in. But because Melville
dispenses with irony by forcing dual consciousness to become one
—so that the profane flows into the holy, the hunter into the
worshipper, the warring savage into the peaceful lover—the
vision of the whale-calves has a divine significance for Lawrence
which he cannot find in Hawthorne's suggestion of Pearl as the
holy child who hovers between two worlds. Hawthorne's caution
is blamed, while Melville's open declaration is praised. In this,
perhaps, Lawrence is bringing to his essays and Melville's 'enchanted pond' the Whitman of 'Facing West from California's
Shores':

> Inquiring, tireless, seeking what is yet unfound,
> I, a child, very old, over waves, towards the house of
>   maternity, the land of migrations, look afar,
> Look off the shores of my Western sea, the circle almost
>   circled.

But for Lawrence the essayist the circle has not been circled. In
his symbolism, the latent life cannot bud or move until the decaying process is really concluded. As the essay on Franklin admits
(p. 40): 'There is, however, the false Now, as well as the mystic
Now. Perpetual youth, or perpetual maturity, this is the false
Now—as roses that never fall are false roses.' Since Dimmesdale
and the other senile 'children' hang on to the point of imbecility,
they block the way of the waiting desires, and in the wish to surpass
what impedes him Lawrence comes dangerously close to the

purposes of Melville. In attempting to escape the knowledge of his full sensibility, Lawrence excludes from the essays the dimension which his novels, at their finest, are concerned to retain. He pushes through in the essays what could not survive in *The Rainbow* or *Women in Love* without being challenged internally or without being betrayed linguistically. On the battlegrounds of these novels, the spurious, one-sided victories in 'sensual cognition' are more readily exposed, just as the real victories can be seen to be earned. Lawrence's comment in his later essay, 'The Novel', is a good reminder for a student of his novels and of the American writers: 'Somehow you sweep the ground a bit too clear in the poem or the drama, and you let the human Word fly a bit too freely.'[1] Therefore, one must look to the relationship between Lawrence the novelist and the Americans if one is to see what he gained and what he could never take, what made for the more subtle 'Word' and what swept 'the ground a bit too clear'.

[1] *Phoenix II*, ed. Warren Roberts and Harry T. Moore (1968), p. 418.

II

The Rainbow and *Women in Love* in Relation to
the Americans

WHEN we come to consider Lawrence's artistic encounter with
American literature, Emerson's essays take on a special relevance
as common literary ground known to both Melville and Lawrence.
The essay 'Circles', in particular, is a valuable point of reference.
Here Emerson puts forward a heroic, evolutionary belief:

> The life of man is a self-evolving circle, which, from a ring imper-
> ceptibly small, rushes on all sides outwards to new and larger circles,
> and that without end. The extent to which this generation of circles,
> wheel without wheel, will go, depends on the force or truth of the
> individual soul. For it is the inert effort of each thought, having formed
> itself into a circular wave of circumstance—as, for instance, an empire,
> rules of an art, a local usage, a religious rite—to heap itself on that
> ridge, and to solidify and hem in the life. But if the soul is quick and
> strong, it bursts over that boundary on all sides, and expands another
> orbit on the great deep, which also runs up into a high wave, with
> attempt again to stop and to bind. But the heart refuses to be im-
> prisoned; in its first and narrowest pulses, it already tends outward
> with a vast force, and to immense and innumerable expansions.

Men cannot rest upon the already achieved, for, with unnerving
persistence,

> every action admits of being outdone. Our life is an apprenticeship to
> the truth, that around every circle another can be drawn; that there is
> no end in nature, but every end is a beginning; that there is always
> another dawn risen on mid-noon, and under every deep a lower deep
> opens.[1]

The American essayist outlines the premises, but the American
imagination in *Moby Dick* deals with the results of the heroic
prospect. One sees how far Melville has to stretch to place his
consolation—' "on the starboard hand of every woe, there is a sure

---

[1] *Essays and other Writings* (London, 1907), pp. 187–9.

delight; and higher the top of that delight, than the bottom of the woe is deep"'—beyond the grip of his narrowing, materializing consciousness and its ambitious encircling of life. 'Valour consists in the power of self-recovery,' says Emerson, 'so that man cannot have his flank turned, cannot be out-generalled, but put him where you will, he stands.' To work out the implications of resilient fearlessness, Melville has to conceive the mad swivellings of an Ahab or the strange beatitude of an Ishmael.

Again, in yet another instance, one can see how Emerson touches on a premise while the literature takes the burden of disorder: for if everything that man achieves so quickly becomes the mouldering past, then all is only relative to the hour and values fleetingly proportionate to their newness. Emerson realizes the implication: 'And thus, O circular philosopher, I hear some reader exclaim, you have arrived at a fine Pyrrhonism, at an equivalency and indifferency of all actions.' He agrees with his reader's possible exclamation, but deliberately offers no solution: 'I unsettle all things. No facts are to me sacred; none are profane; I simply experiment, an endless seeker, with no Past at my back.' The dead load is easily disposable, as it is for Pearl and Holgrave, but the weight of past consciousness is not to be shed without a cry when it is piled so thickly and meaninglessly on Ahab. Hawthorne does not feel the need to take on the inordinate literary responsibility which Melville assigns himself, when he makes his appeal (*Moby Dick*, p. 394): 'Friends, hold my arms! For in the mere act of penning my thoughts of this Leviathan, they weary me, and make me faint with their outreaching comprehensiveness of sweep, as if to include the whole circle of the sciences, and all the generations of whales, and men, and mastodons, past, present, and to come, with all the revolving panoramas of empire on earth, and throughout the whole universe.'

Lawrence's course is different, inevitably. When his art portrays a movement forward from the past it cannot help knowing more fully than the Americans the terms of human progress, and hence the conditions of disaster. Lawrence is bound to a continuity in his sense of experience, to *all* the steps in the sequence, so that in his finest art one knows the distance an individual has come in his being, and at what price. Only a knowledge like Lawrence's of the phases of growth could give him the confidence to see, when distortion begins to assert itself, the quality of the assertion, or how the individual comes to arrogate absolutist power to himself. Lawrence's critical sensibility can still remain in action when the tragic state exercises its hypnotism and demands that its grand inevitability should be accepted. He will not let the sense of disaster escape into the closed system, without past or future, which modern fatalism would like for itself. Lawrence denies this vacuum, this seeming finality, when he insists on the explicit analysis of failure in the consciousness, when he reaches for the whole truth through the play of inner being in personal relationships.

In his art, man may point ahead with a feeling of Emersonian adventure, to 'the dogged leaping forward of the persistent human soul, on and on, nobody knows where'; yet his progress is vitally related to his tie with the woman of his experience. With her, he knows his limits, and his possibilities, his anchorage and his reality. If he cannot lead her with him and 'answer' her doubts, she breaks away in disillusion, anarchy, and scorn. And in breakdown a tragic mystery clouds over. Man, left on his own without the woman's creative link, goes on 'nobody knows where' into a courageous but blind incoherence. Lone, self-reliant heroism, of the kind which Emerson admires, has always, in Lawrence's art, a moral qualification attached to it. This makes Lawrence's literary responsibility more organically disciplined than Melville's. When the circles of consciousness widen throughout *The Rainbow* and *Women in Love*, Lawrence is concerned that the insights he now admits shall make a sane whole—and only the relationship between man and woman, as he knows it, can test the truth of the new inclusions. It is this aspect of Lawrence which brings his art, in several important ways, so close to the purposes of Hawthorne.

I

In the first version of his essay on Hawthorne, Lawrence speaks of the myth of *The Scarlet Letter*: the collapse of the spiritual consciousness in America, the Second Fall. But this view of Hawthorne is not as useful as the remarks on myth, legend, and romance with which Lawrence opens his discussion of *The Scarlet Letter*. 'The primary or sensual mind begins with the huge, profound, passional generalities of myth, and proceeds through legend and romance to pure, personal art' (*The Symbolic Meaning*, p. 137).

To Lawrence, Hawthorne, in failing to understand as deeply as he feels, covers the discrepancy by calling his work romance. Indeed, there is an uncertainty in *The Scarlet Letter*, an unwillingness in Hawthorne to be too definite in assigning significance; this refusal to close options too finally is concealed and justified by the historical setting. Hard, specific explanations are not expected in an atmosphere of conjecture, unendorsed rumour, and varying interpretations of events—as, for instance, the speculations which surround the revelation of Dimmesdale's stigma, or the different versions of the tale about Pearl's experience with the wild animals of the forest. The conjectures and generalities are more subtly insinuated than in the superstitious picture-morality of *The Return of the Native*, but Hawthorne's predicament has at least this in common with Hardy's: neither can offer a more exact description of the activity which their arts engage in, but in refusing to describe it in terms of commonplace, inadequate values, they offer a token of a moral view, something which mediates uneasily between the commonplace and the original, between the communal and the private reality.

The legendary atmosphere in *The Scarlet Letter* is, one can see from Hawthorne's Preface, the result of compromise. When the moonlight affects the familiar, domestic room, the latter (p. 45) becomes 'a neutral territory, somewhere between the real world and fairyland, where the Actual and the Imaginary may meet, and each imbue itself with the nature of the other.' By the time of the Preface to *The House of the Seven Gables*, Hawthorne is declaring his work (pp. vii–viii) as 'Romance' that is moving towards the Actual: 'It is a legend prolonging itself, from an epoch now gray in the distance, down into our own broad daylight, and bringing along with it some of its legendary mist.' The curse that comes down to the present age from the time of the sinning American Adam is here ended, but the legendary atmosphere is dispersed and replaced by a consciousness that Hawthorne cannot save from disappointing glibness. He has lost the old ambiguity and duality in order to gain a diffuse oneness. Only by such loss, however, can he attempt to realize Hester Prynne's hope 'that, at some brighter period, when the world should have grown ripe for it, in Heaven's own time, a new truth would be revealed, in order to establish the whole relation between man and woman on a surer ground of mutual happiness.'

Interest in 'happiness' is too limiting a description of Lawrence's purposes in the making of *The Rainbow*: 'I can only write what I feel pretty strongly about: and that, at present, is the relation between men and women.'[1] Yet Hawthorne's and Lawrence's purposes are comparable, certainly as regards the movement from 'passional generalities' to a more individualized, conscious, 'personal art'. The terms by which a 'whole relation' can be achieved are as radically different for Hawthorne and Lawrence as the cultures from which they, as artists, emerge; but this is not to deny the focus which *The Rainbow* gains from *The Scarlet Letter*—the sense which Lawrence seems to attain, that he is writing initially amongst 'passional generalities', in the 'realm of the myth and the morality play' where, to him, *The Scarlet Letter* belongs. He is writing at the level of the 'primary mind', knowing, however, the further course of his development.

Hester Prynne's estranged state and the legendary insinuations surrounding her are important for Lawrence in the first chapters of *The Rainbow*. According to Hawthorne (*The Scarlet Letter*, pp. 87–8), Hester is 'banished, and as much alone as if she inhabited another sphere, or communicated with the common nature by other organs and senses than the rest of human kind. She stood apart from moral interests, yet close beside them, like a ghost that revisits the familiar fireside and can no longer make itself seen and felt.' Hawthorne refuses to be less oblique when he suggests, in his conjectural fashion, that 'perhaps there was more truth in the rumor than our modern credulity may be inclined to admit' that Hester's symbol could be seen glowing at night with infernal fire. In the same way he cannot be more explicit about the evil with which Hester communicates as she wanders 'without a clew in the dark labyrinth of mind'. Yet he does reveal the suffering of the situation, where an old consciousness has been transposed into a new scene without at the moment having taken root. There is an unearthly, flickering quality about the first scaffold scene, when Hester stands arraigned before the Puritans (pp. 64–5) and her memory brings up the past—herself as a girl in England, her parents, her life in a continental city with Chillingworth:

[2] Letter to Edward Garnett, c. 18 April 1913 (*Collected Letters*, vol. 1, p. 200).

there were intervals when the whole scene, in which she was the most conspicuous object, seemed to vanish from her eyes, or, at least, glimmered indistinctly before them, like a mass of imperfectly shaped and spectral images. Her mind, and especially her memory, was preternaturally active, and kept bringing up other scenes than this roughly hewn street of a little town on the edge of the Western wilderness; other faces than were lowering upon her from beneath the brims of those steeple-crowned hats. Reminiscences, the most trifling and immaterial, passages of infancy and schooldays, sports, childish quarrels, and the little domestic traits of her maiden years, came swarming back upon her, intermingled with recollections of whatever was gravest in her subsequent life; one picture precisely as vivid as another; as if all were of similar importance, or all alike a play.

It is like the strange incandescence of Lawrence's vision of a drowning man—'all I have become, and ceased to be', and one remembers the way in which he sees the settlement in *The Pioneers*: 'England lost on the edge of the unknown'—'the long, raw street of wooden houses, with wood-fires blinking and flashing through the uncurtained windows, in the winter nights' (*The Symbolic Meaning*, p. 97). Through Hawthorne's picture of Hester one can also see the exaggerated brilliance in the memory of Lydia Lensky, demanding her girlhood in Poland again and yearning in the snows of alien England for the sight of 'the peasants coming out like new people, in their sheepskins and their fresh, ruddy, bright faces, that seemed to become new and vivid when the snow lit up the ground.' Her deeper consciousness cannot bear to come to life in this English exile. Implicitly she denies its new reality for her, whatever her outward acceptance. When Tom sees her at church, 'She was strange, from far off, yet so intimate. She was from far away, a presence, so close to his soul. She was not really there, sitting in Cossethay church beside her little girl. She was not living the apparent life of her days. She belonged to somewhere else. He felt it poignantly as something real and natural. But a pang of fear for his own concrete life, that was only Cossethay, hurt him, and gave him misgiving.' (*The Rainbow*, p. 27.) His sympathies must draw back from what he cannot completely understand in her brooding and remoteness, as if he were denying the truth of his experience by following her too far beyond the flesh and blood.

After the death of Lensky and her sufferings, she is cut off from

life's growing interests, and like Hester she is wandering ghost-like
through an alien land: 'She was like one walking in the Underworld, where the shades throng intelligibly but have no connection with one. She felt the English people as a potent, cold,
slightly hostile host amongst whom she walked isolated. . . . She
walked without passion, like a shade, tormented into moments of
love by the child. . . . In the superficial activity of her life, she
was all English. She even thought in English. But her long blanks
and darknesses of abstraction were Polish.' (Pp. 46–7.) To this
abstracted state belong her puzzling, foreign memories of an
unfulfilled past with Lensky whose total meaning she cannot yet
comprehend. The abstractness is also a ceasing to care, a fatal
leaning towards the deathly and some incomprehensible evil. It
is a 'dread-worship' which Lydia seems to share with Hawthorne's
Hester, an urge to lapse 'into a sort of sombre exclusion, a curious
communion with mysterious powers, a sort of mystic, dark state.'

Pearl, in all her freakish imbalance, derives from Hester's
situation, as if the child were a product of her mother's breach
with familiar 'moral interests'. The mother's crisis in the spirit
creates the abnormality of her 'elf-child' and 'demon offspring'—
a restlessness in Pearl which Lawrence translates as an unconscious
anxiety in Lydia's child, Anna. Tom and his sister see Lydia and
her daughter after church (p. 28):

'She's *somebody* very funny,' said Effie, almost in condemnation.
'That child's like one bewitched . . . '
'Bewitched—how bewitched?' he repeated.
'You can see for yourself. The mother's plain, I must say—but that
child is like a changeling . . .'

Pearl's rapid 'mutability' enables her to inhabit a variety of forms
but to be circumscribed by none. She is for ever 'darting up and
dancing . . . in a state of preternatural activity', a skittish 'airy
sprite' who, after playing at her sports and talking to her 'visionary
throng' of imaginary people, will 'flit away with a mocking smile'
in her 'wild, bright, deeply black eyes'. Hester cannot be sure
that Pearl is really 'flesh and blood, and not utterly delusive.'
Lawrence's Anna is no semi-tangible phantasm, yet she suffers
under a similar dilemma of being: 'As a rule, however, she was
active, lightly flitting about the farmyard, only appearing now
and again to assure herself of her mother. Happy she never

seemed, but quick, sharp, absorbed, full of imagination and changeability. Tilly said she was bewitched.' (P. 68.) Later in summer she is seen as 'a brown elfish mite dancing about.'

But although Anna's black eyes, painfully ever-watchful, are not the demonic abyss into which Hester looks, there is a guardedness about both children which acts, in different ways, as a restraint upon the desires of the mothers. In the forest scene with Dimmesdale and Hester, Pearl is the hindrance, the triumphant reminder, when her mother would seek to escape the full working-out of her fate. One sees the will intensified in Anna when her mother drifts into abstraction and gives up the responsibility of her own life. Anna takes on the responsibility for her, and is strained beyond her years and understanding as she persists in recalling Lydia again and again from the deadly nostalgia of 'the life that had been'. She is also preventing the entry of the life that is to come, but since her child's knowledge cannot distinguish between the undefined good and the evil presences waiting for admittance, her one sure instinct is to stop all intrusion upon their shared life for as long as is wakefully possible—as when (p. 38) Tom is forced to bide his time outside the vicarage door while Anna insists on her story from Lydia: 'The fair, strange face of the child looked over the shoulder of the mother, all asleep but the eyes, and these, wide and dark, kept up the resistance and the fight with something unseen.'

It is not just the child who cannot make out the shape of the evil which she resists, for at this point in the novel, Lawrence has so bounded his art that it does not seek to be more clear about the obscure processes with which the child does battle, or with which Lydia's religion struggles in the crisis (p. 48) before she comes to Cossethay—'There was a little agony of struggle, then a relapse into the darkness of the convent, where Satan and the devils raged round the walls, and Christ was white on the cross of victory.' It is sufficient, however, for the combat with the deathly forces to have an elemental, pristine urgency. The danger has to be sensed and fought without analysis, because at this moment, as Birkin says of another state, ' "no understanding has been reaped from that plane." ' And in the life-and-death conflict that goes on with Tom and Lydia, it would be a depreciation of Tom's 'otherness'—an upset of the balance by which he can give stability to her—if he were to reach over to understand more closely the identity of the evil he opposes. Here the instinctive religion can win the day. The time has not yet arrived in the novel when the Lamb with the flag must be challenged by the unsatisfied mind and when the shape of the unseen evil must be realized more consciously by Lawrence if he is to counter it again by any adequate moral criticism.

Lawrence saw Hawthorne and Hardy as makers of 'morality plays' whose outward moral structure contradicted or hid their artistic purposes. Even though one may not agree that Hawthorne is *so* at odds with his purposes as Lawrence suggests, it is clear that Lawrence in the early part of *The Rainbow* knows he is creating the movement of a primal morality play, without offering its concepts as the ultimate description. In the first American essays, he underestimates Hawthorne's difficulty in *The Scarlet Letter*—that of having to contend with an elusive psychological disorder by resort to a conjectural moral method. In the attempt to make the chaos relate back to an outer wholeness, Hawthorne puts an abstract, generalized stamp upon the experience. Lawrence does not have this disadvantage. In the 'morality play' of *The Rainbow*, one is constantly aware of the strenuously felt flesh-and-blood struggle, with its retreats, advances, hopes of victory and disillusion, shifting of sides—as Anna buttresses her mother, then compensates Tom in his outcast state—and the final winning: the adjustment of mother, child, and husband, as each undergoes a subtle change in relation to one another.

Lydia is 'transplanted' as she works out the painful yet living fate. Bearing Tom's child, 'she seemed to lose connection with her former self. She became now really English, really Mrs. Brangwen. Her vitality, however, seemed lowered.' And just as Lawrence knows the cost of the effort to struggle beyond the old conditions of the self, so he appreciates the gain, as regards Anna's new freedom. When she sees her mother with the child (pp. 78–9), 'Anna was at first puzzled, then gradually she became indignant, and at last her little life settled on its own swivel, she was no more strained and distorted to support her mother. She became more childish, not so abnormal, not charged with cares she could not understand. . . . She became an independent, forgetful little soul, loving from her own centre.' It has taken the calming, rhythmic compassion of Tom's knowledge to overcome the fixity of the child's will. But Hawthorne, when making a similar adjustment in the spirit, has to leap too far, too symbolically—from Pearl's abstract, ambivalent values as a sprite to the suggestion of a settled human being, ready for adulthood: 'The great scene of grief, in which the wild infant bore a part, had developed all her sympathies; and as her tears fell upon her father's cheek, they were the pledge that she would grow up amid human joy and sorrow, nor forever do battle with the world, but be a woman in it. Towards her mother, too, Pearl's errand as a messenger of anguish was all fulfilled.' (*The Scarlet Letter*, p. 238.) In this context, the 'pledge' still wears a remote, abstract meaning.

Hawthorne cannot stand far enough back to make a conscious containment of all that Pearl signifies, but Lawrence in *The Rainbow* gives his art the opportunity to widen its realizations as Anna outgrows the settlement made in her childhood. Will Brangwen has not the knowledge to stop her breaking the continuity of the marriage, but Lawrence's art has a rich scale of understanding with which to place and interpret her meaning. In her childhood her fear of the unseen could be pacified by the sane, male power of her stepfather, so that she could move on towards individuality, no longer insistent that the present moment should stand still, in defiance of all to come. But in her breach with Will's less respected manhood, her fears are awakened again, and with them the old wish to arrest life according to her wilful illusion. Only innocence shall exist, and all the angry devils she has provoked in Will shall be excluded from the light, together with those which she chooses not to know in herself. The fears, the absolutism, the self-division, the break in the sequence of reality: these are the aspects which Gudrun inherits (*The Rainbow*, p. 268) from Anna: 'Gudrun was a shy, quiet, wild creature, a thin slip of a thing hanging back from notice or twisting past to disappear into her own world again. She seemed to avoid all contact, instinctively, and pursued her own intent way, pursuing half-formed fancies that had no relation to anyone else.' When she reappears in *Women in Love*, the fancies and unrelatedness have brought the division in herself to a point of intolerable conflict, so that she will advance to challenge the world with her reality, and then retreat in fear, illusion, and artistic self-preservation. From little Anna's flitting and 'changeability' to Gudrun's back-and-forth sensationalism there goes a logic of wilfulness which reaches a further, more concentrated expression in the portrayal of Winifred Crich. And here Lawrence returns directly to the source of his vision of disorder in Hawthorne's Pearl.

This time, however, he sees a new significance and gains a sharper emphasis than was possible in his previous sight of Anna through the focus of Pearl. His actual analysis of Pearl's significance in the essays reveals only a fraction of the gain which comes into *Women in Love*. In the first version of the essay on *The Scarlet Letter*, Pearl continues Hester's revenge on life as the mocking figure who betrays the flesh with the spirit and undermines the spirit with the flesh. She is a demon who makes a null neutralization. But one remark in the essay does indicate how Pearl's meaning applies more closely to Winifred than to Anna— 'surely nowhere in literature is the spirit of much of modern childhood so profoundly, almost magically revealed.' In *Women in Love*, Lawrence is nearer than ever before to the specially American quality of disorder in the child—that restless ambivalence which pervades Hawthorne and Melville, the Protean facility for being everywhere and nowhere, for never being openly caught in unequivocal attitudes, for inhabiting numerous shapes without being identified with any. In Pearl's 'mutability' one sees the shifts of Ishmael and the many faces of the Confidence Man; one sees Holgrave's unfixed career through America— 'putting off one exterior, and snatching up another, to be soon shifted for a third.' 'The unlikeliest materials—a stick, a bunch of rags, a flower—were the puppets of Pearl's witchcraft, and . . . became spiritually adapted to whatever drama occupied the stage of her inner world. . . . It was wonderful, the vast variety of forms into which she threw her intellect, with no continuity.' (*The Scarlet Letter*, pp. 96–7.) In the same vein, she pelts the birds with stones by the sea-shore, breaking one's wing in her play— after which 'the elf-child sighed, and gave up her sport; because it grieved her to have done harm. . . .'

It is Lawrence's unique triumph to have understood the full significance of the 'mutability', to have achieved in the novel and the creation of Winifred the 'parallel rational exposition' of the disorder which, in his Hawthorne essay, he sees the other novelist unable or unwilling to provide. 'The child', says Hawthorne (p. 93), 'could not be made amenable to rules. In giving her existence, a great law had been broken, and the result was a being whose elements were perhaps beautiful and brilliant, but all in disorder; or with an order peculiar to themselves, amidst which the point of variety and arrangement was difficult or impossible to be discovered.' This means to Lawrence that Hawthorne 'did not choose to discover too much, openly.' The 'law' which has been broken is the Seventh Commandment, but even Hawthorne suggests that this is only a formal identification of a principle that has been infringed. And for Lawrence, in the essay and in *Women in Love*, the 'law' broken is a passionate, physical principle, and it has been transgressed by those who have mentally exalted love above all other forms of consciousness, thus creating the mockery of the 'devils' who strike at the mind's presumptions.

One does not have to agree with all of Lawrence's conclusions in the essay on *The Scarlet Letter* in order to see that he grasps the essential meaning of the disorder which Hawthorne's burning letter 'A' can only suggest intuitively to be representative of greater sin than a single broken Commandment. Directly and unmysteriously, Winifred arises out of a mental climate of love, so that the American novelist's intuition—when Pearl skips among the graves 'like a creature that had nothing in common with a bygone and buried generation, nor owned herself akin to it . . . as if she had been made afresh out of new elements'—is translated into the English novelist's realization in Winifred: 'She was quite single and by herself, deriving from nobody. It was as if she were cut off from all purpose or continuity, and existed simply moment by moment.'[1] Pearl's 'mutability', as she hovers between the world of the spirit and the world of flesh and blood, is given further understanding in the portrayal of Winifred's action-reaction, as her divided psyche constantly forces her into rapid alternations of feeling—now making her belittling, witch-craft pictures of the rabbit and the dog, and then shifting back into penitence and 'real grief' at what she has done. Emerson's essay 'Circles' not only speaks for Pearl's meaning but also for the narrator of Poe's 'Berenice', for Ishmael squeezing sperm, for Glimmerglass and the untouchable Deerslayer, when it says: 'The one thing which we seek with insatiable desire is to forget ourselves . . . to lose our sempiternal memory.' In the American disorder which brings

---

[1] Cf. England as seen after the first World War: 'The younger generation were utterly unconscious of the old England. There was a gap in the continuity of consciousness, almost American: but industrial really' (*Lady Chatterley's Lover*, Penguin ed., 1961, p. 165).

Lawrence to the refined creation of Winifred, Emerson's wish is wickedly enacted: 'She . . . could never suffer, because she never formed vital connections, she . . . could lose the dearest things of her life and be just the same the next day, the whole memory dropped out, as if deliberately' (*Women in Love*, p. 212).

This is her value to her family at their moment of crisis. She is a compensation, a balance, to her father just as little Anna has been to Tom after Lydia has borne his child; just as Ursula has been to Will Brangwen after he has been emotionally cast out by his wife. But one does not have to realize the difference between Will's use of Ursula as an addition to himself and Thomas Crich's exploitation of Winifred to see how far Lawrence's analysis has carried him since *The Rainbow*. Absolutism of the will and its purposes are now seen with a new courageous subtlety, and it is Melville, as well as Hawthorne, who is the source for the subtlety.

2

While engaged on *Women in Love* in 1916, Lawrence wrote to a correspondent: 'I loved Melville's *Moby Dick*. I read Thucydides too, when I have the courage to face the fact of these wars of a collapsing era, of a dying idea. He is very good, and very present to one's soul.'[1] In another letter (to Ottoline Morrell, from whom he had borrowed the Thucydides) he admires the Greek historian's 'true classic dignity and self-responsibility'.[2] Thucydides is admired as a brave forerunner in a similar historical situation, and it is consistent that Lawrence should use his book as a symbolic shield for Birkin's spirit when Hermione tries (*Women in Love*, pp. 98–9) to murder him: 'Hurriedly, with a burrowing motion, he covered his head under the thick volume of Thucydides, and the blow came down, almost breaking his neck, and shattering his heart.' This is a detail, but the attitude that the Greek symbolizes here is important for Lawrence the novelist. He expresses it more amply through Somers at the end of *Kangaroo* (p. 390), when his character is asked if he will 'give in' to America after he has resisted Australia. Somers replies that he will not go back on '"our real civilised consciousness. . . I'm the enemy of this machine civilisation and this ideal civilisation. But I'm not the enemy of

---

[1] Letter to Barbara Low, c. 30 May 1916 (*Collected Letters*, vol. 1, p. 454).
[2] Letter of 7 April 1916 (ibid., p. 444).

the deep, self-responsible consciousness in man, which is what *I* mean by civilisation. In that sense of civilisation, I'd fight forever for the flag, and try to carry it on into deeper, darker places." ' It is that kind of awareness which has the staying power to follow out the fate of the *Pequod*—'symbol of this civilised world of ours' in the early essays on the Americans—and yet has the sanity to be present, in critical health, at the heart of the disintegration. The 'self-responsibility' is not forsaken when Lawrence regards the Americans through *Women in Love*, because he sees them in two ways—as his contemporaries whose knowledge can explain the processes at work in his own time, and yet as his forebears, figures of the previous century who have already gone through the experience which Europe is still toiling in. They are advanced in decay and hope: 'America, being so much *worse*, falser, further gone than England, is nearer to freedom.'[1] The manner in which Lawrence contemplates the American past as the present leading on to the future relates to an important aspect of *Women in Love*—the way in which Gerald leaps ahead in experience, abbreviating normal time, and the 'old laborious way of working things to their conclusion'.

The understanding of abbreviation, compression, foreshortening is Lawrence's gain from the American experience, because at the same moment he still possesses a sense of time and scale. His historical feeling for the size and length of a process gives him the perspective to remark, in the essay on Whitman: 'The Americans have finished in haste, with a certain violence and violation, that which Europe began two thousand years ago or more.' Ahab speeds unswervingly to destruction in Melville's novel and charges Lawrence's novel with a succinct understanding, which Poe's art intensifies: the further logic of the wilful, post-creative state. With Gerald, the soldier, explorer, and master-industrialist, Lawrence quickly advances to a position which *Women in Love* (p. 215) can take for granted, and, therefore, can see beyond: 'His vision had suddenly crystallised. Suddenly he had conceived the pure instrumentality of mankind. . . . As a man as of a knife: does it cut well? Nothing else mattered.' So, 'Without bothering to *think* to a conclusion, Gerald jumped to a conclusion.' Unerringly the functional knife-edge of Gerald cuts through everything in fulfilment of his new industrial philosophy. In the transformation

[1] Letter to Catherine Carswell, 7 November 1916 (ibid., p. 481).

of the collieries, 'New machinery was brought from America, such as the miners had never seen before, great iron men, as the cutting machines were called, and unusual appliances.' It is inevitable that the 'iron men' should come from an America that produces Ahab's Promethean suggestion to his carpenter on the ship: ' "I'll order a complete man after a desirable pattern . . . no heart at all, brass forehead, and about a quarter of an acre of fine brains." ' For the 'iron men' of human reality in both novels, the fineness of the cutting-edge depends on the sharpness of the blade and the pressure behind it. Gerald's youth shares with Ahab's age the common feature, that the sharp-edged quality of both is the forceful tip of an immense wedge.

The condensed energy in Gerald which unleashes him into space—'He is several generations of youngness at one go'—makes him more than an English phenomenon. Like the savage carving in Halliday's flat, with its 'void, peaked' face, he carries for his white race an immensity of pressure and experience. He also is 'abstracted almost into meaninglessness by the weight of sensation beneath.' Birkin remarks of the savage figure (p. 72): ' "There are centuries and hundreds of centuries of development in a straight line, behind that carving; it is an awful pitch of culture, of a definite sort." ' One remembers Ahab's load: ' "I feel deadly faint, bowed and humped, as though I were Adam, staggering beneath the piled centuries since Paradise." ' Ahab comes to vindicate his complaint against life, as one of mankind's 'proud gods', leading and outstripping the democratic principle which he represents. In his address to the flames burning on the yardarms, he boasts that his mind has encircled and materialized their mysterious significance: ' "all thy eternity is but time, all thy creativeness mechanical." ' And with ghastly absurdity throughout the novel Ahab is constantly replacing the organism in himself or in life with its materialized equivalent. The destructive aims of Poe's lovers in the *Tales* are brought to a clumsy, tragic fantasy in *Moby Dick*, where the 'bird of heaven' caps the sinking ship and becomes part of its mechanism, a helmet for the Promethean defier. About Gerald, however, there is a deadly plausibleness which makes him less mythically amazing than Ahab but which makes his achievements more recognizably immediate. Like the Promethean captain, with 'the mechanical humming of the wheels of [Ahab's] vitality', Gerald representatively proceeds 'to fulfil the will of mankind as a whole', by substituting the mechanical principle for the organic, making a synthetic 'God-motion' in which he is a functional God-head: 'He found his eternal and his infinite in the pure machine-principle of perfect co-ordination into one pure, complex, in-finitely repeated motion, like the spinning of a wheel' (p. 220).

It is impossible for Lawrence to present Gerald's actions in the posturing kind of drama in which Ahab moves for Melville. As Lawrence says of Dana (*The Symbolic Meaning*, p. 212), so might it be said of Melville: 'Dana is wonderful at relating these mechani-cal, or dynamic-physical events. He could not tell about the being of men: only about the forces.' Because of the advantage he holds, his ability to tell of the effect on being as it passes into abstraction, Lawrence cannot divorce Gerald from a context of relatedness with the aplomb with which Melville cuts out the *Pequod's* carpenter: 'He was a stripped abstract; an unfractioned integral; uncompromised as a new-born babe; living without premeditated reference to this world or the next' (*Moby Dick*, p. 404). Even Pearl, as seen in Winifred, cannot achieve such mechanical indifference without her dualism and activity revealing the psychic disturb-ance which has brought it about. Gerald's blast on the conch shell at Shortlands may be an act 'without reference to anybody', but his development towards abstraction in the novel is paralleled by the sense of repercussions to the organism—the sense of how much of his being must be sacrificed before he reaches the state (*Women in Love*, pp. 411–12) where his muscles are 'elastic in a perfect, soaring trajectory, his body projected in pure flight, mindless, soulless, whirling along one perfect line of force.'

Because Lawrence's moral awareness still works at such extremes —with its knowledge of what is and what is not possible for the inner being; with its pursuit of the would-be absolute by a larger reference—it is not enough for Gerald to be an advanced expres-sion of mankind's will and disgust at life. Ahab is already far gone in self-mechanization when he first appears, but even though Gerald seems to be horrifically detached from the effects on his own body, so that he is undismayed by his wounded hand which he has 'trapped' in machinery, he is not free of the context of sensitive moral reproof in which Ursula's response is set: ' "I hate people who hurt themselves." ' Nor is Gerald's industrial achieve-ment free of the cynical response it engenders, the deep, hideous boredom of despair with which Gudrun at the last sees the irony of his England. Following through the structure of the machine, from the simplest wheelbarrow, to the truck, the donkey-engine, the winding-engine, the miner, the electrician, the underground manager, the general manager, Gudrun arrives (p. 458) at the great complexity of Gerald himself, her would-be 'young hero', 'with a million wheels and cogs and axles. Poor Gerald, such a lot of little wheels to his make-up! . . . What weariness, God above! . . . So many wheels to count and consider and calculate! Enough, enough—there was an end to man's capacity for complications, even. Or perhaps there was no end.' Emerson does not halt at the implications when he says 'that around every circle another can be drawn; that there is no end in nature', and Melville cannot express the full emotional detail of his own or Ahab's general weariness in the 'outreaching comprehensiveness of sweep'. For Melville there is a 'tall tale' freakishness of humour, a quietly grotesque joy, in his presentation of Ahab's mechanical success—' "my one cogged circle fits into all their various wheels, and they revolve" '—or in the description of (*Moby Dick*, p. 404) the carpenter: 'He was like one of those unreasoning but still highly useful *multum in parvo* Sheffield contrivances, assuming the exterior—though a little swelled—of a common pocket-knife; but containing, not only blades of various sizes, but also screw-drivers, corkscrews, tweezers, awls, pens, rulers, nail-filers, counter- sinkers.'

In his vision of compactness and functionalism Lawrence cannot allow Gerald to be the thought-hero which Ahab is for Melville. Ahab, the 'anaconda of an old man', with his ability to draw men and things into himself, to compress them into his mechanism, has the grappling power of the great white squid. But Gerald's far-ranging consciousness is judged more critically when his meaning appears in 'Water-Party' as the white cuttle-fish which stares out from the lantern—cold, intent, but blind. His myth is not Promethean, therefore, with self-creating man as the tortured, bound, undaunted hero. It is with a sense of relatedness that Gerald takes on for Lawrence a Dionysian meaning, in which he is perpetually wounded like Ahab but as the victim of his era, of himself, and the woman whom he unconsciously provokes against himself. Gudrun has the fury of the Bacchae when she tears again and again at the Dionysian child-god. Gerald's tragedy and the demonic retaliation he causes are ultimately related to a failure of realization at a personal level. He may have the attributes of Dionysus,

Cain, or Siegfried in the *Nibelungenlied*, but above all he is Gerald, with the processes of his destruction still visible, not yet swept up into a fascinating, incontestable archetype.

In admiring Gerald's courage in negativity, Lawrence does not applaud the arrogance entailed in the proud following-out of his fate. There is not the satisfied thrill at his doom and its inevitability which Melville receives from the portrayal of Ahab. Too much of his author is committed to Ahab, the seeker for ultimate Truth (in the Timon or Lear fashion, as Melville hints in his essay, 'Hawthorne and his *Mosses*'), the great refuser who declares for that unremitting side of Melville which says 'NO! in thunder.'[1] In saying 'Yes' in recoil, Melville creates Queequeg, but all the loose, beatific feeling has no relevance to Ahab's onward drive. As an abstract idea, the sword intervenes upon the fixed pattern of necessity and free will, or the life-buoy is fashioned from the coffin, but this is only a dream-like way of accepting the unalterable circumstances. Ahab does without such dreams, and since the external, material forces are more real than human tissue and relationships, his vision is more ugly and stark, but more compelling in its stubbornness. The positive cannot authentically intervene upon Ahab, because no one else has any greater *conscious* wisdom which can effectively dispute the main negative contentions. The alternative philosophy offers survival (and only tenuously, the suggestion of a superior truth), but Melville cannot completely resolve his gambler's kind of admiration for the Promethean hero who, ignoring perpetual mutilations and shrugging off attempts at dissuasion, stakes all on a last, desperate throw. In the chapter 'The Symphony', Ahab is only temporarily recalled, and then by a figure whose uneasily-held Christianity has been discredited. Starbuck's appeal from the basis of human affection, love, and the family—' "See, see! the boy's face from the window! the boy's hand on the hill!" '—seems for a moment to persuade Ahab to turn back on a homeward course. But the hope is an illusion, for to Ahab the storm, the thunder, the mechanical vision, and dead matter are the triumphant realities, not the temporary Pacific calm in which he and Starbuck converse. So the circular madness rotates again (p. 466): ' "By heaven, man, we are turned round and round in this world, like yonder windlass,

[1] Letter to Hawthorne, c. 16 April 1851 (*The Melville Log*, ed. Jay Leyda, New York, 1951, vol. I, p. 410).

and Fate is the handspike. And all the time, lo! that smiling sky, and this unsounded sea!" ' When inner being is dead—like Ahab's 'last cindered apple' of creative belief dropping here—and when human relationships have also rotted away (as in the sperm-squeezing), then man cannot act upon man in confident reality, only slide and melt together in a dream.

Lawrence is attracted by the idea of a great, regenerative brotherhood, yet cautious. If he can see that the fatalistic vision of external, manipulating forces only comes to dominate the human imagination when the organic relationship has been brutalized into a mechanical one, he is also aware that the call for a whole-sale amorousness comes out of the damaged being. His letter to Henry Savage in 1913 speaks for this awareness better than the early version of the Whitman essay: 'the bitterness of it is, that while one is brother to all men, and wrote *Macbeth* with Shakespeare and the Bible with James the First's doctors, one still remains Henry Savage or D. H. Lawrence, with one's own little life to live, and one's own handful of thoughts to write. And it is so hard to combine the two, and not to lose oneself in the generalisation, and not to lose the big joy of the whole, in being narrowly oneself.' Going on to talk about Whitman's making a mental idea out of his own flesh and blood, he says:

The fault about Whitman is, strictly, that he is too self-conscious to be what he says he is: he's not Walt Whitman, I, the joyous American, he is Walt Whitman, the Cosmos, trying to fit a cosmos inside his own skin. . . . The flesh and blood must go its own road. There is something wrong with Whitman, when he addresses American women as his Stalwart brides in whom he is to pour the seed for stalwart sons. One doesn't think like that. Imagine yourself addressing English women like that, in the mass. One *doesn't* feel like that—except in the moments of wide, gnawing desire when everything has gone wrong.—Whitman is like a human document . . . a self revelation of a man who could not live, and so had to write himself. But writing should come from a strong root of life: like a battle song after a battle.—And Whitman did this, more or less. But his battle was not a real battle: he never gave his individual self unto the fight: he was too much aware of it. He never fought with another person—he was like a wrestler who only wrestles with his own shadow—he never came to grips.[1]

[1] Letter of 22 December 1913 (*Collected Letters*, vol. 1, pp. 257–8).

With this letter, Lawrence does not rid himself of the idea of Whitman's wide embrace, not even when he has later shot down the cosmic inflation in the Whitmanesque figure of Ben Cooley in *Kangaroo*. But the letter is interesting in the way that Lawrence envisages the coming to grips with the truth of a feeling as a fighting test.

Between the men and women of the novels up to *Women in Love* the fight develops into a contest of emotional and intellectual subtlety, but in trying to place the theme of male comradeship on a similar basis, Lawrence seems to need an essentially physical struggle as his starting point. It is as if he fears in the 'Gladiatorial' wrestling-match of *Women in Love* that unless he makes the terms of the struggle a matter of flesh and blood—a give and take, naked and without mental defences—he will have nothing concretely established on which to guarantee the value of the love between men. Here Birkin comes to Gerald to intervene in his doom with an application that Melville's seamen cannot bring to Ahab or Poe's narrator to Roderick Usher, and the wrestling seems a deliberate effort to prove artistically, and believe undoubtingly, the desire which in Melville remains a shadow-struggle, where the cell walls of separate tissues disintegrate and allow a luscious meeting: 'Squeeze! squeeze! squeeze! all the morning long; I squeezed that sperm till I myself almost melted into it; I squeezed that sperm till a strange sort of insanity came over me; and I found myself unwittingly squeezing my co-labourers' hands in it, mistaking their hands for the gentle globules.' What Ishmael slides into by chance and without memory Lawrence can only imagine as the result of a hard-fought intentness, with the hope of a new but endurable consciousness emerging from the conflict: 'So they wrestled swiftly, rapturously, intent and mindless at last, two essential white figures working into a tighter, closer oneness of struggle, with a strange, octopus-like knotting and flashing of limbs' (*Women in Love*, p. 263).

But though there is a reciprocity there is still an 'essential' quality perceivable in among the oneness. The flesh and blood meets in the two men, but not to lose itself in the generalization. Birkin's hand unconsciously grasps Gerald, and is warmly grasped in return (like Hawk-eye and Chingachgook in *The Last of the Mohicans*); then they withdraw to stand apart in mutual recognition of each other's specially 'single' nature. Yet the element of self-consciousness of which Lawrence accuses Whitman and also Melville, in the essay on *Moby Dick*, after Ishmael worships with Queequeg—'The sophistry with which he justifies his act of idolatry is amusing, and very characteristic of Melville'—is not completely absent from 'Gladiatorial' by virtue of its declared expulsion by Birkin, who says to Gerald that they should be both spiritually and physically intimate without shame: ' "I don't know why one should have to justify oneself." ' The hand-clasp across their distance is too tenuous to survive the disbelief in Gerald and Ursula and Birkin's uncertainty. It takes another cycle of novels to describe the unsure desire at a more fully explored level; and it takes that cycle of active work for Lawrence to be able to abandon the theme.

There is always a Judas force waiting to betray the love, a volcanic anger ready to erupt in denial of the structures which Lawrence proposes to himself in the later novels. But in *Women in Love* the demonic questioner is still part of the moral interplay, as the idealistic generalizing is countered by acute inspection, as the regenerative vision which Lawrence has from America is crossed with the disintegrative knowledge which America also offers him. Writing in a letter of 1917 about America's capacity for destroying the old race of men and creating a new, he re-expresses the idea which is found in *Women in Love*: 'To me, the thought of the earth all *grass* and trees—grass, and no works-of-man *at all*—just a hare listening to the inaudible—that is Paradise.'[1] As his account of *The Pathfinder* indicates—'the insuperable glamour of sailing the sweet-water seas in the early days when the continent was still virgin to white man'—he has behind him Mabel Dunham's feeling for 'that softened solitude, that calm grandeur and eloquent repose that ever pervade broad views of natural objects which are yet undisturbed by the labors and struggles of man' (*The Pathfinder*, p. 103). This is the mood of the mythical 'enchanted pond', the mood which acclaims Glimmerglass, and which ventures to dream in *Aaron's Rod* (p. 299) of rowing 'upon a great lake in the underworld country, a lake of dark blue water, but crystal clear and very beautiful in colour'—a foresight of the Mexican lake in *The Plumed Serpent* from which a new 'religion' emerges. But when Birkin in *Women in Love* puts forward his 'beautiful clean thought' to Ursula, the proposition of 'a world empty of people' is only

[1] Letter to Waldo Frank, 15 September 1917 (ibid., p. 525).

momentarily attractive, because it is 'actuality', the sense of the personal individual inside the clean, futuristic sweep, which is the doubter: 'Her heart hesitated, and exulted. But still, she was dissatisfied with *him*.' The myth runs ahead, but the flesh and blood goes its own felt road. Even Aaron on his dream-lake has an 'anxious second self' which watches over him when the boat passes out into deep water and when 'the flesh-and-blood Aaron' unheedingly lets his elbow be struck by the marking stakes in the shallows. Aaron wakes up from the dream, and looks at his watch in the darkness. 'He had one of those American watches with luminous, phosphorescent figures and fingers. And to-night he felt afraid of its eerily shining face.'

3

Ursula knows from her 'subtle, feminine, demoniacal soul' that humanity has 'a long way to go yet, a long and hideous way', and the sense of the depraved lengths that *can* be reached is something that perhaps only Poe could intimate so thoroughly and only Lawrence could evaluate so perfectly. The feeling of endless, corrupt consciousness is given by Melville in the futility of the circles, but Poe's art shows the break with the organism in process of taking place.

Lawrence first treats the idea of post-mortem consciousness in the essays in his interpretation of 'Usher' and 'Ligeia', where he concentrates on the meaning of destructive love, the wish to murder and so possess in mental knowledge another's living being. *Women in Love* employs that analysis in the portrayal of Gudrun's and Gerald's relationship, but the essay does not reveal as fully as the novel the understanding of Poe's *Tales* as a whole. Lawrence understands Poe's need for a constant supply of mental nourishment, and this gives a particular keenness to the vampirism of Gerald and Gudrun. The kind of thrill which excites Morella's widower when he sees his dead wife through her daughter's phrases and expressions—the thought that he has found 'food for consuming thought and horror—for a worm that *would* not die'— is amplified and morally comprehended by Lawrence when he portrays Gudrun's sensations as her hands rove over Gerald's face in 'Death and Love'. She reaches for 'the glistening, forbidden apple', more conscious than Morella's husband of the need to restrain her greed, to keep back supplies for a further time: 'How much more of him was there to know? Ah, much, much, many days harvesting for her large, yet perfectly subtle and intelligent hands upon the field of his living, radio-active body. . . . But for the present it was enough, enough, as much as her soul could bear. Too much, and she would shatter herself, she would fill the fine vial of her soul too quickly, and it would break.' (*Women in Love*, pp. 324–5.) This is the 'absolute beauty' which Will Brangwen knew in *The Rainbow* brought to a point of chaotic complexity, to the 'general intricacy and confusion' of the kind which Poe enjoys in his dream-cities.

Melville shows the same corrupt complexity, but Poe gives it its real scale—its miniature mental proportions, its subdivision and reduction of possible experience to gain the effect of a mechanical infinite. 'So many wheels to count and consider and calculate!' Gudrun feels in later despair; 'Enough, enough—there was an end to man's capacity for complications, even. Or perhaps there was no end.' It is Poe, not Melville, who cannot help exposing the dimensions of the folly to Lawrence, so that the appearance of inorganic endlessness is seen to come about by a narrowing process. One misses the sense of human limits in *Moby Dick*, whereas for Poe their transgression is still a real factor to be reckoned with. Morella and Ligeia suffer the effect of partnership with their husbands in the delight of corrupt knowledge. In the same way Gudrun and Gerald are co-students, 'implicated with each other in abhorrent mysteries', who play dangerous games with their sensations and bring the over-filled 'vial' of their souls near to the breaking point reached by the aesthete's 'cracked and blackened' goblet of poison in 'The Assignation'.

But although Poe is intensely aware of the boundaries he is leaving behind or staying within, his analysis is as numb as Melville's and Dana's: he cannot 'tell about the being of men: only about the forces.' Since Lawrence's portrayal of demonic cruelty and lacerated nerves inevitably and morally takes account of the organic repercussion, Gudrun and Gerald cannot afford the detachment with which Poe's victim of the Inquisition in 'The Pit and the Pendulum' reflects on the descending blade: 'I forced myself to ponder upon the sound of the crescent as it should pass across the garment—upon the peculiar thrilling sensation which the friction of cloth produces on the nerves. I pondered over all this frivolity until my teeth were on edge.' In contrast, the indulgence of Gerald and Gudrun in 'Rabbit' has its cost counted in terms of physical suffering and felt consequence to the inner being. One knows the price of the sensation when the rabbit's clawing provokes a welling-up of cruelty in his tormentors, so that they meet (pp. 234–5) across the tear, comparing scratches: 'it was as if he had had knowledge of her in the long red rent of her forearm, so silken and soft. . . . The long, shallow red rip seemed torn across his own brain, tearing the surface of his ultimate consciousness, letting through the for ever unconscious, unthinkable red ether of the beyond, the obscene beyond.'

The hurtfulness, the torture of this experience, are reminders of the period in which *Women in Love* came to be written—that point in Lawrence's life when the disaster of the War, the sense of civilization's imminent collapse, were interpreted through his vision of the American precedent in downfall. It is significant that Lawrence, in conveying the feeling of spiritual confinement during the War in the 'Nightmare' chapter of *Kangaroo*, looks (p. 289) in retrospect to Poe for an image of the experience: 'It had been like Edgar Allan Poe's story of the Pit and the Pendulum —where the walls come in, in, in, till the prisoner is almost squeezed. So the black walls of the war—and he had been trapped, and very nearly squeezed into the pit where the rats were. So nearly! So very nearly!' And that same pressure, in the novel which comes from the War years, is also depicted by a specifically American image of spiritual crowding—as when Birkin's words at Breadalby strike viciously into Hermione. The effect, like that in 'Usher' or 'The Cask of Amontillado', is that of a premature burial: 'The terrible tension grew stronger and stronger, it was most fearful agony, like being walled up. . . . And then she realised that his presence was the wall, his presence was destroying her. Unless she could break out, she must die most fearfully, walled up in horror.' (*Women in Love*, p. 97.) In the gloom of Shortlands, personality crowds upon personality, as Gerald's unthinking, blind will slowly hems in Gudrun: 'He shifted slightly on the hearth, crunching a cinder under his heel. He looked down at it. Gudrun was aware of the beautiful old marble panels of the fireplace, swelling softly carved, round him and above him. She felt as if she were caught at last by fate, imprisoned in some horrible and fatal trap.' (P. 318.)

The trap of marmoreal beauty is comparable to the psychological captivity of Breadalby where Hermione sits in state, like an Usher waiting for a sound from the vaults, controlling the extravaganza she has set in motion for herself, after suffering (p. 82) 'the ghastliness of dissolution, broken and gone in a horrible corruption . . . pallid and preyed-upon like a ghost, like one attacked by the tomb-influences which dog us.' As a setting of beautiful confinement, Breadalby's 'static prison' is like the English abbey in 'Ligeia', the English school in 'William Wilson', or the 'magic prison-house' of the Valley in 'Eleonora'—the place of elaborately-sustained existence, where the enclosed sensations give the illusion of boundless space, where Hermione feels ' "so *uplifted*, so *unbounded* . . ." ' At Breadalby the dead live on beyond their time—like the decayed fruit of Birkin's accusation, who ' "won't fall off the tree when they're ripe" '—and here, as with Gerald, the American feeling of antique decay which informs the atmosphere is translated into Lawrence's concept of race-age. The Gothic theatricalism of the English abbey in 'Ligeia' houses the narrator's second wife and contains, besides its mechanically-stirred draperies and contrived lighting effects, in each of its angles 'a gigantic sarcophagus of black granite, from the tombs of the kings over against Luxor, with their aged lids full of immemorial sculpture.' Hermione, dogged by 'tomb-influences', is seen at dinner, 'strange and sepulchral', tightly enshrouded in 'a dress of stiff old greenish brocade', looking as powerful and tall as when she is seen later (pp. 91–2) at breakfast by Birkin:

How well he knew Hermione, as she sat there, erect and silent and somewhat bemused, and yet so potent, so powerful! He knew her statically, so finally, that it was almost like a madness. It was difficult to believe one was not mad, that one was not a figure in the hall of kings in some Egyptian tomb, where the dead all sat immemorial and tremendous . . . how known it all was, like a game with the figures set out, the same figures, the Queen of chess, the knights, the pawns, the same now as they were hundreds of years ago, the same figures moving round in one of the innumerable permutations that make up the game.

Hermione's creation, as a person of inward disorder who catches her thoughts 'from off the surface of a maelstrom of chaotic black emotions and reactions' and who surrounds herself with colours, sounds, and dresses of strange variety, might well be said to originate directly from Lawrence's understanding of Poe. Speaking in the essay of Poe's unfailing 'bad taste' as an artist, Lawrence remarks that Poe 'seeks a sensation from every phrase or object, and the effect is vulgar'—a remark which is deepened in meaning when he interprets the organic disorder which underlies Poe's 'extraordinary facility in versification' (what Poe calls Usher's 'fervid facility'): 'The absence of real central or impulsive being in himself leaves him inordinately mechanically sensitive to sounds and effects, associations of sounds, association of rhyme, for example—mechanical, facile, having no root in any passion' (*The Symbolic Meaning*, p. 127). Lawrence is thinking of the 'Haunted Palace' verses in 'Usher', but his analysis of the vulgarity would be relevant to this passage, from the tale, 'The Assignation':

In the architecture and embellishments of the chamber, the evident design had been to dazzle and astound. Little attention had been paid to the *decora* of what is technically called *keeping*, or to the proprieties of nationality. The eye wandered from object to object, and rested upon none—neither the *grotesques* of the Greek painters, nor the sculptures of the best Italian days, nor the huge carvings of untutored Egypt. Rich draperies in every part of the room trembled to the vibration of low, melancholy music, whose origin was not to be discovered. The senses were oppressed by mingled and conflicting perfumes, reeking up from strange convolute censers, together with multitudinous flaring and flickering tongues of emerald and violet fire. The rays of the newly risen sun poured in upon the whole, through windows formed each of a single pane of crimson-tinted glass. Glancing to and fro, in a thousand reflections, from curtains which rolled from their cornices like cataracts of molten silver, the beams of natural glory mingled at length fitfully with the artificial light, and lay weltering in subdued masses upon a carpet of rich, liquid-looking cloth of Chili gold.

(*Tales of Mystery and Imagination*, pp. 149–50.)

If such writing is only possible in the 'absence of real central or impulsive being', then the mechanical association of sounds, colours, and ideas in the international anarchy of Breadalby is brought about, Lawrence suggests in the novel, by the same deficiency in Hermione. After she has been rendered 'witless, decentralised' by Birkin's words, she presides at dinner like one returned from the dead:

The party was gay and extravagant in appearance, everybody had put on evening dress except Birkin and Joshua Mattheson. The little

Italian Contessa wore a dress of tissue, of orange and gold and black velvet in soft wide stripes, Gudrun was emerald green with strange net-work, Ursula was in yellow with dull silver veiling, Miss Bradley was of grey, crimson and jet, Fräulein März wore pale blue. It gave Hermione a sudden convulsive sensation of pleasure, to see these rich colours under the candle-light. She was aware of the talk going on, ceaselessly, Joshua's voice dominating; of the ceaseless pitter-patter of women's light laughter and responses; of the brilliant colours and the white table and the shadow above and below; and she seemed in a swoon of gratification, convulsed with pleasure, and yet sick, like a *revenant*. She took very little part in the conversation, yet she heard it all, it was all hers. (*Women in Love*, pp. 82–3.)

Later in the evening when Hermione's will sets her guests moving in a dance—first the Contessa, Ursula, and Gudrun in a ballet clothed in extravagant oriental robes; then all in a 'convulsive' rag-time—she seems to share the same detached, presiding force as the monarch in Usher's 'Haunted Palace' before madness overpowers:

> Wanderers in that happy valley
>   Through two luminous windows saw
> Spirits moving musically
>   To a lute's well tunèd law,
> Round about a throne, where sitting
>   (Porphyrogene!)
> In state his glory well befitting,
>   The ruler of the realm was seen.

Hermione's 'fervid facility' is not for versifying but for chaotic connections, as she bears down on Ursula, making some inarticulate attempt at communication through the 'corrupt gorgeousness' of some Indian silk shirts. Ursula's response to the appeal ('crying mechanically' of a red and blue shirt, ' "who would dare to put those two strong colours together—" ') has the same non-organic foundation as her other sympathetic responses to Hermione in the novel, when she makes temporary, rootless allegiances with the other woman.

At the fête Gudrun's extravagant colours are also 'put together' with a gaudy, striped effect, implicitly weighing down the mind with sensations—like her sash 'of brilliant black and pink and yellow colour wound broadly round her waist', and the 'black and pink and yellow' decoration on her hat-brim. The bars of colour encaging her have no organic relation to one another in their showiness, and since they are only juxtaposed in mechanical equilibrium, one has the impression that they are constantly in danger of flying apart or reacting frictionally upon one another at the instant of attack. Only the strength of the will can maintain the appearance of unity. The Rainbow vision is brought to a visual, disintegrative shimmer in *Women in Love*, as if the arc of whole being cannot stand firm again in Lawrence's imagination until it has fully absorbed and surpassed the corruption: hence the prism-like consciousness, the absolutist's eye, which produces the strange hallucinations of the novel by splitting the light of wholeness into constituent, separate colours—all shamelessly, bizarrely unmodified.

American absolutism is the key to Lawrence's understanding of this, and so it would not be wrong to suggest that the presentation of Hermione in 'Water Party'—macabre, almost unfocused, precariously poised as a human *fleur du mal* 'in a handsome gown of white lace, trailing an enormous silk shawl blotched with great embroidered flowers, and balancing an enormous plain hat on her head'—is an artistic employment of the realization which Lawrence comes to in his remarks on Poe's 'Eleonora'. The Valley of the Many-Coloured Grass in the tale is the place where Lawrence sees that life and love have turned destructively poisonous, 'the valley of prismatic sensation, where everything seems spectrum-coloured.' The Valley of the tale is the setting for Eleonora and her spiritual lover, where among the 'serpent-like', insidiously phallic trees, the changes take place which lead inevitably to the girl's death. As 'Love' progresses through its stages, there are corresponding shifts of hue in the landscape: the white daisies of innocence are now overborne by the red asphodels and 'strange brilliant flowers, star-shaped'. The shades of red in the flora, fauna, and clouds—ruby, crimson, scarlet, gold—give way, after the death of Eleonora, to an erotic dissolution in the 'dark eye-like violets that writhed uneasily and were ever encumbered with dew.'

One may well think of Lawrence's comment on Turner in the Hardy *Study*, that his purpose was 'to make the light transfuse the body, till the body was carried away, a mere bloodstain.' It has already been indicated that Hardy attempts just such an effect (in the cause of equanimity) by means of the 'spectral, half-compounded, aqueous light' of *Tess*. So in the Valley of the

Many-Coloured Grass and in the Talbothays garden there is the same effect of decomposed sensuality, the same prismatic blur and break-up. The spiritualizing kaleidoscope of 'Eleonora' is brought about by the same kind of vision which produces the spectrum of weeds round Tess, plants 'whose red and yellow and purple hues formed a polychrome as dazzling as that of cultivated flowers.' But Lawrence's comment on Turner cannot be applied to Hardy with the exactness that it could apply to Poe: 'If Turner had ever painted his last picture, it would have been a white, incandescent surface, the same whiteness when he finished as when he began, proceeding from nullity to nullity, through all the range of colour.' Hardy will not go to the extreme which Poe reaches in other tales, and it is instructive to note the point at which Hardy turns back from the full 'incandescence' which the Americans know so much more intensely.

With a laborious insistence which is characteristic, Hardy sets a limit to the interests of his art, as if deliberately warning himself off from developing consciousness to a level where he cannot sustain it. He will often let it be seen that he is turning back to a continuity which he *can* sustain, where the scope is smaller, where the interests of humanity are levelled down to a quieter purpose, among the basic needs of food, humble work, and shelter. In the same novel that turns Clym back from the unsupportable 'moon-lit' dreams of his ambition, Diggory Venn sees a wild mallard on the wintry Heath, 'just arrived from the home of the north wind. The creature brought with him an amplitude of Northern know-ledge. Glacial catastrophes, snowstorm episodes, glittering auroral effects, Polaris in the zenith, Franklin underfoot . . . But the bird, like many other philosophers, seemed as he looked at the reddleman to think that a present moment of comfortable reality was worth a decade of memories.' (*The Return of the Native*, p. 101.) Under the big sky of the desolate uplands farm in *Tess* (p. 369), the girls are hacking for swedes in the frost-bound earth when there begin to arrive 'strange birds from behind the North Pole . . . gaunt spectral creatures with tragical eyes—eyes which had witnessed scenes of cataclysmal horror in inaccessible polar regions of a magnitude such as no human being had ever conceived, in curdl-ing temperatures that no man could endure; which had beheld the crash of icebergs and the slide of snow-hills by the shooting light of the Aurora; been half blinded by the whirl of colossal storms and terraqueous distortions. . . .' But for all the knowledge which they bring back—and which the pursuing wind also suggests, with its smell of 'icebergs, arctic seas, whales and white bears'—the birds are intent on less thrilling interests: 'The traveller's ambition to tell was not theirs, and, with dumb impassivity, they dismissed experiences which they did not value for the immediate incidents of this homely upland': that is, the chance of food being turned up by the humble endurance of the girls on the soil.

The Americans do not turn back from the spiritual extremity. Their art is centred amongst the 'glittering auroral effects' and the 'terraqueous distortions', whereas Hardy only approaches such intensity symbolically, deliberately at second-hand, so that Tess's experience on the bleak upland farm serves to parallel and suggest the quality of Angel Clare's experience in South America. When she blows out 'a passionate kiss upon the snowy wind' it goes to Angel far off amongst his spiritual harrowing, and he returns at last, like the birds from the Pole, gaunt and hollowed, from an Arctic of the spirit, rather than from an actual South America. He is ghostly: 'He matched Crivelli's dead *Christus*.' Yet Lawrence rightly sees that Angel is not conceived by Hardy with the knowledge that Hawthorne is able to suggest in Arthur Dimmesdale: 'He is far more refined than Angel Clare in *Tess*, perfect as a moonstone emitting the white and sacred beam of the spirit and the holy mind.' In Dimmesdale's consciousness, the 'preternatural activity' of Hester's mind upon the scaffold has reached a more luridly brilliant phase when he later stands with Hester and Pearl at midnight on the scaffold. The meteor 'burning out to waste in the vacant regions of the atmosphere' is an unearthly American light playing destructively beyond the reach of the customary, modest satisfactions to which Hardy can still relate himself: 'It showed the familiar scene of the street, with the distinctness of midday, but also with the awfulness that is always imparted to familiar objects by an unaccustomed light', thus illuminating the things of the everyday consciousness with 'a singularity of aspect that seemed to give another moral interpretation to the things of this world than they had ever borne before.'

In the 'strange and solemn splendor' of this Judgment Day light, Hawthorne attempts to give moral explanations of the phenomenon—an attempt that is psychically impossible for Poe when he describes Usher's picture, with its 'ghastly and inappropriate splendour'. But Hawthorne's interpretation wavers, going back and forth between popular myth and private reality, or between the sacred outer belief and the profane, undermining knowledge of the interior. Suggestions therefore circulate: between the idea that the light is an omen of the destiny of nations and the idea that it is the projection at large of the guilty individual who has 'extended his egotism over the whole expanse of nature'; between the sinful consciousness of Dimmesdale for whom the burning light signifies spiritual corruption and the belief of the people that the letter 'A' in the sky stands for the Angel that their dead Governor seems to become that night. But when the corposants burn upon the *Pequod* in the 'Candles' chapter of *Moby Dick*, there is no ambivalent flicker of meaning. The whole profane ship has become a church, electrified by the lightning fire which feeds on the stored whale-oil below decks and burns on the three masts 'in that sulphurous air, like three gigantic wax tapers before an altar.' In this revelation of the Trinity, of 'God's burning finger', the spiritual flame is burning upon the flesh, as if cauterizing the diseased or maimed sensuality of mankind. The crew's eyes are seen 'gleaming in that pale phosphorescence, like a faraway constellation of stars', and among the aboriginal harpooners 'lit up by the preternatural light, Queequeg's tattooing burned like Satanic blue flames on his body.' Ahab, above all, knows the meaning of the fire: that knowledge of Moby Dick is the end of the spiritualizing process—' "the white flame but lights the way to the White Whale!" ' And to bring that Judgment Day nearer, Ahab grasps the lightning in the flesh of his hand, testing his pulse against the flames, thus closing the ironic gap between sinful exultance and blessedness: ' "defyingly I worship thee!" '

The 'white, incandescent surface' which Lawrence saw as Turner's ultimate aim is striven towards with a violence by the Americans, and it is a measure of Lawrence's increased awareness of this after the Hardy *Study* that he should conjecture more systematically in the first version of his essay on *Moby Dick*. Speaking of the white albatross in *Moby Dick*, he says: 'We attribute whiteness to refraction. The sheer mechanical reaction between water and light, or Matter and light, or Matter and fire, causes white incandescence, whether of foam or of burning.' Ahab's grasp of the mainmast links—' "blood against fire!" '—is behind these ideas, and, equally, the 'white fire' of the foaming squall in the 'First Lowering' chapter. But the 'terraqueous distortions' are, perhaps, even more spectacularly present in Poe's *Tales*. In The 'Assignation', the natural light of day is decomposed, whittled into the chaos of a thousand reflections by the panes of glass, before it mingles with the artificial light of the chamber and lies 'weltering in subdued masses upon a carpet of rich, liquid-looking cloth of Chili gold.' In 'The Conversation of Eiros and Charmion', there is a momentary 'wild lurid light' penetrating everywhere before the world ends by bursting into 'intense flame' of 'surpassing brilliancy'. It is probably on the basis of such passages that in his essay Lawrence interprets Poe's 'sensationalism' as 'a process of explosive disintegration, phosphorescent, electric, refracted. . . . The combustion of his own most vital plasm liberates the white gleam of his sensational consciousness.' For Lawrence, however, whiteness is not the undecorated, ultimate truth beneath the variegated colours of existence which it is for Melville and Poe in their materialism. The art which creates Gerald Crich sees the whiteness as a limited totality, the result of ultimate disintegration, which cannot, therefore, include any organic truth; it is what remains when all the colours explode, not what is always there in life as the blank container of them all.[1]

In Gerald's portrayal one sees the hints of Hardy's 'Northern knowledge' brought to confirmation out of the American experience. He has the refraction 'gleam—'In his clear northern flesh and his fair hair was a glisten like sunshine refracted through crystals of ice'—and there is a frictional, elemental inter-reaction at work when he appears as a human water-plant in 'Sketch-Book', 'surging like the marsh-fire' on the surface of the water and voluptuously controlling his boat 'like the rocking of phosphorescence', or when he is Gudrun's lover 'glistening with uncanny white fire'. As with Hermione in 'Breadalby', so with Gerald in 'Water-Party', Lawrence's writing takes an important part of its psychological basis from an understanding of Poe or Melville. Gerald is here like Hermione, an aloof but controlling force behind the 'sensationalism' and festivities, one who is responsible

---

[1] Cf. Lawrence's letter to his American friends, Earl and Acsah Brewster, c. 8 May 1921: 'white does *not* include all colours. It is only pure colourless light which includes all colours. And of even that I am doubtful. I doubt the exact sciences more than anything else.' (*Collected Letters*, vol. II, p. 651).

'for the amusements on the water'. But here, in contrast to the refinements of Breadalby, the 'decentralised' pleasures—the play of lights, sounds, and dance—are nearer explosion point, nearer with the working people to the outright, flaunted vulgarity of Poe's mechanical taste: 'In the distance, the steamer twanged and thrummed and washed with her faintly-splashing paddles, trailing her strings of coloured lights, and occasionally lighting up the whole scene luridly with an effusion of fireworks, Roman candles and sheafs of stars.'

Just as the dinner, the ballet, and the swimming party at Breadalby resemble Poe's masquerades in the outlandish dazzle of colour, so the pleasure-seeking here is like a masked dance from Poe on the verge of the inevitable break-up that occurs in the *Tales*. The detached position which Gudrun could hold at Breadalby is threatened at the fête, because she is swamped and diminished by the masses. Again Poe's American sense of spiritual confinement, of democratic crowding upon the intense individual, is translated into English as Gudrun's social nausea when she refuses to join the pleasure-craft on an excursion because it reminds her of the vulgarity of the Thames steamer. One recalls the situation of 'Mellonta Tauta' where a would-be superior is overwhelmed and trapped, 'cooped up in a dirty balloon, with some one or two hundred of the *canaille*, all bound on a *pleasure* excursion.' (The narrator of Poe's tale also speaks of a railway trip across the North American continent which, in its puerility, provides an ironic comment on the passengers streaming off the launch in 'Water-Party', 'clamouring as if they had come from America.')

In the masquerades of other Poe tales there comes the inevitable moment when all the dancing must cease, when all the cheats are shown up, when all the illumination is extinguished. 'Out—out are the lights—out all!' and the curtain comes down on Ligeia's verse-picture of the human theatre where 'the tragedy, "Man"' reaches its worm-eaten end in 'the lonesome latter years'. But the full destructive forces in 'Water-Party' are held off from their triumph. The climax of the demonic excitement is the death of Diana and her young man after the reckless dance on the roof of the launch. The 'prismatic sensation' intensifies with their fall, and then is switched off. After all the lurid refraction of colour—with the launch's lamps as 'sinuous running tongues of ugly red and green and yellow light'—and after the explosion of the gaudy spectrum when the couple drown—'as if the night smashed, suddenly there was a great shout . . . warring on the water'— most of the colours vanish under Gerald's 'sudden and mechanical' order: ' "Put the lights out, we shall see better." ' The elemental inter-reaction ceases to burn, and the only colours left on the lake at this moment of the evening are soft bluey-greys, just before the ascendance of the moon's 'grey sheen'. It is not stark, complete whiteness: for the last, irretrievable refraction one must wait until the last chapters when the sledge-blade burns through the snow and Gerald seems to rush into the sky, almost taking wing. But for the moment the 'sensationalism' is stopped. As Gerald dives for the bodies the moon shines only 'with faint luminosity on his white wet figure.'

In the end Gerald and Hermione are surpassed by Loerke in their capacity as masters of ceremonies at Poe-like masquerades. The *Götterdämmerung* mood of the final chapters suggests a Loki significance in Loerke, but he must also be seen as the culmination of Lawrence's artistic debt to Hawthorne, Poe, and Melville in *Women in Love*. Once more the sense of American Proteanism is extended by Lawrence—from Anna the 'changeling' to Winifred 'the changeling' to Loerke. Like Pearl with her witchcraft puppetry, or like Poe's Hop-Frog who is 'inventive in the way of getting up pageants, suggesting novel characters and arranging costume for masked balls', Loerke is the last of the child-absolutists, the last of the unidentifiable, equivocal actors of detachment, as he gives mocking impersonations for the guests at the mountain hotel, as he instigates, without partaking in, the frenzied dance ('everywhere at once, like a gnome, suggesting drinks for the women, making an obscure, slightly risky joke with the men, confusing and mystifying the waiter'), and as he stands apart in aesthetic nonchalance from the implications of his granite frieze.

In Loerke one can see Poe's social hatred, the satiric disgust, which is present in Hop-Frog and which underlies Loerke's role as a 'clown', a 'maker of mischievous word-jokes.' Hop-Frog, who 'more resembled a squirrel, or a small monkey, than a frog', is strangely represented in Loerke as the end of a reducing process for mankind, after the heroic spirit has left the scene, leaving creatures like Loerke in possession—a bat, a rat, a rabbit, an insect with 'the understanding of a flea.' Birkin's letter in the

Pompadour speaks of 'the great retrogression, the reducing back of the created body of life . . . reducing ourselves part from part . . . reducing the old ideas, going back to the savages for our sensations,—always seeking to *lose* ourselves in some ultimate black sensation, mindless and infinite' (*Women in Love*, pp. 375–6). It is that reduction, that miniaturizing and enclosure, that scrutiny of sensational particles, which makes William Wilson find in restriction 'a wilderness of sensation, a world of rich incident, an universe of varied emotion.' Now in the game of 'infinite suggestivity' which Gudrun plays with Loerke, she finds what she craved all along in Gerald, but with the conceited lust of her search fulfilled at a safe, impersonal level, obscenely and securely '*in petto*' with the little wastrel figure.

When the walls close in on the victim of 'The Pit and the Pendulum' or when the *Pequod* sinks in a whirlpool of ever-narrowing circles, there is a survivor from the American disaster to tell the tale. In Lawrence's novel, in this white place of the 'eternal closing-in', Loerke is the European version of the American psychological escaper, playing games similar to those mental puzzles of Dupin and his friend inside their crumbling Parisian mansion, as they solve crimes, reverting from effect to cause. But, like his other transformations from American fiction, Lawrence provides in Loerke a sense of *effect*, the dimension of inner consequence, noting 'the black look of inorganic misery, which lay behind all his small buffoonery.' It is the ultimate end of the sequence, the effect, which Gudrun and Loerke avoid when they play mentally with the past culture of Europe. Pearl with poor materials inhabits a 'vast variety of forms . . . with no continuity'. The continuity of Gudrun and Loerke finishes abruptly in the mid-air of the future when they play (p. 444)

a sort of little game of chess, or marionettes, all to please themselves. They had all the great men for their marionettes, and they two were the God of the show, working it all. As for the future, that they never mentioned except one laughed out some mocking dream of the destruction of the world by a ridiculous catastrophe of man's invention: a man invented such a perfect explosive that it blew the earth in two, and the two halves set off in different directions through space, to the dismay of the inhabitants: or else the people of the world divided into two halves, and each half decided *it* was perfect and right, the other half was wrong and must be destroyed; so another end of the world. Or else, Loerke's dream of fear, the world went cold, and snow fell everywhere, and only white creatures, Polar bears, white foxes, and men like awful white snow-birds, persisted in ice cruelty.

The last 'dream of fear' seems to take one directly to the 'Whiteness of the Whale' chapter in *Moby Dick*, to Melville's vision of terror at the 'heartless voids' of the universe, to his footnotes on the polar bear, the white shark, and the albatross. And the 'mocking dream' of the world's division by explosion or ideology—the absolutist's fear throughout the novel of a *reductio ad absurdum* to his purposes, the fear that the mind and senses will completely break apart when the mind triumphs—might well look back to 'The Fall of the House of Usher'. Here the consciousness of Usher is finally shattered as the mansion cracks open with a zig-zag fissure running through it to admit the beams of the blood-red moon. It is like the visual rip across Gerald's brain in his game of cruelty with Gudrun—'letting through the for ever unconscious, unthinkable red ether of the beyond, the obscene beyond'—or like Gerald's situation in the final chapters as 'a victim that is torn open and given to the heavens', finally stripped from his old consciousness and pursued to the white end by 'a painful brilliant' moon. In 'Usher', the narrator tells how the 'fissure rapidly widened—there came a fierce breath of the whirlwind—the entire orb of the satellite burst at once upon my sight—my brain reeled as I saw the mighty walls rushing asunder.' Through the 'mocking dream' of world-division, Gerald's fate, and Loerke, Lawrence in *Women in Love* not only makes the implications of the American literature *his* contemporary understandings. They become ours as well.

III

Studies in Classic American Literature, 1922–1923

As the previous chapter suggested, the Americans' experience of disintegrated consciousness both informs and confirms Lawrence's moral intuition in *Women in Love*. But one effect is especially witnessed by him in the other literature—the way in which the past can endure in the mind of the present as 'refracted' remains, as a phosphorescent marsh-fire light which plays over decomposing matter. In this respect, the 'sempiternal memory' which is 'heaped' behind Emerson, or Ahab's 'piled' centuries of corrugated thought, become particularly relevant to Lawrence's analysis of breakdown in the sensuous understanding. Because of the Americans, Lawrence in *Women in Love* knows more keenly how sensuous understanding can lose its integrity and living discrimination, becoming a thickened, cruder consciousness, a mass of sensations which gleam incomprehensibly and meaninglessly while at the same time weighing down the life of the present. When sensuous integrity dies away to become sensation and oppressive weight, the past menacingly reappears in the present as a series of disconnected memories which cannot be evaluated because they are heavy, fragmentary reminders of what was unfulfilled, never grasped, evaluated, or made conscious in the past life.

Such are the abstract memories which clutch at Lydia at the beginning of *The Rainbow*. They weigh upon Gudrun also in the 'Death and Love' chapter of the following novel, and are especially dreadful because she cannot escape them, cannot fly off into a non-sequential forgetfulness, since Gerald is there as her lover. It is in 'Death and Love' that one again sees Lawrence's understanding of the implicit meaning in the first scaffold scene of *The Scarlet Letter*. Here (p. 65) Hester Prynne's memory is invaded by past scenes—a string of pictures to which the present consciousness can bring no discrimination or evaluation:

Reminiscences, the most trifling and immaterial, passages of infancy and schooldays, sports, childish quarrels, and the little domestic traits

of her maiden years, came swarming back upon her, intermingled
with recollections of whatever was gravest in her subsequent life; one
picture precisely as vivid as another; as if all were of similar importance,
or all alike a play.

It would be relevant to add to these memories the 'unearthly
reminiscence' of the whale-calves in Melville's 'Grand Armada'
chapter, for with them, as with Hester, a pre-American life is
remembered, not a heavenly. But the whales have escaped the
past's heaviness and dead constriction, whereas it still weighs
upon Hester. What she endures as a ghastly illumination Gudrun
knows in *Women in Love* (p. 339) as a 'state of violent active
superconsciousness':

She was conscious of everything—her childhood, her girlhood, all the
forgotten incidents, all the unrealised influences and all the happenings
she had not understood, pertaining to herself, to her family, to her
friends, her lovers, her acquaintances, everybody. It was as if she drew
a glittering rope of knowledge out of the sea of darkness, drew and
drew and drew it out of the fathomless depths of the past, and still it did
not come to an end, there was no end to it, she must haul and haul at
the rope of glittering consciousness, pull it out phosphorescent from the
endless depths of the unconsciousness, till she was weary, aching,
exhausted, and fit to break, and yet she had not done.

Meanwhile Gerald sleeps beyond time, obliviously a child again
at a mother's breast, 'a pebble far away under clear dark water',
as Gudrun counts out the unendurably slow movement of the
hours. And so, in like manner, the dreaming Aaron passes into the
deep water of the lake, into the 'enchanted pond' of new birth, and
the later, waking Aaron tells the time by his American watch,
with its 'luminous, phosphorescent figures and fingers'. It is 'the
great white clock-face' of life as mechanical consciousness which
persists as an endless taunt in Gudrun so long as she serves
Gerald's desires. In shifting to the 'odd little boy-man', Loerke,
she gains the illusion of forgetfulness. The clock appears to stop
in the new whimsicality.

But for Lawrence not all the past is 'unrealised', a glittering
incoherence. As Ursula travels across a ghostly, desolate Europe
with Birkin, she has a momentary intimation of how far her life
has come, and as she looks back across 'the great chasm of memory'
one is reminded of how far Lawrence has projected his art since

The Rainbow. So many selves in Ursula have been outgrown and so many widenings to the consciousness of the art have taken place: yet there is a constancy, an unbroken thread, which runs through all the past experience and the discarded claims. As with Lydia in her widowhood looking back upon Lensky in a realizing way that would have been impossible before her marriage to Tom, one sees that what Ursula is now has come about by her struggle to go forward through experience. The seed may push through the husk, skin after skin may be displaced, yet the new consciousness which emerges does so in the knowledge that the struggle has modified, marred, or contributed to the strength of the individual. A price has to be paid for emergence, and when this is organically realized the value of past achievements can be sifted.

Ursula is more conscious, constant, not discontinuous like her sister, and so, even if she would have the past as a total meaningless mass which one evades in illusion, she cannot break off. There is a logic, a reality, an essential meaning, which will not be dismissed. It is the persistence of the *valuable* past in the present which she sees again when walking with Birkin near the guest house:

They drew near to their home. They saw a man come from the dark building, with a lighted lantern which swung golden, and made that his dark feet walked in a halo of snow. He was a small, dark figure in the darkened snow. He unlatched the door of an outhouse. A smell of cows, hot, animal, almost like beef, came out on the heavily cold air. . . . It had reminded Ursula again of home, of the Marsh, of her childhood, and of the journey to Brussels, and strangely, of Anton Skrebensky.

Oh, God, could one bear it, this past which was gone down the abyss? Could she bear, that it ever had been! She looked round this silent, upper world of snow and stars and powerful cold. There was another world, like views on a magic lantern; the Marsh, Cossethay, Ilkeston, lit up with a common, unreal light . . . as unreal, and circumscribed, as a magic-lantern show. She wished the slides could all be broken. . . . She wanted to have no past. She wanted to have come down from the slopes of heaven to this place, with Birkin, not to have toiled out of the murk of her childhood and her upbringing, slowly, all soiled. She felt that memory was a dirty trick played upon her. What was this decree, that she should 'remember'! Why not a bath of pure oblivion, a new birth, without any recollections or blemish of a past life.   (P. 399.)

As in 'memory's picture gallery' which imposes English faces and Old World scenes on Hester's mind, the 'magic-lantern show' in Ursula's memory is a moment of poise between two lives and consciousness. The most important link between the interests of Hawthorne and Lawrence in these similar contexts is the word 'home'— the home that one has left and the suggestion of new roots that must be painfully sunk elsewhere. Hester looks back to her native village and decayed paternal house, Ursula to the English 'republic set in invisible bounds' of Tom and Lydia, to a meaning encircled by the Rainbow, the Covenant, but which now is so far off and seems so confined in its intimacy that the Rainbow appears as a small 'halo', a distant grace. The alien snows of Ursula's new existence set off the past achievement in brilliance and limitation, but the clue of the meaning persists: 'Let the leaves perish, but let the tree stand, living and bare.' Ursula can let go the inessential as she journeys with Birkin into the abstract 'Nowhere', yet she fears the loss of too much in the stripping and transplanting. The vision of the Marsh is a reminder of a rooted ideal that the present cannot easily realize anew. The circle of fulfilment which Ursula and Birkin make between them has its moral bounds but no anchorage in a place or community. 'Oh, if he were the world as well, if only the world were he!' Ursula thinks of her husband. 'If only he could call a world into being, that should be their own world.' To imagine Ursula's desire as credible, to envisage Birkin's earlier recommendation to Gerald as serious, Lawrence must expand the circle beyond the man–woman relationship: thus comes the pondering of action, the tentative re-making of the world in the brotherhoods and mystic leaderships of the American essays and the novels up to *The Plumed Serpent* (1926).

In these years, Lawrence seems unsure whether the continuity he is following from past to future is a straight growth ahead or a swerving, a necessary bias, a side-track that will eventually lead back to justification on the main course. There is a fear that in attempting to believe in male comradeship, he has lost the belief of the woman in the other relationship. It is the half-guilty sense of himself, as the possible betrayer of trust, which seems to be felt in the dream of Richard Lovat Somers in *Kangaroo* (1923). Here again in the terrible face of an accusing, repudiating woman, is the return of the past *and* present, both demanding fulfilment, satisfaction. In the dream-face Somers sees his dead mother and his wife, his two loves: but ' "They neither of them believed in me." ' The demon of disbelief returns, and it is with this that Lawrence attempts to settle in the later American *Studies*.

I

When Lawrence writes again of the Leatherstocking novels, it is with a sense of actual, painful effort, of organic consequence. Mythic, easy victories of the Melville kind are not sought, for 'when you are actually *in* America, America hurts, because it has a powerful disintegrative influence upon the white psyche.' It is as if the reckoning that Lawrence had instinctively dreaded and procrastinated over were now painfully upon him. No shadow-struggles with America are relevant to the mood in which he writes the new version of the 'Spirit of Place' essay: 'It is the shifting over from the old psyche to something new, a displacement. And displacements hurt. This hurts. So we try to tie it up, like a cut finger. Put a rag round it. . . . It is a cut too. Cutting away the old emotions and consciousness. Don't ask what is left.' (Pp. 1–2.) The false pattern of love and reconciliation in the early essays is now broken: in truth, the land cannot yet be loved, nor its inhabitants, the white Americans and the Indians who are resistant in unremitting malice against the whites. 'There is no mystic conjunction between the spirit of the two races. . . . There seems to be no reconciliation in the flesh.' He does want a 'reconciliation in the soul', but by means of 'some strange atonement', the conditions of which he will only vaguely envisage.

What is seen in the *Studies*, in fact, is the breaking of the former wholeness, the race-unison, together with a plea for truce while the damage is being repaired. There is a modest movement forward at the end, in the Whitman essay, but throughout, the effect is of sternly sober consolidation while the former extravagance is cut away. The *Studies* are very much an emergency measure in their apparent aggressiveness: they warn off while the wound has a chance to heal. So much has been stripped from the former essays: the belief in mythic miracles, the belief in the Americans at last expressing themselves in perfection and then disintegrating to be reborn out of fusion and race-love. All this vanishes, except for vestigial reminders, and with it the symbols by which Lawrence formerly felt out his imaginative logic: the seed, the tree, the jewels, the ripple-motion. 'Don't ask what is left' is the real *caveat* of the essays, for though the pattern of unison has been broken, Lawrence still insists on the deeper truth of the ideal, even in the 'rag' of nervous, hurried prose. The note is stoic staccato. He will retract so much and so far, but will turn to defend his very integrity under pressure.

When he stops giving ground, the 'Holy Ghost' is the touch-stone of belief, the one religious injunction that Lawrence must allow himself. Since he is caught at a moment of indecision, not completely confident of the identity and full value of the positive to which he refers by gesture, the Holy Ghost becomes a flexible symbol of wholeness, a gauge of emotional situations as they come and which refuses to be taken unawares, off balance. It is completely relativist, limiting assertive scope in one way, and, in another, making room where none has been before. With the idea of the Holy Ghost as credit rather than displayable funds, Lawrence approaches the problems of the American literature from another direction. In these essays he is not involved in the problem of false harmonies and pseudo-victories in 'sensual cognition', but in the problem of authority: man's seeking a direction in himself and liberty from the encroachment of other men's chaos. This is Cooper's interest, and therefore it is not surprising that in the new realignment of the essays, Lawrence no longer looks towards *Moby Dick* as the centre of justification. The Leatherstocking novels are now the hard, sober guide.

In the new reading of motives, the Pilgrim Fathers came to America borne by the invisible winds of fate and by the urge to rid themselves of any masters or constraint, to set up a 'free' democracy—a negative reaction, Lawrence sees, since for the Americans this kind of freedom only resulted in the return of constraint. 'It is never freedom till you find something you really *positively want to be.*' Against this false freedom, as Lawrence conceives it, is set the shadowy positive of authority, the 'deepest self', the 'IT' of purposeful integrity: 'If one wants to be free, one has to give up the illusion of doing what one likes, and seek what IT wishes done.' From this position Lawrence wants to speak and behave, as if the democracy of the United States and the Mexicans uttered a challenge to his nature. 'When I'm challenged,' he writes in the essay on Cooper's 'White Novels', 'I do feel myself superior to most of the men I meet. Just a natural superiority.' If the other man ('even if he is an ignorant Mexican pitted with small-pox') will recognize in Lawrence the 'very me', then Lawrence will be glad 'to salute the brave, reckless gods' in the other man. It is mutual deference for which Lawrence asks, like Cooper in *The Pathfinder*, for nothing over-emotional or highly charged, no arrogant claims, but *perhaps* a little recognition of the higher source of authority by the other man.

However, Lawrence prefers breathing space to comradeship. This is the leeway he urges in the name of the Holy Ghost: to be allowed to unbend from too rigid a position, recuperate and change. The post-Renaissance Puritans, he sees, 'hated the flowing ease of humour in Europe', and it is this deficiency which, in the new Poe essay, he declares (pp. 69–70) to be the cause of the downfall of Ligeia and her lover. They sinned against the Holy Ghost—'the thing that prompts us to be real, not to push our own cravings too far, not to submit to stunts and high-falutin, above all, not to be too egoistic and wilful in our conscious self, but to change as the spirit inside us bids us change, and leave off when it bids us leave off, and laugh when we must laugh, particularly at ourselves, for in deadly earnestness there is always something a bit ridiculous. . . . Everything has its hour of ridicule—everything.' Ligeia and her lover sinned because they could not 'laugh and forget' as the Holy Ghost bids, and the Ushers sinned in their desire to merge with one another. They could not be separate because they could not 'listen in isolation to the isolate Holy Ghost.' The Holy Ghost is also an oracle of inner strength against the outer pressures of democracy: a man can resist all murderous encroachments on him 'if he can laugh and listen to the Holy Ghost.' But the laughter of the essays has none of the quality suggested in the 'flowing ease of humour'. Instead one sees a scourging passage of ridicule, the effort of a man attempting a purgative, confessional laugh at himself, with the wives of Hawthorne and Crèvecœur enlisted (in Harriet Somers style) for the attack on dreamy, idealist husbands.

The first version of the Hawthorne essays saw Dimmesdale as the representative of the white, spiritual consciousness which, having apparently triumphed over the sensual being, is finally brought down by Hester and Chillingworth, the representatives of the suppressed knowledge, the aboriginal powers. In the final version, Dimmesdale is still the scapegoat, but the motives for revenge upon him have changed, brought closer by Lawrence, one suspects, to his own personal predicament as an indecisive leader. Now the Red man pursues the White as a taunting ghost, not in reaction to the latter's past assumption of superior consciousness, but because the White has died 'disbelieving' in his own civilization. As Lawrence sees it now, fulfilment and appeasement can be attained, not by the union of opposing spirits and opposing flesh but by belief—'the only healer of the soul's wounds . . . Only those that die in belief die happy.' Therefore, the 'grinning, unappeased aboriginal demons' who return to persecute are a disbelieving 'mystic enemy'. Lawrence cannot fully answer their mockery, except by moving back in humorous resilience, there to stand firm in hope of reconciliation by means of the Holy Ghost. The demons seem to plague the uncertainty that Lawrence is caught in when trying to seek sources of new, civilized authority from the blood-consciousness of primitive peoples. The Red mockery is a danger signal, a horrible suggestion that the White delivers himself too vulnerably to ruin when he betrays his civilized sensibility—either by discarding too much and becoming a renegade, or by going down with the fall of an obsolete vision.

Into the new Dimmesdale, a man who has lost his integrity and manliness, a hypocrite who disbelieves in his own spirituality, Lawrence diverts his apprehensions of personal disaster, especially the fear that he might not be able to back out of a fatal direction: 'man must either stick to the belief he has grounded himself on, and obey the laws of that belief, or he must admit the belief itself to be inadequate, and prepare himself for a new thing' (p. 86). (Upon this premise, Melville is attacked in the essay on *Typee*: 'Melville was, at the core, a mystic and an idealist. Perhaps, so am I. And he stuck to his ideal guns. I abandon mine.') Dimmesdale invokes revenge upon himself because he has failed to keep Hester bound by belief, not because he is a spiritual despot: 'Unless a man believes in himself and his gods, *genuinely*: unless he fiercely obeys his own Holy Ghost; his woman will destroy him.'

By this reading, Chillingworth is no longer Hester's ally in the destruction of Dimmesdale, because, as a man, he is equally hollow. No more the believer in the old, sensual knowledge, symbolically crippled by Christian spirituality, he now belongs to the old order of merely intellectual, passionless belief in the dark sciences. The male authoritarian, not the sensual man, is crippled in him now, trodden under by the womankind to whom he has surrendered the leadership. And the anarchic, disruptive side of woman rides triumphant, according to Lawrence, because the power of male authority is too effetely unsure of itself, too discredited to stop the chaos of Hester and Pearl. They elude the judgements of the New Testament law just as much as those of the Old: 'And the world is simply a string of Pearls to-day. And America is a whole rope of these absolutely immaculate Pearls, who can't sin, let them do what they may, because they've n god to sin against. Mere men, one after another. Men with no ghost to their name.' (P. 96.) But again the conception of the Holy Ghost catches up with the female anarchists: 'The Father forgives: the Son forgives: but the Holy Ghost does *not* forgive. So take that.'

The story of revenge in the first versions of the essays is changed into a drama of disbelief and its consequences. Correspondingly, the new myth of atonement in the Leatherstocking novels becomes, in answer, the barest statement of a hard core of possible belief. It is not merely the idealism of believing in Red and White love which Lawrence attacks in himself through his attack on Cooper, but the idealism of believing that his earlier conceptions of America had already gone past the stage of idealism. He feels that he has not been sufficiently radical—'the deepest self is way down, and the conscious self is an obstinate monkey'—and that he has not thrown enough away to get at the core—'This popular wish-fulfilment stuff makes it so hard for the real thing to come through, later.' His mockery is therefore deployed in ruthlessly cutting away the trimmings in order to come at the minimum of belief which he can allow himself. 'Evasion!' he says of Cooper's 'glamorous pictures' of frontier life; 'Yet even that doesn't make the dream worthless.'

He must cut away in order to know what to keep: 'Now let me put aside my impatience at the unreality of this vision, and accept it as a wish-fulfilment vision, a kind of yearning myth. Because it seems to me that the things in Cooper that make one so savage, when one compares them with actuality, are perhaps, when one considers them as presentations of a deep subjective desire, real in their way, and almost prophetic.' (P. 48.) Therefore, in the new interpretation of the Leatherstocking novels, Lawrence can allow himself to accept the 'yearning myth' on condition that he is at the same moment mockingly guarded, over-cautious even, in his ridicule against the return of the earlier tendency to indulgence. 'Perhaps my taste is childish, but those scenes in *Pioneers* seem to me marvellously beautiful. . . . Alas, without the cruel iron of reality.' Where the guarded reservations are now so close to hand, even the 'leap of enchantment', the geographical spaciousness of the first versions of the essays, has had its extravagance severely curtailed: previously Lawrence saw Natty dying in *The Prairie* and touching the Pacific myths through the 'Asiatic or Polynesian quality' of the hill Indians, but one now reads that 'Cooper could see no further than the foothills where Natty died, beyond the prairie.' Lawrence's imagination refuses to flow out to Melville's Pacific, and the Glimmerglass quality of *The Deerslayer* can be accepted again so long as the earlier acclaim and imagery have undergone a mocking restriction. The previous acceptance—'flawless as a jewel and of gem-like concentration'—can only be the later acceptance when Lawrence has made his position qualifyingly clear: 'It is a gem of a book. Or a bit of perfect paste. And myself, I like a bit of perfect paste in a perfect setting, so long as I am not fooled by pretence of reality.' The mocking demolition of Cooper's poor forest realism is necessary for Lawrence before he has earned the right to 'put aside' his cavilling and accept the 'deeper' realism: 'But it is a myth, not a realistic tale. Read it as a lovely myth.'

Against Dimmesdale, the betrayer of the Holy Ghost, are opposed the heroes of the Holy Ghost, Natty and Chingachgook. In their new myth, severely disciplined, they are men who have dived down beyond love and idealism and arrived at 'the stark, loveless, wordless unison of two men who have come to the bottom of themselves. . . . And each is stark and dumb in the other's presence, starkly himself, without illusion created.' Their 'unison' is devoid of the intensity and fire which Lawrence had recently conceived in *Kangaroo* as the binding power that social man knows, like a telepathic vibration, when great leaders appear. The 'Grand Armada' and 'Schools and Schoolmasters' chapters of *Moby Dick* had given Lawrence in *Kangaroo* a vital analogy when he thought there (pp. 336–7) of leadership in terms of the Sperm whale for whom 'intense is the passion of amorous love, intense is the cold exultance in power, isolate kingship. With the most intense enveloping vibration of possessive and protective love, the great bull encloses his herd into a oneness.' But (*Kangaroo* had continued) when the leaders of human society upset the equilibrium of Love and Power by stressing one part of the twin mastery at the expense of the other, then society loses its great guiding clue and regroups to form a new, destructive unity. Directionless mob-passion takes over, or the more aimful destructiveness of revolutionary passion, when men 'are reduced to a great, non-mental oneness as in the hot-blooded whales, and then, like whales which suddenly charge upon the ship which tortures them, so they burst upon the vessel of civilisation. Or like whales that burst up through the ice that suffocates them, so they will burst up through the fixed consciousness, the congealed idea which they can now only blindly react against.' In the new *Studies*, however, Lawrence keeps away from the heatedness, the ideal of loving oneness and turmoil which Melville recalls in him. He removes from Natty and Chingachgook the charged interflow of feeling by which the first version of the Cooper essay had linked them. Now, as the words 'stark' and 'stoic' continually suggest, he insists on a drier, harder compactness in the self. The white man and the Indian are no longer called 'single', with the word's old overtones of pride and extravagance, and their new 'isolate' strength is not intended to suggest the 'isolate kingship' of the whale bull but a power which is more quietly centred, withdrawn to an internal certainty.

Natty is no longer the 'mystic destroyer' of the aboriginal sensuality and the eagle of the spirit. Without grandeur now, he destroys the spiritual-mental consciousness as 'the stoic American killer of the old great life.' He is now more static, no longer the onward adventurer moving out into space on his race-voyage. When he falls in love with Mabel Dunham, Lawrence now sees that this is not because he is flinching from his racial destiny but because he is suffering from the infatuated idealism to which 'men of an uncertain age' are liable (Lawrence included, perhaps?). When Deerslayer rejects Judith Hutter it is not now because (*The Symbolic Meaning*, p. 109) he 'represents the heroic spirit of his race passing in singleness and perfection beyond his own race, into the pure unknown of the future.' He rejects her because he wants to keep himself whole, intact, private, isolated. In disapproving of the falseness which he sees in the relationships of Hetty and Harry, Dimmesdale and Hester, Lawrence says of Natty: 'Rather than be dragged into a false heat of deliberate sensuality, he will remain alone. His soul is alone, for ever alone. So he will preserve his integrity, and remain alone in the flesh.' (*Studies*, p. 58.)

It is this static stoicism, immovable and integral, which Lawrence admires in 'the stark, enduring figure of Deerslayer'. Unlike the 'spiritual type' he had been in the earlier essays, Natty is now 'neither spiritual nor sensual'. He is the 'deep' realist which Lawrence would wish himself to be: 'He is a moralizer, but he always tries to moralize from actual experience, not from theory.' Lawrence dislikes Deerslayer's ethic of killing, yet he admires the internal consistency, the abiding integrity, which it represents: 'The essential American soul is hard, isolate, stoic, and a killer. It has never yet melted.' And here, at the end of the essay, Lawrence is deliberately contradicting the end of the earlier myth in which Natty disintegrates into the consummation of death 'as a pearl dissolves in wine'. There is to be no melting, no dream-flow and merging, just the discipline of keeping faith with the inner voice of the 'deepest self'. In fact, 'what true myth concerns itself with is not the disintegration product. True myth concerns itself centrally with the onward adventure of the integral soul.' But the tracing of further motion is not the interest of the Cooper essay, with its concern to maintain the 'integral soul' whole and hard, without love, self-delusion, over-extended claims or excitements.

2

The essay on Cooper ends with a significant warning: 'when *this* man breaks from his static isolation, and makes a new move, then look out, something will be happening.' The direction of the move is suggested later, but the terms on which it will be made are already to be found in the essay on the Leatherstocking novels. Having drastically curtailed the range of his previous vision, Lawrence has contracted the over-wide circle to an 'isolate' centre from which he can envisage future expansion on surer principles. This is where the sense of personal, honest, painful effort intrudes. The old fluid ease of symbolism is forsaken for a tougher symbol of struggle. The previous ripple images of the 'enchanted pond' are no longer apt for the new idea of possible rebirth in America, with its businesslike and painful necessity. Men came to America for two reasons:

1. To slough the old European consciousness completely.
2. To grow a new skin underneath, a new form . . .
The two processes go on simultaneously. . . . It needs a real desperate recklessness to burst your old skin at last. You simply don't care what happens to you, if you rip yourself in two, so long as you do get out. . . . It also needs a real belief in the new skin. Otherwise you are likely never to make the effort. Then you gradually sicken and go rotten and die in the old skin.   (P. 50.)

The myth of America involves a struggle in substitution: 'She starts old, old, wrinkled and writhing in an old skin. And there is a gradual sloughing of the old skin, towards a new youth.'

The image of painful 'writhing', the tearing open and abandoning of the old skin, is a description of Lawrence's own reassessment process in the essays, as he destroys through mockery the former idealisms of the self and of the Americans. But the new myth of atonement, having eschewed easy miracles, can now only conceive belief in the 'new skin' of appeasement and reconciliation as belief in a calm, tolerant space, freed of injurious pressure. There is to be no fusion of white man and Indian on the edge of death, but on his side the white man's spirit 'can open out a new great area of consciousness, in which there is room for the red spirit too.' Lawrence's anti-idealism having through Cooper pared down enthusiasm to a clear, minimal centre, he is now able to demand again, after austerities, a version of Cooper's moral space in his plea for width and tolerance. The right to be temporarily indefinite, not to be hustled into false adventures, is the position sought in the Franklin essay, where Lawrence addresses himself rather than his subject as he gives his Whitmanesque retort (p. 9) to the idea of narrow limitation: 'Who are you? How many selves have you? And which of these selves do you want to be? . . . every man as long as he remains alive is in himself a multitude of conflicting men. Which of these do you choose to perfect, at the expense of every other?'

Room to manœuvre is wanted, the right to change and soberly know where one stands, undistracted by external chaos and pressures. In coming closer to Cooper's purposes, by removing the belief in love-reconciliation and stressing the lone blankness of Leatherstocking, Lawrence is able to regard the love between Ishmael and Queequeg as 'renegade' wish-fulfilment, to see Ishmael, in the final version of the *Moby Dick* essay, as clearly as

he sees Winifred-Pearl in the novel. 'You would think this relation
with Queequeg meant something to Ishmael. But no. Queequeg
is forgotten like yesterday's newspaper. Human things are only
momentary excitements or amusements to the American Ishmael.'
(P. 140.) It is as if in finding the value of Cooper's sense of ordered
apartness, Lawrence has felt for himself a new meaning in the
'enchanted pond' of Melville's Grand Armada. The vision of love
seen there is not as important as the spacious centre of stability
which the 'pond' now seems to imply to Lawrence. In *Moby Dick*
(pp. 333-9), one remembers, the whale-boat is dragged and buf-
feted through the outer ring of panicky whales—'In all directions
expanding in vast irregular circles, and aimlessly swimming
hither and thither . . .' Steered by Queequeg 'through their
complicated channels and straits, knowing not at what moment
it may be locked in and crushed', the boat enters 'that enchanted
calm which they say lurks at the heart of every commotion.'
Through the mental labyrinths and American confinements of the
being, Queequeg leads the hunters into the wonderful, charmed
space of the centre. But the moral space is soon destroyed. The
war in the outer circles, with its torments, entanglements, and
confusions, brings the whales packing in violently, and leadership
in the boat changes over to Starbuck. The Christian steers the way
back into chaos as the whales begin 'to crowd a little, and tumble
against each other'. Then 'the submarine bridal-chambers and
nurseries vanished; in more and more contracting orbits the
whales in the more central circles began to swim in thickening
clusters.' One is returned to the world of external, physical commotion and the diminished inner reality, without the total space
that Emerson's vision saw as the reward of man's expansion as he
'rushes on all sides outwards to new and larger circles.' One is
back to the violent purpose of the American ship, where material
expansion and externalizing means the paradoxical horror of
further contraction for moral reality. In the 'Try-Works' chapter,
Ishmael is at the helm of 'the rushing *Pequod*, freighted with savages,
and laden with fire, and burning a corpse, and plunging into that
blackness of darkness'. When he awakes (p. 368) his moral
compass has gone: 'Uppermost was the impression, that whatever
swift, rushing thing I stood on was not so much bound to any
haven ahead, as rushing from all havens astern. A stark, bewildered
feeling, as of death, came over me. Convulsively my hands

grasped the tiller, but with the crazy conceit that the tiller was, somehow, in some enchanted way, inverted.'

The externalism, the frantic outgoings and the insane narrowings of *Moby Dick* are Lawrence's reference in *Kangaroo* when Richard Lovat Somers refuses to let himself be swept away by his involvement in political brotherhoods. If he listens to the deeper, steadier voices within him, he is in touch with a rooted centre, making all the other calls seem superficial excitements; and now (pp. 170–1), with the centre in him reassured, 'he could remember the frenzied outward rushing of the vast masses of people, away from themselves, without being driven mad by it. But it seemed strange to him that they should rush like this in their vast herds, outwards, outwards, always frenziedly outwards, like souls with hydrophobia rushing away from the pool of water.'[1] It is Melville's inverted knowledge which also informs the uprushing vision of evil which Lou Witt experiences in *St. Mawr* (1925). There as the horse rears over backwards at the sight of the crushed snake, pinning his rider under him, it seems as if mankind's sane control has been utterly overthrown, and evil has been turned fully uppermost. 'It had come to her as in a vision, when she saw the pale gold belly of the stallion upturned, the hoofs working wildly, the wicked curved hams of the horse, and then the evil straining of that arched, fish-like neck, with the dilated eyes of the head. Thrown backwards, and working its hoofs in the air. Reversed,

---

[1] Immediately after the 'Nightmare' chapter in *Kangaroo* (where Somers has remembered 'the black walls of the war' moving in like the crowding motion of 'The Pit and the Pendulum'), he asks himself why these memories should boil up in him so angrily now, in Australia. Somers wonders (pp. 292–3) whether the feelings have come back so virulently now because of

the inversion of the season, the climate. His blood, his whole corporeal being, expected summer, and long days and short nights. And here he had wilfully come into the Southern hemisphere, with long starry nights of winter, and the late sun rising north-east behind the sea, and travelling northwards up the sky, as if running away . . .

Perhaps it was just this: the inversion of the seasons, the shock to his blood and his system. For, of course, the body has its own rhythm, with the sun and with the moon. . . . He had had an inkling of what it would be when, from the ship in the Indian ocean he had seen the great and beloved constellation Orion standing on its head as if pitching head foremost into the sea, and the bright dog Sirius coursing high above his heels in the outer air. Then he had realised the inversion in the heavens.

And perhaps it was this inversion which had brought up all that corrosive and bitter fire from the bowels of his unconscious, up again into his full consciousness.

and purely evil.'[1] When Kate Leslie reflects in *The Plumed Serpent* (p. 73), the rushing *Pequod* of 'The Try-Works' is still persistent in Lawrence's mind as the image of mankind broken from its swivel and flung outwards in centrifugal horror: 'White men had had a soul, and lost it. The pivot of fire had been quenched in them, and their lives had started to spin in the reversed direction, widdershins. That reversed look which is in the eyes of so many white people, the look of nullity, and life wheeling in the reversed direction. Widdershins.' At Lake Sayula, she finds she can no longer bear the 'American flippant toughness' of her companion Villiers. It is as if he belongs with Ahab, with the excited turmoil and materialism of the outer circles, not with the mystery of this 'enchanted pond':

He was nice, she liked him. But he, too, was widdershins, unwinding the sensations of disintegration and anti-life. No, she must send him away . . . she must free herself from these mechanical connections. . . . Every one of them, like Villiers, was like a cog-wheel in contact with which all one's workings were reversed. Everything he said, everything he did, reversed her real life-flow, made her go against the sun.

(P. 100.)[2]

---

[1] *The Short Novels* (1956), vol. II, p. 65. Of course, the idea of unnatural reversal—of the world turned upside down, in particular—is an ancient one. (See E. R. Curtius, *European Literature and the Latin Middle Ages*, London, 1953, Chapter V.) What I suggest, however, is that though the idea may have been vivid for Lawrence in sources apart from American literature it is Melville's immediacy which makes it especially potent to him.

[2] Cf. Lawrence's treatment of 'reversed' life and the problem of authority in the short story 'England, My England'. In the original version (published in the *English Review*, October 1915, pp. 238–52) Evelyn Daughtry and his family live out a precarious idyll of cottage-life on an 'ancient, shaggy heath' in the south of England—a dreamy, Egdon-like scene which is sharpened, in the final version (published in 1922 in *England, My England*), into a more dangerous, primeval setting. The nostalgia for the English past is transferred into a voyaging mood of forwardness, so that the family in the cottage ('lost all alone on the edge of the common') now seem like a small colony of civilization planted in the wild, supported by the emotional authority of the father-in-law. But the husband (now called Egbert) cannot move forward into his own original authority, and it is inevitable, after his daughter has been crippled, that he should become cruelly retrogressive, an 'Ishmael' outcast reverting to an old, uncreative authority: 'His heart went back to the savage old spirit of the place: the desire for old gods, old, lost passions, the passion of the cold-blooded, darting snakes that hissed and shot away from him.' The War, when it comes, is like a fulfilment *en masse* of the spiritual reduction, the recoil from life, which has

Even after the 'stunts and high-falutin' which follow in *The Plumed Serpent*, where Lawrence is swept off into external excitements of a different nature, his position in the *Studies* is a centre which he can still find in himself. The comment on Melville's *Typee* is like a prophetic warning issued to himself, whose truths persist beyond the strain of the Mexican experience:

We can't go back. We can't go back to the savages: not a stride. We can be in sympathy with them. We can take a great curve in their direction, onwards. But we cannot turn the current of our life backwards, back towards their soft warm twilight and uncreate mud. Not for a moment. If we do it for a moment, it makes us sick.

(*Studies*, p. 130.)

In the *Studies*, the 'curve' suggests no drastic veering off course, no loss of sane momentum, no capture by the mud-life or the mass-generalization. Here the unambitious journey takes in the isolated figures. Each has his allowed room: the new skin is flexible enough to contain them, without pressure. The neutral word 'sympathy' expresses the only kind of feeling permitted between the figures of the space; it is more like a symbol of the desired modest truce of the moment than an active sentiment. Such cooling brings Lawrence to Whitman without a vision of 'ultimate comradeship' or male relationships of 'singleness'. Since love has gone as a factor in the essays, only 'sympathy' exists, the mere 'recognition of souls', with (possibly, but not essentially) 'a great soul seen in its greatness, as it travels on foot among the rest, down the common way of the living.' And this 'common way' leads to Whitman's 'wide, strange camp at the end of the great high-road'. Here Lawrence pauses before entering and recoiling from the disaster of *The Plumed Serpent*.

But to reach the momentary impasse at all, Lawrence must contend as a novelist with a resistance in himself which the Americans do not know. When he goes against his full intelligence and forces spurious victories in 'sensual cognition', he undermines

---

taken place in Egbert individually. Fatally he serves the war-machine as a gunner, finding in the snake-bite motion of bombardment–'The shot went, the piston of the gun sprang back'—almost an American kind of freedom in reduction: 'It left the soul unburdened, brooding in dark nakedness. In the end, the soul is alone, brooding on the face of the uncreated flux, as a bird on a dark sea.' (*The Complete Short Stories*, 1955, vol. II, p. 330.)

a markedly different quality of consciousness. His discovery of personal mistakes can never have the same touch of mental bitterness, of black disorder, as those of the Americans. He is self-deceived from a different quarter. He cannot for long put a phantom wholeness round experience, like Whitman who, 'seeking what is yet unfound', looks over the Pacific, 'the circle almost circled'. He cannot completely share with Ishmael the self-souring note of futility when all the rushing expansions are meaningless contractions:

> Round the world! There is much in that sound to inspire proud feelings; but whereto does all that circumnavigation conduct? Only through numberless perils to the very point whence we started, where those that we left behind secure, were all the time before us.
>
> (*Moby Dick*, p. 207.)

Lawrence's way to reckoning is by a different course. His 'straying and breaking away' is related inevitably, inescapably, to an organic reality. Because of this, he can say with Somers in *Kangaroo* (p. 388):

> 'You have got to go through the mistakes. You've got to go all round the world, and then halfway round again, till you get back. Go on, go on, the world is round, and it will bring you back. Draw your ring round the world, the ring of your consciousness. Draw it round until it is complete.'

Bibliography

Following are sources refered to in the text, in the editions indicated; the place of publication is London unless otherwise noted.

D. H. LAWRENCE

The Phoenix Edition of the novels and stories published by Heinemann, London:
The White Peacock (1955)
The Trespasser (1955)
Sons and Lovers (1956)
The Rainbow (1955)
Women in Love (1954)
Aaron's Rod (1954)
Kangaroo (1955)
The Plumed Serpent (1955)
Lady Chatterley's Lover (1963) (Penguin ed., 1961)
The Complete Short Stories of D. H. Lawrence, 3 vols. (1955)
The Short Novels of D. H. Lawrence, 2 vols. (1956)

The Complete Poems of D. H. Lawrence, ed V. de Sola Pinto and Warren Roberts, 2 vols (Heinemann, 1964)
The Symbolic Meaning: the Uncollected Versions of 'Studies in Classic American Literature', ed. Armin Arnold (Centaur Press, 1962)
Studies in Classic American Literature (Heinemann, 1964)
Fantasia of the Unconscious and *Psychoanalysis and the Unconscious* (Heinemann, 1961)
Phoenix: the Posthumous Papers of D. H. Lawrence, ed. Edward D. McDonald (Heinemann, 1961)
Phoenix II: Uncollected, Unpublished, and Other Prose Works by D. H. Lawrence, ed. Warren Roberts and Harry T. Moore (Heinemann, 1968)
The Collected Letters of D. H. Lawrence, ed. Harry T. Moore, 2 vols. (Heinemann, 1962)

THOMAS HARDY

Far from the Madding Crowd (Macmillan, 1964)
The Return of the Native (Macmillan, 1942)

The Life and Death of the Mayor of Casterbridge, A Story of a Man of Character (Macmillan, 1941)

Tess of the d'Urbervilles, A Pure Woman Faithfully Presented (Macmillan, 1928)

Jude the Obscure (Macmillan, 1949)

The Life of Thomas Hardy, 1840-1928, by Florence Emily Hardy (Macmillan, 1962)

EDGAR ALLAN POE

Tales of Mystery and Imagination (Dent: Everyman, 1963)

NATHANIEL HAWTHORNE

The Scarlet Letter (New American Library, New York, 1964)

The House of the Seven Gables, A Romance (New American Library, New York, 1963)

The Blithedale Romance (Dell, New York, 1962)

The Marble Faun, or The Romance of Monte Beni (New American Library, New York, 1961)

HERMAN MELVILLE

Moby Dick, or The White Whale (Dent: Everyman, 1939)

Pierre, or The Ambiguities (New American Library, New York, 1964)

JAMES FENIMORE COOPER

The Pioneers, or The Sources of the Susquehanna (New American Library, New York, 1964)

The Last of the Mohicans, A Narrative of 1757 (New American Library, New York, 1962)

The Prairie (New American Library, New York, 1964)

The Pathfinder, or The Inland Sea (New American Library, New York, 1961)

The Deerslayer, or The First Warpath (New American Library, New York, 1963)

Index